THE RISE OF ITALIAN FASCISM

THE RISE OF ITALIAN FASCISM
1918-1922

by

A. ROSSI

With a Preface by

HERMAN FINER

Translated by

PETER AND DOROTHY WAIT

NEW YORK

Howard Fertig

1966

Translated from *La Naissance du Fascisme,*
L'Italie de 1918 *à* 1922

First published in English in 1938
by Methuen & Co. Ltd.

HOWARD FERTIG, INC. EDITION 1966
Published by arrangement with Methuen & Co. Ltd.

First American edition

Library of Congress Catalog Card Number: 66-24355

PRINTED IN THE UNITED STATES OF AMERICA
BY NOBLE OFFSET PRINTERS

IN MEMORY OF

MY FATHER

A METALLURGICAL WORKER
WHOSE LATER YEARS WERE DARKENED
BY THE VICTORY OF FASCISM IN ITALY

PREFACE

THOSE who still persist in the belief that faithful history can and should be an indispensable counsellor in civic behaviour and state policy, will find the present work of extraordinary and enduring importance. Nothing in the literature of Italian Fascism compares with this as an account of origins, a judgment of significance, and the highly skilled appreciation of cause and effect. It stands besides such works in political history and science as Heiden's *History of National Socialism*, Rosenberg's *History of the German Republic*, and Mr. Chamberlin's works on Soviet Russia. It corroborates and is corroborated by the works of Salvemini, Nitti, and Lussu.

' In fifteen years ', declared Mussolini in 1925, ' Europe will be fascist or fascistized ! ' The grim results of dynamic fascism, with its goal so confidently predicted, are to-day evident to all—even to some of those deceived by the cleverly incessant propaganda that the Comintern will get you if you don't look out ! But its import and present works—threat or joy according to one's outlook—were discernible in its origins and early years. Plutarch attributes to Cicero the opinion that the character of Cæsar was sufficiently established in his youth for a valid prediction of the harm he would do to the Republic : he should have been dealt with appropriately before and not after he wrought untold mischief. The things which Signor Rossi tells should have been known to our rulers, for our safety ; and it is interesting to speculate on the causes of their deficiencies of knowledge, or understanding, or resolution.

Signor Rossi (a pseudonym) is an example of the highest type of Italian : a subtle, searching, analytical mind, combined with warmth of feeling and expression, and a noble, humane sympathy for mankind. Few have so good a title as he to reveal the nature of fascism by the investigation and recording of its genetic years. He was born in Piedmont in 1892, the son of an artisan, the metallurgical worker to whose memory the book is dedicated. He progressed, through years of bitter poverty as a child and youth, up the educational ladder, by scholarships. His doctorate at the University was obtained for a thesis on *Leopardi and French Philosophy of the Eighteenth Century*. As was naturally to be expected, he began an active participation in politics in early youth. In 1913 he was an active socialist *with Mussolini*—i.e. when Mussolini had arrived at the editorship of the *Avanti*, and was an extremist in his demands, and violently revolutionary in tactics. This was in the days when Mussolini was an utter pacifist, anti-imperialist, anti-militarist, and an applauder of regicide.

When Italy was faced with Europe at war, Rossi broke with Mussolini in order to continue his deeply felt and sincerely held repudiation of war. Mussolini, it is interesting to remember in the era of the Rome–Berlin axis, advocated the participation of Italy on the side of France and England, and especially on the side of France (Mother of Revolutions for Liberty, Equality, and Fraternity !) because, he declared, if there were to be a little more liberty in Europe after the war, that supreme good was to be obtained only by laying Germany low. Rossi, who preached the gospel of goodwill among men, served at the Front from May 1915 to August 1918, that is to say for nearly three years longer than his former colleague, Mussolini. The war over, Rossi settled in Turin and there founded an advanced Left political group and a journal called *Ordine Nuovo*. In 1920 he was appointed director of the Turin Co-operative Alliance, the largest co-operative society in Italy. This post he held till the autumn of 1922. At the same time he was political secretary of the Socialist Party of Turin and leader of the socialist minority on the Municipal Council. It was from this position that Rossi was able to understand fascism and to contest its advent.

Perplexed, and wishing to learn, he paid a visit to Russia in October 1922 and met Lenin, Trotsky, and, after them, the lesser of the first generation of bolshevik leaders. On his return shortly afterwards to Italy, fascism had triumphed. Thenceforward, he led the life of a fugitive until the end of 1926, when he left Italy. He travelled all over Europe. He was made a member of the Secretariat of the Communist International, but having the extraordinary temerity to disagree with Stalin in open debate, he was expelled. He settled in France and became editor of the review, *Mondo*. He is a foreign editor of the *Populaire*. He has written booklets on *Marxist Humanism* and *The Political History of the Comintern*.

The importance of this book is threefold : as a contribution to the history of Italy since the war, as an explanation of contemporary international policy, with especial regard to the relationship between Great Britain and Italy, and as a theory of the future of national and international government.

In its first aspect, Signor Rossi skilfully distributes the burden of causation between the pre-war history and institutions of Italy, its political immaturity, the social and economic effects of the war, the defective functioning of the parliamentary system and the political parties, and the character and will of Mussolini. He is not fond of the several compendious definitions of fascism now in political currency, and defines his own purpose most aptly thus :

' Our way of defining fascism is to write its history. We have tried to do this for Italian fascism of the years 1919–20. . . . It is not a subject with definite attributes which need merely be selected, but the product of a situation from which it cannot be considered separately.'

He is therefore able to reveal that fascism did not inevitably arise out of the existing political difficulties. No inevitability lay there ; but the material possibilities were converted by Mussolini's ambitions, power-lust, and homicidal ruthlessness, into a deadly certainty. No one could imagine such a tyranny in the Italy of the twentieth century, and therefore not enough citizens were prepared to resist the brutal seizure of their liberties. With figures and facts, character sketches, and depiction of local circumstances, economic and social conditions and opinion, the author demonstrates (though this is not a deliberate thesis), that the cry of danger from bolshevism was a deliberately adopted lie, adopted for its value as a psychological lever. He shows that far from being dangerous, moderate socialism as well as extreme socialism was, in its leaders, its hopes and tactics, innocently humane. The leaders were too noble to envisage the coming ignobility, too humane to imagine the advent of crushing inhumanities. Those who excelled in cruelty won. Since then, their victories at home and abroad have accumulated and they have gone from strength to strength. The mendacity of danger from bolshevism, concocted for use at home, and successful there, has been every bit as serviceable in international relations.

As we read this record we become acutely aware of the character of Mussolini in action and the strategy and tactics of fascist aggression, at first domestic. Political demands are made, so abnormal and far-reaching, that opponents are staggered into a state of shock, hypnosis, and self-doubt, causing retreat and disastrous fumbling. Secondly, the intellect and character, private and public, of opponents are vilified in terms so unscrupulous and disgusting that the non-political masses come to believe that there must be some truth in what they are told. The paradox is that the very monstrosity of the allegations sways to belief therein, as average men cannot believe that people can be so wicked as to make such terrible charges without a basis of truth. Particularly did and do the fascists stigmatize the most capable leaders on the other side. Thirdly, occurs the unscrupulous fomenting of agitation and violent assaults on fellow citizens who, according to plan, are enraged, whereupon, facing provoked retribution, the fascists claim the right of armed self-defence—and another cycle of violence begins. Fourthly, they make a fake noble appeal for justice for their own cause to move their opponents to make concessions to them, but do not yield a reciprocal concession to their opponents. This is sometimes dignified by the title of ' relativity ' of principle. Fifthly, the fascists, especially influenced in this case by the personal character of Mussolini, practise, as they regularly promise, revenge. No phrase is more common in the speeches of the leaders

than, ' We will settle accounts with all.' Sixthly, there is
the stratagem of putting the burden of responsibility on the
other side. Illegal, unconstitutional, or outrageously un-
civilized acts are practised, promises and alliances are
disregarded, and when in the natural course of events,
resentment produces the possibility of reprisal or punishment, the disturber of the peace declares that the responsibility for the threatened violence in defensive or punitive
measures rests, not with the aggressor, but with the defender !
Seventhly, it is continually claimed that only constitutional
means will be used, but in fact there is such an accumulation
of arms and organization of terror, that within the constitutional forms, men and women act contrary to that
constitution's spirit and intention. Eighthly, there is the
unqualified denial of sanctity or sovereignty to any standard
of justice, honour, pledged word or principle, other than
the personal and public interests of the dictator. Finally,
there is the cool, deliberate annihilation, by imprisonment,
exile, maiming, and murder of those who in opposition
are brave to the limit.

When this has been said, Signor Rossi, without express
discussion, has made clear to us the spirit and aims of
fascist foreign policy. We are far from denying that international justice has not been fully conceded to Italy by the
great Powers. But over and above what is reasonable,
the temper and tactics sketched above have since 1922
been brought into action in world affairs with consummate
cynicism and selfishness, and delight in making mischief.
Mussolini's declaration just before his advent to power in
Italy that ' the succession is open, and we must hasten to
seize it,' applied perfectly to the Italian fascist conception
of the international order. It has been expressed in many
forms, but always with the same frank brutality. Unfortunately for our generation, British and French diplomats, and
we may even say the British and French governing classes,
did not realize clearly enough that after the war the world
was in flux, the balance of power disrupted, with axes and
levers everywhere unattached, that not merely a piece of
land here or there, or an unredeemed population was the
issue—but the very succession to the status of predominant

(which does not mean the exclusive) determiner of the *kind* of peace in which the world was to live. Even now it is in the highest degree doubtful whether our rulers ever studied the inward audacity of the fascist advent to power, and especially its accumulation of arms and organization of political support at critical localities, to be used at critical junctures where their available force could be exercised out of entire proportion to their real material and psychological strength. The identity of the tactics of aggression at home and abroad is perfect, except that to the former two necessary additions were made—to divide allies and associates on the opposing side, and parties and classes in hostile nations, and to seal hermetically the fascist country from the truths which might filter in from outside. If those who have our destinies in their hands have understood these verities, and nevertheless have not taken the appropriate measures to safeguard us, then the only other conceivable explanations are too dreadful to contemplate.

In a final chapter, the Epilogue, Signor Rossi, reflecting on his personal struggle and the moral issues, contemplates the future. We need not epitomize the conclusions since the chapter is quite short. We offer only two quotations as evidence of the serenity and force of the author's mind and the quality of the rest of this book.

> ' The fascist experiment proves that an idea is jeopardized when its background is destroyed. " Ideas cannot be killed," is a sublime and dangerous commonplace, which ignores the fact that an idea needs material support if it is to last. An idea is a generation, or a succession of generations. If the generation disappears and the succession is cut, the idea is submerged and the inheritance lost. When the fascists kill, banish, or imprison their enemies, burn their houses, and destroy their institutions, they know what they are about and they do not strike in vain. . . .'

And again :

> ' In point of material and military strength we must be superior to the fascists since that is the ground on

which they are trying to force a decision. But unless some great moral force emerges to prevent war altogether, or if it comes, to keep its aims clearly defined, some force that endures unchanged through all events, however frightful or overwhelming, victory cannot be won, or, if won, signifies nothing. Such a force is only to be found in the popular masses, the common people, the workers. Theirs are the fundamental feelings : love of peace, desire for social justice, respect for humanity, the sense of brotherhood which are the mainsprings of humanity. Naturally these feelings do not predominate all the time ; they have often to be unearthed, and they can be suppressed or deflected. But not a single man of the people in any country really believes that war is " the hygiene of the world," or joins in the jeers of the fascist leaders at the massacres of Addis Ababa or the martyrdom of the children of Madrid. He has to be educated up to this stage, trained to forget his genuine impulses.'

HERMAN FINER

CONTENTS

MAP

On November 16, 1919, in the first general election since the war, Mussolini obtained 5000 votes out of a total of 268,000 at Milan, where the executive committee of the fasci had its headquarters and ran a daily paper, the Popolo d'Italia. The socialists won more than half of this total, and celebrated their victory on election night by marching up and down under his windows chanting funeral dirges. Their paper, Avanti, announced ironically that a corpse had been fished up from the bottom of the Naviglio canal in an advanced state of decay—Mussolini's.

A year and a half later the 'corpse' whom, in November 1919, no other party or group had been willing to put on its list, was elected at the head of the candidates of the national bloc in two constituencies, Milan and Bologna.

After the beginning of 1922 the fascist advance became an avalanche, and Mussolini left Milan in a sleeping-car on the evening of October 29 to 'march' on Rome, where he had been invited by the king to form a cabinet. This rapid success, which on the face of it seems little short of miraculous, was the result of a combination of factors, dating from medieval Italy, from the Risorgimento and above all from the world war and its repercussions.

But this result, favoured as it was by the accumulated apathy of centuries, was not inevitable. It is the aim of this study to explain, or at least resolve as far as possible into its elements of inevitability, more or less conscious purpose, and luck, the social drama which preceded it.[1]

---

[1] To prevent the text from becoming a patchwork of references, sources are mostly omitted. Every fact and judgment, however, is based on wide documentation and a mass of evidence used with the scrupulous impartiality of a historian and a militant.

ITALY'S INTERVENTION IN THE WAR AND HER INTERNAL CRISIS

WHEN Serbia received the Austrian ultimatum Italy was in a state of political and social crisis. Some months earlier in March the Chamber had debated the balance sheet of the Libyan campaign, as finally drawn up. The socialists thus had their chance of taking some sort of revenge, and of condemning the war, which had embittered the party and class struggle and endangered the moderate policy followed since 1900 by Giovanni Giolitti. To escape his budgetary difficulties and a threatened railway strike Giolitti resigned on March 10, 1914, nominally on the score of a hostile resolution put through by the radicals, thus avoiding a debate, although he had a strong majority in the Chamber. He assumed that he was certain, as always, to return to power after a short interregnum, once the storm was over. But this time his calculations were to be defeated.

The trend to the left was becoming more and more marked at Socialist Party meetings ; between the meetings at Reggio Emilia in 1912 and at Ancona in 1914 the free-masons and a group of reformists were expelled from the party. On the eve of the war Mussolini had been a member of the party executive for two years and editor of its paper, *Avanti*, for one and a half. He was distrusted by veteran socialists, adored by the young. The swing to the left favoured his purpose, which was to forge the party into an instrument for his own use, ridding himself of the old guard, who were too full of scruples and were paralysed by routine. The ' red week ' at Ancona[1] in June 1914

---

[1] Following a fight in which the state forces had fired on demonstrators, serious rioting broke out in Ancona in June 1914 ; from this town, where for several days the anarchists had the upper hand, the revolt spread to the provinces of Ravenna and Forli, and lasted for a week.

widened the rift between him and the circle grouped round
Turati and Treves in Milan.   Mussolini favoured anarchistic
revolt ; ' a hundred dead at Ancona and all Italy is in
flames ', he thought, without, incidentally, stirring from his
editorial office.   Left to itself and disowned by the General
Confederation of Labour, the revolt flickered out.   Here
and there sparks from the conflagration flared up into
strikes of protest.

From Milan Mussolini viewed the spectacle with keen
satisfaction. ' We record events ', he wrote, ' with something
of the legitimate pleasure that an artist must feel on contemplating his own work.   If the proletariat of Italy is now
acquiring a new psychology, fiercer and more unrestrained,
it is to this paper that it is due.   We can understand the
fears of reformists and democrats faced with a situation
which time can only make worse.'   This on June 12, a few
weeks before Serajevo.

When the world war became inevitable, the whole of
Italy was in favour of neutrality, that is unwilling to intervene on the side of the central powers, which at that
time was the only danger.   The whole of Italy, with the
exception of the nationalist group, which was afraid of
letting slip the chance of a ' good war ', and of Sonnino,
who judged—wrongly—that the Treaty of the Triple
Alliance must automatically come into play.

For months Italian diplomacy carried on simultaneous
negotiations with both sides ; Salandra, in October, invoked
' sacred egoism '.   At the beginning of 1915 Sonnino, who
had been at the *Consulta* since November, was still in favour
of an agreement with Austria, and if she had made up her
mind at once to yield ' the Trentino and something beside '
the Salandra government would have anticipated and
carried out the *parecchio* policy.[1]   Austria's hesitations drove
the Italian government towards the Entente, and intervention on this side was virtually decided on in March, by
three people : the king, Salandra, and Sonnino.   The
Treaty of London, signed on April 26, was known only to
them ; the other ministers were ignorant of it, and its

---

[1] This was the policy advocated in January 1915 by Giolitti, who thought
Italy might gain all she wanted by remaining neutral.

text was not communicated to the Italian parliament until March 1920.

The Socialist Party merely followed the current already created by its opposition to the Libyan war. At first Mussolini made a few vague protests against the ' Teutonic hordes ', but as soon as he realized that the party was practically unanimous in its support of neutrality he beat a retreat, made a violent attack on what he called, at the end of August 1914, the nationalist *delirium tremens*, and put his attitude to the party vote. At the beginning of September he proclaimed : ' We are asked to weep over martyred Belgium. We are watching a sentimental farce staged by France and Belgium. These two gossiping old women would like to exploit the gullibility of the world. From our point of view, Belgium is only a belligerent power like all the others.'

But as in private he had spoken quite differently—in favour of intervention—on several occasions, he was shown up as a hypocrite in the paper *Resto del Carlino* by some-one who had overheard him and was annoyed at his double-dealing. Mussolini, after a preliminary denial, feared his prestige would suffer, and sought to save himself by his favourite method of escape by rushing forward. If he stayed on in the Socialist Party, his standing would be im-paired, but if he left it he would lose his paper, he who needed to ' talk to the people every day '. So he went to see Filippo Naldi, who controlled the paper which had attacked him, and came to an agreement with him to found a new paper. The *Popolo d'Italia* appeared at Milan on November 15, 1914, as a ' socialist daily ', and Mussolini made his début with a bitter and malignant onslaught against the party he had just deserted. His sudden change of face struck the party and the workers, who had followed him so far in blind confidence, as an act of treason. In the so-called country of Machiavelli this raised an insurmountable barrier, not only between the working classes and Mussolini, but also between the working classes and the policy of intervention.

Both industrial workers and peasants, socialist and catholic, opposed the war. The Italian people felt that war was being prepared without their consent and against their interests. The government itself could think of nothing better than to appeal to ' sacred egoism '. National territory had not been invaded, which, as Clemenceau said, was unfortunate. A group of former socialists and anarcho-syndicalists demanded war in the name of the ' revolution ', but in this the working class could not follow them. Musso-lini, who had driven them down the road of absolute neutrality, was least qualified to bring them back. Not for him was the part of the apostle, proclaiming his error and winning by his confession the right to preach the new truth. Embittered and vengeful, he left the Socialist Party : ' you shall pay for this ', he promised on the evening of his expulsion. He found himself opposed not only by the extremist feeling on which he had relied up to the last moment, but by the moral revulsion which his attitude provoked. In this way Mussolini, in 1914–15, contributed more than anyone to the wall of prejudice which grew up between the Italian people and the war.

On the other hand the supporters of a ' revolutionary ', ' democratic ' war were soon swamped by a flood of adherents from the most reactionary quarters, who saw in any sort of war their opportunity of reversing the red verdict of the 1913 elections. The conservative spirit of the *bourgeoisie* inclined them to neutrality, but with the threat to their authority in commune and parliament they became converts to the war, hoping to be done with a policy of reform which encroached on their privileges and raised new social strata into the political life of the country.

For here was a fundamental weakness, due as much to the absence of a real ruling class as to the gulf between the masses and the new state. The Italian *bourgeoisie*, as it has often been pointed out, succeeded in organizing the state less through their own intrinsic strength than because a series of international events had hastened their victory over the feudal and semi-feudal classes : the policy of Napoleon III in 1852–60, the Austro-Prussian war of 1866, the defeat of France at Sedan and the resulting development of the German empire. The *Risorgimento* was carried through by the tiny Piedmontese state as a 'royal conquest,' without the active support of the people and on occasion in face of their opposition.

The Roman question[1] kept the catholics outside the new state ; the social problem ranged the masses against it. From the ' transformism ' of Depretis to the emergency laws of Pelloux and from the ' collaborationism ' of Giolitti down to the dictatorship of the right in 1914–18, the policy of the ruling classes was dominated by the necessity of controlling the masses while avoiding any decisive change of course in a democratic sense.

The Italian social system suffered above all from its lack of the slow evolution, the storing up of experience, the resiliency and social stability that gave scope to the democratic impulse in England and France. The people were only just emerging from centuries of servitude and poverty to which they were still held by a primitive economic system based on low wages in industry and feudal exploitation on the land. Democratic revolution had still to be achieved, and it was the task of the socialist movement. National history only began with the action of the socialists in awakening the masses to national life. Giolitti understood this very well, for he had long studied the problem of how the masses should be represented in the state. In 1913 he granted almost universal suffrage, and made a pact with the Vatican (*patto Gentiloni*) which enabled the catholics to vote in the elections based on the new system which took place the same year. This was a bold step, but it was doomed to failure by the reactionary motives which inspired it. Giolitti was concerned less with the creation of a modern state than with the securing of a parliamentary majority. This was made up of a group of deputies from the south, ' askaris ', elected by corrupt and violent methods, and of industrial members from the north, won over by high protective tariffs. The benevolent neutrality of the socialists was ensured by a sprinkling of reforms and the concession of public works ; while, for election day, the catholics were held in reserve against them and led in serried files to

[1] Dating from 1870, with the occupation of Rome by Victor Emmanuel II, and settled by the Lateran Treaty between Mussolini and Pope Pius XI.

the ballot by their priests. The result was political emasculation, with a blurring of programmes and a decay of parties, which hindered and falsified the healthy working of universal suffrage.

But the splitting of public opinion into two extremes, begun by the Libyan war and accentuated by the economic crisis of 1914, broke with the tradition of compromise and the methods employed by Giolitti since he came to power. The situation became more and more tense. The stopping of emigration, the transport crisis, and the feverish preparation of armaments all combined to provoke crises in industry, over raw materials and in public finance. The price of bread was beginning to rise, in a country where rioting has always begun in front of bakers' shops. Numerous demonstrations and clashes showed an increasing aversion from the war amongst the masses, especially in the country districts.

The '*fasci* of revolutionary action', created towards the end of 1914 by revolutionary supporters of intervention, and amongst whom Mussolini was already playing the part of a leader, carried on a fierce campaign and breached working-class and socialist organization. If the socialists objected, they must be crushed. The government, deceived by the prospect of a short war, undertook to come in on the side of the Allies (Treaty of London, April 26) without taking thought for the future. They bound themselves to action within a month, leaving no time for military or political preparation. They passed measures against the right of assembly and the liberty of the press, prelude to a regime of absolute power. This only widened the gap between the masses and the state. According to Ivanoe Bonomi, minister during the war and President of the Council in 1921 :

'When Italy's intervention in the war finally alienated the socialist proletariat from the state and drove it into implacable opposition, the Italian crisis began. And the crisis appeared extremely dangerous, when the manner of Italy's entry into the war also detached Signor Giolitti and his friends from the existing government.'

For even Giolitti, the master of compromise, was to go. On May 9, 1915, three hundred deputies to the Italian Chamber—the majority—left their cards on Giolitti, who had come to Rome, unaware that the die was cast, to defend his *parecchio* proposal, which Sonnino had adopted a few months earlier. The government, which had signed the intervention agreement in the meantime and was only continuing to negotiate with Vienna and Berlin the better to guard its secret, encouraged demonstrations by 'interventionists', especially in Rome, Milan, and Bologna. In Quarto d'Annunzio made a great speech in favour of war ; in Rome nationalists and 'fascists' mobilized and demonstrated against parliament. Salandra resigned, but the king assured him of his confidence, and the government summoned the Chambers, but only to tell them what had already been settled. War had come, and Giolitti was to wait five years before returning to power.

So the Chamber, elected on a universal suffrage in 1913 when the swing to the left was considerable, and with a majority in favour of neutrality, brought about intervention and a dictatorship of the right. One cannot avoid a comparison with the post-war situation, when the 1921 Chamber, democratic and anti-fascist, ended with the government of Mussolini. From several standpoints the 'glorious days' of May 1915 were the counterpart of the march on Rome. The overriding of the will of parliament by the king and a handful of men, and the impression that the government had been bluffed into giving way by a minority that had been allowed to demonstrate, unchecked, in the streets. made the people feel wronged and deceived, and led directly to the anti-parliamentary and maximalist sentiments of the post-war years. ' The whirlwind of the war will blot it out for the moment,' as Croce says in his *History of Italy*, ' but its consequences are irrevocable '. The carelessness, the unconsciousness almost, with which the ruling class plunged Italy into the war prepared the way for the disappointments of peace which contributed so much to the birth of fascism. And in the course of the struggle for intervention the *fasci* of 1914–15 began to acquire the mixture of demagogy, inflamed nationalism, anti-socialism and reaction which appeared again in the *fasci* of 1919–22. Embarked on amid party strife, the national war ' will be waged in an atmosphere of civil war ', said senator Vincenzo Morello. Between May 1915 and October 1922 this process was direct and uninterrupted.

II

THE DEMOCRATIC REVOLUTION OF 1919

ITALY, which had only been a united nation for fifty years, was dealt a terrible blow by the war. She was left with 680,000 dead,[1] half a million disabled, and more than a million wounded. Lacking a great accumulation of reserves, she had to import everything : coal, oil, rubber, leather, raw materials for textiles, and a proportion of minerals and foodstuffs.

On the other hand, there had been no great national ideal to support this effort or transfigure these sacrifices. The government's ' sacred egoism ' had been fundamentally neither egoistic nor sacred. Begun and carried on like a civil war, the war left a legacy of violent passions and insatiable hates. The day of victory brought no relaxation, and the defeats of 1916 and 1917 were only sparsely and belatedly avenged by the victory of Piave.

To no other country did demobilization bring such difficult problems. The traditional outlet of emigration, through which, in 1913, had passed about 900,000 workers, chiefly landless peasants, had become more and more restricted. What was to be done with those returning from the front, and how long could the wartime factories keep on the million hands who worked there ? The change from war industry to peace industry is notoriously hard. How, in the midst of general disorder, persistent upheavals, and growing hunger, could the way be found back to a world trade already wrecked and impoverished, and guarded by ruthless competitors who were better prepared and better equipped ?

Everyone faced the future, though, with a heart full of

---

[1] The figure given by fascist statisticians. M. Pierre Renouvin, in his work, *La Crise Européenne et la Grande Guerre*, puts it at 460,000.

hope. The war had so turned and sifted the soil of existence, created such landslides and outcrops that it was felt that at the end of this geological epoch the sun would rise on a new world. Had not Lloyd George himself announced : ' The post-war world is to be a new world. . . . After the war the workers must be inexorable in their demands.' Even the pronouncements of the government invested the war with the mystic meaning of a revolution which had just begun. ' This war ', proclaimed Orlando, the President of the Council, on November 20, 1918, ' is also the greatest politico-social revolution recorded by history, surpassing even the French revolution.' Salandra, on the same day, spoke even more forcibly. ' Yes, the war is a revolution ; a great, a very great revolution. It is the hour of youth. Let no one think that a peaceful return to the past will be possible after this storm.'

During the war the most revolutionary catchwords had been allowed, without scruple, to circulate. To one who was concerned as to the consequences of such propaganda, a fanatical advocate of intervention gave the following reply : ' It does not matter if, in order to beat the Austrians, the proletarian troops need to call the *bourgeoisie* dirty traitors, so long as they fight.' This same propagandist came to realize that ' this *bourrage de crânes* was not entirely inoffensive '.

Mussolini himself had kept throughout the war on the front page of his newspaper Blanqui's maxim, ' he who has steel has bread ', and Napoleon's, ' revolution is an idea that has found bayonets '. After the armistice he set his sails to catch the rising wind :

> ' The war has brought the proletarian masses to the fore. It has broken their chains and fired their courage. The people's war ends with the triumph of the people. . . . If the revolution of '89, which was both a revolution and a war, opened up the world to the *bourgeoisie* after its long and secular novitiate, the present revolution, which is also a war, seems to open up the future to the masses after their hard novitiate of blood and death in the trenches.'

And again :

' May 1915 was the first episode of the revolution, its
beginning. The revolution continued, under the name
of war, for forty months. It is not yet over. It may or
may not follow this dramatic and striking course. Its
tempo may be quick, or slow. But it goes on. . . . As to
methods, we have no prejudices ; we accept whatever
becomes necessary, whether legal or so-called illegal. A
new historical epoch is beginning, an epoch of mass
politics and democratic inflation. We cannot stand in
the way of this movement. We must guide it towards
political and economic democracy.'

Such was the exalted atmosphere to which the demobilized
soldiers returned, after four years of war, which had brought
them nothing but suffering, bitterness and disillusion. The
The peasants, particularly those of the south, came back to
insist on their right to the land. The workers looked to
Russia, where for two years the bolsheviks had carried on a
superhuman struggle.

The outlook in Europe became daily more tragically
dramatic.

' The fall of the Hohenzollerns in Germany,' writes
Pietro Nenni, an ex-combatant, ' the break-up of the
Habsburg empire and the flight of its last emperor, the
Spartacist movement in Berlin, the Soviet revolution in
Hungary and Bavaria : in short, all the extraordinary
and sensational events of the end of 1918 and the beginning
of 1919 fired the imagination and inspired the hope that
the old world was on the point of crumbling away and
that humanity was on the threshold of a new era and a
new social order.'

The ex-soldiers were for the most part Wilsonian and
democratic, with a vague but sincere desire for reconstruction
mixed with distrust for the old political cliques. Groups of
ex-soldiers uniting here and there were shortly joined
together in the National Association of Ex-service Men,
with an independent part to play, outside the traditional
parties. ' No party, no class, no vested interest, no paper

enjoys our confidence ', it proclaimed, ' organized and independent, we formulate our own policy '. In January 1919 the central committee of the Association launched an appeal for the formation of an ex-service men's party. At the first meeting which took place in June feeling against the fascists, whose movement had been under way for some months, was strong and a manifestly democratic programme was adopted. This included the setting up of a constituent assembly, the abolition of the Senate and its supersession by councils elected by all classes of workers and producers ; the reduction of military service to three months ; the proclamation of a fatherland ' free from national egoism and at one with humanity ', etc. The programme, as a member, Emilio Lussu, remarks, seemed ' specially designed for collaboration with the Socialist Party '. He adds : ' The ex-servicemen were in short embryo socialists, less through a knowledge of socialist doctrine than through a deep international feeling acquired through the experience of war, and the yearning for the land which was felt by most of them, being peasants.'

How was the Socialist Party going to make use of this situation ? Everything was in its favour ; there seemed to be no opposition ; and everybody—members of the government, fascists, ex-servicemen—used its catchwords and waited to see what it was going to do. Its opposition to the war seemed to single it out as the official heir to power.

In March 1917, a few months before Caporetto, the executive of the Socialist Party, together with the parliamentary group and the General Confederation of Labour, had published a paper setting out their immediate demands for *Peace and the Post-war Period*. This programme was conceived in anticipation of new social and political ideas which were in the air. In foreign policy the party, which had taken part in the Zimmerwald conference,[1] demanded a peace without forced annexations and ' respectful of the rights of nationalities ', immediate and simultaneous disarmament, the abolition of tariff barriers and the institu-

[1] In September 1915 forty left-wing socialist delegates from all the European countries met at Zimmerwald, near Berne, and launched an appeal ' to the proletariat ' to stop the war.

tion of 'federal juridical relations between all civilized states'. Such a policy could only be carried through if the proletariat were to achieve the first position in the state, through a series of 'social, political and economic reforms', including 'republican government based on the supremacy of the people'; the abolition of the Senate; universal, equal and direct suffrage; free rights of association, assembly, strike and propaganda; election of judges and the chief officers of the state; a complete system of social insurance; collective labour contracts and minimum wages; a great programme of public works; expropriation of badly cultivated land, etc. This remained the programme of the Socialist Party until half-way through 1918, but while waiting for its fulfilment a proportion of the masses became more radical in outlook, as a result of what they had suffered in the war, and more especially in reaction to the loathsome way in which the 'home front' shirkers had taken advantage of wartime discipline to carry on the struggle against the working class and the Socialist Party. In the party, the swing to the left became more and more pronounced, and at the national congress in Rome in September 1918 obtained a crushing majority. This new majority dismissed the programme of 1917 as far too feeble and 'reformist', without considering it in relation to the problem of the character and historic content of the Italian revolution.

In the Italy of 1918–19 there was undoubtedly the need for a bourgeois-democratic revolution, such as was experienced by the bolsheviks in March 1927, and which they tried to consolidate after their victory in October.[1] In Italy, too, it was essential to break the supremacy of the old social castes, whose influence had been strengthened by the war, and lead the masses to take a share in political life and build a popular state. In this way her national revolution, left

---

[1] In an article devoted to the fourth anniversary of the October revolution, Lenin remarks : 'The most exacting task of the revolution was *bourgeois* and democratic in nature. This was the destruction of survivals of the Middle Ages, the final removal of shameful barbarism, shackling all culture and progress. . . . We went through with this revolution to the end. With one purpose in view we advanced towards social revolution, well aware that there was no impassable barrier before us. The measure of our progress depends on our efforts ; to-morrow the struggle will decide which of our conquests are for ever assured.'

incomplete by the *Risorgimento*, could be rounded off. Radical reforms were inevitable, and no one dared openly oppose them. Even the governmental question was no longer a serious obstacle ; nearly everybody either wanted the abolition of the monarchy or was resigned to its disappearance. The war had set the masses on the move and their momentum was easily sufficient to overthrow the existing structure. Republic, political and economic democracy, common ownership of the land : these were the essentials of the first stage of the revolution.

Almost all parties were in favour of a constituent assembly and the most sweeping social reforms. At the beginning of January 1919 the Italian Labour Union, which was national-syndicalist in tendency and later provided the framework of fascist syndicalism, called for a ' national constituent assembly conceived as the Italian section of the constituent assembly of nations '. In March Mussolini demanded a ' constituent assembly of the Fourth Italy ', and insisted that the deputies returned at the next elections should ' constitute the national assembly summoned to decide on a form of government '. In April the Republican Party and the independent socialists (Bissolati's group) called on the ruling class to ' yield their power quietly to the people ', demanded a ' national constituent assembly, with full power to decide on the new forms of representation ; the assembly to nominate without delay a provisional government which should remain in power until the new national statute of the Italian people came into force ', and pronounced itself in favour of the inauguration of a ' social republic '. The Radical Party launched an appeal for ' a thoroughly comprehensive renewal of the state ', and ' an immediate and wider participation of the working classes in the government '. Even the congress of ' Liberal ' Associations (i.e. conservatives) recognized the necessity of ' speeding up the course of events '. The strength of the current swept along the most widely differing groups. The first congress of the National Association of Ex-servicemen rallied to the idea of a constituent assembly, and the congress of freemasons which was being held in Rome at the same time (June 1919) resolved that ' in the political and social sphere all changes which would democratize the character, direction and structure of the state should be carried out '. Again in October, in Florence, the national congress of *fasci* demanded almost unanimously ' a constituent assembly, by whatever means, for a fundamental alteration of the law, with the aim of achieving politically, socially and economically an entirely new state of affairs '. The idea of a constituent assembly caught on chiefly amongst the more politically minded groups of soldiers returning from the war zone, who were now just beginning to be seen about again at home. Pietro Nenni, in a book which is certainly the best that has been written on the post-war crisis in Italy (*Storia di Quatro Anni*), writes :

' Everyone who lived through those feverish months when the joy of peace was mixed with profound dissatisfaction with social and political conditions in the country, when all differences were merged into an almost mystical exaltation of the *rights* of those who had fought, everyone who can remember the first withdrawal of the fighting forces to their home districts, will recall that there was never a reunion or meeting or torchlight procession without talk of the constituent assembly. The phrase was passed on from zone to zone and was impressed on the minds of the demobilized troops. Each man gave it what meaning and value he liked. It was everything, and it was nothing ; or, better, it could have been everything, and came to nothing.'

Why did it come to nothing ? Because a ' mystical ' constituent assembly, of which so many component parts were already in existence, could not really come into being or function without action from the party which controlled the masses. This party, however, had just removed the constituent assembly from its programme. In the discussions of December 1918 the majority of the parliamentary group of the General Confederation of Labour had renewed their claims of 1917 and declared for the constituent assembly ; but the party executive, elected at the Rome congress, announced that henceforward their goal must be ' the creation of the socialist republic and the dictatorship of the proletariat '. The dispute broke out again the following January and was complicated by the equivocation which made ' reformists ' and ' revolutionaries ' equally powerless.

In order to overcome the post-war social and political crisis successfully, the Socialist Party ought to have taken office at the earliest possible moment. The ' reformists ' of the party and of the General Confederation of Labour had revived the 1917 programme, to counterbalance the empty theories of the left, and above all to avoid the dangerous ground of the struggle for power. But the right-wing socialists voted in their January session for the Turati-Prampolini resolution against taking office, so as not to ' absolve the classes who willed the war from the terrible responsibilities of its results '. Actually this argument applied equally well against the 1917 programme and against every other step towards power, and resembled the theory of the maximalists[1] that nothing should be attempted ' within the framework of capitalism ', since in any case the *bourgeoisie* was doomed, and it was better to let it collapse under the weight of its own mistakes and impotence. Besides, although some of the ' reformists ' found the constituent assembly useful to oppose the ' dictatorship of the proletariat ', they were certainly not prepared to fight for it, since they were contemplating an alliance with Giolitti—far easier within the limits of constitutional monarchy.

The ' revolutionaries ' objected to a constituent assembly, for the very reason that made their opponents accept it. The fact that it was common talk, a password on everybody's lips, alarmed them. If they had possessed a spark of revolutionary spirit this should have led them to adopt it, as in 1871, when ' the Commune acquired a kind of mysterious potency in the confused mind of the mob ', and when, as C. Thalès was not the first to remark, ' rational ideas were eclipsed by the extraordinary appeal of such a shibboleth '.

These revolutionaries, however, wanted above all to ' copy Russia ', and this amounted to a bemused repetition of the catchwords that the bolshevik success had set in

---

[1] This section of the Socialist Party was dominant from the time of the armistice until the March on Rome ; see also Chap. VI, etc.

circulation. Instead of making the problems of the Italian revolution the basis for their own ideology, they tried to build a revolution on a ready-made and ill-digested ideology, and this accounts for their complete failure. The soviets of which the bolsheviks spoke actually existed, and had come into being quite independently of them, dating back to the cherished tradition of 1905 and expressing the profoundly democratic tendencies of village and factory whose roots grew deep in the past. The Soviet Executive Committee was formed in Petrograd at the same time as the Provisional Committee of the State Duma : February 27, 1917. The bolsheviks were reckoning as late as July on a ' peaceful development—preferably—of the revolution ' ; they went through the phase of dual power, shared and disputed between soviets and provisional government, and fought the mensheviks and social-revolutionaries to win a majority inside the soviets. Even after the slogan ' All power to the soviets ' had been issued, they continued to demand that the constituent assembly, which they dissolved a few months after the October victory, be summoned. Every one of these decisions, with its corresponding code of action, grew out of the living drama of the revolution, on which its entire significance depends.

In 1919 the Italian working class had neither programme nor leaders. The 1917 programme, adopted by the socialists, had no revolutionary fervour, while what fervour existed was dissipated in borrowed slogans : on the one side a disembodied soul, on the other a soulless body. Meanwhile the masses continued to dream ; ' for some weeks ', says Mario Missiroli, ' the people became children again and went back to the pure springs of faith '. They only asked to be led somewhere, so long as it was forward, towards a new world, for which their feverish longing was stimulated by the still unhealed wounds of war, but their faith found no interpreter. Against the constituent assembly myth was set the soviet myth, without either becoming a reality. The clash was an imaginary one, between shadows which overcast the political horizon and obscured, on right and left, all paths to power.

Meanwhile Italy's economic situation was getting worse. Between March 7 and December 22, 1919, eleven classes—

from 1896 to 1916—were demobilized. Discontent was general and strikes were on the increase.

'Several factors helped to create and prolong this discontent : the difficulty of starting regular work again after so many years spent in danger and suffering, but also partly in idleness ; the inertia caused by the exhaustion of will-power which had been over-worked and over-exploited ;[1] the reaction against over-strict discipline too long maintained ; the irritation caused by the non-fulfilment of the lavish promises of radical economic reforms made to encourage the troops to the supreme sacrifice ; the revulsion against the squandering of ill-gotten wealth. But the chief cause of unrest was unquestionably the constant rise in the cost of living. The rise in prices was hastened by the effects of monetary inflation, hitherto artificially mitigated, and by the dearth of goods imposed on a population eager to throw off wartime restrictions. The rise in the cost of living, by increasing the discontent of the working classes, forced them to make continual demands for higher wages and kept them in a state of constant irritation and uncertainty about the future which often broke out into violent demonstrations.' (See G. Mortara, *Prospettive Economiche*.)

Strikes, which were on the increase towards the middle of 1919 (200,000 metallurgical workers in the north, 200,000 agricultural labourers in the provinces of Novara and Pavia, printers in Rome and Parma, textile workers at

[1] This fit of laziness was epidemic in all countries that had taken part in the war. In France it was referred to by M. Gabriel Séailles in a pamphlet issued by the *Ligue des Droits de l'Homme* : 'From all parts of the country we hear the same complaint : there is unrest at home ; the workers are passing through a fit of laziness ; they want to earn more and produce less. Some want to blame this entirely on the working class. Laziness takes many forms . . . it is to be found in the negligence of an administration which lets itself be governed by events it has not the skill to foresee, in its lack of any economic or financial policy and its postponement of fiscal measures which should have been passed long ago ; in bureaucratic inertia, unable to abolish out-of-date methods which smother the country's energies with red tape ; in the craving for pleasure of war-profiteers who have decided that earnings give a right to repose ; in lack of enterprise amongst heads of industry ; in the increase of middlemen who augment the high cost of living ; in willingness to speculate on industrial profits rather than increase production by proper organization.' This picture of France in 1919 exactly reflects the grievances felt at the same time during the crisis in Italy.

Como, sailors at Trieste, etc.), only raised wages to the new high level of the cost of living.[1]

The struggle for better conditions was no longer sufficient to calm the general discontent. During several weeks, beginning in June, indignant crowds would pour into the shops, insisting on price reductions and sometimes looting merchandise. Mussolini and the recently formed *fasci* proclaimed their complete solidarity ' with the people of the provinces of Italy in revolt against those who would starve them ', and praised ' the firm and resolute gestures of the righteous vengeance of the people '. The *Popolo d'Italia* expressed the hope that ' in exercising their sacred rights they would not be content with striking at the criminals through their possessions, but would also start to attack their persons ', for ' a few profiteers strung up on lamp-posts and a few hoarders smothered under the potatoes and bacon they wanted to hide would make a good example '. The bewilderment of the socialists and of the General Confederation of Labour, who were harassed and ineffective, invited the abuse of Mussolini, who poured scorn on the manifesto in which they determined ' to create no false hopes '.

All Italy was out in the streets. The government could do nothing, since it had not sufficient forces to intervene everywhere at once.

> ' I was impressed ', writes Signor Tittoni, minister in Nitti's cabinet, ' by the fact that to muster sufficient forces to face the storm it was necessary to send for *carabinieri* and police from other districts, which were thus left unprotected. I have often wondered what the government would have done if revolt had broken out simultaneously throughout the peninsula.'

The agitation against the high cost of living rapidly became a national movement, but there was no one to organize and guide it towards a definite goal, and so make use of the force it represented. The maximalist executive of

---

[1] Even school-teachers struck during the first fortnight of June. What were their demands? Minimum initial salary of ten lire a day and an indemnity against the high cost of living for those on the retired list, some of whom were still receiving, after forty years of service, between forty and sixty lire a month.

the Socialist Party, in order to avoid ' creating false hopes ', postponed all action (and continued to do so until the march on Rome) until the ' approaching revolution ' : the real thing, which would have the authentic stamp of Moscow. Meanwhile, as in Bologna, tradesmen took the keys of their shops to the Chambers of Labour, while the socialist adminis-tration enforced price control. The communes and Chambers of Labour : these were the ' second power ' which were rising up against the state, and might take its place ; these were the Italian ' soviets ', formed by the far-reaching traditions of municipal life and by the recent history of the working-class movement. But they were not copied from Russia, and the so-called leaders persisted in wanting to form soviets exactly to the Russian pattern. Because the revolution was Italian and popular in form the ' revolu-tionaries ', who wanted ' soviets everywhere ', passed it by without recognizing it.

On the other hand there was organized for July 20–21 a general strike, which was to have been international : a demonstration of solidarity with the Russian and Hungarian soviet republics. This had been decided upon at the South-port Conference, but at the last moment the French General Confederation of Labour withdrew, and the Italian socialists alone carried out their agreement. Something serious was expected and the atmosphere was oppressive and uneasy, but nothing happened. The political strike was nothing but a show, staged without enthusiasm or any of the pas-sionate interest which launched the attack against the high cost of living. The premonitions of the ruling classes were dispelled ; with new confidence they prepared for battle.

While the towns were being shaken by strikes, agitation against the cost of living, and industrial riots, there were in the country the makings of a revolution which escaped equally from the control of the socialist and syndicalist leaders. Mobs of recently demobilized peasants took possession of uncultivated estates (*latifundia*) and settled on them. ' During the war there was plenty of talk of " the land for the peasants ". There are some promises which cannot be broken with impunity. When the peasants over-ran several estates of the *Agro Romano*, soldiers of a regiment famous for its heroism were seen cheering on the invaders, who were wearing their war medals.' (Nitti.) During August the movement grew in the Rome district and spread over the south. The Socialist Party, its eyes still turned towards Russia (where, however, the peasants' hunger for the land had been the deciding factor of the revolutionary victory), remained aloof from this thrust made by the rustic mob, which belonged to no party or union and sometimes took the field behind a tricolour flag.

In November the general election revealed the new Italy. It was, thanks to Nitti, the first really free election since the unification of the kingdom. Proportional representation, which had just been adopted, favoured the increase of the big parties, socialist and *Popolare* (catholic). The second, barely a year old, had already attained an important position in Italian political life. In spite of the Roman question, Catholics were permitted by the Vatican to vote and play their part in national life under a united state. It was a revolution within the revolution. The year 1919 was in fact the year of the Italian democratic revolution. The masses had begun their struggle for bread, land and freedom. The ties with the past seemed finally broken ; from this revolution a true nation, a popular state, must at last emerge. All signs pointed clearly to the Fourth Italy.

III

MUSSOLINI AND FASCISM OF THE 'FIRST HOUR '[1]

WITH the armistice Mussolini felt that the day of reckoning had arrived for the whole world, himself included. The dictatorship of the *Fronte Interno*, which had protected him during the war, was over, and nothing stood between him and the growing indignation of the masses. After the demobilization he was forced to play a lone hand, on which his life depended. He had no theoretical or sentimental considerations to hamper him, and was known to have neither scruples nor convictions. He read in order to acquire, not ideas, but the political strategy of which he was in need. The process of thought inspired him with a kind of suspicious embarrassment which made him seize upon anything that justified illogicality and incoherence. He appropriated, often at third hand but with an unerring instinct, Nietzsche's 'will to power', Stirner's 'unique', Bergsonian intuition, Sorel's 'myths', pragmatism and, his latest discovery, Einstein's theory of relativity. His only use for ideas was to enable him to dispense with ideas. He was accused of a betrayal of principle ? The whole object of his researches was to collect everything which detracted, or appeared to detract from the reality or binding nature of principles, and if principles were meaningless so was their betrayal. Only action counted, and on the plane of action betrayal did not exist, only victory or defeat. Mussolini knew very well that he could not even carry on the daily struggle without some general ideas, and he picked them up wherever he could to suit each emergency. He became a cheap-jack philosopher, raking up ancient platitudes which he would bring out with

---

[1] 'Fascismo della prima ora.'

a challenging air of self-satisfaction reminiscent of Monsieur Jourdain or Erostrates. He scorned fixed principles and asserted that ' imperialism is the eternal and unchangeable law of life ' ; he criticized Marxism for its over-simplification of history while proclaiming that ' it is blood that turns the bloodstained wheels of history '. In this way he abandoned dogma for platitude, but platitudes, vividly expressed, circulated rapidly in the vast province which is Italy, and there was nothing easier to replace, without troubling about past or future commitments.

This is what Mussolini needed, while on January 29, 1919, he described himself as ' a cynic, insensible to everything except adventure—mad adventure '. Could he be taken at his word and judged on his own definition ? An adventurer, yes, since his only end in life was personal success, to which everything must be subordinated. A cynic too, since, according to one of his friends, who nevertheless remained loyal to him, ' friendship and sentiment have no place in his heart '. But there was nothing in him of the Titan storming heaven or the romantic hero carried away by the violence of his convictions. He inclined to the classical, ' since he can interpret all the grand passions without feeling them ' : passions both individual and collective on which he played as on a keyboard. Angelica Balabanoff, who knew him well, tells of occasions when he seemed a miserable creature, scared of the prick of a hypodermic needle ; others describe him fearlessly making his way through a hostile mob. But to talk in terms of current psychology of his cowardice or courage is to miss his real personality. Mussolini was too shrewd to be really brave, but he was shrewd enough not to be the slave of his nerves. He had a fine instinct for the road to success and eventually always managed to take it. With no love of danger for its own sake, he would do all he could to avoid or reduce it, but when it was a question of asserting himself, or of self-preservation, he was ready to accept whatever the situation dictated. When the world war broke out he was careful not to follow the Garibaldists into the Argonnes, nor did he commit himself after May 1915 as his friend Corridoni did. He waited to go to the front with his own class, and when he was wounded in a minor accident during hand-grenade practice after a few weeks in the trenches he went back to Milan and stayed there till the end of the war. He never took part in any engagement, for his life was too precious to run the risk of a ' senseless bullet ', but his thirty-eight days in the trenches were just enough to permit him to return, without too much embarrassment, to his paper and his career. This would have been finished if he had not gone at all, but never for a moment did he consider sacrificing himself, like Corridoni or Battisti, in the cause of victory. The only cause he recognized was his own.

Mussolini needed something more than his own unscrupulousness and lack of principle, if he was to advance further. For in spite of his stupendous pride (' I have never yet met my equal,' he confided to a friend before the war), he knew that he could do nothing alone. On November 10, 1918, day of the ' victory procession ', he rode with a lorry full of *arditi*.[1] After driving round the streets of Milan they all fetched up at a large café in the middle of the city, where Mussolini addressed his men. ' *Arditi*, comrades : I have defended you against the slanders of cowardly philistines. . . . With shining daggers and bursting bombs you shall wreak vengeance on the miserable wretches who would prevent the advance of greater Italy. She is yours . . . yours ! ' The *arditi* raised their daggers and drove them into the table round the flag which had been spread over it, shouting : ' Long live Italy '. Thus for the time being, a rough-and-ready bodyguard was formed.

But Mussolini was wise enough to realize that he needed allies, and a proper organization to support him. The Socialist Party and the branches of the General Confederation of Labour were hostile. There was, however, the possibility of a split in their ranks. The socialist leaders and the executive committee of the Confederation did not see eye to eye. The Confederation had just revived, at the Bologna congress at the end of January 1919, the 1917 programme,[2] including the constituent assembly. Mussolini,

---

[1] The *arditi* (*ardito*=brave) were a special body of shock troops in the Italian army, started during the war.
[2] Pp. 12, 13.

inspired with hope, gave his support. The General Confederation of Labour would perhaps break its recently
concluded alliance with the Socialist Party, and regain its
independence. It might aim at the creation of a labour
party modelled on the British Labour Party, a project
favoured by a good many Confederation leaders ; and
Mussolini would then be able to collaborate, with his
newspaper, transformed meanwhile from a ' socialist daily '
to a ' producers' daily '. He carried on a campaign in the
Popolo d'Italia for a syndical coalition, and in particular for
the amalgamation of the General Confederation of Labour
with the Italian Labour Union, whose leaders were his
friends and preached with him a kind of ' national socialism '.
The Italian Labour Union had supported Italian intervention in the war, but with its return to the arms of the
Confederation the question of principle would be overcome,
and supporters of the war would be admitted both to the
new General Confederation of Labour and to the new labour
party. Mussolini hoped to profit by this ruling and at one
stroke win back the contact with the masses that he had
lost during the war.

   Mussolini did not commit himself too deeply in this
direction, partly because the difficulties encountered were
greater than he expected—the General Confederation of
Labour shortly rejected the coalition with the Italian Labour
Union precisely because of its attitude during the war—
and partly because he never liked putting all his eggs in one
basket. In seeking a reconciliation with the socialist movement he aimed at the right wing, and in particular at
the leaders of the Confederation. At the same time he did
not wish to share with the right-wing socialists the risk of
being swamped by a popular movement, so he combined
his ' national socialism ' with demagogy. In this he was the
still unconscious evangelist of all fascist creeds. As early as
January he supported the strike of the postal workers, the
claims of the railwaymen, etc. ' We must grant their
demands at once ! If two, three, or five milliards are needed,
they must be found. At home by a census of national wealth,
abroad by borrowing.' The railwaymen must unite ' from
inspector to navvy ' in one syndical union. And when they

presented their list of claims, in March, he supported them all unreservedly, including the right to strike, although the Italian railways are a state service.

During the same month another event favoured his flirtation with the working-class movement. The factory hands employed by Messrs. Franchi and Gregorini at Dalmine (Bergamo), members of the Italian Labour Union, had presented a memorandum in which their chief demand was for the English working week. When it was refused they shut themselves up in the factory, hoisted a tricolour flag on the chimney and continued production, declaring that they would not quit until their demands had been fully met. It was the first post-war factory occupation in Italy. Mussolini welcomed it in his paper :

> ' The refusal of the metal workers to leave their factories signifies the translation into action of the new tendencies of the international working-class movement, whose distinguishing characteristics have been taken up and studied by this paper. The traditional method of the strike, harmful to class and nation alike, is discarded. The formation of the workers' council, which for three days has managed the concern and kept every department going, represents an honest and painstaking effort and a praiseworthy ambition to supersede the so-called *bourgeois* class in the control of production.'

After their victory Mussolini was summoned to Dalmine, where he praised the workers' action in ' inventing the creative strike which does not interfere with production ' and encouraged them to continue with the new method. ' The conditions with which the industrialists have surrounded you have prevented you from showing all you are capable of, but you have proved your good will, and I assure you that you are on the right road.' Afterwards a speech was made by Michele Bianchi, future general secretary of the Fascist Party and *quadrumvir* of the march on Rome. Thus the first factory occupation took place under the auspices of budding fascism.

During the June and July riots against the high cost of living, Mussolini and the *fasci* devoted themselves, as we

have already noted,[1] to frenzied attempts to outbid the
socialists and the General Confederation of Labour.
Mussolini raised the cry of all demagogues whose demagogy
is a cloak for their fundamental opportunism : 'Squeeze
the rich'. He knew very well that to save Italian finances,
lower the cost of living, satisfy all popular needs, old and
new, and overcome the crisis, it was not enough to decimate
capital or string up a few profiteers. But a sop had to be
found for the proletarian Cerberus. 'The coffers are
empty', he wrote on June 10. 'Who is to fill them ? Not
we, who have no houses, no cars, no factories, no land, no
workshops, no money. Those who can, must pay. Here is
our immediate proposal : let the owners expropriate themselves, or we will call up the army of ex-service men and
storm our way through all obstacles.'

All this served doubtless to make the situation even worse,
but it did not mean that Mussolini's socialist tendencies
were again in the ascendant, or that he was really a socialist
gone astray, a reactionary in spite of himself. Between
Mussolini and his own past stood a barrier of hatred, contempt, and bloodshed. No less infamous than the betrayal
was the manner in which it had been carried out : the
acceptance of blood money on which his newspaper was
founded. *Il modo ancor m'offende*. Repentance in sackcloth
and ashes would have availed him nothing, even if his pride
had allowed it, which was out of the question. But he had
never been a real socialist ; only a mussolinist. While a
member of the party he had belonged to the left wing, chiefly
because the old leaders, who, in his interest, had to be
eliminated, belonged to the right. Directly he acquired the
Avanti he got rid of Claudio Treves, refusing his articles
because he wanted to manage the paper, his paper, alone.
This actually resulted in a duel. After his expulsion from
the party he dreamed only of repaying the humiliation he
had suffered, and his ruthless attack on it was inspired by
spite and his obsession for revenge.

Mussolini had done more than change sides, like a
Renaissance soldier of fortune : he had given up his
bohemian existence and begun to live a life of luxury, to

[1] P. 19.

have mistresses, to combine the 'will to power' with a life of ease, far from dirt and misery. Money was not the sum of his desires nor the deciding factor of his policy, but he had come to realize that it was the sinews of war, and as war was part of his programme he could not dispense with it. He was not likely to forget that without money from Naldi and Barrère in 1914 he would have been powerless. No one who had known him as he was in 1912–13, shabby, hollow-cheeked, with burning eyes, would recognize him to-day in the *Galleria* in Milan, dressed in black, his powerful neck set on his thickened torso, his face squat and swollen. . . . He appealed to mob opinion not because he agreed with it, but because he wanted to gain time and avert summary destruction. He ran with the mob, sometimes ahead of it, but was never swept away. He stirred it up, in order to outwit it, for all his tastes and needs called him to the other side of the barricades.

Thus Mussolini hesitated no longer to break with the 'interventionist' democrats, who with Bissolati remained faithful to their ideals, even after the armistice, and continued to oppose Sonnino's short-sighted policy. Bissolati, himself an ex-editor of *Avanti*, had been one of the four socialist deputies expelled from the party in 1912, at Mussolini's instigation, for their excessively nationalist attitude during the Libyan war. After taking part in the agitation for Italy's intervention, he joined up in May 1915, at the age of fifty-eight, with his old rank as sergeant, and got himself sent straight to the front. Twice wounded in July, during the attack on Monte Nero, he refused to stay in Rome, though weakened by a series of operations. He went back to the front in mid-winter, still as a sergeant, and for his valour won another medal in the great Austrian push of spring, 1916. The grave political crisis of June compelled him to join the newly formed 'national' government. As a minister he unceasingly opposed the policy of 'sacred egoism', insisting that they were fighting for a nobler ideal than mere national unity, and preaching the necessity of close collaboration with the peoples of the Austrian empire in their struggle for independence. On the eve of the Paris Conference the hitherto concealed differences between him

and Sonnino developed into open discord, and he resigned :
Nitti was shortly to follow his example.

By leaving the cabinet, Bissolati hoped to gain a free
hand to carry on his campaign in favour of a genuinely
democratic peace, and he demanded that Italy should not
remain tied by the Treaty of London. ' Baron Sonnino ',
he said in an interview, ' is all for the inviolability of the
Treaty of London, which gives Fiume, an essentially Italian
town, to the Jugo-Slavians, so as to demand the possession of
Dalmatia (where Italians are in a tiny minority). I hold the
opposite view : Fiume must form part of the kingdom of
Italy, and Dalmatia be given to Jugo-Slavia.' Respect for
the principle of nationality coincided with Italy's interests.
By observing the terms of the Rome Pact, signed in
1918 with the representatives of the succession states of the
Austrian empire,[1] she could become the leader of the smaller
powers, and contribute to the stabilization of a new and
peaceful Europe.

But when the time came, Sonnino and the Italian
nationalists persisted in their desire to reap the advantages
of the secret Treaty of London—by annexing Dalmatia—
while at the same time demanding the annexation of Fiume,
in the name of the very principle of nationality which that
treaty, concluded ' consule Sonnino,' violated by awarding
Fiume to Jugo-Slavia.[2] Mussolini rushed to their support
and began a most violent campaign against any renunciation.
Bissolati, invited by the Italian League of Nations Society,
was due to come to Milan on January 11 to hold a meeting,

[1] At the Rome Conference summoned by permission of the Italian government, Italian, Polish, Romanian, Czech, and Jugo-Slavian delegates had
agreed on the necessity of a joint struggle against the Habsburg monarchy,
so that ' each people might realize its complete freedom and national unity
within a free state '. Italians and Jugo-Slavians, in a separate agreement,
acknowledged ' that the unity and independence of the Jugo-Slavian nation
are of vital interest to Italy, just as the achievement of Italian national unity
is to the Jugo-Slavian nation '. Both sides undertook so to act ' that during
the war and on the conclusion of peace the aims of both nations might be
fully attained '. They agreed at the same time on the joint defence of
the Adriatic against foreign control. Amongst the members of the Italian
delegation which concluded this agreement was Benito Mussolini.

[2] Article 5 of the treaty of April 26, 1915, read precisely : ' The territories
listed below will be allotted by the four allied powers to Croatia, Serbia, and
Montenegro : in the upper Adriatic the entire coast from the Bay of Volosca
on the borders of Istria up to the northern frontier of Dalmatia, including
the present Hungarian coastline, and the entire Croatian coast, including the
port of Fiume, etc.'

first of a series intended to explain and disseminate ' Wilsonian conceptions of a peace based on law and justice '. Mussolini mobilized his friends, denounced Bissolati's pusillanimity, and broke up his meeting at the Scala. This marked the final severance of the fascist movement from any possible connection with democracy ; henceforward, taking as usual the line of least resistance, it adopted the cause of discontented nationalism.

But the government had got itself into a fix over this question. It had arranged for hundreds of telegrams demanding annexation ' in the name of the population ' to be sent off by Italian officials in Dalmatia, it had permitted demonstrations in favour of ' Fiume or death ' in Italian towns, and declared in the press that ' the rights ' of Italy would be defended to the death. Meanwhile in Paris Orlando and Nitti were not only unable to force the acceptance of this squaring of the circle—the Treaty of London plus Fiume—but found that the actual validity of the treaty was menaced, since Wilson and the Serbs, who had not been informed of it, refused to recognize it. The Italian delegation was paralysed—completely absorbed, as M. Tardieu remarked, by the Fiume question—and the Conference was reduced to ' a three-cornered dialogue ' : Wilson, Clemenceau, Lloyd George. So, when Orlando and Sonnino decided on April 23 to leave Paris as a protest, their gesture fell flat, for it did not affect the situation. But Italian national feeling was stirred, and Orlando made fiery speeches to cheering crowds at railway stations. Parliament approved the action of the government, and Italy lived again in the atmosphere of *maggio radioso*. To complete the effect d'Annunzio came to Rome to demand annexation in a speech at the ' Augusteo ' : ' Our epic May begins anew ', he proclaimed. ' Do you not hear, far away on the Roman roads of Istria and Dalmatia, the measured tread of an army on the march ? With eagles aloft and tricolour flag, in the dawn of another May Italy sweeps down from the Capitol.'

D'Annunzio, Mussolini, and the nationalists demanded that the government should immediately annex Fiume, Dalmatia, the Tyrol, and present the Paris Conference with the *fait accompli*. 'We must put a *fait accompli* before the three powers', wrote Mussolini on April 29. 'The *fait accompli* is a decree of annexation to which the Jugo-Slavs, though they gnash their teeth, will have to submit. They cannot make war on Italy. They have no artillery, machine-guns, aeroplanes, or munitions. They will go no further than a more or less vigorous diplomatic protest. It would be calamitous for the government to miss such a unique opportunity. If the question is not settled at once in accordance with the simple requirements of necessity, it will never be settled.' It was even threatened that Italy might ally herself ' with all the victims of the Entente : Hungarians, Bulgars and Turks '. The government propagated the belief that its gesture had been successful ; the newspapers emphasized ' the void created at the Conference by the absence of Italy', its 'disorganization', the ' complete confusion ' caused by the departure of the Italian delegates, which had destroyed the ' Wilsonian dictatorship'. But it was gradually realized that the Conference was not only continuing to work, but was settling a great many important questions : the foundation of the League of Nations, the status of Schleswig, of Luxemburg, the Anschluss demanded by Austria, etc. Orlando and Sonnino, without any further invitation, made a headlong departure from Rome when Barrère informed them that the frontiers of Austria and the Brenner were going to be fixed in their absence.

Orlando, ' ce tigre végétarien ', as Clemenceau called him, found no more crowds to cheer his journey back. Disappointment and humiliation brought to many Italians a vision of Italy defeated in spite of victory, with the fruits of victory ' stolen ' by the allies. This sense of injustice and loss was cold-bloodedly exploited to a pitch of frenzy by Mussolini, and was perhaps the most important of the psychological factors contributing to the success of fascism. Mussolini and the nationalists had everything to gain by making out that Italy was a defeated nation. It was quite untrue, for probably no country gained or could gain so many advantages from the war. With the achievement of national unity the work begun with the *Risorgimento* was completed, while the fall of the house of Habsburg destroyed her

hereditary enemy and chief rival. Germany, in spite of the
hard conditions imposed on her, remained on her feet, and
one day would regain her place in Europe ; England and
France, victorious now, would have to reckon with her once
more. If the ruling classes had had the necessary breadth
of vision, if they had not yielded before the threats of
Mussolini and the nationalists, if they had placed themselves
at the head of the peoples of the old empire, Italy would
have taken the place of Germany, the Habsburgs, France,
as the arbiter of Danubian and Balkan politics. She might
have been the pivot of the Little Entente. On the contrary,
while the allies were sharing out amongst themselves the
German colonies in Africa and the former Turkish empire
in the near east, liberals, fascists, and nationalists were
working themselves into a frenzy over a few rocks in the
Adriatic. For new difficulties were arising, for which the
responsibility lay with those who had signed the Treaty of
London, giving Fiume to Jugo-Slavia, and who could think
of nothing, after the armistice, but the renewal of the
policy of ' sacred egoism '. But the judgments of history
do not distinguish between guilty and innocent victims ;
like those of Jehovah they are visited on both alike. Those
responsible for evil profit sometimes from the blind reactions
provoked by the harm they have done, and this was the
case in Italy, where the ' diplomatic defeat ' which Bissolati
had foreseen and tried in vain to avert was made use of by
those who had rendered it inevitable. The ruling classes,
fascists and nationalists, who had ' mutilated ' the Italian
victory, found in wounded national feelings the most
efficacious method of clinging to power and carrying on the
struggle against the democratic revolution.

   Mussolini had more than this one string to his bow.
While demanding of the government an ultra-nationalist
foreign policy he was initiating his campaign against the
state. This appealed to the inherent anarchy of the Italian
people and of the middle classes in particular : disgruntled
ex-officers, students fidgeting in University lecture-rooms,
shop-keepers struggling against taxation, *déclassés* of every
sort who wanted something new, helped to give to growing
fascism its invaluable halo of lawlessness and heresy. But,

which was most important, it favoured the claims of the industrialists and merchants and the capitalist classes generally. The *Popolo d'Italia* stressed the incapacity of the state for carrying on public services and proposed that they should be handed over to private industry, while the state gave up all commercial activity. This became the *leitmotiv* of fascist agitation, and of the meetings of economic ' congregations ' such as that which took place in Genoa at the beginning of April 1919, when Italian industrialists and landowners agreed to combine against state monopolies, the remains of war-time economy and ' bolshevism '. This meeting was the first step towards a reorganization of capitalist forces to face the perils of the situation. Mussolini welcomed it and offered his co-operation. He wanted money, a lot of money, and this was the only way he could get it. The ideological duality which was one of Mussolini's chief assets enabled him in this way to satisfy both the vague passions of the mob and the more precise interests of the capitalists.

This duality is incidentally one of the essential characteristics of all fascist ideology and propaganda, and was naturally evident in the discussions and announcements of the congress of March 23, 1919, in Milan, where the delegates and supporters of the *fasci* met to found a national organization. The meeting took place in the Piazza San Sepolcro, in a hall lent by the Association of Industrial and Commercial Interests. Not many more than a hundred fascists answered the summons sounded by the *Popolo d'Italia ;* anarcho-syndicalists, *arditi*, freemasons, and futurists jostled ultra-conservatives, but the great majority were survivors of the ' *fasci* of revolutionary action ' of 1914–15, and of the former left-wing ' interventionists '. Their influence was noticeable in the programme born of this meeting and issued in June by the new organization, the ' Italian *Fasci di Combattimento* ', which reflected the heat and excitement of the moment. The *fasci* made the following demands :

For political reform :

Universal suffrage, with proportional representation and votes for women.

Abolition of the Senate.

Convocation of a national assembly with the initial task of deciding the form of the constitution.

Creation of national technical councils with the object of extending and improving political democracy, in accordance with the ideas conceived in Bavaria by Kurt Eisner.

For social reform :

Eight-hour day.

Minimum wage.

Participation of workers' representatives in the technical management of industry.

Compulsory retirement of workers at fifty-five.

For military reform :

Replacement of the regular army by a national militia with short periods of training, to be used for purely defensive purposes.

Nationalization of all arms and munitions factories.

A foreign policy emphasizing the value of Italian participation in the peaceful rivalries of the civilised world.

For financial reform :

An extraordinary levy on capital, substantial and graded, amounting to a partial expropriation of all wealth.

Confiscation of all the possessions of religious communities, and abolition of episcopal revenues.

Revision of all contracts for war materials, and a levy of 85 per cent on all war-time profits.

This programme, issued by the central committee of the *fasci* with an eye to the general election, was obviously much further to the left than Mussolini would have liked. But he needed an organization behind him, and he did not want to risk the immediate alienation of those who, thanks to their common memories of ' revolutionary interventionism ', had just rallied to him. He did, however, take precautions against the programme acquiring too much significance.   While appearing to accept the propositions of his friends, he ' interpreted ' and watered them down to such an extent that they lost their meaning, and even ended by leading to quite different conclusions.   At the meeting of March 23 Mussolini drew up the following declaration :

' The Congress of March 23 declares its opposition to the imperialism of other peoples at the expense of Italy, and to the contingent imperialism of Italy at the expense of other peoples.   It accepts the chief principle of the League of Nations, which presupposes the integrity of each nation ; integrity which, so far as Italy is concerned, must be realized in the Alps and the Adriatic through her claim for Fiume and Dalmatia.'

This declaration already violated a principle of the League, by demanding Dalmatia, where the Italians were a tiny minority, while in the Tyrol and Julian Venetia the frontiers already assured to Italy included hundreds of thousands of Germans, Slovenes, and Croats.   But the arguments used by Mussolini in the commentary he added, and the spirit which inspired it, effectively purged the declaration of any League content.   Mussolini, though temporarily forced to lodge under the sign of the League, introduced the explosive which was to shatter it.

' We have a population of forty millions in an area of 287,000 square kilometres, cut across by the Apennines, which reduce still further the cultivable land at our disposal.   Within from six to twenty years we shall be sixty millions, and we have only a million and a half square kilometres of colonies, of which the greater part is desert and quite unsuitable for settling our excess population.   But if we look round we find England, with a population of forty-seven millions and a colonial empire of fifty-five million square kilometres ; and France, with a population of thirty-eight millions, has an empire of fifteen million square kilometres.   And I have figures to prove that every nation in the world has a colonial empire, which it is far from ready to give up for the sake of trans-atlantic creeds. Lloyd George speaks openly of the British Empire. Imperialism is the basis of life for any nation seeking economic and spiritual expansion. We say that either everyone must become an idealist, or no one. Let us seek our own interests. We want our place in the world, because we have a right to it. Let us be frank : the League must not become a trap set by the wealthy for the proletarian nations as a means of perpetuating the present conditions of the world balance of power.'

After such an ' explanation ', what was left of the seven or eight lines of the declaration ?

Since the principles adopted, even in such a curious fashion, might still lead to embarrassment, Mussolini saw to it that the meaning and scope of every programme was limited in advance by the avoidance of all labels and definitions. Fascists were neither republican nor monarchist, catholic nor anti-catholic, socialist nor anti-socialist ; they were ' problemists ' and realists, and practised in turn, according to the needs of the situation, ' class collaboration, class struggle, and class expropriation '. And since the idea of a party involved a doctrine and a programme, they were ' anti-party '. This put the old parties at a dis-advantage, satisfied those who were after something new, and avoided the dangerous ground of principle, as well as the difficulties of being coherent. Emphasis was laid on ' action ' rather than on ideas. This attracted many of the young advancing ' towards life ', impatient of obstructions and eager to have a good time, to sacrifice themselves, to acquire self-confidence. Fascism drove them along the easiest way. Everything was simplified, for thoughts had no time to form themselves, connect, or conflict before they evaporated in action, exalting and melodramatic. The inner life reduced itself to the simplest reflexes, shifting from the centres of feeling and becoming externalized. Doubts and uncertainties ceased to exist. The youthful fascist in a world full of contradictions joyfully affirmed : ' I need not think ; therefore I am '.

Thus the first real fascist congress, held in Florence in October 1919, was able to accentuate the republican note and propose, with Marinetti, the expulsion of the papacy and the ' devaticanization ' of Italy ; all of which was nullified by a single remark made by Mussolini during his speech : ' We fascists have no preconceived doctrine : our doctrine is based on facts.'

But events in Italy during 1919 were far from encouraging for the fascist movement or for Mussolini, who retained nevertheless his sound sense of realities and did not lose his head. He had prophesied at the ' Fascist Constituent Assembly ' in March : ' In two months a thousand *fasci* will have arisen throughout Italy.' At the beginning of July he was far more modest. ' Fascism ', he wrote, ' is pragmatical, it makes no assumptions, it has no ultimate objects. It will not necessarily go on for ever, or even for very long.' Having completed its task, which is concerned with the present crisis, ' it will not cling to life, but will know how to vanish without fuss '. ' Fascism ', he continued, ' will always be a minority movement. It cannot spread beyond the towns. But soon each of the three hundred principal towns of Italy will have its own *fascio di combattimento* '. Even this more modest prospect was not realized. At the Florence congress only 137 *fasci* were represented, with 62 in course of organization, and 40,000 adherents. These figures are obviously faked ; the report of the third National Congress held in Rome in November 1921, when fascism could afford to be frank, announced officially that at the Florence congress there had been represented only ' 56 *fasci*, with 17,000 adherents '. In any case the figures came nowhere near the 1000 *fasci* foreseen in March 1919, or the 300 hoped for in July. The movement seemed to be flagging rather than progressing. Mussolini's fear of isolation was greater than ever, especially in view of the approaching elections, when he would have to come out into the open and reveal his true position.

At the beginning of July he began in Milan a campaign for the creation of a ' committee of agreement and action '. The first meeting, summoned at the instigation of the *fascio*, was attended by representatives of the Syndical Union (pro-Corridoni), the *fascio di combattimento*, the Socialist Union (reformist), the Association of *Arditi*, the Union of Demobilised Soldiers, the National Association of Ex-servicemen, Corridoni's Revolutionary Society, the Republican Youth Society, the National Association of War Volunteers, the Federation of Garibaldists, the *fascio* of Social Education, and the Italian Labour Union. This miscellany was a fair reflection of the circle in which fascism gained its first recruits ; left-wing interventionists, reformist and anarcho-syndicalist, and ex-servicemen, democratic and Wilsonian, formed the majority, but they rubbed shoulders with nationalists, reactionaries, and even ordinary strike-breakers.

Mussolini proposed the formation of a permanent committee to resist the socialist monopoly. ' It must be made clear that these gentlemen cannot start the revolution against us. They might manage without us if they had the necessary organization and resolution, but they lack both. If they want to turn the results of the economic collapse into reprisals against us, we will give them something to think about that will make them bitterly regret it.'

The violence of this language shows a certain lack of balance ; Mussolini's attitude was dictated by a defence reflex. The disturbances against the high cost of living had not ceased, and the atmosphere was charged with revolution. Mussolini and the other delegates decided that ' if this food crisis were to become a political movement ' they would attempt to ' divert it into the revolutionary and progressive direction ' followed by the associations present at the meeting.

Mussolini even hoped to bring about an alliance between the one-time interventionists and the conservatives to drive the socialists out of the Milan Corporation at the forthcoming elections. Electoral reform was in force, and proportional representation would favour the advance of socialists and *Popolari*, while the small intermediate parties risked extinction. He proposed therefore a ' left concentration ', which should ally itself with the right-wing interventionists (nationalist, liberals, and democrats). But the fascist movement was still so chaotic and circumstances were so unfavourable that the tactics adopted by the *fasci* for the elections varied widely in accordance with local conditions and opposition. In Rome a candidate was put forward on the National Alliance list, which was composed of nationalists and conservatives, while the republicans, reformists, and the National Association of Ex-servicemen formed a left-wing bloc. The fascists abstained at Verona and Padua, were included in the national bloc at Ferrara and Rovigo, and joined the ex-servicemen at Treviso. Nearly everywhere else the ex-servicemen made their own separate lists and excluded the fascists from them.

In Milan, after lengthy negotiations, the left-wing parties (Republican Party, Socialist Union, Association of Ex-servicemen) had broken with the *fascio*. The *fascio* refused to make a common list with them ostensibly because of a disagreement over the electoral programme, in which it rejected the principle of the ' legal recognition of working-class organizations ', because that would bring about their ' strangulation '. What was making Mussolini so fastidious about a programme, when he had declared a hundred times that programmes were of no importance, and a few weeks ago had proposed an alliance with the conservatives in order to defeat the socialists ? The fact was that the left-wing parties had said that they would willingly form a joint list with the fascists on condition that Mussolini did not stand. Mussolini was hated and despised by all the workers, while the ex-servicemen considered him a traitor and a renegade, whose name would weaken their whole list. The groups which had formed the co-ordinating committee did not want to begin the fight with such a handicap, hence the veto on Mussolini. Consequently he broke off the negotiations and put forward his own list, which gained some five thousand votes out of about 270,000 Milanese voters.

This was a bitter blow for Mussolini, since it involved his personal failure. He had hoped to break through the wall of enmity that confronted him, and now he found himself dangerously isolated. For the first few weeks his reactions were those of a hunted animal. A short while ago he had sent two parcels containing bombs, one to the prefect, the other to the archbishop of Milan. Now, on November 17, the day after the elections, he incited a gang of *arditi* to throw a bomb at the procession celebrating the socialist victory, wounding nine people. Mussolini was arrested and it was proved that he was behind the outrage, but the prosecution was not pressed and he suffered only a day and a night's imprisonment. At the same time he fell a prey to a kind of 'ideological' exasperation, meditating on his personal isolation with a mixture of bitterness, despair, and pride. He spoke his thoughts aloud, free as he was from any immediate preoccupation, and once more at the beginning of his journey on a new road that seemed both difficult and long.

'Detesting as we do', he wrote in his newspaper on December 12, 'all forms of Christianity, that of Jesus as well as that of Marx, we feel an intense sympathy with the modern revival of the pagan worship of strength and courage. Enough, red and black theologians of all churches, enough of your false and cunning promise of a paradise that will never come. Enough, you ridiculous saviours of the human race, which doesn't care a damn for your infallible receipts for happiness ! Leave the field clear for the sheer force of individualism, since the individual is the only human reality.'

At the same time he sent his hearty greetings to the anarchist Malatesta, who had returned secretly to Italy towards the end of December. And on January 1, 1920, he began the new year with a repetition of the same creed :

'*Navigare necesse est* . . . against others and against ourselves. . . . We have destroyed every known creed, spat upon every dogma, rejected every paradise, flouted every charlatan—white, black or red—who deals in miraculous drugs for restoring happiness to the human race. We put no faith in any system, nostrum, saint or apostle ; still less do we believe in happiness, salvation or the promised land. . . . Let us get back to the individual. We stand for everything that exalts and ennobles the individual, gives him more comfort, more liberty and a wider life. We fight against everything that restricts and harms the individual. Two religions, one black, one red, are fighting to-day for the mastery of our minds and of the world ; two vaticans are sending forth their encyclicals, one in Rome and the other in Moscow. We are the heretics of both these religions.'

Their failure at the elections disconcerted and demoralized the *fasci*, though Mussolini did not yet feel that all was lost. After all he was not entirely alone, and there was one department in which he was, for the time being, superior. Against the vast but undisciplined crowds who swelled the socialist demonstrations and voted red, Mussolini employed armed groups of reckless hooligans who did not hesitate to break the law. These were the *arditi*, whose association had an office in every town, which had become almost everywhere a centre of armed organization closely connected with the *fasci*. The *arditi* had confidence in Mussolini, who flattered and encouraged them. From the war area, while waiting to be demobilized, they used to send him telegrams such as the following, signed by the N.C.O.s of the 27th Storm Battalion : ' Bravo, Mussolini ! Keep on striking hard, by God, for there is a lot of rubbish in our way. We are with you in spirit and will soon come and give you a hand.' The relations between *arditi* and fascists were particularly close in Milan, and resulted in the *arditi* leaving their hiding-place in April 1919 to make a surprise attack on the offices of *Avanti*, the socialist daily, which they sacked and set on fire. This serious action, coolly carried out, with the unmistakable Mussolini touch, provoked no direct response. There was a general strike in which, outraged, the entire working-class population took part, but which led to nothing, and a collection which brought in more than a million towards a new building ; but there were no reprisals. A year later, on the anniversary of this event, Mussolini was able to write :

' On April 15, 1919, the maximalists of Milan were shown in their true colours as philistines and cowards. No attempt at revenge was so much as planned, and neither the money collected, nor the votes gained can wipe out the memory of the day when the maximalist weathercock, knocked off its perch and broken into pieces, fell into the muddy waters of the Naviglio.'

In the meantime his alliance with the *arditi* became closer, and his body-guard was swollen by new members whom he had summoned to Milan towards the end of 1919, and whom he paid with the money subscribed for Fiume. A committee of inquiry investigated, on February 20, charges made against him by two former editors of the *Popolo d'Italia*, including one concerning the formation of gangs drawn from ' mercenary elements collected from Fiume and several other Italian towns, paid thirty lire a day and considerable sums for expenses, and organized for purposes of intimidation and violence.' Mussolini had no alternative but to admit it, and told the court committee : ' There were some hundreds of men in all, divided into squads commanded by officers, and naturally all under my command. I was a sort of commander-in-chief of this little army.' A commander who controlled it without ever leaving the offices of his paper.

When the Fiume subscription was used up, or no longer available as a result of the scandal raked up by the two dismissed journalists, it was big business money that enabled Mussolini to keep up his ' little army '. Towards the end of the year large sums were coming in from industrialists, and Mussolini began a big drive for naval and aerial armaments and for the development of the mercantile marine. On December 23 he declared that he was going to press for an expansionist foreign policy, and announced at the same time that the *Popolo d'Italia* would ' in the new year be provided with the indispensable typographical resources for a paper with a huge circulation '. Clearly he had no doubt that he could get all the money he wanted. Further, the Fiume adventure of d'Annunzio and his ' legionaries ' was an unexpected blessing. Mussolini, by supporting it at first and then turning traitor, was to profit from it greatly.

IV

REVOLUTION CROSSES THE ADRIATIC

ON September 12, 1919, while Nitti, the President of the Council, all unawares, was speaking in the Chamber, he received a telegram informing him that d'Annunzio had occupied Fiume. The fate of this city had never ceased to handicap the whole of Italy's foreign policy. On April 26, after the theatrical withdrawal of Orlando and Sonnino, the National Council of Fiume had proclaimed the annexation of the town to Italy and placed itself under the orders of the king's representative, General Grazioli. Orlando and Sonnino having hastily returned to Paris the day before, d'Annunzio, who had come to Rome to organize and lead the agitation in favour of annexation, made a flamboyant speech on May 6 from the top of the Capitol. He appealed to Italian heroism, unfurled the flag that had covered the remains of Randaccio, the airman killed on the Timavo, and declared that he would present it to the city of Trieste, after consecrating it in Italian Fiume. The Orlando government, caught between Rome and Paris, resigned as soon as possible, while the newspaper war went on, and each successive attempt of the Peace Conference at compromise over the Adriatic question fizzled out.

The Nitti ministry was formed on June 22. The nationalists were frenzied with rage, since all hope of forcing the government's hand over Fiume had to be abandoned. Consequently their anger was vented on the new ministry, and on Parliament, which d'Annunzio wanted to replace by ' a form of representation which would bring to the fore the real producers of national wealth, the real sources of national strength '. Thus the policy of expansion was linked with nationalism and anti-parliamentarism, thanks chiefly to the Poet, who predicted for the new ministry ' a retribution, swift and unerring as the jet of a flame-thrower '.

In this over-heated atmosphere there were grave incidents in Fiume at the end of June and the beginning of July. Soldiers of the French forces in occupation were murdered or wounded. The nationalist press hailed the ' Fiume vespers ', and Mussolini made the threatening suggestion of ' an alliance with the proletarian republics of the east, and a rapprochement with Germany '. An Allied commission of inquiry was appointed, and unanimously recommended the reduction of the Italian contingent and the increase of the Allied one ; steps were to be taken against the responsible Italian officers and the ' battalion of Fiume Volunteers ' disbanded. The Sardinian Grenadiers were also to be removed from the town, and on August 24 Major Rejna, their commanding officer, received orders to leave with his unit that night. A party of officers decided to disobey, and offered their services to the National Council of Fiume. The Council hesitated, and the troops left for the barracks at Ronchi, whence they were to return a few weeks later with d'Annunzio. At a meeting held in their new quarters, eight grenadier officers took the oath ' Fiume or death '. Active propaganda in the press, among politicians and in the army prepared the way for the expedition. A letter containing the oath and the eight signatures was sent to d'Annunzio, who arranged a meeting with one of the officers in Venice and took command of operations. Transport was requisitioned, and on September 12 the column consisting of some thousand men—other officers joined it *en route*—marched, singing, into Fiume. From the Palace, the headquarters of the government, d'Annunzio declared the town annexed to Italy. Each day parties of volunteers of every description arrived with batteries of artillery, squadrons of aircraft, and motor boats, and on September 14 the ' Commandant ' appealed to the officers and men of the Italian ships in the harbour to form ' the first squadron of the free Quarnero '. On the 19th a body of officers and *arditi* boarded the *Pannonia*, which had a cargo of food, took possession of her, and brought her to Fiume ; so began a practice which was to stock the town with food, money, and arms. D'Annunzio's freebooting allies supplied him from their captures : the *Persia* gave him arms ; the *Taranto* two million lire intended for Albania ; the *Cogne*, later, a large cargo of assorted merchandise which was sold by auction in the markets of Fiume.

Demonstrations for Fiume took place all over Italy ; nationalists and fascists as well as officers in uniform took part. Nitti issued orders, inflicted punishments, and dismissed the commanding officer of the Turin army corps, none of which had any effect. Army discipline was severely shaken, and even those officers who upheld it sympathized privately with the successful conspirators.

It was only at the last moment that d'Annunzio took command of the Fiume expedition, but like the Creator he formed it after his own image and likeness. For him Fiume became the scene of a marvellous adventure, through which he lived in a state of delirious excitement. The hero, the man of letters, and the tragedy king took the stage one after the other, and sometimes all together.

At the time of the despotic laws of Pelloux[1] in 1900, though representing the Abruzzi conservatives, d'Annunzio had thrust himself into a meeting of left-wing deputies, and announced that he was advancing ' towards life '. His conversion was never completed, for to d'Annunzio to advance ' towards life ' meant to seek new sources of emotion. In the same year 1900 he wrote his ' Hymn ' *On the Death of a Destroyer*, celebrating the ' great Barbarian ', who has risen above Good and Evil, and left on the plains below ' the slavish mob and lifeless multitude ' to climb the last peak, from which he sees the promised land.

> Man must be his own star,
> A law unto himself, and the avenger of his law.

D'Annunzio was his own star, and followed no other. He had only offered his services to Rome in order to obtain

---

[1] In February 1898 General Luigi Pelloux, President of the Council, put before the Chamber a series of extraordinary bills against the freedom of the press, of meeting and association and instituting the penalty of ' banishment ' (*domicilio coatto*) for opponents of the régime. The left-wing parties and even the liberals carried on a fierce struggle against these bills which went on until the middle of 1900, when the June elections resulted in their victory. It was in March 1900 that d'Annunzio joined the opposition to these laws.

a setting and an audience worthy of his greatness : ' Each day will be marked for you by a mighty deed, wherein you will see, as though engraved on a seal, the quality of my soul.' And twenty years after at Fiume he still dedicated himself to Glory, whose service he recognized before that of Duty.

Once installed at Fiume d'Annunzio intended to play the star part. As ' Commandant of the city of Fiume ' he issued a decree on November 20 by which he left in power, though with strictly limited authority, the National Council which had been elected by plebiscite on October 30, 1918 : ' All decisions and agenda of the National Council which in any way concern public order and may have a political effect, must be submitted for the approval of the military command, and may not be put into force until the day after they have been approved.' Fiume became a centre for idealists, idlers and rogues of every kind, some drunk with patriotic emotion, others attracted by a taste for adventure or a desire for amusement.

In Rome Nitti, as President of the Council, stated in an early speech in the Chamber on September 13 that soldiers who had joined d'Annunzio would be regarded as deserters, unless they returned to their units within five days. He turned at the same time to ' the workers of Italy, to the artisans and the peasants, to ask for their help ', and ' to the nameless masses, to make the great voice of the people a warning to all '. Three days later, in another speech, he adopted a different tone, one almost of retractation, and appealed to the soldiers instead of to the proletariat. At a Royal Council in Rome on September 25, Giolitti advised the occupation of Fiume by regular troops, and an immediate general election. Nitti only accepted part of this advice : he dissolved the Chamber on the 29th, and fixed November 16 for the elections. As to Fiume, he contented himself with declaring a blockade by land and sea ; a blockade which, incidentally, was not at all strictly maintained.

In Fiume d'Annunzio found himself up against a number of the inhabitants, particularly those who in varying degrees wanted autonomy, whose leader was the deputy Zanella. To gain local support, the ' Commandant ' decided to dissolve the National Council and hold new elections ;

meanwhile, by declaring martial law in the town, he anticipated possible opposition. Ten days before the elections he published an edict to the effect that Fiume was ' a war-time stronghold ', that military law would be enforced against ' anyone professing sentiments hostile to the cause of Fiume ' and that the death penalty would be promptly inflicted upon the guilty. On the other hand, in spite of his declaration that he did not recognize the Nitti government, he permitted himself to treat with it. Admiral Cagni, General Badoglio, in command of the blockading troops, the Duke of Aosta, who was always on the look-out for a surprise attack, and members of d'Annunzio's own circle, such as his secretary Giurati and Major Rizzo, all intervened or rushed backwards and forwards between Rome and Fiume.

Nitti never intended drastic intervention, and he saw to the provisioning of the town by means of the Red Cross. In point of fact he was not averse to acquiring, thanks to d'Annunzio, a bargaining point to use in his discussions with the Allies about Fiume, while on the other hand he feared the unpopularity in which a ' strong man ' policy would involve him. D'Annunzio remained obstinate, and proceeded in an Italian warship to Zara, where he obtained a promise from Admiral Millo, the governor of Dalmatia, not to evacuate that region in any circumstances whatsoever. Since the National Council of Fiume announced itself unanimously and unreservedly in favour of an accord with the Rome government, d'Annunzio decided to try for a plebiscite in his favour. But on the evening of December 18, after the voting had taken place, he realized that the result would be unfavourable, and stopped the count. Three days later he broke off all negotiations, and several of his supporters, including his secretary, his press agent, Pedrazzi, and Major Rizzo, deserted him. Immediately after his departure, Pedrazzi published in an Italian newspaper on December 24 a picture of the situation which is worth preserving :

' At d'Annunzio's side there stand only brave young officers, decorated or wounded, bold and enthusiastic, but quite irresponsible . . . to them war has become a necessity of life, fighting a moral practice. To put an end to this enterprise is to put an end to their delightful rebel existence, a little comic perhaps, but still a rebel existence, a life of songs, processions, meetings, military celebrations at once gay and warlike.

' This atmosphere of generous and hot-headed youthfulness has certainly affected d'Annunzio, and turned his head. Hailed by all as a conqueror, to himself he seems a victim. Fiume is victorious, not he. His dream was greater : too great. Coming to Fiume to save the city he has involved himself little by little in dictatorship, not through personal ambition, but for the good he hoped to do. His vision stretches ever further afield—beyond the bounds of the Adriatic. He dreams of noble crusades wherever the spirit of rebellion dwells.'

Such was the situation until the fall of the Nitti cabinet in May 1920.

Let us in the meantime consider the views of the various parties. The nationalists fanned the flames, for the Fiume affair might at any moment provoke a war with Jugo-Slavia, and they hoped by this means to strengthen Italy's territorial claims in the Adriatic. The freemasons did the same, from patriotic and revolutionary (in the 1848 manner) motives, and because they reflected the mental confusion of the average lower middle-class Italian. The Palazzo Giustiniani Lodge urged the government to provision Fiume by means of the Red Cross, an organization in which masonic influence was very great, and whose president, Ciraolo, a deputy, was himself a mason. The freemasons of Piazza del Gesù sent to d'Annunzio at Fiume an award of thirty-three grades of their own order.[1]

Mussolini carried on a campaign for Fiume, not only because it involved a perfervid nationalism which favoured

---

[1] After 1908 there were in Italy two kinds of freemasons, corresponding to the Grand Orient and the Grande Loge de France. Both were subsequently dissolved by the fascist government. Domizio Torrigiani, Grand Master of the Palazzo Giustiniani branch, was deported. Raoul Palermi, ' Commander ' of the ' ancient Scottish and traditional rite ' and an accomplished and unscrupulous adventurer, whose name became familiar in France at the time of the Caillaux affair, became an associate of Mussolini.

his designs, but because he realized that Fiume was ' anti-state ' and the possible starting point for a reconquest of the peninsula. For the moment d'Annunzio was in the lime-light, reaping the prestige of his *coup ;* he had at his disposal armed forces, and was himself a fighter. He must, therefore, be humoured and treated with caution. In September Mussolini started a subscription for Fiume, the proceeds of which he diverted two months later, as we have seen, into the pockets of his ' little army '. He was not prepared to play second fiddle, though, and if d'Annunzio marched on Rome he would establish there, as at Fiume, his own dictatorship. This must be prevented at all costs. In the *Popolo d'Italia* of September 25 Mussolini wrote : ' Revolution is here. Begun in Fiume, it *may* be completed in Rome ', but in private he did his best to dissuade d'Annunzio from any such project. Before the court of honour of the Milan Press Association he stated, early in 1920 : ' There existed in Fiume a kind of club which called me a traitor to Italy, because it knew that I discountenanced a march of any description.'

Most people had considered the possibility of such a march : particularly the legionaries, who sang verses about going to Rome *fare la festa* to Nitti, and one of whose leaders, Giurati, wrote to the Trieste *fascio*, on September 19, that ' the exploit of Fiume *must* be consummated in Rome ' ; certain industrialists, too, who sent Borletti to Fiume to spy out the land ; various royal and military cliques ; and Admiral Millo himself, the governor of Dalmatia, who was in close touch with the Duke of Aosta's circle. The expectation was so general that Nitti handed over the com-mand of the entire Adriatic coast to General Caviglia, in order to prevent a possible landing of legionaries.

Only the socialists had not considered the possibility. There was, it is true, a ' conspiracy ' early in 1920, which was quickly suppressed. D'Annunzio had just appointed as his secretary, to succeed the nationalist Giurati, Alceste de Ambris, a syndicalist and leader of the Italian Labour Union, which had supported the war, and whose adhesion the General Confederation of Labour had consequently refused. When the general railway strike broke out in January, various members of the extreme left, including Malatesta and Giulietti, conceived the idea of turning the situation created by the occupation of Fiume to revolutionary ends. Malatesta, the anarchist, who was aged about sixty-seven and had returned from exile only a few days before, was the only real revolutionary in Italy in the 1919–20 period. For him the word 'revolution' had a definite meaning, and implied a course whose final goal was Rome.

The starting point mattered little; Fiume would serve, for d'Annunzio might be won over, and there were arms to be seized. The revolution, according to Malatesta, must be brought about at once, for, he said : 'If we let the right moment slip we shall pay with tears of blood for the fright we have given the *bourgeoisie*.' A survivor of the 'Alliance' of Bakunin, he had taken part in the attempted rising of the 'Band of Benevento' in April 1877, and had been the moving spirit of the 'red week' of 1914. Now that all Italy was in ferment swift action was wanted, and unhesitating use must be made of anything which could ensure victory. So Malatesta got into touch with d'Annunzio. For go-between he had Captain Giulietti, head of the Federation of Marine Labour. Giulietti, who had contrived the secret return of Malatesta to Italy and supplied money for the anarchist daily, *Umanità Nuova*,[1] was at the same time a valuable ally of d'Annunzio's. In October 1919 his Federation had seized the *Persia*, which was loaded with arms for the White armies fighting the Soviets, and brought it to Fiume.

It was both an advantage and a disadvantage for Malatesta that he had no official connection with the working-class movement. He was unhampered by routine and had a will of iron. But the socialists, who still had the confidence of the masses, were as suspicious of him as of d'Annunzio. Some of the 'conspirators', at their secret meetings in Rome, refused to support him without the co-operation or at least the approval of the Socialist Party and the General Confederation of Labour. The latter, alarmed, withheld approval from the scheme, and it went no further; particularly as Mussolini, who had wind of it, and wanted no

[1] Which appeared first in February 1920 in Milan.

march on Rome without Mussolini, hastened to tell the whole story in the pages of the *Popolo d'Italia*.

In this way any chance of associating the Fiume enterprise with a popular revolution in Italy was ended. The 'march on Rome' was to come from the right. The occupation of Fiume, as time went on, provided fascism with a model for its militia, its uniforms, the names of its units, its war cries and its creed. Mussolini borrowed the whole of d'Annunzio's scenario, including his crowd scenes. Realizing that d'Annunzio was above all a poet, and as such could not get very far, he waited patiently to succeed him. D'Annunzio was the victim of the worst plagiarism ever known. 'For the fascist conquest of Italy,' said Count Sforza, with his usual discrimination, 'has been the most literal and the least original copy of d'Annunzio's wild epic, the Fiume adventure.'

V

NITTI, GIOLITTI, DON STURZO

AT the general election of November 1919, the Italian masses showed their disapproval of the war and their need for social justice by voting for the socialists and the *Popolari*. These two parties alone had between them a majority in the new Chamber : 256 out of 508 seats. There were only three possible ways of assuring a parliamentary majority : socialists and *Popolari* ; socialists, democrats, and liberals ; *Popolari*, democrats, and liberals. The socialists had gained 1,840,600 votes and 156 seats—32 per cent in the country and in parliament ; they were consequently far from having an absolute majority. The proportional voting system had saved the conservative parties from a worse defeat ; the south, in spite of the war, remained their chief source of votes. Of the 156 socialists, 131 had been elected in the north, in the Po valley and in Tuscany ; only ten came from the inland districts of the south, five of whom were from Apulia. The islands returned no socialist deputies. The socialists, however, were nearer to power than the figures showed, by the extent to which they could interpret the will of the whole Italian people and voice their profound discontent. Three courses seemed open to them : to leave parliament and have recourse to direct action in the country ; to remain there while creating a second power in the country to replace it ; to win over in parliament and in the country the allies which were indispensable to the accomplishment of the democratic revolution. In actual fact the Socialist Party, incapable alike of direct action and of large-scale political manœuvres, shilly-shallied for three years until the fascists stepped in and solved the problem without them, and in spite of them.

Mussolini, who was lying low, exasperated by his electoral

defeat, realized very well what he stood to gain from such a situation. Commenting on an article in *Avanti*, according to which the Socialist Party must ' leave to the *bourgeoisie* the task of liquidating the liabilities resulting from the war ', he wrote, a week after the elections :

' No, my dear sirs, the socialists who hold the party ticket may—some of them—understand the reasons for this dilatory policy, but the electorate will not. The masses who voted for you did so in the belief—we shall see whether or no it was an illusion—that you alone were capable of solving their problem and leading the Italian people towards greater prosperity and greater freedom. You cannot decently withdraw from this undertaking. There are two ways of fulfilling your obligations : either by winning absolute power through open insurrection, since you have not a clear majority in parliament, or by a coalition with other parties, arranged on intelligent and advantageous terms, and based on an agreed common programme. The first alternative would mean civil war, with the inevitable destruction of the party and the working class, and the rise of an armed dictatorship ; the second, on the other hand, would lead to the fulfilment of the greatest expectations. We are loath to suggest a further possibility, deadlock in parliament and chaos in the country.'

Three months later Mussolini was convinced that this third hypothesis would be realized.

' The marvellous victory at the polls has simply shown up the inefficiency and weakness of the socialists. They are impotent alike as reformers and revolutionaries. They take no action either in parliament or in the streets. The sight of a party wearing itself out on the morrow of a great victory in a vain search for something to apply its strength to, and willing to attempt neither reform nor revolution, amuses us. This is our vengeance, and it has come sooner than we hoped.'

The Socialist Party could not escape from this impasse, which forced it to waver from one policy to another, taking two steps backward for every one forward. The manifesto issued in August by the maximalist section, which dominated the party, plumped for revolution without any transition period :

> ' The establishment of a socialist society ', announced this manifesto, ' cannot be achieved by decree, nor by the decision of a parliament or a constituent assembly. Hybrid forms of collaboration between parliament and workers' councils are equally to be condemned and rejected. The proletariat must be incited to the violent seizure of political and economic power, and this must then be handed over entirely and exclusively to the workers' and peasants' councils, which will have both legislative and executive functions.'

At the national congress of the Socialist Party, which took place at Bologna in the beginning of October 1919, this section had abolished the old party programme, because it recognized ' the struggle for the control of centres of power (the state, communes, etc.) and their transformation from instruments of aggression and exploitation into instruments for the economic and political expropriation of the ruling class.' The new programme, however, asserted that ' these bodies cannot conceivably be utilized for the liberation of the proletariat '. What then was to be done with parliament and the municipalities after they had been conquered ? The manifesto quoted above explains : the party must strive ' in the constituencies and the institutions of the *bourgeois* state for the intensive propagation of the principles of communism, and for the rapid overthrow of these instruments of *bourgeois* domination '.

Thus the 156 deputies and, a few months later, the 2800 socialist communes were apparently to confine their energies exclusively to revolutionary propaganda and sabotage of the state. In actual fact the socialist deputies and mayors devoted their best efforts, as in pre-war days, to the advocation of public works, the creation of syndicates and co-operative enterprises, and to everyday, sometimes excellent, administration. Everything went on as if there were no distinction, or connection either, between this practical and almost shamefaced reform and the maximalist proclamations.

Everyone worked on his own by a sort of division of labour to which none raised any objection. In Moscow the results of the Congress of Bologna, unanimously ratifying adhesion to the Third International, were hailed as a great achievement. Lenin, however, wrote to Serrati[1] towards the end of October, to warn the Italian proletariat against a ' premature insurrection ', adding his praises and one piece of advice : ' The marvellous work of the Italian communists assures us that they will win over to the cause of communism *the whole industrial and agricultural proletariat, as well as the small proprietors*, which is essential for their victory.' The praise was unmerited and the advice was ignored. The party's work was far from ' wonderful ', and instead of trying to win over ' the *whole* of the industrial and agricultural proletariat, as well as the small proprietors ', the party remained drunk with words, drawing up paper plans for soviets, and taking no notice of the factory councils in the north or the land-hungry peasants of the south.

A great number of the small landowners were coming under the influence of the ' Italian Popular Party ', the *Popolari*, which had just been formed. At the November elections it had obtained more than a million votes and a hundred seats. The Vatican had approved its creation at the end of 1918 to stem the rising tide of socialism. In addition, ' a fair number of liberals ', writes Signor Tittoni, ' counted on its support as an ally against socialism '.

The *Popolari* thus began life with two souls, one democratic and eager for great reforms, the other profoundly reactionary. As time went on the conflict between these tendencies became more marked. The conservative elements, Don Sturzo remarked, ' will leave the party when the agrarian-fascist phenomenon materializes '. But quite apart from this initial equivocation, the attitude of the *Popolari* and the confusion of the socialists resulted in the former being called upon to play a chiefly conservative role during the years 1919–20. Mussolini took the measure of the party exactly in January 1919, a few days after its creation :

' The event of the day in national politics is the creation of the Italian Popular Party. . . . Its programme is demo-

[1] Then editor of the *Avanti*.

cratic. Too democratic, we dare say. It has much in common with other party programmes. But the *Popolari*, in choosing their weapons, must observe the strictest legality. By so doing they can play a very great part in national life. They alone can hope to compete with the socialists for the rural vote at the next election.'

And so it fell out. For two years the socialists had no opponents—apart from their own stupidity—except the new party. The *Popolari* alone opposed the constituent assembly and breached the socialist monopoly in the syndical sphere, especially in the country districts ; and Italy was still, in spite of the war, an essentially rural country. In so far as any ' bolshevik danger ' existed at all in Italy it was the *Popolari* who checked it.

The dual character of the *Popolari* made it difficult for them to collaborate with the socialists, who for their part were not ready for any such thing. This was the fundamental cause of the successive ministerial crises which used up the only two leaders then at the disposal of the Italian *bourgeoisie*, Nitti and Giolitti.

By the time of his accession to power Nitti had accomplished a great deal. He was an honest liberal, widely read in history and economics and, which was unusual in an Italian statesman, thoroughly acquainted with the great modern states, particularly England, Germany, and the United States. He was abreast of modern movements and tendencies in international finance. At the same time— and this curious combination explains to a large extent both his merits and defects—he remained, by extraction and temperament, a typical Italian of the south, brought up in primitive social surroundings, where organized parties and advanced labour movements were quite unknown. Consequently he came quickly to the fore, like many of the pick of the south, who did not have to win their spurs in local campaigns. They were bound to their native soil by ties of common feeling, local prestige, or social rank, and there was no connection between their intense, often cosmopolitan culture and the local life. They were self-made men, and when they returned from Naples, Rome,

or London they found themselves in a sort of family atmosphere, among faithful friends, who were an essential part
of their background and with whom they shared a certain
philosophy built on common sense, cunning and adaptability. It was through their own study and intellectual
effort that they were able to jump straight from the small
provincial world into the great capital, avoiding the
longer road of human experience. It was not surprising
that Nitti should be as sceptical and canny as a big business
man and as fatalistic as a peasant of the Basilicata. The
colossal lag of the south behind northern Italy compelled
its statesmen to adopt a constant gradualism, though, on
the other hand, thanks to their lively intelligence and
culture, they had a taste for high politics. They could only
reconcile these two tendencies by resigning themselves to
patience and caution in home affairs and reserving their
initiative for foreign policy.

A broadly paternal policy is what Nitti always wanted
to put into effect. He would have made a perfect ' commis '
under Louis XIV or Joseph II, but could not adapt himself
to the clash of party and class struggle, which in the post-
war period made it impossible to ' do good ' for the people
without coming into close contact with them, and letting
them feel that their role was important and that a new era
had begun. Nitti, like Giolitti and Turati, kept his pre-
war outlook. His economic and social programme was
still that of his *Discorsi ai Giovani d'Italia* which he had
collected in his *L'Italia all'Alba del Secolo XX*, the most
significant document of the prescient liberalism of the
nineteen hundreds. Nitti did not believe in the possibility
of revolution in Italy. ' Italy ', he liked to say, ' is perhaps
the only European country which in two thousand years
has not had a real revolution or a great war of religion '.
He had a fundamental mistrust of political change, partly
through ingrained conservatism, partly through scepticism
derived from a study of history and economics. He disapproved of the conception of a constituent assembly with
which everybody had flirted, and as a liberal of the old
school, unchanged by the war, he opposed any idea of state
socialism and control of industry or banking. He was

compelled to go further along the road of prudent and rather opportunist reform by the grave economic situation, which confronted the government with problems so urgent that they allowed no respite.

The economic crisis, so far delayed and partly disguised by temporary distractions, broke upon Italy at the beginning of 1920 and immediately reached a climax. The difficulties of the food supply began to be felt ; the coal problem became more and more acute. England now only supplied 300,000 tons a month instead of 800,000, and charged a high import rate. The number of trains had to be reduced, factories could only work half time. Other imports had to be cut down : corn, sugar, frozen meat. The food question was complicated by the rise in the rate of exchange, over which control had to be established in the middle of April 1920. Besides, the Italian economic system had not yet adapted itself to the new conditions. People continued to speculate feverishly and start new businesses, for with peace a new era of expansion and prosperity was expected. Hence the demand for credit increased, and with it the fiduciary issue. Abroad the fall in wholesale prices was a sign that a new adjustment was inevitable.

Nitti made real efforts to cope with the situation, the seriousness of which, particularly with regard to public finance, he did not attempt to conceal. He warned his electors in a letter written in October 1919 :

> ' Present state expenditure exceeds receipts more than three times ; all state concerns are in debt, and thousands of millions a year are lost owing to the fixing of the price of bread ; the national debt is increasing at the rate of a milliard a month ; each month our expenditure on the army is greater than it was each year before the war.'

Nitti introduced numerous measures of control and showed great activity, launching a loan in November 1919 which was very successful and brought in 21,000,000,000 lire in a few months. Later, after his fall from power, he recalled the long list of his decrees to prove that it was he who had made the first most difficult and ungrateful efforts to avoid the storm. This was true, but did not and could not avert his fall. In the atmosphere of 1919–20 his slogan : ' Produce more and consume less ', offered no prospects to Italy and her people. In a world becoming increasingly impoverished, with new needs created in war-time and liberated by peace, such a formula had no psychological meaning and would soon have no economic meaning either.

Moreover, Nitti could not get the necessary political support for his administration. In common with Giolitti he would have liked to persuade the socialists to form a government with him. The bitter struggle between these two statesmen was partly over the question as to which was to succeed first in taming the monster. The socialists, many of whom remained faithful to their old liaison with Giolitti, disliked Nitti for his internal policy. He had reorganized the police force, almost non-existent at the beginning of 1919, and created the ' Royal Guard ', which was to play a very active part in the suppression of popular demonstrations, however peaceful. (Between October 1919 and May 1920 several hundred working men and peasants were killed and wounded in all parts of Italy. Socialists and fascists alike abused the police.) But the socialists shunned the responsibility of power, and the only way of doing without them was to put their 1917 programme into practice with the aid of other supporters.

Nitti was not the man for such a task. This is clear from an examination of his agrarian policy. In 1917, when he was Minister of Finance, he had founded the National Ex-servicemen's Plan, and he now allotted it a large grant for the purchase of land, to be handed over to members who were farmers. This idea, though generous in its original conception, was now totally inadequate to satisfy the land hunger that possessed every peasant in the country. Nitti's hand was forced by ever-increasing seizures of land, and he brought in two successive measures which aimed rather at stopping the seizures than at carrying out genuine reform.[1] The first gave prefects power ' to allow in certain conditions the occupation of uncultivated land, where agricultural production needs stimulating ; and to put an end to violent and arbitrary occupation by the people '.

[1] Decrees Visocchi of 2.ix.1919, and Falcioni of 22.iv.1920.

The second, published when the situation had become worse, was still more repressive, since it specified that ' only uncultivated or under-cultivated land may be *temporarily* occupied ', occupation being only permitted by consent of ' legally constituted associations which already possess and cultivate land '. Within these limits Nitti could hardly counter maximalist ' nihilism ' by bold social planning.

The only other possible allies were the *Popolari* ; but Nitti's training made it difficult for him to understand this new party which had sprung up like a mushroom in the post-war forcing-house. His outlook was too personal to suit the political requirements of the *Popolari*, whose secretary, Don Sturzo, wanted to create a great party on the English model, with a definite programme to which its tactics in the country and in parliament would be subordinated. Besides, the members, who had almost all favoured neutrality and owed their success at the elections chiefly to this fact, considered Nitti too deeply compromised by his share in war-time administration. They accused him too of ' weakness ' towards their rivals, the socialists. During the railway strike of January 1920, when the ' white ' unions had ordered work to be resumed, not only had the strike been terminated by an agreement signed with the single ' red ' organization which had started it, but the Minister of Labour had left to the mercies of the Railwaymen's Union all those catholics who had refused to obey its orders.[1] The *Popolari* therefore took advantage of the first ministerial crisis, in March 1920, to demand the resignation of the entire government and to lay down their minimum programme.[2]

---

[1] The minister was Chimienti. Nitti was away from Rome all January attending the Inter-Allied conference, which was discussing Italo-Jugo-Slav differences.

[2] It consisted of nine points, of which the following are the most important : (1) Foreign policy of conciliation with all nations, and recognition of the principle of self-determination ; at home, respect for individual and collective freedom, combined with firm opposition to all anarchistic elements aiming at the liquidation of the existing social order. (2) Proportional representation for the coming administrative, municipal and provincial elections ; political and administrative votes for women. (3) Recognition of all class organizations and their proportional representation on all central and local councils or commissions. . . . (5) Creation of a state examination for secondary schools ;

Nitti, who had the support of the Vatican, with which he was negotiating over the Roman question, was for a time under the impression that he could dispense with the help of the *Popolari*, and formed his new ministry without them. It only lasted a few weeks, and although he was joined by the *Popolari* after the third crisis it was too late to save the government from its fate. To relieve the budget from the heavy charge of the bread subsidy, Nitti issued an ordinance raising the price of bread by fifty centesimi a kilogram. This provoked violent opposition from both left and right. Mussolini's attitude in his paper was that ' those who have more must pay more : the present price must be maintained for the sake of the poor, the workmen, and the office-workers '. Faced with this storm Nitti withdrew the ordinance with the intention of drafting it into a bill, but the hostility of practically all groups in the Chamber forced him to resign.

Nitti's fall caused no surprise, since so many influences and events had been combining to bring it about. When he came to power Mussolini, following his usual custom, had declared that he was expecting action, and had approved his fiscal measures, as he later approved Giolitti's ; but he was now out for his blood, because Nitti had had him detained a few hours in November 1919 and had ordered a search for arms at fascist headquarters. Nitti was equally unpopular with the army, having axed hundreds of super-fluous generals and thousands of officers, and refused to carry out the expedition against the soviets of Georgia that the previous Orlando government had planned. The nationalists were furious with him because of his views on the Fiume question and his desire for conciliation with Jugo-Slavia, and organized endless demonstrations. On May 24, the anniversary of Italy's entry into the war, which was not officially celebrated, a delegation of Dalmatians and Fiumans came to Rome. This gave rise to a

abolition of all regulations restricting the development of private education. (6) Foundation of regional chambers of agriculture, and reform of the machinery of arbitration in collective disputes ; agrarian legislation for the division of large properties, internal colonization, and purchase of land by the peasants for small-holdings. (7) Fiscal reform to solve the financial problem by increasing the rate of taxation, and imposing a heavy tax on fortunes made during the war. . . .

violent demonstration which was severely repressed with many victims on both sides, eight dead and thirty wounded, an event which considerably weakened the government.

His right-wing opponents felt that the moment had come to redouble their efforts to defeat Nitti and reverse his foreign policy. In the early months of 1920, while strikes were increasing in the country and d'Annunzio was in full blast at Fiume, Nitti was striving in London, Paris, and San Remo to secure an intelligent policy of European reconstruction from which Italy would be bound to profit. Together with Lloyd George he supported a return to normal conditions, the resumption of trade relations with the Soviets, and the fixing of reparations at a reasonable figure. The French government persisted in the policy which led to Millerand's sabotage of the Cannes conference : hostility towards any concession to Germany ' who must pay ', and towards any accord with Russia around whom the *cordon sanitaire* must be kept drawn. Consequently Italian nationalists and fascists obtained every help and encouragement in their opposition to Nitti from the French ambassador at Rome, M. Barrère. He had his instructions from Clemenceau, who had announced after the November 1919 elections that he would ' do anything and sanction any means ' of preventing Italy from being submerged by the tide of revolution. The French embassy at Rome was accused in the press and in the Chamber of having become ' the headquarters of the campaign against the socialists ', who remained ' dangerously ' Wilsonian. The Spa conference was summoned for May 25. ' Signor Nitti ', said M. Barrère, ' will not be present ', and Nitti was defeated on May 11, the very day on which the Italian and Jugo-Slav delegates had at last made contact at Pallanza.

The succession was open ; at the beginning of June, after some weeks of crisis, Nitti was definitely turned out, chiefly because there was a successor all ready : Giovanni Giolitti. Giolitti, like Mussolini, had private scores to settle. He had not wanted Italy to intervene in the war in spring 1915, particularly at that moment and in the existing circumstances. He had been expelled from the government as the result of a palace intrigue, and subsequently abused and threatened. Salandra had incited the fascists and nationalists against him, and had given them the freedom of the streets. It was Giolitti's wish to return to power, combine with the socialists, carry out a number of political, economic and fiscal reforms and finally restore order in the country. He tolerated Nitti and even lent him his supporters, but he looked upon him as a lieutenant who would give way to him when he was ready. Nitti had quite different views.

On October 12, 1919, before the general elections, Giolitti set out his claims to power in his famous speech at Dronero. This largely consisted of a devastating tirade against the Italian ruling class, ' against the impudent minorities, the witless and soulless governments that had dragged a nation into war against its will ', against those who had ' flung Italy blindly into war, without well-defined agreements on political and colonial questions, without even realizing the existence of her economic, financial, commercial, or industrial needs '. After enumerating Italy's losses in life and wealth, Giolitti launched his own programme : to make every effort in foreign affairs to render another war impossible ; to call upon all nations to join the League ; to take advantage of international working-class solidarity ; to abolish secret diplomacy, and leave to parliaments alone the right of declaring war and making peace. As for the past, he looked forward to immediate official inquiries on the subject of war-time responsibilities, the use to which plenary powers had been put, the way in which large contracts had been ordered and carried out, ' to show the country how billions of money had been wasted '. To meet the financial crisis he proposed the abolition of military expenditure, a graduated tax on total income and on inheritance, and an extraordinary levy on capital, especially war profits. He launched a violent attack on the forces of reaction, ' which ', he said, ' can prevail no longer, since the privileged classes of society, which led humanity into disaster, can no longer rule the whole world alone ; its destiny must lie henceforth in the hands of the people '.

This speech raised a great hullabaloo in the nationalist and conservative press. Nitti hastened to oppose such a programme, especially the inquiry into the war, which would

only serve to ' revive ill-feeling ', and he replied in a letter
to his constituents on October 31. From this moment the
papers noted that ' the break between Signor Nitti and
Signor Giolitti may be considered as final '. It was in fact
the beginning of an extremely bitter struggle between
the two statesmen. Their rivalry was complicated by the
conflicting interests of the two biggest Italian banks, the
Banca Commerciale Italiana and the *Banca Italiana Sconto*, and
took the most astonishing forms. Giolitti managed to get
a deputy to blackmail Nitti by bringing a petition in the
Chamber against him for his pretended connection with the
B.I.S., and had leaflets denouncing him secretly printed ;
while Nitti had all Giolitti's dealings on the stock exchange
watched. They did their best to eliminate one another.
At every ministerial crisis each vetoed the other's candidature, thus preventing any solution, paralysing and
discrediting parliament, and aiding the machinations of the
fascists and conservatives.

In this struggle Giolitti consistently had the upper hand.
He had a profound knowledge of the art of government,
to which he had devoted the greater part of his life, and
great experience in handling men, though he was more
successful at exploiting their weaknesses than at making use
of their good qualities. A bureaucrat, he did not share
Nitti's dislike of state economic intervention. As a supporter of neutrality he was nearer the socialists and the
Popolari. On the eve of his return to power he asked the
socialists to join his government, for he hoped to do ' great
things '. Turati replied : ' We are not ambitious. If we
accepted, it would be for personal reasons, and our people
would not follow us.' Giolitti retorted : ' I am convinced
that I can serve the country at this moment, and I shall
form a government. I shall get a majority wherever I can.'
He also appealed to the *Popolari*. Don Sturzo did not like
the idea of joining Giolitti. He had a profound distaste
for the arch corrupter of Italian politics, which was returned
in full by Giolitti : the anti-clerical Piedmontese wished
never to meet a party chief in canonicals. Don Sturzo
feared Giolitti's methods, knowing that he was ready to
make use of the catholics, as he had done in 1913, to split

up and weaken the other parties, and not to initiate, as Don Sturzo wished, a policy of large-scale party alliances based on well-defined programmes. The Vatican, which had tried in vain to save Nitti, opposed Giolitti, fearful of his financial programme and his conception of the ' two parallels ', church and state, which need never meet. Amongst the measures proposed by Giolitti, that enforcing the registration of all bonds by the holder especially concerned the church, which had so far been able to evade the laws regarding ecclesiastical possessions by holding bearer bonds and owning property through intermediaries.

Nothing, however, could stop Giolitti's accession to power. He was looked upon and trusted almost everywhere as a saviour. The Italian *bourgeoisie*, which in 1914 had supported the war to rid themselves of the working-class movement, which was getting too powerful, now rallied for the same reason to the supporter of neutrality, the ' traitor ', Giolitti. Even those who had been his fiercest enemies, such as Sonnino, begged him to take office. It was remembered that in those happy times before the war Giolitti had proved himself able to charm the socialist serpent. ' Those who in 1915 ', wrote Guglielmo Ferrero, ' snatched the magic wand from his hands and broke it, are now calling on the old magician to renew his former marvels.' The nationalists, who had been his most violent opponents during the war, accepted him now, since they hoped that by devoting himself chiefly to internal affairs he would abandon Nitti's excessively pan-European policy. Mussolini was inclined to support him if by so doing he could bring himself nearer power. He announced that Giolitti's ministerial proclamation ' coincided almost exactly with the fascist postulates '. As to the *Popolari*, their parliamentary group had decided, in spite of Don Sturzo's advice to the contrary, to join the new government.

With his accession to power the serious break of 1914–15 which had split the *bourgeoisie* in two was mended. There was no more talk of ' neutralists ' and ' interventionists '. Giolitti, the war-resister, ' demagogic ' financier and man of the Dronero speech, had achieved a real, if temporary, revival of national unity.

VI

THE RISE AND FALL OF MAXIMALISM

AFTER the armistice, and particularly after the elections of November 1919, there was a rush to join the ' red ' General Confederation of Labour, which swept in all classes of labour, including private employees, skilled labourers, state employees, and in many districts the local societies of small shop-keepers. The 321,000 members of the General Confederation of Labour at the beginning of the war had increased to 2,200,000 by the end of 1920. The same thing was happening in every country. In France the *Confédération Générale du Travail*, from a million members in 1914, reckoned 2,400,000 early in 1920 ; in Germany the two and a half millions of 1913 leapt to eight millions in 1920 ; even in England the careful calculations of the Trade Unions showed over the same period an increase of 1,572,391 to 4,317,537 in their membership. An epidemic of strikes broke out and reached its peak in 1920 in Italy as elsewhere, although it was soon put an end to by the cold douche of the economic crisis.[1]

[1] This is illustrated by the statistics of strikes in the years 1919–22 taken from the *Annuaire* of the *Statistique Générale de France* :—

		1919	*1920*	*1921*	*1922*
ENGLAND	(a)	1352	1607	763	576
	(b)	2400	1779	1770	512
GERMANY	(a)	3719	3807	4455	4785
	(b)	1938	1429	1489	2046
FRANCE	(a)	2026	1832	475	665
	(b)	1161	1317	402	290
ITALY	(a)	1871	2070	1134	575
	(b)	1554	2314	724	448
U.S.A.	(a)	3630	3411	2385	112
	(b)	—	—	—	—

(a) Number of disputes (strikes and lock-outs). (b) Number of strikes and workers locked out in thousands.

Germany is the exception which proves the rule, for the number of strikes did not begin to fall until 1925, when the economic crisis occurred independently of inflation.

In January 1920 there was a strike of railwaymen and post office employees, and between the end of February and the end of May increasing numbers of agricultural workers in the provinces of Ferrara, Mantua, Novara, Pavia, Padua, Verona, Arezzo, and Parma, went on strike. The 'white' (catholic) organizations of Soresina (Cremona) were also affected. All these strikes had a definitely economic aim, to make wages meet the ever-rising cost of living. They followed no preconcerted plan ; the railwaymen went out on January 20, while the post office employees returned to work on the 21st ; the agricultural strikes of the north took place unrelated to each other or to the seizure of land which was going on in the south. It was a huge dissipation of energy, a wave of movements which ended by holding up productive work for weeks and months in some rural districts, but whose political effect was nil. But this readiness and persistence of the masses who struck was a sign of the times and evidence of their restlessness and their hopes. The least thing might lead to a cessation of work, though at times strikes were linked with a more widespread discontent, as in Carnia, during May, where the Austrians had been in occupation during the war and too many problems had been left unsolved. In some cases 'political' claims of the first importance were made, as in the general strike at Turin during April, the object of which was the recognition of factory councils by the employers, and which resulted in a severe defeat for the workmen.

This strike arose out of an incident which shows what the atmosphere was like in some industrial centres. The government having just adopted 'summer time', the management of the Fiat motor-works had put on the hands of the factory clock one hour. The workers' committee put it back, so the directors appealed to them to keep to winter hours if they liked, but to let the clock show the same time as the others in the town. No agreement could be made, the workers' delegates were dismissed and the strike broke out. Summer time was a relic of the war, an intrusion by the state into the workers' daily life which they would not tolerate. At Turin the outbreak was spontaneous, but in other centres, such as Bologna and Cremona,

the Chambers of Labour[1] refused officially to accept the
legal time. Mussolini gave the movement his full support,
calling it ' The first revolution of the Italian people against
their ruler.' On April 6, 1920, he wrote in his newspaper :

> ' I, too, am opposed to the " legal time ", because it
> represents a form of state coercion and interference. It
> is not a question of politics, nationalism, or utility ; I
> am for the individual and against the state. Down with
> the state in any shape or form : the state of yesterday,
> to-day, and to-morrow, the *bourgeois* state, the socialist
> state. For us then, the last survivors of individualism,
> nothing remains to carry us through the night of the
> present and the future save the religion, absurd but always
> comforting, of anarchy.'

And the article ended with the word ANARCHY in bold type.

Clashes between demonstrators and authorities increased,
but the former always came off worst, for though excited
they were unarmed. While the dead lay in the streets—
and there were nearly always some—the workers retaliated
by calling a general strike. Sometimes the railwaymen
stopped trains carrying the Royal Guard or vans loaded
with arms for the war against the Soviets. Early in 1920
there took place the first occupations of factories[2] since
those of Dalmine in March 1919.[3] Tension became extreme
in June with a revolt at Ancona, when soldiers, supported
by the working class of the town, refused to embark for
Albania. But in spite of the resistance put up in various
places the revolt was quickly suppressed.

These upheavals disconcerted the workers' and socialist
organizations, whose method with the over-excited masses
was alternately to advise calm and promise them revolution.
A manifesto was drawn up by the Socialist Party, the

---

[1] The Chamber of Labour (Camera del Lavoro) was the meeting-place of
all the local syndicates of every description. Generally speaking, there was
one in every provincial capital and in other places of importance.

[2] Between February and June factories were occupied, and more or less
successful attempts made to run them, in Sestri Ponenti and Viareggio
(Ansaldo), at the Ilva (Naples), in the Mazzoni textile works at Torre Pellice,
in Asti, at the Miani and Silvestri machine shops in Naples, in Sesto San
Giovanni, at the Ilva (Piombino).

[3] P. 26.

parliamentary socialists, and the General Confederation of Labour on June 25, 1920, immediately after the Ancona affair, opposing local action :

'The present situation,' it said, 'shows that the *bourgeois* crisis is getting worse, and that the great clash between *bourgeoisie* and proletariat is near at hand. In view of the necessity of marshalling our full forces for coming battles, the organizations controlling the proletarian movement in Italy warn the workers against action which may spoil the concerted movement. . . . Workers ! the proletarian revolution cannot be the work of a single group of men ; it cannot be accomplished in an hour. It must be the result of vast preparation, achieved by unprecedented efforts and an iron discipline.'

'Great clash ', 'vast preparation '—behind this boasting there was absolutely nothing. The ship, with all its cargo of hope, was adrift, and while the syndical and socialist leaders shuffled and hesitated the *bourgeoisie* began to pull themselves together. There were various encouraging signs : in April 1919 the *arditi* had managed to burn the *Avanti* offices, and in November to bomb a socialist procession, without provoking any serious reaction. During a royal session of the Chamber on December 1, the socialist deputies had walked out crying : ' Long live the Republic ', and the same evening had been chased through the streets of Rome by students and officers, several of them being wounded. This had led on one side to a demonstration in the king's favour in the Piazza del Quirinale, and on the other to a general strike in protest.

The working class raised protests nearly everywhere ; every town had its general strike and its dead. Sometimes popular fury broke out, as in Mantua, where in consequence of the Rome affair the mob invaded the railway station and pulled up the rails, beat up all the officers it met, attacked the prison, released the prisoners, and fired the buildings. In Rome on May 12, 1920, the scavengers went on strike and teams of students and other volunteers took their place. In July the tramway-men brought out their vehicles beflagged in red to celebrate a successful strike. Many exasperated people who had been obliged by the strike to walk miles in the heat of summer, climbed on to the trams, tore down the flags, and beat up the drivers. The same afternoon students, nationalists, and *arditi* sacked the *Avanti* offices and broke up the machines—with the usual result : the Chamber of Labour called a general strike. None the less it was only thanks to the police that the *Epoca* presses, which had produced the Rome edition of the *Avanti*, were not broken up. That evening some socialist deputies, among them Modigliani, were seriously wounded, and during the same month fascists, *arditi*, and legionaries burnt the *Balkan*, the headquarters of the Slovene organizations at Trieste.

These were but the first signs, outpost skirmishes, left to local initiative and enterprise, and carried out by the fascist and nationalist irregulars. Meanwhile the capitalist classes were steadily organizing themselves. On March 7, 1920, when labour troubles were at their worst, the first national conference of Italian industrialists assembled at Milan and formed the General Confederation of Industry. This included all the great and three-quarters of the lesser industries, and being closely allied with the Association of Limited Liability Companies was to have a preponderating influence on national life. During this conference a complete and detailed plan of campaign was drafted and everything, from the centralized organization of all manufacturers to the methods of combating the workers' syndicates, and the political restoration of Giovanni Giolitti, was laid down. At the beginning of April the new alliance won its first success by crushing the general strike at Turin—the strike over ' summer time '. Soon afterwards, on August 18, the General Confederation of Agriculture was formed and rapidly expanded to embrace every form of agricultural property and industry, great and small. No longer would manufacturers and landlords fight in stray units. To the erratic and localized efforts of the workers they could now oppose a defensive and offensive force organized on a national and strongly centralized basis.

Giolitti's return to power[1] was the chief symptom of the

[1] P. 65.

new situation. While among the populace the war question still divided the organized proletariat from numbers of ex-servicemen and certain middle-class groups (students, officers, members of learned professions) in higher circles, supporters both of war and of neutrality were working in complete unity to regain control of the situation.

The socialists had not joined the new government, but Giolitti had not given up hope of gaining their support. In his speeches in the Chamber he went as far as he could to win their confidence. He hoped to repeat the methods which had won him success before the war : to reconcile the conflicting interests of manufacturers and farmers by an apt adjustment of customs duties, and give a share of the benefits of this protective tariff to certain groups of industrial workers in the north and the wage-earning agricultural workers of the Po valley, who formed the backbone of the political and syndical power of the socialist movement. But 1920 was not 1910. The Socialist Party and the General Confederation of Labour no longer represented the *élite* of labour. Hordes of new members had joined, and the makeshift plans of earlier days were no longer sufficient to control them. The economic crisis, daily getting worse, made it difficult for him to carry out his former policy of compromise and left no margin for the satisfaction of everyone's demands. Besides, the Socialist Party, which had promised revolution without raising a finger to prepare it, and had jumped straight from the 1917 programme into their ' soviets ' policy, expected that the ' insoluble ' crisis would thrust power upon them. When Giolitti suggested that the socialists should join his cabinet Turati, the leader of the ring wing, refused because he knew the party would not follow him.[1]

Turati had absorbed from Marx his realization of the close alliance between economic evolution and political change, and his conviction that the emancipation of the workers must be the action ' of the workers themselves '. The task of the socialists was to educate and prepare the working classes for self-government. The persistence with which he had fought for the eight-hour day in Italy was not mere zeal for reform. The reduction of hours, which

[1] P. 64.

Marx had hailed in 1864 in his ' Inaugural Address ' for its ' immense physical, moral, and intellectual benefits ', would allow the working classes to educate themselves and prepare for the struggle. Turati saw the advance of socialism as a stream which absorbed all progressive tendencies, moving harmoniously forward, unhurried, thriving on compromise, and guided by enlightened good will. The masses more and more conscientious, the *bourgeoisie* more and more intelligent : the former patient, the latter resigned to the inevitable : joint executors to a world whose end was to be desired and accepted. Consequently he could not bring himself to join the government without the masses behind him, still less against their will. This was not through lack of courage, like Dante's pope, ' *che fece per viltade il gran rifiuto* '. When Bissolati responded to the king's summons in 1911 Turati asked : ' Take a share in the government ? Perhaps we ought, but certainly we cannot.' The unpreparedness of the masses was an insurmountable obstacle. ' What is socialism in Italy to-day ? ' he asked himself. ' Socialism has barely touched the surface of the masses, and even where it has gone a little deeper, through better organization, it serves interests worthy of respect, but narrow and limited.' How could he take office with such an instrument ? He wanted a policy, not a personal adventure. In 1911–12 he had, for the same reason, opposed the war in Tripoli, because it distracted the Italian people from the slow and painful development of their civic conscience. Again, despite his sympathy for Belgium and the Entente, he had opposed intervention in 1914, because he feared the effect on the public mentality. The mass movements of 1919–20 seemed to him to be merely the outcome of a ' war psychosis '. But the classic proportions of the socialist creed as he had conceived it were shattered now, and Turati felt that the political weapon he needed was farther from his hand than ever. When he rose in the Chamber on June 28 to answer Giolitti's first ministerial pronouncement, he had to do so as a private individual. He proclaimed the necessity of ' rebuilding Italy ' by a combination of measures ' organic, planned, and prompt, capable of arousing her latent vigour, and renewing the state and the Nation'. But his admirable speech was received with general indifference, and, because the mountain would not come to him, Turati did not go to the mountain. The fate of Italian socialism was indeed tragic, for it suffered as much from the insight of some of its leaders as from the obtuseness of the rest.

Another socialist leader, Claudio Treves, for many years Turati's colleague on his review, the *Critica Sociale*, in a speech in the Chamber on March 30, at the time of the first Nitti crisis, described the situation thus : ' This is the crux of the present tragic situation : you can no longer maintain your existing social order and we are not yet strong enough to impose the one we want.' But actually the old social order was digging itself in, while the new one was befogged. Seeking a way out a group of young intellectuals in Turin, headed by Antonio Gramsci, had gone far both in theory and practice to base an organization on the factory councils which had achieved a fair degree of maturity and power in that town. But their efforts were wrecked by the obtuseness of the Socialist Party and by their own inexperience and isolation. The maximalist party leaders, unmoved, continued to sleep on their paper schemes for soviets. The National Council at Florence had directed the party executive in January 1920 to draw up within two months definite plans for Workers' Councils. At the National Council at Milan in April—long after the time limit had expired—the ' need for soviets ' was once more affirmed, and the party leaders once more called upon to ' create these proletarian organizations '. To lighten their task, they were supplied with a set of regulations for drawing up soviets, wherein, in a few dozen clauses, every provision for their efficient functioning was laid down. Only the soviets themselves were missing. . . . Was it in order to seize power and destroy the counter-revolution at birth that the party leaders had to impose these soviets from above, in bureaucratic style ? On the contrary, it was chiefly to ' obstruct and paralyse the experiment of social democracy ', to prevent ' the establishment of the *bourgeois* parliament ', and to destroy those illusions of democracy—' the most dangerous kind '. With these objects in view they must

' intensify and complete their preparations for the forcible overthrow of the *bourgeois* state and the inauguration of the dictatorship of the proletariat '. ' Complete their preparations ' : this was not easy, for how could they complete what had never been begun ? Such preparations could only mean one thing : political action rallying to its programme all whose sufferings, illusions, and need for justice urged them towards a new order. The party leaders were incapable of seeing the problem in such a light. Brave words helped them to maintain their popularity with the mob, but ended by befogging the minds, never very stable, of those who used them. Mixed drinks intoxicate, but do not give courage or decision, and generalizations about the ' inevitable and early crisis ' of the administration, which it was impossible for the *bourgeoisie* to escape, acted as narcotics. For contact with reality they substituted a kind of frenzied and harmless monomania which the *bourgeoisie* placed under forcible restraint at the first opportunity. These extremist clichés derived from a fundamental inertia, which they helped to perpetuate. While the socialists awaited their inheritance, now assured to them, at the bedside of the dying man—the *bourgeoisie*—who was not worth putting out of his agony, political life in Italy became one long meeting at which the capital of the ' coming ' revolution was squandered in orgies of words.

But the masses, still ' awaiting ' the revolution, took the game seriously. The General Confederation of Labour, whose reformist leaders had signed in Moscow in the summer of 1920 a pact which was to bring about ' the triumph of the social revolution and the world-wide republic of the soviets ', had at the same time invited the Italian working class to accept the new law of social insurance, based upon contributions by state, employers, and insured. The workers who had rejected summer time refused to pay their contributions. What was the good of social insurance if there was just going to be a revolution ? Why pay, since they would soon be all powerful ? The gap between social insurance and the world-wide republic of the soviets was too wide. The masses could not understand. Further, while the Confederation led a campaign in favour of the law, the

Chambers of Labour in Bologna and Turin decided that employees should not pay, and the workers at the Bianchi factory in Milan went so far as to call a strike in protest. So began a crisis of authority inside the labour movement, parallel to that in the state, of which the second was to be solved first.

As soon as he took office Giolitti stifled the Ancona revolt[1] and decided to withdraw the Italian forces from Albania. In this way he began the task of settling the *bourgeois* crisis, which in September brought him up agianst the alarming occupation of factories by workers all over the country. In May the Federation of Metallurgical Workers (F.I.O.M.[2]) had begun discussing a collective wage agreement with the employers, who were determined to make no concessions. ' Until now we have always given way ', they said. ' Now things are going to be different, and we shall begin with you.' This attitude showed that there was some change in the situation. On its side the F.I.O.M., which had already had to carry on long strikes to settle local agreements, did not wish to face a new strike which might last many months, exhaust the workers, and bring victory no nearer. A substitute for this blunted weapon had to be found, while, as the increasing symptoms of crisis showed, the field of battle was getting more restricted. It was then that the strategists of the Federation, who all belonged to the right wing of the Socialist Party, decided to combat the persistent and clumsy stubbornness of the employers with a stay-in strike. The employers were prepared to meet obstructionism with lock-outs, so as to drive the workers into the ordinary strike they now wanted to avoid. On August 30 the management of Alfa-Romeo cleared out its workshops in Milan and shut its doors in order to suppress a lightning strike. The Federation ordered its members to occupy the factories, thus snatching their most formidable weapon from the employers' hands by forestalling and preventing a lock-out. This occupation of factories, often represented as some critical stage of revolutionary fever, was in its inception simply a substitute for a strike which had become too

---

[1] P. 68.
[2] Federazione Italiana Operai Metallurgici.

difficult, and a more economical method of enforcing labour's new collective contracts. The Federation leaders had chosen the line of least resistance, and they thought that the occupation would provoke government intervention, while some of them, though they did not admit it, cherished the hope that its political outcome might lead to the socialists taking a share in the administration.

On August 31 the workers occupied 280 machine shops in Milan, and in the next two days the movement spread all over Italy, at times even forestalling the orders of the leaders. It began with the metallurgical trades, but the factories wanted raw materials and accessories supplied by other industries, so, to ensure the continuance of their work, these had to be won over. The control of the factories passed into the hands of workers' committees, who did all they could to maintain output. In this they had only themselves to rely upon, for all the engineers and nearly all the technicians and clerical staff had left on the order of the directors. Work in progress went on well enough, but the difficulty of replenishing with raw materials was soon felt. Money for wages was also wanting, for little had been found in the safes opened after occupation. Once the first enthusiasm had evaporated many of the workers got tired of spending all their time in the factories, until finally, towards the end of the campaign, they were not allowed out for fear they should not return. So the ' red guards ' at the gates, to defend the factories against possible attack, served equally to prevent a large number from deserting.

The workers' committees often displayed admirable activity, combined with a keen sense of responsibility, a care for ' proletarian honour ' in all questions of labour discipline, and respect for property become communal, and made incessant appeals to the workers' consciences, of which less and less notice was taken. The few weeks the occupation lasted called forth in the workers, those ' appendages of the machines ', a flood of moral energy, a striving towards higher activities, which the impartial historian must preserve among the brightest pages of proletarian idealism, or of any form of idealism. But the picture had its shadows, which deepened as enthusiasm

waned. Scenes of violence—engineers held by force in their
factories, etc.—were few and quickly checked. Little blood
was shed, murders could be counted on the fingers of one
hand, and were in every case due to the isolated acts of a
few over-excited individuals : a small matter in proportion
to the extent and seriousness of the upheaval which had
occurred, and the thousands of factories and millions of
workers involved.

Thoroughly alarmed, the employers dissolved their
delegation, which by its high-handedness and obstinacy
had provoked the movement, and replaced it with a fresh
one, more conciliatory and determined to come to an
understanding. Overtures were made from all quarters to
the syndical and socialist chiefs, to get them to agree to a
compromise. The editor of the *Corriere della Sera*, senator
Albertini, betook himself to Turati and told him that the
time had come for the socialists to assume power. The
directors of the *Banca Commerciale* assured the F.I.O.M. of
their benevolent neutrality, and offered and asked for
assurances in case of a revolutionary outcome to the movement. The prefect of Milan, acting for the government,
did his utmost to bring together the two parties to the
struggle. Mussolini, too, took his precautions, announcing
in his paper that the fascists had no intention of attacking
the occupied factories, and so far forgot his pride as to go in
person to the hotel where Buozzi, secretary to the F.I.O.M.,
was staying, to tell him he would continue to support the
movement.

Should negotiations with the employers, now prepared
to yield on every point, be resumed ? A negative answer
would give the signal for a general insurrection, since it
was no longer possible to keep the workers in the factories
without giving them something further to aim at. The only
way out was by escaping in a forward direction. Armed
insurrection was out of the question, for nothing was ready.
The workers felt safe behind the factory walls, not on
account of their arms, often ancient and inadequate, but
because they looked on the factories as hostages which the
government would hesitate to shell to bits in order to dislodge the occupants. It was a long step from this defensive

attitude to open street fighting, as the workers were, if confusedly, aware. Even in Turin, where there was a venturesome advance-guard, better armed than elsewhere, the communist leaders took no active steps, and restrained the groups which had prepared lorries for a sortie from the Fiat works.

The National Council of the General Confederation of Labour met in Milan on September 10 by agreement with the executive of the Socialist Party, and faced the question of what tactics they should adopt. The two bodies had decided, a few days earlier, that ' if as a result of the continued obstinacy of the employers no early solution can be reached ', the workers' struggle must take as its objective ' the control of firms, in order to bring about collective management and the socialization of every form of production '. The immediate claim was for control ; socialization was put off into the distant future. By defining control as their objective they made it clear that they had no intention of going further, but would evacuate the factories as soon as it was granted. Not for nothing were the Socialist Party leaders maximalists ; they were unwilling to face the inevitable disillusion of the masses. A treaty of alliance concluded at the end of 1918 between the General Confederation of Labour and the Italian Socialist Party had left to the latter the management of *political* strikes. There now took place a pointless discussion as to whether this was a political or a syndical strike, which really masked a joint shrinking from responsibility. The Confederation offered the control of the movement to the maximalists and communists at the head of the party, knowing quite well that they had no desire to take it on.

The National Council in Milan voted for the syndical view, and Gennari, the secretary of the party, confined himself to saying :

' The agreement lays down that the party executive may make itself responsible for action, and the General Confederation of Labour undertakes not to interfere. At the present moment the party executive does not wish to assert these powers. Possibly, in the course of time and if circumstances alter, the executive may decide to appeal to the agreement, and I am certain that it will be honoured.'

This vague allusion to possible future events committed them to nothing ; it was quite irrelevant to the present situation. The executive had wasted months in preaching revolution, but had foreseen nothing and prepared nothing. After the Milan decision in favour of the Confederation viewpoint the leaders breathed a sigh of relief. Relieved of all responsibility, they could now scream themselves hoarse about the ' treason ' of the General Confederation of Labour. Thus they had something to offer to the masses whom they had abandoned at the critical moment, and were able at the same time to save face.

But the working classes saved nothing. They believed themselves to be on the threshold of power ; they had got out of the rut to catch only a vanishing glimpse of something fresh beyond their old horizon. Everybody said they had won, including Mussolini.

' A revolution has taken place,' he wrote, ' or to be precise a phase of the revolution that we began in 1915. It has lacked the 1848 manner which, according to outworn romantic ideas, should accompany revolutions. . . . Nevertheless there has been a revolution, and one may add, a great revolution. A legal relationship that has stood for centuries has been broken.'

But the workers felt tricked and beaten, and they were right.

The occupation of the factories marked the decline of the working-class movement, and the inglorious end of ' maximalism ', though its corpse continued to litter the ground until the fascists swept it up. A distinct change soon came over the workers' psychology, ' the beginnings of wisdom ', in the words of Mussolini. Instead of disarming their adversaries it had the effect of making them more aggressive and drove them to reprisals. The *fasci*, feeble and almost non-existent before September 1920, multiplied in the last three months of the year. It was not fascism that defeated the revolution, but the inconsistency of the revolution that gave impetus to fascism.

How and why did such a phenomenon occur ? Because the occupation of the factories gave the *bourgeoisie* a psychological shock, which explains their fury and guided their successive steps. The sense of property and the authority of the industrialists was hit ; evicted from their factories, they saw work going on, for better or for worse, in their absence. Now that the shadow of death had passed away, life flowed back into them. After a few days of bitterness and uncertainty, during which their chief feeling was a deep grudge against Giolitti,[1] who ' had failed to back them up ' and had forced control of their industries on them by decree, their reaction took the form of a fight to the death against the working class and the ' liberal state '.

But the so-called victors were demoralized. After superhuman efforts they had tasted the joys of free production, only to find themselves no better off than they were before, and, worse still, with no prospect of improving their lot. The arms manufactured or brought into the factories during the occupation were gradually all found and confiscated by the police. Nothing seemed changed ; work was resumed and the F.I.O.M. had signed its ' better agreement ', while the workers' factory committees were the same as those which had managed production. But the barriers between workers and employers had broken down, and neither side could resume work on the old footing. The employers felt the occupations as a blot on their escutcheon. The factories were haunted by evil spirits which must be exorcized. At Turin Senator Agnelli, chairman of Fiat, hoped to do so by arranging a co-operative administration of the factory with the employees. Similar schemes put forward nearly everywhere came to nothing. The F.I.O.M.

---

[1] On September 15, seeing that ' the General Confederation of Labour has demanded the modification of existing relations between employers and workers, in order that the latter, acting through their syndicates, should achieve the possibility of some form of control in industry ', that the Confederation ' by means of this control ' was proposing ' to secure an improvement in disciplinary arrangements between employers and workers and an increase in production, upon which the whole economic revival of the country depends ', Giolitti issued a decree forming a commission on which both sides were equally represented, to draft ' proposals on which a government bill might be based for the reorganization of industry, to provide for the participation of the workers both in technical and financial control and in the general administration of firms '.

leaders wanted to consolidate their victory by joining the government, thinking that a coalition resulting from such events would give the masses a definite token of success and would save them from demoralization. They felt, too, that the agreement they had won was the last which their organisation would be able to conclude, and that they could not hold the position they had gained against the inevitable attack of the exasperated *bourgeoisie*. But the occupation of the factories had for the time being ' radicalized ' the masses and, so far from imposing their participation in the government, had rendered it psychologically impossible.

The evil spirits were to be exorcized by direct and violent action ; the hour of fascism had come.

VII

THE 'POSTHUMOUS AND PREVENTIVE' COUNTER-REVOLUTION

THE end of the factory occupations left both the workers and the employers with the feeling that they had been beaten. In addition to the collective agreement the workers had gained ' syndical control of industry '. But what was this vague committee set up by the September 15 decree in comparison with the mirage they had seen during the weeks spent in the occupied factories ? The employers had been forced to give in without a soldier or a gendarme stirring to dislodge the workers from the factories ; they had been made to sign blindly an agreement which they had recently refused to discuss, and submit by Giolitti's orders to the control of industry. Both sides were disgruntled and saw no hope in the future, but the industrialists and landowners were livid with rage and ready for anything, willing to sell their souls for revenge. The bloodshed and the fires which were to destroy the offices of hundreds of working-class and socialist organizations and the homes of ' red ' and even ' white ' workers seemed to them the ritual of an atonement ceremony, necessary to purify the violated temple of property.

Giolitti ignored the abuse that was heaped on him and set about making the best use of a situation which, so he thought, favoured his designs. A *bourgeois* bloc was formed, based on patriotic sentiment, and on November 4, 1920, for the first time since the armistice, victory celebrations, unbroken by any disturbance, took place in Rome and all the big cities. At the administrative elections, which took place soon after, the *bourgeois* parties fought nearly everywhere on a ' national bloc ' platform. The *Popolari*, on the other hand, decided to form a separate list, but the Vatican disapproved of this perversity and censured it publicly. In a few large towns such as Turin and Milan the *Popolari* joined the bloc as a result of pressure from Rome. In Turin Cardinal Gasparri wrote a letter proclaiming that ' wherever co-operation is necessary to resist the socialist advance, such co-operation is a duty ', and in Milan Cardinal Ferrari intervened in the same way. The fascists, still a negligible quantity, supported the lists of the national bloc everywhere. In Milan Mussolini, who had learned prudence from his experience of November 1919, resisted his friends who would have liked a fascist list : ' For us to take part in the struggle would enormously increase our opponents' chance of success, for to present a list including fascists would be enough to start a rush to the poll to vote against it. That is obvious as you know very well. We could not even get a minority list through.' Which shows, once again, that when the ' maximalist ' advance was beginning to weaken, the forces of fascism, which later claimed that they had ' saved Italy from revolution ', were still disunited.

The administrative elections took place at a time of suspense and transition. The socialists obtained majorities in 2162 communes out of 8059, and in 25 provinces out of 69. They won the greatest number of communes in Emilia and Tuscany, where, a few weeks after the elections, the fascist offensive was launched. The socialist success, however, had its drawbacks. It was too definite to allow the Socialist Party to go on marking time, but not sufficient to make it face its responsibilities boldly. The *bourgeois* coalition, on the other hand, had fought hard and succeeded in stemming the red tide in several important centres : Rome, Spezia, Brescia, Genoa, Pisa, Naples, Bari, Palermo. It won significant victories at Florence and, greatest of all, Turin, the ' red town '. In the year 1919–20 the tide was showing signs of ebbing.

On the strength of these results Giolitti decided to carry his policy a step further, and to do so it was necessary to settle the Fiume question, a permanent source of trouble and indiscipline in the army, and a cancer in the body politic. Giolitti attempted a master stroke and brought it off : the buying off of Mussolini and his separation from d'Annunzio. So successful was he that he thought he had Mussolini in his pocket ; in which he was much mistaken. The negotiations took place at Milan through the prefect Lusignoli, who was to be the connecting link between Giolitti and Mussolini until the march on Rome. The Treaty of Rapallo with Jugo-Slavia was signed on November 12, 1920. Dalmatia, except for Zara, remained Jugo-Slavian, and part of the port of Fiume, Sussak, was also ceded. Mussolini, whose attacks on Bissolati[1] in January 1919 will be recalled, wrote on the same day : ' We declare ourselves satisfied as far as the eastern frontier is concerned, and we believe that this satisfaction will be shared unanimously by Italian public opinion. As for Fiume, the Rapallo solution is not the ideal one, which would be annexation, but it is the best so far put forward '. Next day he went still further : ' Italy needs peace to recover and refresh herself and to pursue the way to her inevitable greatness. Only a madman or a criminal would consider unleashing new wars not forced on us by sudden aggression. For this reason we thoroughly approve of the settlement of the eastern frontier and Fiume questions.' In the same article Mussolini set himself against the nationalists, whom he accused of imperialism and reproached for ' being hypnotized by the sight of a few islands and beaches in the Adriatic '. This article dumbfounded the Fiume legionaries, who called Mussolini a ' parasite ' and a ' traitor ', adding, ' the great man of the Via Cannobio[2] has fizzled out '. At the Central Fascist Committee in Milan a breath of revolt was felt. To cut the ground from under the opposition Mussolini himself introduced a motion in favour of compromise, which declared that the Treaty of Rapallo was ' Sufficient and acceptable as to the eastern frontier, insufficient as to Fiume, inacceptable as to Dalmatia '. One member of the central committee, Cesare Rossi, voted against it ' because he was in complete agreement with the tendencies and opinions expressed by Mussolini himself some days ago in the *Popolo d'Italia* '.

By this manœuvre Mussolini avoided a break with the *fasci* and at the same time brought off his pact with Giolitti,

[1] P. 28 ff.
[2] The Milan office of the *Popolo d'Italia* was in this street.

for from now on Italian public opinion hesitated and dropped all active opposition to the Treaty of Rapallo. Giolitti's money had been put to a good use. But money was not the chief part of the bargain. For Mussolini the new arrangement presented other personal advantages. He was free of the agreement he had made in the summer with d'Annunzio for some vaguely defined form of action to be made under the latter's direction. In addition, he thought Giolitti could form a government consisting of liberals, *Popolari*, fascists, and perhaps right-wing socialists, with himself a member of the cabinet. Besides, Giolitti and his war minister, Bonomi, were very well disposed towards the fascists, whom they hoped to use against the socialists. Mussolini, therefore, postponed for the time being any idea of a ' march on Rome '. He would reach Rome in any case by way of a parliamentary alliance which only Giolitti could bring about. Protected on the left by the socialists who were hostile to d'Annunzio, and on the right by Mussolini, Giolitti could now attempt his great *coup*.

The same day that the workers in the peninsula occupied the factories d'Annunzio published at Fiume the ' Constitution ' of the ' Italian Regency of the Quarnero '. It was a mixture of medieval guild and modern syndicalism, personal government and vague sovietism, which alienated the sympathy of the nationalists, who were reactionaries first and patriots afterwards. In particular, Article 9 of this constitution said :

> ' The state does not recognize property as an absolute domination of individual over matter, but looks upon it as the most useful of social functions. No property can be reserved by any person as if it were part of him ; it is inadmissible for a lazy proprietor to leave his property unused or badly used, to the exclusion of others. Labour is the only title to power in any means of production or exchange. Labour alone is master of the goods it has rendered fruitful in their highest degree and most profitable to the general economy.'

It was all rather hazy, and Mussolini has written more subversive prose. But d'Annunzio was a poet, and poets are sometimes slaves to their dreams. Such a ' constitution ' ran the risk of over-valuing certain social claims by linking them with national claims, at a moment when the *bourgeoisie* were setting national claims aside while they made a clean sweep of the social claims of the masses. The *bourgeoisie* and even the nationalists deserted him, and at the crucial moment Admiral Millo went back on his engagements.[1]

On September 9, 1920, d'Annunzio proclaimed simultaneously the independence of the ' State ' of the Quarnero and his new constitution, thus provoking a breach with the National Council of Fiume. The economic situation of the town was becoming difficult ; there was a shortage of water, gas, electricity, and coal. Negotiations for a loan between d'Annunzio and a group of financiers fell through. Towards the end of October the legionaries, with the assistance of the Federation of Marine Workers, seized the *Cogne*, an Italian vessel loaded with Swiss merchandise which was put up for auction in Fiume. As soon as he learned of the conclusion of the Treaty of Rapallo,[2] d'Annunzio ordered the occupation of the islands of Orbe and Cherso, transferred by this treaty to Jugo-Slavia. But Giolitti now decided to put an end quickly to this chaos. General Caviglia started a blockade of the Fiume coast to prevent further raids by legionaries. A delegation of Italian members of Parliament approached d'Annunzio to suggest a compromise. D'Annunzio rejected any agreement and demanded as a preliminary the recognition of the Regency of the Quarnero by the Rome government. Two destroyers and a torpedo-boat deserted from the Italian fleet, came to Fiume and placed themselves at the ' Commandant's ' disposal. The actual blockade of the town was begun and d'Annunzio replied by declaring a state of war between the Regency and Italy. On Christmas Eve the Italian forces advanced, but a few shots fired at the governor's palace, the hostility of the National Council, and of the population, brought about d'Annunzio's surrender. Doubtless he had sworn to shed the last drop of his blood on the sacred ground, but he convinced himself quite easily that ' it was not worth devoting one's exertions to a people who, when battle is

[1] P. 47.   [2] P. 84.

joined at Fiume, will not for a single moment leave their Christmas gluttony and festivities '. D'Annunzio was an actor who could not play to an empty house, the super-man in him could not do without his public.

On December 31 an agreement was signed and a provisional government formed in Fiume. D'Annunzio left the town and went to Italy where, in spite of all his and his friends' efforts, he was no longer able to play a leading part. The *fasci* made a great deal of noise about events in Fiume, and Mussolini in the *Popolo d'Italia* spread himself in headlines and abusive language, but no gesture of sympathy was attempted. While the Fiume affair was going on and he was dreaming of leading a national and social crusade, at the head of an army of the oppressed, d'Annunzio had lost touch with the country.

' The horizon and spirit of Fiume ', he had declared, ' is as wide as the earth. Wherever one of the oppressed sets his teeth under the oppression, wherever a rebel keeps watch, armed with a stick or a stone against machine-guns and cannons, there shines the light of Fiume . . . and force will be met with force . . . and the new crusade of the poor and the free against the predatory races and the tribe of usurers who yesterday exploited war in order to exploit peace to-day, our *nobilissima* crusade, will restore true justice.'

This resembled the revolutionary nationalism that the genuine leaders in Moscow were preparing to exploit : the congress of eastern peoples was held in Baku in September 1920. But the workers who had occupied the factories and the peasants who were still occupying the land knew nothing of d'Annunzio, and the socialists looked on the Fiume episode merely as a grotesque adventure. Serrati, the editor of *Avanti*, was astonished and quite shocked when Lenin described d'Annunzio to him as a revolutionary. An Italian maximalist could never recognize an ally, even a temporary one, in the d'Annunzio, ' who has never hesitated to lead the most dangerous forces in the service of a noble cause '. The more d'Annunzio saw of the chaotic state of the world, the more he turned away from Italian politics. Once more the thread between Fiume and Rome was cut, only to be joined again at Milan by Mussolini.

Since the General Confederation of Labour was involved in the deadlock of the committee of workers and employers, and the Fiume question was settled, Giolitti had nothing to wait for but disruption in the ranks of the socialists in order to complete his plan. At the end of 1920, the socialists still had an imposing force at their disposal : one hundred and fifty-six deputies in parliament, about a third of the communes, more than a third of the provincial councils, eight thousand co-operative societies, and two million members of the General Confederation of Labour. How could this force be used to make a real power in the policy and destiny of the country ? Could the experience gained during the occupations help the party towards a definite goal at last ?

The time for ' direct and violent ' seizure of power was past. During recent events it had not been considered, and Lenin himself did not think it possible. ' We do not want a second Hungary ', he declared. But he hoped the situation would become more favourable, and he demanded the expulsion of Turati and his friends from the Socialist Party. ' Expel the Reformists from the party and then support a Turati government ', he advised Serrati. But the Italian maximalists could only carry out the first part of this plan, and that only two years later. The campaign against the ' Reformists ', which led to the first split at Leghorn, made the second part inapplicable. How could they drive out Turati in the name of the struggle ' against all compromise ' and then contemplate a fresh compromise with him ? The result was a split which added a fresh difficulty to those which already embarrassed the Socialist Party, namely the communist question. The Socialist Party at the end of 1920 reckoned 4367 sections and 216,327 adherents. At the Leghorn Congress in January 1921 the maximalists (centre party) won a majority with 98,028 votes, the communists were second with 58,183, while the right only obtained 14,625 votes. This split resulted in no increased freedom of action for the tendencies it liberated. The communists who led the party in September were as incapable as the rest. A new party, they were driven to the left by immaturity and the desire to be different. The maximalists, harassed from the left by the communists, dared not face the situation, and remained inactive between the two extreme tendencies, still repeating the old refrain : ' In the present situation, as Serrati says, the only result of taking power would be that the present responsibilities of the *bourgeois* would be transferred to the socialists.' Nor did the right-wing socialists, at their conference at Reggio Emilia, dare to have the courage of their conclusions, or indeed to arrive at any conclusions. They even voted, without conviction, simply as a political manœuvre, for adhesion to the Third International, only claiming ' independence in their interpretation of the twenty-one points and their application according to conditions in each country '. The right wing was concerned with safeguarding the unity of the party and especially that of the syndicates (bound to the party by the pact of alliance), and consequently took refuge in a smoke-screen of procedure. Each party was the slave of its own time-worn slogans, regardless of the great change in the situation. The old fear of responsibility, the same fundamental insincerity which had prevented them from putting their theories into practice, now prevented them from bringing these theories down to the level of facts. The split was as pointless as it was inevitable.

The economic situation continued to make inroads on the strength of the syndicates, though there were signs of approaching stability.

' Just as a total economic breakdown in Italy seemed inevitable ', wrote Professor G. Mortara in his *Prospettive Economiche*, ' a concatenation of circumstances altered the course of events. The return to normal conditions was largely helped by the reduction in the factors of economic disturbance. The price fall in the world market, the control of the note issue and the progress towards exchange stabilization checked the rise in the cost of living and diminished its wide fluctuations. On the other hand industrial depression, by causing a vast amount of unemployment which was aggravated by the slowing up of emigration, prevented workers who still had jobs from taking the risk of losing them.'

During the first quarter of 1921, the number of strikers, compared with the same period in the preceding year, fell from 493,914 to 148,796, and the number of working days lost from 6,268,900 to 1,644,250, a decrease of about 77 per cent and 80 per cent. Mussolini remarked in an article at the end of 1920 : ' Within the last three months the psychology of the working-class masses has been profoundly modified.' In February 1921 Giolitti managed to do away with the control of the bread price, and the socialist deputies who had turned Nitti out over this very question only made a show of opposition, pleading ' apathy on the part of the masses for this battle that had been fought in their name '.

Fascism became stronger towards the end of 1920 and particularly during the first half of 1921, when post-war unrest had largely subsided and ' order ' was being restored by the combination of economic events and the decay of the Socialist Party. The great fascist advance began in the Po valley and in Tuscany, where the landowners were at grips with the farm-labourers in the one and with the *mezzadri* (share tenants) in the other. A decisive factor dating from this period was a rush of country-folk to join the fascists. In 1919 Mussolini had thought that the *fasci* could only flourish in towns.[1] But towards the end of 1920 the landowners ' discovered ' fascism, took it up and left their mark on it. All their grudges and bitterness went into it : ' The old spirit of hatred and mistrust of anyone who wants a new distribution of the land has revived in the landowners and wealthy peasants ', it was said : ' The enemy to-day is the organized wage-earner, as yesterday it was the vagabond. Against him everything is permissible.' In some places the proprietors had already built up fighting organizations whose traditions and example influenced the newly formed *fasci*. The clash soon reached a pitch of extreme violence ; it was like a barbarian ' ordeal ', concluding a twenty years' feud with a ' judgment of God '

---

[1] P. 37.

by which the victor took possession of the body and chattels of the vanquished.

The Po country, where the clash took place, is highly cultivated ground with a rich harvest yield. The work of reclaiming the land from swamps, rushes and malaria had been going on for centuries. This splendid work was intensified towards the end of the nineteenth century thanks to new technical processes, private capital, state loans and the new conditions in the home market. The water was drained off, leaving fertile alluvial land on which roads, houses and plantations sprang up. The yield per hectare was high : 17 quintals of corn as against 10, the average elsewhere, and on the artificially developed land up to 25 and 30, sometimes even more. The cultivation of other crops had been widely extended, such as hemp, and particularly beetroot, with high profits guaranteed by tariffs on sugar. This agricultural system and the industrial one that developed beside it brought in a very good revenue, of which both landowners and workers scrambled to get all they could. But what was for the owners only a question of extra profits was a matter of life and death to the workers. The country was over-populated and the people had no desire to emigrate ; after the war they could not. Consequently work had to be found on the spot, and since there was only an average of 120 or 130 days' work available for each labourer it was essential for wages to be high enough to keep off starvation during the rest of the year. After memorable struggles which often broke out just before harvest time and sometimes went on for months, the workers' organizations obtained that the hiring of labour should be done through the local syndical employment office. Other clauses, relating to the number of labourers employed per hectare, threshing arrangements, direct exchange of services between farmers, had the same end in view. Agreement was often reached at the expense of the state, whose protective policy kept up the price of agricultural produce and instituted public works to absorb some of the labour. Such a solution was not so easy just after the war when prices had fallen and there was a general economic crisis. The struggle for revenue grew into one for the ownership of capital, and the landowners, who had always put up an obstinate resistance, were less and less inclined to yield.

On the workers' side the system was only possible with strict discipline, even with the control over the employment of labour. This combination of rules as meticulous and as closely enforced as those of a medieval gild with a highly advanced technique was not the least oddity of this huge region. Anyone who did not join the peasants' league, who accepted lower wages and worked all the year round, depleted the share of the others and was consequently pitilessly harassed by them. The blackleg was boycotted, refused bread by the baker, treated as an outcast with his wife and children, until he gave in or left the district. Penalties and fines were imposed on landowners who employed him and broke the labour contract.

Such a system could only function if it was universal, for any breach of its terms brought other workers to starvation. At the same time small farms were disapproved of and their development hindered : not from any theoretical objection, but because they were partly exempt from the *imponibile della mano d'opera*,[1] for the wealthy peasant or small farmer and his families did not keep to the legal day and made scarcely any use of the working shifts of the wage-earners. Conditions on the plain favoured economic development by large-scale enterprise where the labour contract really functioned and could be more easily enforced. After the war the peasants, who had heard much talk about their ' right to the land ', and particularly the sons of small owners and farmers, many of whom had risen from the ranks, wanted to be independent and make their own way, and this brought them up against the collective regulations. The Federation of Agricultural Labourers engaged in long strikes in which they forced the farmers and *mezzadri* to take part. The latter were allowed to harvest half their crops, the half which was their due, but the landlord's share they had to leave in the fields. However necessary or justifiable such tactics might be, the sight of such wealth abandoned

---

[1] The *imponibile della mano d'opera* means the obligation on the landowner to employ a minimum of labourers per hectare, a minimum which varied with the type of farm and the nature of the ground. The minimum was fixed in the collective labour contract.

and often lost deeply wounded the peasants' love of the land and shocked even the hired labourers. Such methods were resented by the public, who saw no reason in them, and were only carried out by the strikers under compulsion and with qualms of conscience. Gaps immediately began to show in the ranks of the forces directed by the Federation, and it was through these that the fascist offensive was able to penetrate. Its monopoly made the red organization all-powerful, but as soon as a group of labourers in any one place succumbed to the temptation of being able to work all the year round or of owning a patch of land, the land-owners had won the day, since the system broke down and there was nothing to stop the rout once it had begun. How were the workers' leagues to prevent it? How were they to re-establish their unity? The old tactics were no longer effective against the attack of the landowners, having nothing better to offer than one, two, three months spent every year in a strike to ensure that everybody got his allotted number of working days. The system could only be saved by extending the old scramble for a share of the inadequate revenue to an actual conquest of the ' land for the peasants '.

Some of the Federation leaders realized this, and at the General Confederation of Labour congress in February 1921 a proposal for making a start with the ' socialization of the land ', drafted by the socialist deputy Piemonte, was adopted. In each province an ' agricultural community ' was to be set up, and all the land, except that of the small proprietors, was gradually to pass into its hands. The bodies administering this community were drawn exclusively from the direct representatives of the agricultural labourers and their associations. Their powers were very wide ; they could order, through one of their officials, the expropriation of a property and its transfer to the agricultural co-opera-tives. The proprietors were to receive as indemnity securities bearing an interest of 3 per cent, redeemable after a maximum of fifty years. The state was to provide the necessary hundreds of millions a year for the purchase and cultivation of the land. Everything was provided for, as in Gennari's and Bombacci's plans for soviets.

It was the dream of Lassalle turned into a genuine bill which the socialists were to introduce and support in the Chamber. Consequently the agrarian revolution depended on the governmental majority. But the socialists formed no part of this majority and would not or could not approach the government. Moreover the *rapporteur*, to defend himself against criticism from the left, which denounced the bill for ' drugging revolutionary spirit ' and for providing an expropriation indemnity, took care to explain that the securities given to the ex-proprietors ' can easily be kept in sight, despite change of ownership, and confiscated when communism triumphant judges it opportune to tax them further or to annul them '. Since it was out of the question for the Chamber to pass such a bill, the principles behind it should at least have been used to compel further action on the part of the masses, who were set on agrarian revolution. But the bill had been drafted precisely to replace direct pressure from the people by a gradual and legal conquest ; no means of enforcing it had been considered, nor of attaining the same goal by different means in the event of failure. Apart from this the bill, at least for the time being, practically left out the peasants of the south, and made no provision for the small proprietor, who could not add to his portion, even if it were insufficient ; while the farmers and *mezzadri* had to give up all hope of owning their land, since expropriation affected them equally with their landlords. At best, if the act took effect during the agricultural year, they would be left alone till the end of the year, then expelled with no corresponding indemnity. Their only hope was to become proletarian members of the agricultural co-operative, formed by others, which was to work the land. This meant, in the immediate future, complete loss of independence and forfeiture of all their rights. So the bill succeeded in being too revolutionary ever to get through parliament, while it left out of the revolution, and even forced into opposition, millions of peasant families, the great majority of Italy's rural population.

Out of 280 communes in Emilia 223 were in socialist hands. The landowners, living in town or country, with their sons, their friends, their contractors, and their customers were impotent before the all-powerful workers' syndicates. In the country the prizes and distinctions of public life were almost entirely denied to the whole *bourgeoisie*, and also to members of the lower middle class who were not members of the socialist organizations. The country landowner who for years had been cock of the walk, head of the commune, manager of all local and provincial bodies, was ousted from all of them. On the land he had to reckon with the ' League ' and the employment office, in the market with the socialist co-operative society which fixed prices, in the commune with the red list, which won crushing majorities. Profit, position, power, were lost to him and his children. Hatred and bitterness were welling up, ready at any moment to overflow. Some of the Chambers of Labour, as at Bologna, Reggio Emilia, Ravenna, exercised complete control over the economic life of their province. They had organized the labourers, the small-holders, and the tenant farmers ; they fixed the price of the goods which they distributed throughout many communes by means of their network of co-operatives. Landowners, shopkeepers, con-tractors, and middlemen of all kinds found their positions being daily sapped by the co-operative and municipal socialist movement. This was why their hatred was chiefly directed against the admirable conversion schemes which the workers' organizations introduced and worked success-fully everywhere. ' The man we fear most ', as a great landowner of the province of Ravenna said, ' is not the communist Bombacci, but Nullo Baldini, who, with his Co-operative Federation, is cutting us out everywhere.' For this reason also fascist violence was chiefly directed against the institutions set up by reformist socialism. These institutions were spreading, and little by little were monopo-lizing the entire economic and political life of their districts. The old ruling classes felt that they were being swept away to make room for the new social structure. The success of socialist enterprise reminded them daily : *vita mea, mors tua ;* and faced with this dilemma, clinging desperately to life, the condemned classes reached by the same logic the conclusion, *mors tua, vita mea.*.

In the country the socialists had always been opposed by

the great landowners ; now they were losing their grip on the smaller fry, whose sons, just back from the war, wanted to run their own concerns. In the towns, too, they were losing the support of this class, who after waiting in vain for some time for the socialists to ' do something ', were beginning to have their doubts, while the old animosity between the black-coated worker and the man in shirt-sleeves, no longer restrained by their common hopes, flared up again. In addition, the party's attitude towards the returned soldiers was inspired by purely sectarian motives. The ' Proletarian League of Ex-servicemen ' which it had created in 1919 was merely a branch of the party, and indeed of the maximalist section which dominated it. Its aim was to prevent ex-servicemen from being ' led by government concessions into the path of collaboration and compromise '. Its political aims were identical with those of the party : preparation for social revolution, soviets, the dictatorship of the proletariat. The General Confederation of Labour included in its programme an ample list of claims on behalf of the ex-servicemen, but the party postponed all this to a later date. How could the ex-servicemen confide their interests to a party which publicly recommended to its branches ' the greatest strictness in the admission of old and new members ', because it ' considered the membership of all those who had given practical support to the war as incompatible with socialism '? In this case, as was remarked by one ex-serviceman, ' the cry " down with the war " practically amounts to " down with the soldiers " '.

There were hundreds of thousands of ex-soldiers in Italy, without any special political views, who had gone to the war very young and brought back with them nothing but the memory of their sufferings and their adventures. Why should they turn their backs on such memories when the socialists could give them nothing in exchange ? What crime had they committed to turn everyone against them ? ' If it is a lie or a piece of sectarian exaggeration ', wrote another ex-soldier, ' that the demobilized soldiers have been constantly attacked and abused, it is at least indisputable that we have been shunned, spied on, mistrusted, treated as if we were plague-stricken.' Mussolini was quick to realize the chance offered by the blindness of his enemies. ' The socialists are making a mistake ', he said, ' if they believe that those who really fought, that is two or three million Italians, are going to turn round as soon as peace comes and spit on the war in which they fought.' On the contrary, as time went on, and no prospects were offered them, they forgot their suffering, idealized the past, and championed the ' victory ' they had won. This state of mind prevailed especially among the officers, that is to say nearly all those members of the middle classes who had taken part in the war.

A careful study of the newspapers of the period shows that attacks on officers were comparatively rare. The most serious were reprisals for attacks by nationalist or fascist officers on socialist deputies in the streets of Rome. But it would be a mistake to draw conclusions from statistics of this kind. When one officer was booed or beaten up, they all shared his humiliation, and the results of the insult were exaggerated by their over-sensitive nerves. The *bourgeois* press would take care to rub in the insult, inventing the most contemptible lies in order to distort the incident and stir up hatred, just as it did in France with its description of a ' red ' spitting on the tomb of the Unknown Soldier. Moreover, after autumn 1920 the state began to exploit this mentality for its own reactionary ends. Some time ago a colonel had been sent by the war office to travel through Italy, build up groups of officers, and maintain connections between them, and pass the word to divisional commanders. His report, published a year later, already provided a detailed plan for the anti-socialist offensive and a pretty accurate analysis of the strength and particularly the weakness of the movement they had to deal with.

According to this Colonel A. R., in order to combat subversive influences in the army, the authorities ought to shorten the term of compulsory service and create ' a solid framework of long-service officers and non-commissioned officers, well paid and carefully chosen on a volunteer basis '. Since this professional army would not be enough :

> ' We must add to our conscript army and the 250,000 mercenaries which we shall soon possess a militia of

idealists, consisting of the most expert, brave, strong and warlike from amongst us to support and control their action. This militia must be capable of being used both for defensive action and for political purposes, and must be able at this critical period to put fresh blood and life into the national forces and lead them to victory.'

The report insists that such a movement should be under the direction of a special staff formed of political as well as military elements, and goes on to give technical advice : ' Form squadrons, companies and battalions, or at any rate their framework, which responsible members of our class must be made to join.' In this way a progressive training could be given to the inexperienced.

' Minor engagements with the object of chastising the insolence of the more subversive centres will give a fine schooling to our militia and serve to break up and demoralize the enemy at the same time. But care must always be taken to have one or more bases as starting points and as centres for concentrating our resources. These bases must be at a reasonable distance from the place where the blow is to be struck, so that it is possible to return to them without arousing suspicion and to reorganize there in the event of a temporary set-back. This is the procedure to be followed when local punitive action is undertaken.'

Here is another glimpse of the adversary's forces at a time when the decline of the socialist movement had begun, but was not yet evident :

' Discontented and revolutionary-minded people are not capable of organization. They act in heterogeneous masses under the impulse of passing emotion. The arms in their possession are scarce and unevenly distributed. They have no organized bodies capable of making use of them. Their equipment is necessarily inadequate, particularly for prolonged resistance. The political groups that help to keep up mass excitement possess clever and courageous men, but these are interspersed with senseless braggarts, and they all have a very limited grasp of tactics, the use of arms, discipline, co-operation, and even action itself. The very conditions of life of these subversive elements allow them only extremely limited resources ; any attempt at co-ordinated preparation remains local, or at best extends to the district. . . . Long and far-sighted preparation is impossible for them. The more fanatical meet together, spur each other on, choose leaders, issue instructions ; most of the others remain undecided, passive, without initiative. Hypnotized by noise and crowds they delude themselves as to their strength and their prospects. Their first reverse will be followed by disillusion and disorder.'

This sketch of the situation was made before the working-class movement had suffered the collapse which followed the occupation of the factories. By this time the danger of a popular insurrection, already discounted in the report, had totally disappeared, and it was no longer necessary to carry out in its entirety the programme of Colonel A. R., ' military expert in civil war '. But the government did not remain inactive. On October 20 Giolitti's minister of war, Bonomi, the former socialist, whom Mussolini himself had expelled from the Socialist Party in 1912, sent out a circular,[1] announcing that officers in course of being demobilized (about 60,000) were to be sent to the chief centres with orders to join the *Fasci di Combattimento*, which they were to control and staff, and for this they would receive four-fifths of their present pay. In this way the *fasci* themselves would be enabled to carry out the part of Colonel A. R.'s programme referring to ' local punitive expeditions ', and later on to go to further lengths, since they were assured of the effective and indispensable aid of the state.

The contest soon became too much for the socialists, as was shown by events in Bologna on November 21, 1920. Here, at the municipal elections, the socialist list, mainly composed of extreme left-wing elements, obtained 18,170 votes, against 7,985 for the national bloc, and 4,694 for the *Popolari*. This was on a basis of universal suffrage, and the

[1] Later Bonomi denied having taken this step and complained that he had been ' betrayed ' by the military authorities.

victory, even allowing for a great number of abstentions, was decisive. The local fascists were furious at this defeat and gave out that they would prevent the socialist administration from functioning. The day before the installation of the Council they posted up typed notices announcing battle for the next day and asking women and children to keep well away from the centre of the city, where the town hall, the Palazzo d'Accursio, was situated.

The victors had been elected by an enormous majority of the population, but what were they to do ? Appeal to the prefect or the state to have their mandate respected and its result enforced ? Had anyone dared to suggest it he would have been howled down as a traitor by the crowd of windbags who lost their heads at the first shot fired by the fascists. Since the state was nothing but the ' executive committee of the *bourgeoisie* ' nothing could be expected of it. In point of fact socialist deputies and mayors, besides secretaries of syndicates and Chambers of Labour, spent quite a lot of time at ministries and prefectures, asking for all sorts of things : the concession of public works, credit for co-operatives, nomination or dismissal of officials, even orders of knighthood. Such demands were apparently venial or at any rate not against their principles. But how could they ask for state intervention for the defence of a municipality and the enforcement of respect for democratic institutions, in the very town where a year ago the Socialist Party Congress had declared that these institutions must be abolished, and where the party branch was dominated by communists ? There were actually negotiations between the Chamber of Labour and the authorities, which ended in a vague compromise, an undertaking being apparently given not to hoist the red flag. But at party headquarters it was decided : ' We will defend ourselves against the fascists '. Cases of bombs were brought to the Palazzo and revolvers distributed ; but the job was left to inexperienced hands and, as so often happens, to *agents provocateurs*. At the ceremony of installation the communist Gnudi, after being named mayor by the council, stepped on to the balcony, surrounded by party flags, to greet the crowd collected in the square. Pigeons were released with red streamers attached to their tails. It was maximalist

Bologna's greatest moment. When the new mayor appeared the crowd burst into cheers, but the fascists who were lined up, armed, at the corners of the square, opened fire. Panic followed, and on the town hall balcony those entrusted with the 'defence' dropped their bombs. Fascist revolvers and municipal bombs accounted for nine dead and a hundred wounded, all socialists or sympathizers. Indoors the reports and explosions spread panic and rage. From the public balcony revolver shots were fired at the minority benches, mortally wounding Giordani, lawyer, ex-soldier, nationalist and freemason, and one of the most pacific amongst the opponents of the new administration.

The events of the Palazzo d'Accursio precipitated in Bologna, Emilia, and throughout Italy an outburst of accumulated hate and violence. The dead body of Giordani was exploited to the point of hysteria, while the provocation of the fascists, the illegality of arming against a properly elected administration, and the nine dead socialists were forgotten. Nothing was remembered but the ex-soldier with a heroic war record, 'killed in a trap' by the 'anti-nationalists'. Hatred separated the two camps; waverers kept off or joined the fascists. The socialists, incapable alike of profiting by legal or organizing illegal methods, found themselves up against both fascist squads and state forces. The era of violence, reprisals, and 'punitive expeditions' had begun.

In December a clash took place in rather similar circumstances near the Castello Estense in Ferrara, with the same effect on public opinion. In the province of Ferrara, however, another factor contributed to the success of fascism. Here, at the beginning of 1921, took place the first great reverse which was to lead to the total collapse of the organized working-class movement. This province was the electoral home of revolutionary and anti-socialist syndicalism. Between 1907 and 1913 there had been a succession of violent agricultural strikes under the leadership of Umberto Pasella, future secretary-general of the *fasci*, Michele Bianchi, future *quadrumvir* of the march on Rome, and others, nearly all of whom went over to fascist syndicalism. If the employers' resistance were prolonged they knew how to deal with it, for the crops of a recalcitrant landlord could be destroyed, they explained, ' with a single match '. The country-folk of this province had always been the easy prey of demagogues and of Mussolini's friends and colleagues. Socialist propaganda had never made much impression on them, which explains why the district was first to give way to fascist pressure. With a fine instinct for local feeling the fascists adopted as their slogan here : ' The land for those who till it ', without waiting for future socialization. The Agrarian Association let itself be persuaded into leasing several thousand hectares direct to individual workers, who thus escaped their quota of labour service. Generally speaking the land was poor, and not much of it was ceded. These ' Potemkin villages ' only served to enhance the poverty of most of the wage-earners of the province, but the fascists could now say : ' You see, the socialists promised you everything and gave you nothing ; they even prevented you from having your own land to farm. The *fasci* have set up hundreds of families who can farm their own land all the year round.' The country-folk were rallied by this single word of hope, after being frightened by the punitive expeditions. The peasant ' leagues ', no longer under the protection of the traditional system, went over in a block to the fascist syndicates, to join the struggle against ' socialist tyranny '. The first fascist syndicate was created on February 25, 1921, in the commune of San Bartolomeo of Bosco, in the province of Ferrara, at the headquarters in the old socialist *Lega*.[1] The co-operatives soon followed the syndicates, while lorry-loads of blackshirts touring the country forcibly dissolved the local socialist administrations. In November 1920 all twenty-one communes of the province had been won by the socialists ; towards the end of April 1921 only four were left, and it was not long before these were dissolved or forced to resign.

By the end of 1920 the fascists were making habitual use of ' punitive expeditions ' to extend their influence. These were employed on a large scale in Julian Venetia, where the fascist groups were openly supported by the local authorities,

---

[1] The *Lega* was the farm labourers' syndicate in each district ; these tended to be socialist.

and where the struggle against ' bolshevism '—i.e. against Workers' Co-operatives, Sickness Funds and Culture Clubs, inherited from Austrian Socialism—was accompanied by a violent oppression of the Slovene and Croat populations. The headquarters of the Slovene associations in Trieste was set on fire in July 1920, and in October the socialist daily, *Il Lavoratore*, was attacked, and the Chamber of Labour in Fiume destroyed. This form of action, while it was intensified in Julian Venetia, where it drew much support from nationalist aspirations, spread into the Po valley, where it acquired the characteristics which were dominant up to the time of the march on Rome. In the Po valley, the towns were on the whole less red than the country, being full of landowners, garrison officers, university students, officials, *rentiers*, professional men, and tradespeople. These were the classes from which fascism drew its recruits and which officered the first armed squads. Thus an expedition would usually set out into the country from some urban centre. With arms provided by the Agrarian Association or by some regimental stores, the blackshirts would ride to their destination in lorries. When they arrived they began by beating up any passer-by who did not take off his hat to the colours, or who was wearing a red tie, handkerchief, or shirt. If anyone protested or tried to defend himself, if a fascist was roughly treated or wounded, the ' punishment ' was intensified. They would rush to the buildings of the Chamber of Labour, the Syndicate, or the Co-operative, or to the People's House, break down the doors, hurl out furniture, books, or stores into the street, pour petrol over them, and in a few moments there would be a blaze. Anyone found on the premises would be severely beaten or killed, and the flags were burnt or carried off as trophies.

The expedition usually had a definite object, which was to ' clean up ' a neighbourhood. They would then draw up at once outside the headquarters of the red organization and destroy it. Groups of fascists would round up the ' leaders ', mayors, and town councillors, the secretary of the ' league ', or the president of the co-operative. These were forced to resign and banished for ever from the district, under pain of death or the destruction of their houses. If they escaped vengeance was taken on their families. ' Punitive expeditions set out every day', says Chiurco in his *History of the Fascist Revolution*.[1] ' The lorry load of fascists arrives in a given district, and they announce themselves to the head of the League. They begin with a discussion ; then either the head of the League gives way or persuasion is followed by violence. He generally does give way. If not, the revolvers have their say.' If he still resisted he was done away with. They would come to his house at night and trick him into coming out ; as soon as he opened the door they would shoot him down on his own doorstep. Such people would often let themselves be taken away in order to spare their families the tragic sight. Next morning they would be found dead in the field to which the fascists had brought them. Sometimes the fascists amused themselves by taking away their victims in a lorry and, after torturing them, leaving them naked, tied to a tree, hundreds of miles away. To maintain the terror they used to send out and publish all kinds of threats and orders, without the slightest sign of interference from the magistrates or the government. Thus the Marquis Dino Perrone Compagni[2] could with impunity send the following letter, in April 1921, to the mayor of a village in Tuscany :

' Sir, Since Italy must belong to the Italians and cannot therefore permit herself to be governed by people of your sort, speaking for your fellow-citizens who are under your administration I advise you to resign your office of mayor before Sunday, April 17. If you refuse, you alone are responsible for the consequences. If you take it upon yourself to draw the attention of the authorities to this generous, kindly and humane advice your time allowance will expire before Wednesday the 13th—a

[1] This *History*, from which we shall make frequent quotations, deals with the events of 1919–22, is an ' official ' work compiled under the auspices of the Government Press Bureau and published in 1929 with a preface by Mussolini.

[2] This man had under him squadrons consisting of disgruntled patriots side by side with rogues and professional criminals. ' A century earlier ', writes Pietro Nenni in his *Six Years of Civil War in Italy*, ' the noble marquis would have been a famous brigand. In the post-war period he became a defender of order in the service of the landowners. The fascist government made him a prefect.'

lucky number. Signed, Dino Perrone Compagni, 1 Piazza Ottaviani, Florence.'

The author signed his own name, on paper stamped with the *fascio*, and added his private address, quite certain that there would be no interference with him and his friends and no official veto on the proposed expedition.

During the first weeks of 1921 the fascist offensive reached its highest pitch of violence and ferocity. The meaning of the events of this period cannot be grasped without a clear realization of how this phenomenon broke out and of the wideness of its territorial distribution. In Julian Venetia the offensive was complicated and intensified by a struggle against the ' outlanders ' who made up almost the entire population of the country districts and the Carso plateau. Here the role of the *fasci* was almost official, for they represented the Italianization that was to be imposed on peoples and administration ; the police force and the army openly co-operated with them. They had in addition the money and the support of the shipowners who wanted a firm hand kept on the workers in the numerous building-yards from Trieste to Pola, and on the miners' unions of the Carso. In the southern, most fertile zone of Istria, the landowners took the offensive. The whole of this district, whose long-discussed frontiers had only just been fixed and where the Fiume question was still an open one, was still mobilized. There was no contact between the Slav population and its landowning rulers, and except in one or two towns the Italians felt they were in occupied territory. The *fasci* were largely composed of garrison officers, officials, and other elements imported from the peninsula, who carried on the war of ' liberation ' against the Slavs and the ' communists.' Working-class institutions, priests who preached in Slovene and villages where the police were the only Italian inhabitants were the objectives of this war.

The fascists had already,[1] in 1920, attacked the socialist newspaper and the headquarters of the Slav organizations in Trieste, and at the beginning of 1921 they did so again and again. The *Lavoratore*, Socialist Party organ, which had

[1] Pp. 102, 103.

been forcibly seized by the communists on January 29 after
the rupture at the Congress of Leghorn, was set on fire by
the fascists for the second time on February 9. The workers,
as usual, replied with a general strike. But the ' work of
systematic destruction of everything bolshevik '[1] began, with
open state assistance, in the country district of Istria, which
stretches along the coast from Pirano to Pola. Thus, ' on
the evening of January 20, by arrangement with the garrison
troops, an attack was made on the Chamber of Labour at
Dignano '. On February 28 the Trieste Chamber of Labour
was attacked for the third time and entirely destroyed. To
avenge the burning of the Chamber of Labour, the workers
at Muggia, near Trieste, fired the shipyards of San Marco.
These too were destroyed.

> ' Troops of the Sassari brigade were then called in to
> fight the rebels and a fascist aeroplane from the Portorosa
> flying school flew to the scene of the disturbance. During
> the night of March 1 the fascists of Trieste and Upper
> Istria massed in Pirano, seized a ship and went to Muggia.
> The vessel drew near, with masked lights, and the fascists
> landed and set fire to the Chamber of Labour, which was
> completely destroyed.'

At the beginning of April serious incidents took place in
the Carnizza district, south of Istria. A fascist squad from
Dignano arrested and removed a Slav innkeeper. This
arbitrary act caused a revolt. The tocsin was sounded in
the neighbouring villages, peasants hurried to the spot and
the fascist gang was forced to retreat towards Carnizza with
its prisoner. There it was besieged, while soldiers, police,
and fascists were mobilized and a desperate fight took place,
under real war conditions, with barbed-wire and machine-
guns. This guerrilla war lasted several days, until finally
the forces of ' order ' prevailed. ' The rebel populations
were driven from their villages, which were destroyed by
fire, and the districts of Segotti, Vareschi, Zuechi, and
Mormorano were devastated either by fire or battle.' The
struggle was prolonged in the Arsa (Albona) mines, where

---

[1] In this section on the territorial distribution of the movement, quoted
passages where no reference is given are from Chiurco's *History of the Fascist
Revolution*, Vol. III.

the workers were on strike and under arms. The military authorities decided to occupy the district, and attacked it by land and sea. After a few skirmishes the miners' resistance was overcome. The fighting had given the fascist squads a chance to perfect their organization and equipment, and from now on they carried out a ' systematic destruction ' of all working-class institutions, syndical, co-operative, or cultural. All the ' Culture Clubs ' in the suburbs and neighbourhood of Trieste were destroyed. A few weeks later a socialist paper summed up this campaign as follows : ' Out of dozens and dozens of Chambers of Labour and People's Houses, only three or four still exist, of which two, at Trieste and Pola, are carrying on in temporary premises or even in the ruins of their buildings. Of a hundred Culture Clubs not one survives.'

In the Po valley agrarian fascism, supported by storm squadrons raised in the towns of the district, was in full swing. After the events at the Palazzo d'Accursio in Bologna and at the Castello Estense in Ferrara,[1] a period of desperate tension broke out into a storm of punitive expeditions. On January 24 a fascist procession in Modena was fired on and two *squadristi* killed, one of whom belonged to a squadron brought over from Bologna for the occasion. The Chambers of Labour at Modena and Bologna were immediately set on fire. The Minister of the Interior— Giolitti—ordered the cancellation of all licences to bear arms in the provinces of Bologna, Modena, and Ferrara. Mussolini protested violently in the *Popolo d'Italia* against this measure. At Bologna and Ferrara the *fasci*, the liberal associations, and the employers' organizations decided to refuse to give up their arms. At Modena : ' The representatives of he local associations of Soldiers on Leave, the Ex-servicemen, the *Fasci di Combattimento*, State Pensioners, the Order and Liberty Association, the Popolari, the liberal-democratic group, the Liberal Party, the Sportsmen's Society, the provincial Agrarian Association, the Association of Traders and Manufacturers, associated themselves with the resolution passed by the associations at Bologna and Ferrara, refused to recognize

[1] Pp. 99 ff. and 101.

the constitutionality of the ministerial decree or the legality
of the prefectorial order and demanded of the government
instant withdrawal of the decree, failing which they were
ready to resist.   Meanwhile they advised citizens not to
surrender their arms.'   At Ferrara the *fascio* ordered
and secured the closing down of all shops and factories
as a protest, and a general lock-out in the three
provinces was expected.   The decrees were not withdrawn, but a week later at Bologna the ' Committee of
Action against Disarmament ' was able to report with
satisfaction on the small numbers of those who had yielded
up their arms.   The most determined opponents of pacification were the landowners, principal instigators and gainers
by the fascist offensive.

In the province of Bologna raids and acts of terrorism
increased, particularly after the meeting of the fascist
provincial congress (April 3), which was celebrated by the
destruction of numerous workers' and socialist clubs in the
capital.   In the province of Ferrara, operations on a grand
scale began earlier, at the beginning of March, and reached
a peak in May, when the expeditions became ' innumerable ',
there were so many, says the fascist historian, that ' one could
no longer keep count : leagues, organizations, all were
overthrown.'   On May 26 Italo Balbo, who had planned and
directed all the expeditions without any interference from
the local authorities, was arrested at Ferrara for being
found in possession of a revolver.   ' As soon as the news
became known the town was in a ferment.   Columns
of fascists roused the population with patriotic songs,
while the bells of the principal churches sounded
the tocsin.   At one o'clock in the morning the
Castello Estense was besieged by the fascists, who had
mobilized, rounded up their country squadrons and
threatened to occupy it.   The authorities were forced to
free Balbo and he was presented by public subscription
with a new weapon to replace the confiscated one.'   Two
months earlier Arpinati, the leader of the action squadrons
in Bologna, accused of having committed several murders
and other acts of violence, had been set free three
days later after similar demonstrations.

In the province of Mantua, which had enjoyed peace since the tragic days of December 1919,[1] the landowners took advantage of the fascist advance to attack the agricultural labour agreement. In Mantua itself the confederate Chamber of Labour and the People's University were destroyed on April 20, and next day, with the aid of fascists who drove up in lorries from the country, the syndical Chamber of Labour, the Railwaymen's Club, and the flat of the socialist deputy Dugoni suffered the same fate. The Agrarian Association announced that in future work would only be given to those on the fascist register. Punitive expeditions wiped out leagues, co-operatives, workers' associations, special attention being paid to league leaders and their homes. At San Giovanni del Dosso, after the suppression of the league, wages were reduced and hours of work raised from eight to ten a day. It was impossible to get into the country without a fascist pass. At Buscoldo a lorry drew up one night outside the local co-operative club, a handsome building of which the workers were very proud. Darkness had already fallen. The fascists rushed in, shouting : ' Down with the king. Long live d'Annunzio.' Some guarded the main entrance, others entered the café ; with eyes glaring and faces distorted they shouted : ' Hands up.' The workers present, who were playing cards or reading newspapers, obeyed. They were searched, without so much as a penknife being found. The fascists, revolver in hand, forced them to leave, one by one. At the door others lay in wait for them with daggers and bludgeons. The workers all had to run the gauntlet. Blows were rained on their heads and shoulders and they were stabbed in the back. Thirty-eight were thus stabbed, including old men, three disabled soldiers, and a fourteen-year-old child. After this the fascists ransacked the building, broke up the furniture, and destroyed the registers. At a blast from a whistle they got back into their lorry, after emptying the till, and disappeared into the night.

The tradespeople hated the co-operatives as much as the landowners hated the ' leagues '. At Ostiglia, an important provincial centre, there was a flourishing co-operative store

[1] P. 69.

in one of the little town's most beautiful buildings, containing its most popular café. The fascist executive stepped in and announced their decision : ' The management of the co-operative are invited to go into liquidation and dispose of their property before the end of May ; for shopkeepers have the right to carry on their trade without being crippled by the co-operative.' The management with some difficulty secured a month's reprieve, but had to carry out the fascist decree before the end of June.

The successful preaching and practice over a long period of Prampolini's ' evangelical ' socialism could not avail to save Reggio Emilia and its province from the fascist affliction. At Reggio the socialist municipality had organized, with undeniable success and to the great benefit of the population, pharmaceutical services, the distribution of milk and meat and the provision of bread ; while it either ran or controlled numerous food-shops, restaurants, and a flour-mill. In the province agricultural co-operatives farmed 2227 hectares, and there were in 1920 eighty-six co-operative stores with 16,800 members and a turnover of more than 53,000,000 lire. It was a new social system of production and distribution, and it found itself up against a coalition of all those whose private interests it affected. After the middle of March, to quote Chiurco again : ' The fascists were in the ascendant and the red organizations, attacked and plundered, began to decline.' The Reggio Chamber of Labour was set on fire on April 8, and by the middle of May many leagues and syndical employment offices had suffered the same fate ; sixteen socialist municipal councils, including that of Reggio, had been forced to resign, several hundreds of workers had been savagely beaten up and dozens of socialist officials banished from the province by the fascists. During April the People's Houses in Salsomaggiore and Borgo San Donnino among others in the province of Parma were burnt down. In the town of Parma, where resistance to fascism was strong, the People's House belonging to the Syndical Union was sacked. A few shots were exchanged on April 19. The next day a general strike was declared and the police arranged to arrest a large number of ' subversive ' persons and confiscate the arms they used in the defence of their organizations. The fascists thought their way was open and advanced to the attack ; but the workers resisted : ' They fought a real battle in the outskirts of Naviglio and sent a rain of tiles on to their attackers from the roofs ; armoured cars joined in, bombs exploded, and there were several wounded.' Next day there was another police round-up to arrest and disarm those who had tried to resist the fascist attack. On April 23, the date of the inauguration of their *fascio*, a squadron of former Fiume legionaries, preceded by carabiniers with revolvers in their hands, attacked and broke up the vine-producers' co-operative at Piacenza. In a few weeks all the towns along the old Via Aemilia were subjected to the fascist reign of terror.

Firmly installed in the Bologna–Ferrara–Piacenza triangle, the fascist squads also conquered the provinces of Rovigo in the north-east and of Pavia in the north-west. In the province of Rovigo—Polesine—there was no sort of bolshevism to be suppressed. Social disputes had always been settled peacefully. The local socialist leader was Giacomo Matteotti, by conviction and inclination a reformist, in the best sense of the word. On February 28 the old agricultural agreement expired, and the labourers' organizations suggested starting negotiations for a new one. The landowners, inspired by recent events in the Po valley and Ferrara, decided to take the opportunity of ridding themselves of the leagues, employment offices, and all forms of workers' organization, and refused. Expeditions with nothing to ' punish ' but the very existence of a body of working men who had emerged from a state of ignorance and serfdom began to increase towards the end of February, immediately reaching an unheard-of degree of violence. Matteotti and the Chambers of Labour gave the order : ' Stay at home ; ignore all provocation. Even silence and cowardice are sometimes heroic.'[1] This attitude was quite ineffective against the fascist squads touring the country in lorries provided by the landowners or borrowed from the Cereal Requisition Board, which had the services of the army at its disposal. The league offices were closed down or

[1] See Matteotti's speech in the Chamber on March 10, 1921.

destroyed, and socialist town councils forced to resign. The town council of Occhiobelli, for instance, one of the first districts to be influenced by socialist propaganda, had to relinquish its mandate, although it had been elected in November 1920 by 1100 votes to 160 for all other parties. Its retirement did not save this commune from more expeditions. On May 1 the Chamber of Labour and the co-operative were set on fire by fascists who appeared in lorries from every direction. ' More and more Chambers of Labour and other organizations were destroyed daily,' says Chiurco. The fascist squads could be proud of their work, for not a single syndical or co-operative organization was left, dozens of people had been killed, between four and five thousand wounded or tortured, more than a thousand private houses had been broken into, more than three hundred sacked and burnt. The landowners had won. Matteotti stated as much in another speech to the Chamber : ' The whole tenor of civil life is destroyed, each Commune is isolated from the next, each labourer from his neighbour, the agrarian war is lost. One by one the peasants are asking for work, and the Rovigo Chamber of Labour whose buildings are already in ruins is to be dissolved at the beginning of April.'

From Ferrara and Polesine the tide swept over Venetia. Between February and May the Chambers of Labour in Vicenza, Padua, Belluno, and Udine, the provincial capitals, as well as in less important centres, were destroyed. As elsewhere expeditions became more and more like proper military operations. On April 10 for example there was a ' punitive expedition on a grand scale ' in Mossano (Vicenza). ' About four hundred fascists, who had come specially from Vicenza, Montegaldello, Poiana, and Noventa, collected here. They invaded the district from all sides at once, dealing out fire and blood. Seven houses were attacked and their contents destroyed or burnt, some being set on fire. Many bastinadoes were administered.'[1] On April 24 another similar expedition took place at Poiana. ' The fascists arrived in six lorries, occupied the red co-

---

[1] Readers may be reminded that all passages in inverted commas are quoted from Chiurco's *History*.

operative and the theatre, kidnapped the socialist assessors and councillors from their houses and punished them severely. The police drove the fascists off,' but they came back five days later : ' On the 29th a lorry-load of fascists arrived and cut the telephone-wires to prevent possible interruption. The mayor was beaten up and his house set on fire.' On May 10 the Udine fascists made an expedition in lorries to Pordenone. They were met with revolver shots and bombs ; one of them, an eighteen year old student who had been a Fiume legionary, was killed, and others were wounded. ' The fascists received substantial reinforcements from neighbouring districts and forced the revolutionaries to retreat to the Torre country, where they were beleaguered. Machine-guns and even a field-gun were brought into action. Troops from the Udine garrison intervened on the side of the fascists and the bolshevik fortress was stormed.' The engagement was prolonged thanks to the arrival of squads from Vittorio Veneto, Friuli, Venice, and Trieste. ' For the next few days the work of cleaning up the country-side, under the direction of Signor Giunta (leader of the Trieste *fascio*) went on ; they destroyed red (socialist) and black (popular Catholic) headquarters, made arrests and carried out searches.' In these provinces the land occupied by fascism touched on the east Julian Venetia, already under its domination, and on the west the Trentino and Tyrol, which on the other hand resisted up to the eve of the march on Rome.

The province of Pavia, which lies between Emilia and Piedmont, is entirely agricultural. The Mortara section— the Lomellina—forms part of the rice-growing district which covers the whole plain of the province of Novara. Here there was, if possible, an even closer connection than in other provinces between the growth of fascism and the struggle between landowners and ' red syndicates ' and their employment offices. The socialists had gained forty-five out of fifty communes in the November elections and all fourteen seats in the provincial council. The manufacturers of Mortara, who included big war profiteers and two multi-millionaires, had hired, before the elections had even begun, gangs of armed roughs who for forty francs a day terrorized the town. The *fascio* was formed in February 1921, chiefly by people from other districts, a demobilized colonel, a student from Pavia (Lanfranconi, afterwards one of the first fascist deputies), and various other *déclassés*, who were all welcomed with open arms and financed by manufacturers and landowners alike. As in Polesine the agricultural labour agreements were due to expire. The labourers were well organized and supported by an extensive network of town councils, leagues, and co-operatives, and there was no chance of worsting them by legal means. Fascist squads were quickly formed and set to work. The authorities protected them, for as Chiurco reveals : ' The sub-prefect of Mortara sympathized with them ' and in the neighbouring district of Voghera ' the sub-prefect, himself a partisan, was the father of an ardent fascist.' A levy was raised from all the farmers in the district ; for the richer four lire, for the others two lire per *pertica*.[1] They all paid up in the knowledge that once the workers were defeated they would get their money back with a good profit as well. Within a few months the whole system of the workers' organizations was wiped out.

In ' gentle Tuscany ', however, fascist cruelty and violence reached their highest level. Here the agricultural proletariat was smaller than in Emilia (12·8 per cent of the population, as against 23·2). The favourite form of agrarian exploitation was the *mezzadria*, which occupied rather more than half the agricultural population. The socialists and the *Popolari* disputed hotly for influence over the *mezzadri*, and the fascists, standing for the rights of landowners, attacked all ' leagues,' red or white. One of the first punitive expeditions in Tuscany was directed against the ' white ' settlers of the Mugello, and on December 14, 1920 a peasant was killed at San Piero a Sieve. Four fascist leaders, accused of a share in the murder, were released after cross-examination. Two of them, Captain Chiostro and Lieutenant Capanni, both retired, were welcomed as fascist candidates in the national bloc and were elected a few months later in the May elections.

Florence, particularly after the end of February, became

---

[1] Local measure equivalent to 769 square metres.

a fascist storm centre. On the 27th a bomb was thrown at a procession of fascists, who killed a communist leader, Lavagnini, that evening. The next day there was a general strike, fighting, and barricades in the working-class quarter of San Frediano. A young fascist, Berta, the son of a manufacturer, ran into a group of rioters who stabbed him and threw his body into the Arno. In the suburbs the workers threw up barricades to defend the headquarters of their societies. At Scandicci *carabinieri* and fascists were met with bullets and bombs and forced to retire, leaving their lorry, which was set on fire. They returned to the attack :

> ' On the bridge which leads into the district the first barricades were met with. The chief of police gave the order to fire. With the aid of artillery and armoured cars they broke down the barricades and damaged the bridge. After thus succeeding in getting into the quarter they brought up field-guns against the People's House and partly demolished it.'

Then, finding their way open, the fascists ' attacked the town hall and triumphantly carried off arms and red flags to Florence.' Machine-guns were used by the *bersaglieri* at Bagno a Ripoli ; a field-gun was brought into action at the Oema bridge. Violent riots broke out in all working-class neighbourhoods. Soldiers and police were cheered by crowds as they returned from their raids ; but the workers everywhere were becoming angry and frightened, and this made their guns go off by themselves. They developed a persecution complex which in some places drove them like hunted beasts into acts of unprecedented violence. Thus when at Empoli, near Florence, some fascists were reported to be approaching, the whole neighbourhood rose in arms. When a couple of lorries reached the first houses they were overwhelmed by rifle-fire from all round ; tiles were rained on them from roofs, pots, and other missiles from windows. The invaders were merely naval mechanics in civilian clothes on their way to Florence to take the place of railwaymen on strike. One lorry was burnt, the other just managed to get away ; eight men were killed and ten wounded. They were brutally avenged, for soon after a number of troops and fascist squads marched in and burnt down the People's House. Two days later they attacked the People's House at Siena where the workers had taken their stand. Fascists and police surrounded it, together with 200 troops. After a few hours of battle machine-guns were brought up and two shots were fired from a 63 field-gun at the building ; after a last attack the defenders hoisted the white flag and surrendered. The fascists finished their day's work by burning down the People's House ' with petrol provided by several people, including the Cavaliere Morelli of the Landowners' Consortium '. Thanks to co-operation between the *fasci* of Florence, Pisa, and Siena the whole district was soon overwhelmed by the destructive tide of fascism. The Chambers of Labour in the most important centres were burnt down : Lucca on March 31, Arezzo on April 12, Prato on April 17, Pisa on May 2, Grosseto on June 28. The fascist squads also organized the conquest of Umbria. Between March 22, when the Chamber of Labour and all the workers' institutions at Perugia were destroyed, and April 26, when the same thing happened at Terni, the whole district came under fascist control.

In the country round Rome and in the south fascist progress was slow, except in Apulia, where the workers' organizations were strong and class feeling bitter. Agriculture was more progressive here than anywhere else. Wheat, wine and oil were cultivated largely on industrial lines and there was a correspondingly large rural proletariat. As in Emilia, wages, the minimum number of employees per hectare, and the employment offices, were questions of vital importance to the workers and gave rise to frequent disputes. It was not through mere chance that Apulia was the only part of southern Italy to experience immediately a fascist movement on the Po valley scale. The causes were the same ; the landowners had the same end in view, the restoration of their power ; and used the same methods, the destruction of the workers' organizations. Even before the war they had employed gangs of toughs, *mazzieri*,[1] to knock reason into recalcitrant labourers and force them to support the landowners' candidate on election day. These gangs had chiefly consisted of 'wanted' men, whose new job, thanks to collusion between the authorities and the landowners, great manipulators of elections and majorities, guaranteed them immunity from the law. Membership of a gang was a safeguard as effective as the protection of a medieval sanctuary. The workers became so strong after the war that this method became impossible unless applied on a much larger scale with a better organization and more arms. The Apulian *fasci* came into being to carry out this policy; the old lags were enlisted in the fascist squads, officered by students and demobilized officers, mostly sons of landowners or members of the *petite bourgeoisie* of the south, very poor, but greedy for fame and advancement. Their method was to attack the townships, for in Apulia the peasants lived in towns and went out every day to work on the big estates, often several miles away, and came back at night. The landowner's agent used to come to the market-place every morning to hire labour; formerly he had fixed the daily wage, but now this was done, at least in part, by the Chamber of Labour. The destruction of the Chamber would be a death-blow to the resistance of the peasants. Consequently, when on February 22 thirty fascists made a surprise attack on the Chamber of Labour at Minervino Murge and set it on fire, and others collected the next day at Bari to attack the workers' headquarters, the reaction was immediate and violent. The provincial congress of the Federation of Agricultural Labourers was that day sitting at Bari, and a general strike was proclaimed. The labourers felt themselves threatened once more with the abject poverty and slavery from which they had only just emerged. In their large villages, where everyone knew everyone else, it was obvious that fascist, *mazziere* and landowner made common cause. Instinctively they vented their rage on the fascist-owned farms (*masserie*), and scoured the country in armed groups setting fire to them. Gangs of mounted *mazzieri* pursued them and a desperate battle followed

[1] From *mazza*, a cudgel.

which went on after night had fallen. The infuriated labourers butchered live stock and tore up plants, while the fascists struck at the reds' headquarters. The following description appeared in the *Popolo d'Italia* of February 25 : 'After last night's events there is tremendous feeling among the peasants. Many of them stayed in the town[1] without waiting for a general strike to be proclaimed by the officials of the Chamber of Labour, now burnt down. Numerous groups of fascists and peasants are parading the streets, outwardly calm, but ready to fly at each others' throats at the first incident. There is an atmosphere of suspense and it is feared that at any moment something serious may happen. Armed bands roam the country-side to hunt out the fascists. The troops sent are already insufficient for keeping order inside the town and it is impossible for them to patrol the country, where the peasants are committing numerous acts of reprisal. Armed squads of fascists are engaged in ascertaining the state of the farms attacked by the socialists and in avenging their relatives and friends,' and next day : 'Minervino Murge is still in a state of upheaval. A fierce struggle is being waged in the surrounding country. To-night the Chamber of Labour at Terlizzi was burnt down. There is bad news from Conversano, where they are fighting in the streets with hand-grenades. At Cerignola the leaguists have set fire to the *masseria* belonging to the Caradonna brothers, who are fascist leaders.'

But the police and the military intervened to help the fascists' manœuvres and defend them against reprisals, and the struggle quickly became one-sided. Between March and May the Chambers of Labour at Tarento, Bari, Corato, Andria, Barietta, etc. were reduced to charred ruins. The *fasci* created their first 'economic' syndicates, the collective labour agreements were torn up, and the landowners could look forward once more to having their own way in the hiring of agricultural labour. From now on they had a terrible weapon with which to complete the destruction of the free syndicates, for those who refused to leave them

[1] Instead of going to their daily work on the *masseria*.

could no longer obtain a single hour's work, and now that emigration had become almost impossible were condemned, with their families, to starvation.

Thus by the middle of 1921 the fascist ' occupation ' included the whole of Julian Venetia, part of Venetia, the entire Po Valley except Romagna, Cremona, the greater part of Tuscany, Umbria, and Apulia. In Piedmont the whole province of Alessandria was infected, particularly the districts of Casale and Novi Ligure and the rice-growing districts of Novara. The provinces of Como and Turin were hardly affected, but on April 25 in the town of Turin the fascists managed to occupy and burn down the great People's House in the Corso Siccardi, the headquarters of the Chamber of Labour and all the workers' institutions, without provoking any active retaliation. The communists, who controlled nearly all the local organizations after the split in the Socialist Party, had often defied the fascists to touch the People's House, threatening them and the industrialists who subsidized them with ruthless reprisals if they did so. They could do no more than others had done in similar circumstances, and declared a general strike. This allowed the fascists to make off in twenty-four hours with all the honours of war and a resounding victory won at small expense.

Lombardy, except for the provinces of Pavia and Mantua, was as yet almost unaffected. In the capital, Milan, the explosion of a time bomb on March 23 in the Diana Theatre, placed there by anarchists as a protest against the imprisonment of Malatesta, killed eighteen people and wounded a hundred. The fascists retaliated not only by attacking the anarchist paper *Umanità Nuova*, but by taking the opportunity of setting on fire and destroying the new offices of *Avanti*, newspaper of the socialists, who had had nothing to do with the affair. Thus the new offices suffered the same fate as the old, which had been fired by Mussolini's *arditi* in 1919. In the Marches and the rest of central and southern Italy the fascist movement was only just beginning. As may be seen from the table,[1] which is still incomplete, during the first half of 1921 the fascists destroyed 17 newspapers and

[1] P. 120.

printing-works, 59 People's Houses, 119 Chambers of Labour, 83 Peasants' Leagues, 151 Socialist Clubs and 151 Culture Clubs. Nearly all these destructions took place between March and May, chiefly in the country districts, where, thanks to the *fasci*, the landowners were taking their revenge on the workers' organizations. A pro-fascist paper, the *Giornale d'Italia*, brought out the essential character of fascism by calling it a ' Jacquerie bourgeoise '.

District.	Newspapers and printing offices.	People's Houses.	Chambers of Labour.	Co-operative societies.	Peasant leagues.	Mutual aid societies.	Socialist and communist clubs and offices.	Culture clubs.	People's libraries and theatres.	People's Universities.	Workers' syndicates.	Workers' friendly societies.
Piedmont	1	4	9	3	2	1	9	–	2	–	10	8
Lombardy (except Cremona and Mantua)	3	–	1	2	–	–	6	–	–	–	–	1
Liguria	–	–	3	–	–	–	–	–	–	–	–	–
Venetia (except Rovigo)	–	1	9	8	1	–	7	–	1	–	–	1
Julian Venetia	4	2	21	3	–	–	5	100	–	–	–	2
Po Valley												
Bologna	1	6	7	9	5	–	5	–	–	–	–	2
Cremona	–	–	–	–	–	–	–	–	–	–	–	–
Ferrara	–	–	9	1	19	–	5	–	2	–	1	–
Mantua	–	3	4	37	15	–	2	–	–	1	–	1
Modena	–	–	2	–	–	–	–	–	–	–	–	–
Parma	–	5	1	6	–	–	2	–	–	–	–	1
Pavia	–	21	7	9	25	4	8	–	4	–	–	2
Piacenza	1	2	–	7	–	–	3	–	–	–	–	–
Reggio Emilia	1	1	2	1	8	–	2	–	1	–	–	–
Rovigo	–	2	4	3	3	–	2	–	–	–	–	1
Po Valley total	3	40	36	73	75	4	29	–	7	1	1	7
Romagna	–	–	1	–	–	–	1	–	–	–	–	1
Tuscany	3	11	15	11	–	2	70	–	–	–	1	24
Umbria	1	–	5	3	–	1	6	–	–	–	–	–
Latium	–	–	–	–	–	–	–	–	–	–	–	–
South (except Apulia)	2	–	2	–	–	–	3	–	–	–	–	–
Apulia	–	1	13	4	2	–	1	–	–	–	7	1
Sicily	–	–	3	–	3	–	4	–	–	–	9	5
Sardinia	–	–	1	–	–	–	–	–	–	–	–	2
GRAND TOTAL	17	59	119	107	83	8	141	100	10	1	28	53

N.B.—This table does not pretend to a high degree of accuracy. It is based on data taken from *The History of the Fascist Revolution* by G.-A. Chiurco, official party historian, which are very inconsistent. The book often mentions the destruction of ' all the red organizations ' of a locality or region, without any further details. The destruction of a single building, People's House, or Chamber of Labour involves that of all organizations having their offices in it, but except in the case of Turin we have not been able to take this into account. Had we been able to complete the statistical data for all the other localities and regions, figures in the last column but one, the workers' syndicates, would be much higher. The total number of organizations of every kind destroyed in the first half of 1921 is undoubtedly higher by several hundreds than the figure we have given. Even the results of the public inquiry published by the Socialist Party at the beginning of 1922, heavily drawn on by Chiurco, are very incomplete, for they do not always enumerate acts of fascist violence and destruction, for example in Julian Venetia, the provinces of Ferrara, Rovigo, etc. ' The reports we have used ', the preface adds, ' only go as far as May or June 1921 ; and omit all Romagna, the province of Modena, a great part of Tuscany, Umbria, Latium, the province of Mantua, Piacenza, Parma.' This table does not include simple ' punitive expeditions ', of which there were thousands at this time, nor individual violence, lock-outs, forced resignations of town councils, destruction of private houses and shops, banishments, and other forms of terrorism.

In all the ' invaded ' districts there was the closest connection between the forces of the state and the fascists. At Trieste on February 9, 1921, the fascists attacked the paper *Il Lavoratore* and the police interfered to arrest the communists who were trying to defend their paper and printing offices. The fascists of Siena, before setting out on their expedition to Foiano della Chiana, received arms and munitions from the local military headquarters. As a rule there was no attempt at concealment. If the military authorities did not help, such officers as were fascists did. Chiurco records that at Tarento, for example : ' With the sanction of the fascist Nicolo Schiavone, a sub-lieutenant of the 9th Infantry Division, a case of bombs was taken from the arsenal of the Rossarol barracks and twenty-four mark 91 rifles from the San-Paolo military stores, where this officer happened to be confined to barracks.' The state forces not only provided arms, but often, as we have seen, shared in punitive expeditions. In this connection Mario Cavallari, a war volunteer, tells of the following events which took place in the province of Ferrara at the end of March 1921 : ' The fascists are accompanied on their expeditions by lorries full of police, who join in singing the fascist songs. At Portomaggiore, an expedition of more than a thousand fascists terrorized the country with night attacks, fires, bomb-throwing, invasion of houses, massacre under the eyes of the police. Further, as fast as the lorries arrived they were stopped by the police, who blocked every entry, and asked the fascists if they were armed, doling out arms and ammunition to those who were not. Houses were searched and arrests made by fascists, and for two days a combined picket of fascists and police searched all those who arrived at the Pontelagoscuro station, allowing only fascists to enter the country.'

Plenty of similar evidence exists, though it is impossible to quote even a very small proportion of it. Here are two examples supplied by *squadristi*. The first is taken from *Memoirs of a Fascist*, written in 1922 by one of the squad leaders of the Florence *fascio*, Umberto Banchelli : ' It must be admitted that the reason fascism developed so quickly and was given so free a hand was that in the breasts of officials and officers beat Italian hearts, which welcomed us gladly as we marched to the rescue. N.C.O.s and militiamen competed with each other to help the *fasci*.' A fascist student, member of an action squad, wrote a sort of public confession which he sent to a communist paper. Written rather later it is very characteristic of the fascist offensive from the start. It shows the prejudices, hates, interests, in short the essential motives which spurred the fascist leader, when he was not simply a mercenary or a bandit: ' The army officers are on our side and supply us with arms and ammunition. We are powerfully and intelligently organized, and so we can order our movement better, without too great a risk. . . . We have you disarmed by the police before attacking, not because we are afraid, since we despise you, but because our blood is precious and must not be wasted on the vile and despicable masses.' The writer proceeds to give his views on the future of the country : ' Italy cannot go bolshevik. She is not an industrial country, and her workers must adapt themselves to peasant life. We will set them to work at harnessing our water power, and we will send them into the fields to cultivate the marshlands where malaria abounds. This will give wealth to the country and cool their revolutionary ardour. It is time to put an end to the luxury of the peasants whose daughters in their silk dresses set themselves against the foremost ladies of the *bourgeoisie*.' After emphasizing the lack of real leaders among the socialists, he adds : ' If you had anyone really capable and loyal, we should not hesitate to imprison him and—why not ? —do away with him, since the end justifies the means.' This student was the son of a landowner and a typical action squad leader.

It is time to ask how the central government faced this situation. The local officials often sympathized with the *fasci* or their powerful protectors. In Rome Giolitti took no serious action, since he meant to dissolve parliament and incorporate the fascists in the national bloc. The socialists in the Chamber began to move resolutions demanding that the government should enforce the law. On January 31, 1921, Matteotti brought in a motion of this kind, the first of a series which continued at intervals until the march on Rome.[1] Giolitti saw everything in terms of bargaining, compromise, give and take. What offer could the socialists make ? Their participation in the government, which was all he wanted and had long demanded, was more than ever impossible. Even after the departure of the communists the reformists were a minority in the Socialist Party. The maximalists were still on top, more preoccupied with protecting themselves on the left against the onslaughts of the communists, who attacked them bitterly, and consistently tried to outbid them, than with the fate of the Italian people.

The element of force was having a fatal effect on the working-class and socialist movement. Paralysed by an internal crisis which was aggravated by the Leghorn split, it had to fight simultaneously against the fascist army, the revengeful industrial and landowning classes and the state, whose external forces contributed to the success of the fascist movement by shutting their eyes to crime or, more frequently, by lending it their active support. Taking a realistic view of the situation there is nothing inexplicable, mysterious or even unexpected in the weakness which the Italian working class finally displayed before the fascist offensive. But if socialists were still far from agreeing on the causes of this weakness, a few of the leaders and of the

---

[1] During this debate the communists moved that ' The Chamber, considering that the government as representing one class cannot defend the proletariat, but on the contrary is forced to resort to violence to prevent its eventual victory, proceeds to the order of the day.'

people were becoming conscious of it, though they did not yet openly acknowledge the fact.

But the speed and the completeness of the socialist collapse in districts where the system had been long and firmly established are not entirely accounted for by the causes so far mentioned.   There was, besides, the *military* character of the fascist offensive which secured it predominance from the start.   This gave the struggle a character for which its opponents, more powerful though they were in some respects, were quite unprepared.   The fascists adopted at once and carried on with increasingly devastating effect the technique of mobile warfare.   In the first place an expedition against a particular locality was hardly ever carried out by the local fascists, who would be few, isolated and exposed to reprisals.   The lorries came from the nearest big centre and were filled with people entirely unknown in the district.   If the ' reds ' were strong and it was feared that there were still too many arms about, even after searches carried out by the sympathetic police, sufficient armed forces were collected to crush any possible defence.   The offices of the various organizations were destroyed, town councils driven out of office, leaders killed or driven into exile, after which the local *fascio*, previously almost non-existent, would be swelled by the adhesion of reactionaries of all complexions and of those who, lately afraid of the socialists, were now afraid of the fascists.   To conquer the great centres they mobilized the forces of the provinces and if necessary those of adjoining provinces.   Later the scope of the offensive widened, expeditions went from province to province and region to region, and the fascist army, obtaining more recruits after each ' occupation ', and gaining in strength and mobility, stormed the enemy strongholds one by one.

In this way districts, provinces, and groups of provinces united for common action, with a permanent exchange of resources and almost automatic co-operation at the first call from any one which was threatened, or if an attack was to be made on an important centre.   More and more we find cases of pairs or trios of *fasci* regularly acting together : Trieste and Fiume ; Bologna and Modena ; Bologna,

Modena and Ferrara ; Brescia and Verona ; Verona and Mantua ; Florence, Pisa and Siena ; Casale, Alessandria and Mortara. If Grosseto, where the *fascio* was powerless, was the objective, four experienced fascists were first sent from Florence to encourage and train the local fascists. The expedition was then prepared and the secretary of the Siena *fascio*[1] 'ordered two cars to take the mobilization order to the *fasci* along the Siena–Chiusi line for a joint attack on Grosseto.' But the workers of this town laid in wait for the fascists in the country outside. When these arrived their first car was stopped, and after a fight they were forced to retreat, leaving one dead behind them. Meanwhile other squads were arriving and surrounding the town, which was still unapproachable. Reinforcements collected from all directions, even from Florence and Perugia, at least a hundred kilometres away, and the entrance to the town was forced during the night. So Grosseto, where there were hardly any fascists, was occupied and passed under their control. When the Milan fascists wanted to make an expedition to Greco Milanese, a communist centre in the suburbs of the town, they called in the *fasci* of Emilia and Tuscany, who sent several squads. This co-operation increased, snowball fashion, and by extending the field of action helped to reach distant objectives and cover whole regions. How did the fascist occupation absorb the whole of Umbria between March and April 1921 ? The flood spread from Florence, Arezzo, Siena, over Perugia ; swollen with Perugian reinforcements it flowed on to Foligno, Todi, Umberti ; from these to Assisi and Spoleto, until it swept over Terni, the last socialist stronghold, all in a few weeks. The *fasci* had immense capacity for concentrating and spreading their influence. When a new *fascio* was formed, especially in districts as yet unconquered, representatives from many other *fasci*, sometimes from far off, would come and assist at the ceremony, and this in itself sometimes gave rise to incidents and expeditions. For instance, at Casale Monteferrato there were delegates from Turin, Biella, Vercelli, Milan and Genoa. As another example of the wide range of the operations, the Pisa *fascio*

[1] Chiurco himself, author of the *History of the Fascist Revolution*.

organized expeditions to several hundreds of places in Tuscany, some of them very far off. The Parma *fascio* sent men to Reggio Emilia, Ferrara, Modena, Milan, Spezia, various Tuscan centres, and even to Trieste and Fiume. Even the *fasci* in smaller centres had plenty of mobility and initiative. To take one example out of several hundred, that of Poggio Rusco (Mantua), apart from provincial expeditions, shared in expeditions to Crevalcore (Bologna), Pozzolengo, Desenzano and Rivoltella (Brescia), Peschiera and Nogara (Verona), and to Bologna and Verona in May 1921. Later it went as far as Parma, Bolzano and Trente. A very small *fascio* in the province of Mantua, according to Chiurco : ' Took part in innumerable expeditions and its activity is proved by its expenditure of 300,000 francs on petrol.'

On the other hand there is hardly one case of a socialist raid on fascist headquarters, or of anti-fascists rallying to a place threatened by *squadristi*. The pre-war socialist movement and its post-war successor had led to the formation of hundreds of little republics, socialist oases with no inter-communication, like medieval cities without their ramparts. Italian socialism was only a conglomeration of thousands of local ' socialisms ', greatly handicapped by municipal exclusiveness and the absence of fully awakened national consciousness. Fascism also managed to adapt itself to local surroundings, but had one great advantage over the working-class movement : its powers of transportation and concentration supported by military tactics. The sixty-three communes of Rovigo, Matteotti's province, all held by the socialists, succumbed one after another without ever attempting to unite and post superior forces at the danger-points. The bells were never rung, as in the Great Revolution, to give warning to the peasants. In the Po valley the advent of the terror only increased isolation. Thirty, fifty armed fascists, as they came to each district, were too strong for the local labourers. They were almost always *arditi*, ex-soldiers, led by officers ; homeless, as men at the front, they could live anywhere. The labourers clustered round their People's House, like medieval cottages round a castle, but though the castle protected, while it mulcted, the village, the People's House needed protection. The labourers were bound to the soil, where after lengthy struggles they had won valuable concessions. This situation gave the enemy the advantage of the offensive, of mobile as against defensive tactics. In the fight between the lorry and the People's House the former was bound to win.

The workers were further handicapped by psychological difficulties which hindered the efficient organization of their defensive tactics. The Italian people had no revolutionary traditions and no taste for war. Those who had acquired this taste at the front had been flung into the arms of the fascists. When the militant worker took his revolver out of his pocket he put himself and felt himself on the wrong side of the law. A similar feeling paralysed Hanriot's gunners outside the doors of the Convention on the 9th Thermidor. The fascist knew he was safe, and could even kill and burn with impunity. Besides, in the eyes of the workers the People's House and the Chamber of Labour were the fruit of two or three generations of sacrifice, their capital, the concrete proof of the progress made by their class and the symbol of their hopes for the future. They were devoted to them and hesitated involuntarily to use them as mere war material. It is not easy to turn a house one loves into a fortress, and this is why the Italian workers showed none of the fierce resolution of the last defenders of the Paris Commune, building a barrier of fire between themselves and the Versaillais. For the fascists the Houses were simply targets. When their fine buildings went down in flames the workers gave way to bitter despair, while the attackers yelled with delight. The plain of the Po, covered with these socialist oases, was a desert by the end of the civil war.

Could the workers have held up the fascists if they had been properly organized? They could certainly have made life difficult for the fascists. If every expedition had suffered heavy loss the fascists would have ceased to look on murder as a sport, to use Mussolini's own description of certain exploits of the *squadristi*. But the more ground the socialists lost in the political game the greater was the part played by military factors. The events of the second half of 1921 up till October 1922 showed still more clearly that the military inferiority of the working class was the consequence of its political inferiority, due in its turn to the maximalist atmosphere with which it was imbued. The fascist movement, before the period of the great meetings, had been a movement of squads, little companies of men, tactics which the *arditi* had learnt at the front. Italian maximalism, on the other hand, was a movement of inarticulate crowds, chaotic, incoherent and blind. Everyone felt safe in this great crowd, alternately shaken by ecstasy and lost in a rosy mist of facile and insolent optimism, but they were like ants under the feet of a marching legion. Even organized, in order to win power, they would have had to settle matters at Rome. But it was their inability to transfer their power into political terms which both prevented them from organizing and doomed to failure any attempt at armed action.

Encouraged and helped by the relative simplicity of its task, and by making use of the two-edged weapon of legality and illegality presented to it by the socialists, the fascist movement made a prodigious and well-sustained effort during the first three months of 1921. It was declared in July 1920 that there were 108 *fasci* 'formed or in course of being formed'. Towards the middle of October, a few weeks after the factory occupations, there were 190. By the end of the year there were more than 800, and by February 1921, 1000. 277 new *fasci* were formed in April, 197 in May, and at the party congress in November there were 2300. The working class, paralysed by the political split and the economic crisis, was obviously losing ground. The industrialists were taking the offensive in Turin. Strikes at the Fiat and Michelin works were suppressed, and the workers had to give in unconditionally ; in factories which had flown the red flag and where all regulations had been submitted to a workers' council the owners were now getting rid of 'undesirables'. Giolitti was delighted. Now that the factories had been evacuated, the treaty of Rapallo signed, the Fiume affair settled, and the fixed price of bread abolished he thought he would give the socialists a good lesson and escape at the same time from the irksome pressure of the *Popolari*. He would dissolve the Chamber in the hope that a fresh election would reduce the power of both parties. He would still be master, he thought, and later share office with the socialists. For him to succeed in this it was necessary for both parties to be weakened so that they would accept his terms in fear of fascism. He therefore allowed fascism to flourish, supported by the public forces, with officers supplied by the War Office and arms by military authorities. The Minister of Justice, Signor Fera, a freemason, sent a circular letter to magistrates inviting them to shelve their records of fascist crimes. Socialist municipalities which were attacked by fascists were dissolved by ministerial decree ' in the interests of public order ', that of Bologna on April 2, Modena, Ferrara, Perugia, and hundreds of others a little later. The fascists joined the national bloc and were included in its lists. At the same time their terrorist acts were ' legalized ', and the ' liberal ' state took its first and irrevocable step towards suicide. In this sense, Giolitti, not Mussolini, was the true evangelist of fascism.

Socialists, communists, and *Popolari* remained outside the national bloc and, contrary to Giolitti's expectations, the new Chamber was more intractable than the last. The election made no major alterations. The total socialist and communist vote was actually higher, with the new provinces, by 20,000 than the socialist vote in 1919, the ' red ' year. The total number of voters had increased since 1919 by 700,000[1] and the percentage from 52 per cent to 56 per cent of the total electorate. The two workers' parties more or less maintained their position, except in the Po valley where the people were terrorized. Even on its reduced scale the electoral campaign of the workers' parties called for exceptional heroism. In the ' occupied ' districts socialists and communists could scarcely hold any meetings, especially in the country. Their newspapers and leaflets were seized, even in the post offices, and burnt. Canvassers who were known had to get out of the district on election day or lock themselves into their houses.

The older workers' parties were hardly affected, except where the fascists actually prevented voting. But the small parties, as always happens in a political crisis, were driven to the right and vanished. Out of the 700,000 new voters rather more than a fifth supported the *Popolari*, the remainder

[1] Of these 265,000 were in the *redente* provinces voting for the first time.

the national bloc. There was a displacement, therefore, of a little over half a million votes out of a total of six and a half million ; this meant a loss of about twenty seats to the workers' parties, who had 139 in 1921 (123 socialists and 16 communists) to 156 in 1919, and since the number of deputies had risen from 508 to 535 their percentage had fallen from 30 per cent to 26 per cent. The problem of the majority remained almost unchanged. Socialists and *Popolari*, the latter having won more votes and ten more seats, were still the two strongest groups. Giolitti's grand design had completely failed. It was the fascists who really gained most by it. Mussolini was elected head of the list at Milan and Bologna and the new Chamber included a fascist group of thirty-five members.

But the real fight had only just begun and the outcome was far distant. A preliminary swing to the right had taken place. Would the workers' parties learn from their experience ? There were no signs at the moment. The socialists rejoiced in their ' victory ', celebrated by the *Avanti* with huge headlines : *The Italian proletariat has buried the fascist reaction under an avalanche of red posters.* The communists, even more blind, directed their campaign against the socialists rather than the fascists, proclaiming as their slogan : *The May* 1921 *elections must pass the verdict on the Socialist Party.* Mussolini, overjoyed and arrogant in his own victory, felt that the hour he had awaited since 1914 was at hand : the hour of vengeance and power.

VIII

THE INTERNAL CRISIS OF FASCISM

IN the report which preceded the decree dissolving the Chamber, Giolitti wrote : ' We shall be nearer a real solution of the most serious social problems when the working classes get over this period of vague revolutionary hopes, which have been and still are a great hindrance to progress. It would be only logical for them to invite their representatives to take an active part in political life, instead of confining their activities to mere criticism.'

But the result of the elections, deliberately planned against the socialists and the *Popolari*, made it impossible for them to combine with Giolitti. The socialists blamed him, too, for his complicity with the fascists and for the blood which they had shed with impunity ; the *Popolari* bore him a grudge for not having included the representatives of the catholic syndicates in the commission of inquiry into industry, and for abandoning the scheme for a public examination which Benedetto Croce, his minister for education, had planned and which was much favoured by the party and by the Vatican. These fresh grievances, combined with the old ones, created such feeling against Giolitti that he had to abandon the manœuvre for which he had held the elections.

The fascists showed him no gratitude either, although they owed so much to him. On the eve of the elections Mussolini wrote in his paper that the electoral blocs ' are also a platform for the government of to-morrow ', and that men ' capable of standing at Italy's helm ' must be provided. He was presumably thinking of a coalition ministry in which he would take part. But coalition with whom ? In May 1920, at the national fascist conference in Milan, he had put out his first feelers in this direction. He rallied the ' economic assemblies ', by declaring against any experimental 'state socialism', proclaiming that 'the state must be deprived of all economic functions', and brought back into line with 'Manchester school economics'. He reassured the monarchy, the army and the conservatives by dismissing the 'previous question' of a republican regime : 'The republican problem is not an essential question ; to-day a democratic republic would not be enough ; once started the people would go much further.' He did not exclude the possibility of collaborating with the right-wing socialists, provided they 'straightened their aim', and he tried to win over the *Popolari* by passing, in spite of an anti-clerical speech by Marinetti, a motion in favour of free education, one of the Church's principal demands. In all these adjustments of programme the dominating note was an increasingly blatant nationalism. For the time being his sentiments were reminiscent of d'Annunzio's Naval Odes. 'The Italian people must be expansionist, and adopt a bold naval policy. Italy's future must be on the seas.'

A few weeks later, at the beginning of July, he outlined his programme of foreign policy. In this department the work of recasting the 'fascism of the first hour'[1] was complete. In March 1919 at the Piazza San Sepolcro meeting he had accepted the principles of the League of Nations, explaining them in such a way that nothing was left of them.[2] Now he declared that 'fascism believes in neither the vitality nor the principles of the so-called League of Nations'. He demanded the revision of the Treaty of Versailles, wanted Italy to 'withdraw gradually from the group of plutocratic western nations' and draw closer to the 'enemy nations', Austria, Germany, Bulgaria, and demand in the colonial sphere 'the nation's rights and needs'. In February 1921 at Trieste, the home of the powerful armament firms which had subsidized him heavily, after recalling the July 1920 programme, he finished with an impressive peroration : 'Fate demands that the Mediterranean should belong to us again. Fate demands that Rome should once more lead the civilization of Western Europe. Let us raise the flag of empire, of our imperialism.'

---

[1] *Fascismo della prima ora*, i.e. Fascism of 1919.
[2] Pp. 35–36.

Mussolini had many reasons for seeking power, but a mere desire for a portfolio was not one of them. If necessary he would get in by the back stairs, but foreign policy was his great passion and the only way of satisfying his will to power. His imperialism was his own policy, realizable by him alone. How could it be carried out with the Chamber resulting from the elections of May 15 ? The socialists and *Popolari*, who accounted for nearly half the seats, were hostile to Giolitti ; only by abandoning him was it possible to come to terms with them. And Mussolini had other reasons for such a course. In a coalition cabinet Giolitti would play the leading part and had sufficient strength and cunning to outwit Mussolini, who would be compromised in the eyes of his *squadristi* without having gained his object. Profitless betrayal was not his line. So during the electoral campaign he had taken the precaution of separating himself as far as possible from Giolitti, and once elected he came out openly against him.

For some time he considered whether he could down Giolitti and bring in his own coalition government. The manœuvre depended on the *Popolari*, who were still demo-crats after their own fashion and were calling for great social reforms. He prepared the way by separating himself ostentatiously from the right wing, and particularly from the nationalists. With this end in view he persuaded the Fascist National Council in Milan (June 2–3, 1921) to readopt the republican doctrines that he had previously dropped ;[1] on the same occasion he got a motion passed which declared the complete independence of the Fascist Party of the other groups, and in favour of the abstention of fascist deputies from the opening session when the king would be present and would read his usual speech. It was a first step towards the large scale manœuvre he was preparing when he made his first speech in the Chamber on June 21, 1921. The speech was fiercely nationalistic. He referred to the Ticino, Alto-Adige, Fiume and Monte-negro, and roundly abused the policy of Count Sforza, Giolitti's minister for foreign affairs. At the same time he flirted with the *Popolari :* fascism ' neither preaches nor

[1] P. 132.

practises anti-clericalism ', is not connected with freemasonry, accepts most of the *Popolari's* views on divorce, freedom of education, rural property, decentralization. He appealed to the Vatican over the heads of the *Popolari* : if the papacy would renounce its dreams of temporal power, the state would provide it with ' help and material facilities for schools, churches, hospitals, and everything that a lay power has at its disposal '. Besides the relations between the fascists and the *Popolari*, there must be considered the relations between Italy and the Vatican, whose reconciliation and collaboration were necessary, ' for Rome's Latin and Imperial tradition is represented by catholicism '.

Another part of Mussolini's speech dealt with relations between fascists and socialists. At the outset he declared that his speech would be ' completely anti-socialist and anti-democratic ', which made it easier to set out his offers and his threats. He made no concessions to the socialists, but even criticized them on doctrinal grounds. In an article on January 14 he had already stated that ' capitalism is scarcely at the beginning of its history ', and he repeated his articles of faith before the Chamber : ' The true history of capitalism is only just beginning '. Since capitalism is facing its highest tasks the state should renounce all its economic functions : ' We must abolish the collectivist state that the war forced on us, and return to the Manchesterian state '. He took care to point out his own personal success : ' The socialists, after seven troubled years, see before them in the proud attitude of a heretic the man they expelled from their orthodox church '. They will have to admit that they have taken a wrong turning, that they have been and always will be defeated on the ground of violence that they have chosen. It is inevitable, for the workers ' are by nature and I venture to say piously and fundamentally pacifistic, for they represent the standing reserve on which society draws, while risk, danger, and a taste for adventure have always been the business and privilege of aristocratic minorities '. Then there are the extremists of socialism, the communists. ' I know them very well, for some of them are of my making ; I admit with a sincerity that may appear cynical that I was the first to infect those people when I introduced into Italian socialism a little Bergson diluted with plenty of Blanqui.' But they have failed to digest the mixture properly, he added. The fascists make a distinction between the Socialist Party and the General Confederation of Labour : ' Our attitude to the latter, which has never been one of opposition, might be modified if the Confederation as a whole—its leaders have long since considered it—were to separate from the Socialist Party '. Under these conditions mutual disarmament was possible, and Mussolini declared that he desired it, for ' if things go on like this, the nation runs a real risk of plunging into an abyss '.

Was Mussolini sincere in making these very conditional and prudent advances ? If a definite answer were called for, we should say yes. Not because he had the slightest intention of going back to his old love, for Mussolini was convinced that the age of capitalism had only just begun and that, as he wrote a month after his speech, ' the new reality of to-morrow, for the n'th time, is capitalistic '. The news from Russia, where famine raged and the N.E.P. was taking the place of ' war communism ', convinced him that there was a universal Restoration. Since the future belonged to capitalism, socialism had no hope of making headway ; the choice lay between an almost dead past and the unlimited possibilities of the future, and his choice had been made in advance. Besides, he risked nothing by his overtures. If Giolitti brought off a coalition with the socialists, they would enter the cabinet in triumph, and on their own conditions. For this reason Mussolini declared in his speech that he was ' anti-Giolitti, since the flirtation between Giolitti and the socialist parliamentary group has never been so pronounced as now '. But if the wedding should take place on the initiative and under the guidance of Mussolini, the fascists would refuse to act as the poor relations of the new menage, and the socialists would find their demands curtailed.

The majority of the Socialist Party were against participation, fearing the attacks of the communists. If their right wing, the leaders of the General Confederation of Labour, joined the government, they would lose some of their influence with the masses, and in any case the party and the syndicates would be weakened by a violent internal struggle. Once they lost their hold on the people the socialist and reformist syndicalists would be weakened in parliament. Thus, whether the new government was formed without them or with only a part of them, the disintegration of the Socialist Party would be intensified. Mussolini felt finally that it was impossible for him to guide Italy's foreign policy in the way he wanted so long as the country was torn by civil strife. If it ceased, and the socialists, defeated and divided, could be pushed into the government, the fascist offensive would have achieved most of its aims after all. He could therefore calmly await the socialist metamorphosis and ' with all sincerity ' hope that it would take place in the way he had expected and worked for.

Giolitti, for his part, was preparing a similar solution. He had just quashed a strike of officials of the central administration of the Post Office and the Finance Ministry, who had failed completely and had been forced to go back to work unconditionally under a threat of severe reprisals. But at the same time he wooed the leaders of the General Confederation of Labour by yielding up to the ' Metallurgical Labour Consortium ', a producing co-operative society emanating from the F.I.O.M., five great state concerns, the arsenals at Naples and Venice, and the armament works at Terni, Genoa and Gardone, with the idea of running them more profitably and lightening the budget. Henceforward there could clearly be little danger in Italian ' bolshevism ' if it was possible at the end of May 1921 to trust arsenals and armament works to the same Metallurgical Federation which eight months ago had ordered the occupation of the factories.

But Giolitti's master stroke was to get new tariffs worked out and approved by parliamentary commissions (Alessio's bill). This was an important turning-point in Italian economics. Tariff walls were once more to defend national industry and agriculture. Confederation chiefs and leading industrialists were in accord over this, for this step would create employment, and once more provide excess profits to be shared in some measure between the capitalists and the syndical workers of the north.   Giolitti thus initiated the economic policy he had followed before the war, and he hoped that this economic collaboration would result in the socialist leaders, or at least the syndicalist leaders, joining the government.   But he never gathered the fruits he had planted. Five days after Mussolini's speech Giolitti's ministry was defeated over a motion presented by the socialists and backed by the fascists.   He was succeeded by Bonomi.

But even with Giolitti removed, Mussolini's way was far from clear.   Inside the fascist movement itself obstacles rose up and blocked his way to power.   There was discontent among his followers on account of his attitude towards the Treaty of Rapallo and d'Annunzio's Fiume adventure.[1] He was compelled to devote some of his speech at Trieste on February 6 to defending himself : ' In November 1920, the idea of a revolution to annul a peace treaty —that of Rapallo—which for better or worse was accepted by 99 per cent of the country, was out of the question . . . and equally so to become embroiled in armed opposition against the treaty conducted from an outpost of the nation, Fiume.'   And to those who reproached him for not having started a revolutionary movement to save Fiume, Mussolini replied with a summary of his views on tactics which showed his complete superiority in this respect over his followers and also over the so-called revolutionary socialists :

' The *fasci di combattimento*,' he said, ' never promised to start a revolution in Italy in the event of an attack on Fiume, especially after Millo's defection.   Personally I never wrote to or told d'Annunzio that revolution in Italy depended on my whim.   Revolutions are not jack-in-the-boxes, which can be jumped off at will. . . . History, a collection of dead facts, teaches people little, but daily events, which are history in the making, should be more profitable.   They show that revolutions are made with armies and not against them ; with arms, not without them ; with disciplined groups and not with shapeless masses assembled at meetings. . . . Revolutions succeed when the majority surround them with a halo

[1] P. 83–85.

of sympathy, otherwise they cool off and fail. In the Fiume tragedy the army and navy stood firm. There was a certain amount of revolutionary spirit in Fiume at the last moment, but it could find no means of expression ; it wavered between a handful of anarchists[1] and nationalists. According to certain " agents " the devil and holy water could be mixed, or the nation and anti-nation, Misiano and Delcroix. I reject all forms of bolshevism, but if I had to choose one it would be that of Moscow and Lenin, if only because its proportions are gigantic, barbaric, universal. . . . It was not possible, then, to liquidate a single episode of civil war—that of Fiume—by starting a much bigger war, at such a moment ; and no one can artificially create historic situations or prolong them when they are outdated.'

It will be seen that in spite of this defence the question of d'Annunzio and Fiume was to be one of the rallying points of the opposition to Mussolini now visible in the fascist ranks. But the chief difficulty lay in the state of the country. How could he attain power by legal means, which were the only ones possible at the moment, in the prevailing atmosphere of civil war, to which he himself had contributed more than anyone ? On January 28 he had written in his newspaper : ' It is obvious that the fascists must close their ranks, perfect their organization in every detail, and at the first opportunity hit out, without bothering about unnecessary distinctions ', and on February 5, after the debate in the Chamber on fascist acts of violence : ' There is only one remedy : hit hard ! and hope that little by little we shall knock some sense into their skulls.' On April 13, again addressing the socialists : ' We are determined to put you out of your misery with cold steel, or hot.'[2] Again, on May 4, in a speech at Milan, on the eve of the elections : ' We shall go on ramming the truth down our adversaries' throats until they swallow it.'
But by now this policy had already yielded its most important results ; working-class organization was visibly

---

[1] Pp. 49-50.
[2] ' Cold steel or hot,' d'Annunzio's description of the *arditi's* daggers.

damaged and the ' enemy ' driven into a corner or reduced to impotence. Continued fascist violence threatened to compromise Mussolini's plans and destroy any possibility of political manœuvring. On April 28 he had written an article recalling the fascists to a sense of proportion :

' The fascists must not in their turn lose their sense of proportion, or a great victory will be snatched from them. It is dangerous for those who have won to want too much. Fascism must not cause a revival of the P.U.S.[1] in the same way that the latter's countless stupid mistakes helped the development of fascism . . . since the P.U.S. is no longer harmful we must not disturb the country, but help it along its difficult way towards peace at home and abroad. Our present watchword must be : " If fascism loses its sense of proportion it will lose its victory." '

These preoccupations determined Mussolini's successive attitudes and explain why he supported the idea of a ' peace pact ', which was suggested in certain parliamentary and liberal circles. He hoped he would thus be able to kill two birds with one stone, join the government and reassert his influence over the Fascist Party, which was beginning to get out of hand. For him the struggle for the peace pact was a struggle for power both in the fascist movement and in the state.

It was not easy to manage the movement now that it had grown so tremendously, particularly since it owed its rapid growth to its having joined in the election with the frankly reactionary national bloc, and to the solid rising of the landowners in the Po valley and particularly in Tuscany. Mussolini first encountered resistance over the presence of the fascist deputies at the opening session of the new legislature.[2] The right wing and the nationalists wanted to go, to do honour to the king, but Mussolini wished the fascist group to bide their time and not to commit themselves. They were also opposed to any agreement with the socialists, and wanted to form a right coalition government.

[1] The official Socialist Party. A pun is intended here. The party's name was really Partito Socialista Ufficiale.
[2] P. 133.

Against them Mussolini tried to revive fascism ' of the first hour ' with its ' republican trend ', the ' old ' fascists against the new.

' We are faced with the trouble that destroyed the P.U.S. in November 1919,' he wrote on May 25. ' Under the surface of fascism lurks the " illustrious cowardice " of those who were afraid both of the others[1] and of ourselves ; fascism is being used as a mask for the selfishness and greed which rebel at the spirit of national conciliation, and there are many who have used fascist prestige and violence to further their own miserable ends, or who have employed violence for its own sake and not for the ends for which we planned it.'

He ended his article with an appeal : ' Fascists on the eve of power, fascists of action, defend fascism ! '

Two days later the *Popolo d'Italia* came out with the headline : ' Fascists throughout Italy, go forward along the old road, against all dissension.' On May 29 he threatened to put up a new target : ' Why should not fascism, having fired to the left, take a shot at its enemies on the right ? ' He insisted at the same time that the *fasci* should not disarm, but should perfect the organization of their action squads. When the socialist parliamentary group announced its intention of asking the new Chamber for an inquiry into fascist violence, Mussolini threatened a march on Rome to prevent it : ' From now on the *fasci* of Latium, Umbria, Abruzzi, Tuscany and Campagna are morally obliged to concentrate on Rome at the first call from the leaders of our movement.' An armed mobilization against a parliamentary inquiry—such was the situation in Italy in the middle of 1921.

To attain power, Mussolini wanted to be able to draw on both legal and illegal resources. On the one hand he had to keep in with the fascist masses, the *squadristi*. These must not suspect too soon that fascism was being ' parliamentarized '. For this reason fascist deputies drove the communist deputy Misiano out of the Chamber at the point of their revolvers, without, incidentally, provoking any retaliation. In June and July there was a fresh agitation

[1] i.e. the socialists.

throughout the country against the high cost of living, led this time by the fascists. In Trieste fascist squads boarded the boats from Istria with cargoes of vegetables and fruit and forced the peasants to sell at very low prices. In Naples they imposed a reduction of 50 per cent in the cafés and restaurants. In Florence the squads paraded the streets with banners, ' Producers and shopkeepers ! Prices must go down within two days ! ' Violence was on the increase, and the fascists often made something on their own account by exacting ransom from shopkeepers who wanted to be left in peace. Mussolini approved, though making certain reservations to prevent the application of fixed scales so as not to alarm his financial backers too much. ' We must not lose sight, at this stage, of one of the fundamentals of fascism, the abolition of all war economy, all state intervention in business, and the establishment of economic liberty, conditions necessary and adequate for a return to normal conditions.' This was the argument of big business.

But since a new ministry was being formed, Mussolini tried to prepare opinion for a fascist participation in the government, with Salandra, Meda, and even, if necessary, with Giolitti. ' The attitude of the fascist parliamentary group towards the Giolitti ministry,' he declared on June 8, ' might in certain circumstances be modified.' And up till June 27, the day Giolitti was defeated in the Chamber, he left his way in this direction open. He felt he was near his goal, and did not want the newly elected fascists and the old reactionaries to spoil his success. ' I am always on the watch,' he declared for the benefit of friends and enemies, ' particularly when a changing wind fills the sails of my ship of fortune.' At the meeting of the parliamentary fascist group on June 3, however, although he got his own way in the matter of the ' republican trend ', he failed to impose abstention from the ' royal ' session. By 18 votes to 15 the group decided that deputies should have a free hand.[1]

At the beginning of July the peace pact negotiations were started,[2] and on this point Mussolini joined issue with the

[1] The National Council, which was held at the same time, approved Mussolini's wishes on the other hand.
[2] P. 139.

National Council of *Fasci* (July 12–13). With great difficulty he succeeded in getting through a resolution which made a distinction in the exercise of fascist violence between the political organizations and the syndicates, and which authorised the *fasci* to make local agreements ' wherever circumstances allowed, with representatives of working-class organizations '. Opposition to the peace pact came chiefly from the *Fasci di Combattimento* in ' occupied ' territory, who were afraid of losing the advantage gained by the terrorist tactics they had ' invented '. Their doubts were expressed by Farinacci of Cremona : ' If we allow the reds to go on with their propaganda,' he said, at the meeting of the National Council, ' all our work may be undone.' The representatives of Julian Venetia, Emilia, Tuscany, where *squadrismo* flourished, repeated the argument : ' If necessary, blows can be dealt out more judiciously ; but we must not weaken.' Mussolini only just got the resolution through. He emphasized that circumstances had changed and the pact would help to divide the enemy.

> ' It is ridiculous at the present time to talk as if the Italian working class were heading for bolshevism. You all know that the state of mind of the working classes is fundamentally different from what it was two years ago. By making peace with us the socialists will cut themselves off from the communists and anarchists. Our aim must be to divide the enemy and so defeat them. . . . This resolution leaves us prepared for any possibility. . . . We must try to separate the General Confederation of Labour from the subversive parties. Soon, when the syndicates, co-operatives and federations are on their way to independence, we shall hold a strong position in national life.'

Mussolini used every possible argument to win over the opposition ; he believed what he said, but he did not say all that he thought. For he wanted the pact signed as soon as possible, no matter how, so as to get going with his preparations for the political issue that he foresaw and on which he had been banking for several weeks. He had a detailed plan : to separate the General Confederation of

Labour from the Socialist Party, and then form a sort of 'Labour' party by uniting the Confederation with the 'national' syndicates which were springing up everywhere. Independence, which, as he wrote on July 2, would separate the Confederation 'from all socialist and non-socialist parties' and would mean 'a step forward towards the realization of a united proletariat and the creation of a Labour Party which would minimize the importance of the socialist political parties'. Mussolini was resuscitating in the new conditions created by the initial success of fascism the plan he had had in mind during the early months of 1919.[1] For the success of this manœuvre the fascist movement must not be transformed into a political party, or there would be no room for the 'Labour Party' and Mussolini's aims would be endangered. For it would be far easier to form a coalition government with the Confederation chiefs and some of the fascist leaders on the common platform of a Labour Party, than with a Fascist Party, aiming at the creation of a new syndical organization to do away with and replace the General Confederation of Labour. Hence, Mussolini declared that he was absolutely opposed to the transformation of the fascist movement into a political party.

Once started in this direction Mussolini could not turn back, for he was eager for power. On July 19 the parliamentary fascist group, which was, as was to be expected, the right wing of the movement, voted for a resolution in favour of conciliation. After this vote, which he had himself brought about, Mussolini declared that he considered himself personally pledged and that his 'line of conduct as far as fascism was concerned' depended on future events. The fascists were not to be afraid of forced inactivity after the end of the civil war, for fascism 'must agitate for the settlement of the formidable problems of Italy's expansion in the world'.

Various signs warned Mussolini, always on the alert, that he must hurry. Amongst the workers a move towards a united front had begun, and red fighting groups, the *arditi del popolo*, paraded the streets of Rome for the first time at

[1] P. 25.

the beginning of July, while d'Annunzio's legionaries and some of the ex-servicemen *Arditi* had broken away from the *fasci*. Worse still, the Bonomi government, which had succeeded that of Giolitti, seemed determined to limit the exploits of the fascists and the help they had been getting from local authorities. The Sarzana affair made the fascist leaders reflect—such of them as were capable of reflexion—on the real strength of the *squadre di combattimento* when they came up against state forces.

This happened for the first time at Sarzana on July 21 after seven months of violence, tolerated and even approved of, when a fascist ' expedition ' found itself faced by representatives of the state, determined not to let it pass. Five hundred fascists from Florence, Pisa, Lucca and Viareggio had concentrated at Sarzana and occupied the station. Police captain Jurgens was there with eight militiamen and three soldiers. The leader of the little fascist army, Amerigo Dumini, explained to the captain the object of the expedition. The fascists were proposing to surround the town in order to set free ' peacefully or by force ' ten fascists from Carrara who had been arrested as a result of various outrages committed in Lunigiana. At the same time they demanded the person of Captain Niccodemi whom they accused of striking the leader of the arrested fascists, Renato Ricci, to whom Mussolini later entrusted the task of recruiting and organizing the *Balilla*. This accusation was quite false, as Ricci himself admitted later, but the fascist ultimatum was none the less peremptory. While Dumini was arguing with the captain of police the fascists grew impatient and crowded round. ' Enough of this chatter ', they shouted. The militiamen came to the ready, and when a revolver shot was fired on them from the fascist ranks, fired point blank into this menacing and aggressive crowd, killing and wounding a few of their number. The *squadristi*, accustomed as they were to fighting unarmed enemies and relying on the help of the state forces, lost their heads when confronted with a dozen rifles actually pointed at them, and ran away in all directions.

In the subsequent report, the *squadrista* Umberto Banchelli, who signed it in his capacity of the expedition's ' chief of staff', explained the reasons for the adventure. 'The Sarzana expedition is only a normal episode, which was bound to happen once fascism was met by opponents who stood firm. . . . These squads, too often accustomed to conquering enemies who nearly always ran away or offered feeble resistance, did not know how to defend themselves.' Banchelli also explains in his *Memoirs*, already quoted,[1] that fascism only managed to develop because it was helped by police and army officers. The ten rifles put five hundred fascists to flight, not only because they went off, but because by going off they had for once put the *squadristi*, bewildered at suddenly finding themselves on the wrong side of the barricades, outside the law. Further, the presence and action of the representatives of the state dispelled as if by magic the terror which preceded and accompanied the punitive expedition. The inhabitants, who had been warned by railwaymen of a train fired on by fascists, were on the defensive. When they heard what had happened in the station square armed groups marched out into the surrounding country and, aided by angry peasants, gave chase to the fascists, who left a dozen dead behind, strung up on trees or drowned in the marshes, and several dozen wounded. The police interfered again, this time to rescue the retreating fascists from the angry mob.

After this the fascists mobilized and demonstrated in several districts. In the town and province of Bologna, the *fasci*, by agreement with the industrialists, proclaimed a factory lock-out and ordered the shops to close as a protest. In Padua they occupied the tower of the university, sounded the tocsin, and ordered all cafés and shops to shut and display notices announcing 'National mourning', while in the neighbourhood of Carrara, as Chiurco records : 'The fascists, infuriated by the Sarzana massacre, killed two communists.' The fascist leaders, however, issued a manifesto to the nation framed in reasonably cautious language and calling for a truce.

For Mussolini realized that if the dangerous situation caused by fascist terrorism continued there was bound to be a reaction and state intervention, and everything might be

[1] P. 121.

lost. In his speech in the Chamber on the day following the Sarzana affair, therefore, he held out the olive branch, and on July 23 he expounded his future policy to the disconcerted socialists :

> ' Sooner or later I believe it will be necessary to form a grand new coalition of the three really " efficient " forces in the life of the nation. First socialism, which is already beginning to change its form, as is shown by the vote of the General Confederation of Labour against the communists and by its new attitude to strikes in the public services ; then the *Popolari*, whose strength is great, and is derived—with what advantage to religion I do not know—from the immense force of catholicism ; finally it is impossible to deny the existence of a complex, formidable and essentially idealistic movement, which includes the best part of the youth of Italy. To these three forces, united round a programme which will be their common denominator, will be entrusted to-morrow the task of leading the country to a higher destiny.'

This speech was no empty gesture on Mussolini's part. For several weeks his actions had been ruled by a feeling that fascism was losing its grip on the country, and that he personally was losing his grip on fascism. There was a risk of his perishing with it, and he wanted to escape, if necessary even at the expense of the movement. ' If I achieve power,' he confided to the liberal leaders,[1] whose support he wished to gain, ' I shall turn the machine-guns on the fascists, if they do not learn wisdom.' In any case he wanted to prevent the formation of an anti-fascist government supported or shared in by the socialists. He had everything to gain by a truce, both for what it made possible and for what it could prevent. Hence his willingness to treat.

After his July 23 speech he intensified the campaign in his newspaper in favour of his plans. His chief aim was to reassure that section of the *bourgeoisie* who were alarmed at the prospect of socialists sharing in the government. There

---

[1] Including Nitti, with whom he was negotiating over the formation of a coalition government.

was nothing to be alarmed about, he said. If some of the leaders of the General Confederation of Labour were to become ministers to-morrow, ' they will have formidable enemies on their left, the uncompromising portion of the Socialist Party, communist, syndicalist and anarchist ', and would be ' intelligent enough to take into due account the free and undogmatic force of fascism '. Under fire from the left, they would have to come to terms with the fascists, and would fall into their power. Further, ' people like Baldini, Turati, and Baldesi, will not be any more capable of concrete achievements than the others. Being new they will merely make a greater show of goodwill, and will end up by resuscitating the now feeble and decadent governing class. Once socialist unity is impaired the possibilities of the government are likely to be very greatly increased.' On July 27 he took the fascist bull by the horns in an editorial headed ' A Return to First Principles ', the document which illustrates most strikingly the position he had taken up and which he wanted the fascist movement to support.

> ' The question for fascism is one of discipline. The National Council has fixed the limits (in the matter of violence) and we must keep to them or get out. They must be kept to if the nation and fascism are to be saved. The nation welcomed us when our movement meant the end of a tyranny, but they would repudiate us if it were to become a new tyranny. In certain districts fascism to-day is not what it was yesterday. It is no longer inspired by its old ideals as a movement for defending the nation, but is a purely repressive organization working to protect the interests of certain individuals. Fascism in 1919 and 1920 was an almost negligible minority as regards numbers, but it was full of strength and wisdom.'

After quoting the fascism of Milan as an example and recalling a well-known passage of Machiavelli, Mussolini concluded : ' It is urgently necessary for fascism to return to its principles now. To-morrow may be too late.'

The peace pact was signed in Rome on August 2 by the representatives of the National Council of Fascism, the Socialist Party, the fascist and socialist parliamentary groups, the General Confederation of Labour, and by Signor De Nicola, President of the Chamber, who had lent very active assistance in the negotiations. The five delegations agreed, according to article 2 of the pact, ' to take immediate action to put an end to threats, assaults, reprisals, punishments, acts of vengeance, pressure, and personal violence of any description '. The two parties ' agreed reciprocally to respect all economic organizations ' (Article 4). Infringements of the conditions of the pact would be submitted to arbitration, and to this purpose tribunals were to be set up in each province. The first signature at the foot of this document was that of Benito Mussolini.

Mussolini now proceeded to deal with the resistance in the fascist camp. The pact, he proclaimed, was a *fait accompli*.

> ' I hereby declare, assuming all moral and material responsibility for my action, that I have put my heart into it, and that once the essential part was accepted I threw various minor details overboard. Let me add that with all my strength I will defend this Peace Treaty, which in my opinion is an event of historic importance, and that I shall put into practice the old proverb—" Spare the rod and spoil the child ". If fascism is my child, as has hitherto been recognized, I shall correct it or make life impossible for it. We may celebrate a victory. But I am always thinking of the future. I know not where to stop. A victory has been won, and I am now considering what use we can make of it. . . . For me personally the situation is simple : if fascism does not follow me, no one can force me to follow fascism.'

On the same day in an interview with the *Resto del Carlino* he explained :

> ' Peace could certainly have been dictated on more severe terms a month ago, before the star of fascism, which had long been shining on the horizon, had paled a little after the events at Viterbo, Treviso, and Roccastrada. . . . The treaty also settles the internal fascist crisis, in the sense

that henceforward the political element will have a clearly marked supremacy over the military.'

What were the events which in Mussolini's opinion had revolted public opinion? Viterbo had been occupied on July 9 by a squad from Rome commanded by Bottai, future Minister of Corporations and future Governor of Rome ; at Treviso on July 13 columns of fascists from Padua and Bologna had destroyed the offices of a republican and a popular newspaper and committed every sort of violence ; at Roccastrada in Tuscan Maremma, on July 25, a punitive expedition had killed thirteen and wounded some twenty of the population ; the houses of the mayor and councillors, who refused to resign, being set on fire.[1] These outrages were not very different from the hundreds and thousands of others which had been going on for six months in several districts in Italy and which enabled the fascist dictatorship to be established. The *Popolo d'Italia* of the time contained no word of regret, only justification and encouragement to continue. A few days afterwards, Mussolini referred to them in order to explain the necessity for imposing a reversal of policy on the fascists. Actually, to attain his own ends, he judged it indispensable to dissociate himself from such acts. The ' return to normality ' coincided with his own interests and ambitions.

The rank and file of the fascists resisted the pact. The centre of dissent was Bologna. Dino Grandi, now Italian ambassador in London, was the newest and youngest star in the fascist firmament. Barrister, ex-soldier, editor of the fascist paper, *l'Assalto*, he was the theorist of the opposition, the anti-Mussolini. Mussolini came to grips with him at once, and the struggle between the ' old ' Milanese fascism and the neo-fascism of Bologna began. Mussolini charged Grandi with being only a recently joined member of the party, and yet calling Bologna ' the cradle of fascism '. He went on :

' Do the fascists of Emilia want to desert Italian fascism ? Personally I am indifferent, or nearly so. For

---

[1] It was the mayor of Roccastrada to whom the Marquis Perrone Compagni had sent, in April, the threatening letter quoted on pp. 104, 105.

me fascism is not an end in itself, it was a means of restoring national equilibrium and reviving various neglected values. . . . These ends have largely been attained. Fascism may now split up, evaporate, crumble, decline, disappear. If a few hard knocks are wanted to hasten its ruin I will lend myself to the ungrateful task. Fascism which is no longer liberation but tyranny, no longer the nation's safeguard, but the defence of private interests and of the most exclusive, sordid, and despicable classes which exist in Italy ; fascism which takes this form may still be fascism, but not fascism as I conceived it at one of the saddest periods of our country's history. We are becoming too numerous, and when the family increases some are bound to break away. Let it happen if it must, and may the socialists be glad of it. It is not the peace pact which spells victory for them, but this crisis of insubordination and the deplorable blindness which is causing the loss of a section of Italian fascism.

' Did no one notice, then, the circle of hatred which threatened to suffocate fascism both good and bad ? Did no one notice that fascism had become synonymous with terror even to people who were not socialists ? I have broken through this circle, and made a breach in the barbed wire of the thenceforward unbridled hatred and exasperation of the vast mass of the people, who would have defeated us. I have given fascism a future again, and shown it the way to all its greatness, at the cost of a civil truce exacted by the superior strength both of the nation and of humanity. As a result—as in the quarrels of the old parties—the heavy artillery of strife and slander is turned on me ; there is talk of renunciation, surrender, treason, and other pitiful idiocies. It is time for Italian fascism to be frank about its thoughts and desires. The peace pact is the agent which must precipitate a result. . . . Fascism can do without me ? Doubtless ; but I, too, can do very well without fascism. I can allow myself to speak openly, for, having given much I ask absolutely nothing and am ready to start all over again.'

This kind of talk failed to persuade or intimidate his opponents. On the contrary Grandi and his friends organized a meeting of the *fasci* of Emilia and Romagna, which took place in Bologna on August 17. The town was plastered with posters insulting the Duce: 'Once a traitor always a traitor', and anti-Mussolini rhymes were sung. This local *adunata* turned into an opposition conference, many representatives of other provinces being present also. The *fasci* of Bologna, Ferrara, Cremona, Modena, Piacenza, Rovigo, Forli, Venice, declared themselves 'completely opposed to the peace treaty'. The fascism of the Po Valley and of the landowners was proclaiming its dissent. To the latter Mussolini was a coward; he was unsparingly denounced for being on the point of sacrificing fascism and treating with the 'marxists' to satisfy his own ambition. Amongst those who took part in the discussion were Italo Balbo, of Ferrara, the deputies, Oviglio, Farinacci, Vicini, Piccinato, and Marsich. The last announced: 'We have come to the turning point of fascism. Mussolini realizes it, but he appears to me to have lost his way. In effect there are two solutions, one national, the other parliamentary. We are for the national one, he for the parliamentary.' Dino Grandi announced himself in favour of the completion of the fascist revolution and opposed to the parliamentary compromise, in favour of abandoning the outworn principles of 1919 fascism for a fascism 'of the new generation'. The starting-point of this fascism was Fiume. 'I was not a legionary', he said, 'but on the night of Ronchi[1] I saw the first baptism of Italian fascism. It is there, in the constitution of the Quarnero and its national syndicalism that we must seek the foundation plans of the state we have to build.'

Immediately after the Bologna meeting, Mussolini handed in his resignation from the Executive Committee of the *fasci*. He was furious and depressed: 'The die is cast. The loser must go. And I am going, leaving the front ranks. I remain and hope to remain a private soldier in the Milan *fascio*.' A few days later Cesare Rossi, under-secretary-general of the *fasci*, followed his example. In his letter of resignation he declared that the majority of the fascist organizations 'have displayed in their regional conferences, and, what is worse, in their daily actions, a firm and

[1] P. 44.

implacable hostility to the implementing of the peace pact '. No great skill was needed to see that the invasion of late-comers, ' who had joined up for the most part when the enemy was in retreat ', and the suspect enthusiasm of the old ' clerical and agrarian cliques ' would wipe out the original characteristics of fascism. In fact fascism, ' through the action of its local masses, through an infinity of episodes, which make up the whole history of the fascist movement in recent times, dominates the scene only in appearance, for it has become the authentic and exclusive instrument of conservatism and reaction '.

Mussolini was beaten, and the opposition did not stop at its first success. In September it organized two new conferences, one at Ferrara, the other at Todi (Umbria). This was the signal for several provincial federations to denounce the pact, which they had never accepted. The dissentients even organized a ' fascist march ' on Ravenna, for the celebration of the 600th anniversary of Dante's death. Columns arrived from Ferrara, Bologna, and Modena ; setting out on September 10, numbering at least 3000, staffed and organized like an army, after a three-day tour of the roads of Emilia the fascists marched into the ' town of silence ' singing their battle hymns. On the way, to keep their hand in, they wrecked several socialist clubs. In Ravenna they attacked all who failed to salute the fascist banners. Workers and priests were severely beaten up, and with them foreigners who had come for the celebrations, including Johann Joergensen, the historian of St. Francis. There were protests and incidents. On the very morning of the 12th the fascists broke up and sacked five socialist clubs in the town and the neighbourhood, the Chamber of Labour, and the Federation of the Co-operatives. On their return journey the columns destroyed everything they had not had time to destroy on the way. Had Dante been able to rise from his tomb he would have recognized Sordello's apostrophe :

> Ahi serva Italia, di dolore ostello
> nave, sanza nocchiero in gran tempesta.
>
> .   .   .
>
> e ora in te non stanno sanza guerra
> li vivi tuoi, e l'un l'altro si rode
> di quei ch'un muro ed una fossa serra.

The same habits, but without the fierce courage and greatness. The aim of this expedition was to demonstrate the strength of the opposition. All its chiefs were there, Grandi from Bologna, Balbo from Ferrara, Misuri from Perugia, Caradonna from Apulia. They meant to prove their determination to go on with their present methods and adventures. Mussolini felt himself more and more isolated, and though he hid his bitterness, giving vent to it nevertheless on occasions, he began to wonder if he was not making a useless sacrifice of his prestige, and if, after losing his first battle, he was not in a fair way to lose the other, the govermental battle. The meaning of the Ravenna episode was quite clear to him and he made no protest about it. On the contrary, in the *Popolo d'Italia* he abused Nullo Baldini, who had resorted to the feeble expedient of an interpellation in the Chamber. This was the first move in Mussolini's new manœuvre to regain without loss of face the main body of the fascist army, now in mutiny against him. He now realized that the policy he had conceived and which he had inaugurated with his speech of July 23 was unworkable. This policy had antagonized the majority of the fascists without winning him support from any other quarter.

The conservatives were furious, because Mussolini's new attitude gambled on socialist participation in government, and this meant that the state would defend working-class and socialist organizations from the fascist gangs. Those whom Mussolini described as ' until recently imploring the degrading charity of a little socialist collaboration ', now that the danger was past found that Mussolini ' lacked style '. In the *Giornale d'Italia* of August 18—the day after the Bologna conference and Mussolini's resignation—Senator Bergamini[1] wrote :

' Behind Mussolini's fickleness there is perhaps a lack of firm convictions. . . . At any rate this hasty liquidation of fascism shows lack of style . . . the Duce throws in his hand prematurely, with noisy ostentation, while his victorious troops continue here and there their

[1] After the march on Rome Bergamini made the acquaintance of fascist ' style '. He got no mercy from the blackshirt thugs and was forced to resign from his paper.

implacable warfare against the remains of their routed adversaries.'

Mussolini, stung by the cheap gibes of those who had profited by fascism, retorted that he had nothing to learn from any of them, and as to his style ' he did not pretend to act the general, since his army refused obedience or discipline. . . . It was my intention,' he specified, ' my definite intention, to have a peace pact ; hundreds of *fasci* would have nothing to do with it and said so clearly. It is not I who am leaving ; it is these others who force me to leave, because it is I personally who am disqualified by their vote '.

The *Giornale d'Italia* answered by setting out its pre-occupations, or rather those of the landowners who controlled it :

' We are not impatient for the development of the crisis in fascism, on the contrary we have criticized Mussolini for wanting to bring it on. In our view, as we have often said, fascism has only a temporary function, but for precisely this reason it must only be liquidated gradually, when it becomes superfluous. We have spoken of lack of style in connection both with Mussolini's resignation and with the excessive haste he has shown lately, since the beginning of the negotiations for peace. We, who are to-day engaged in a controversy with Mussolini, agree that he is right when he says that the anti-fascist front must be broken, that fascism must not come into conflict with the forces of the state, and that it is important to reconcile public opinion to fascism. But this cleavage of ideas must not lead to the liquidation of fascism at the very moment that *arditi del popolo* are starting up in various districts, and when the Turati socialists are making unprecedented efforts to get their party into the government, or anyhow to capture the government. It is probable that at the approaching socialist congress the collaborationist tendency will be defeated, and this will be a good thing for Italy, for even a socialist *puntarella* in the government would waken the state at this juncture. There is also danger of a coalition of socialists with the reformists, the social democrats, and perhaps the liberal democrats, making possible a liberal-radical-socialist ministry. Efforts towards this end will probably be crushed by the socialist congress, which will confirm its refusal to compromise. But we must not ignore signs of activity on the part of certain left-wing elements who aim at an alliance between democracy and socialism, which would mean a governmental swing towards the extreme left. The premature crisis of fascism is very harmful, and its immediate disintegration would be even more so, since it would weaken national and conservative political forces and leave the ultra-democratic forces in control of the country's destiny. Hence it would be a mistake for the fascists to break up their forces now and leave the ground open for unfettered democracy in which the socialists would be the real masters.'

On their side the nationalists, noted the *Popolo d'Italia*, ' have laid a political ambush ', and their paper, the *Idea Nazionale*, which was also the mouthpiece of heavy industry and the armament manufacturers, discovered that fascism was born, not at Milan in March, 1919, but ' in Bologna in December 1920 '. Mussolini had against him, therefore, his own movement, the big industrial and landowning class and the nationalists ; and he realized that he would never get the socialists to disarm, not even those of the right wing. He was certainly not going to back a policy which he could not himself direct and gain profit from.

The socialists saw nothing in the fascist crisis but the embarrassing position in which Mussolini found himself, and instead of making political capital out of it they looked on, blinded by their grievances, and enjoyed the unhoped-for revenge which they regarded as final. In his speech in the Chamber about the Sarzana episode (July 22), Mussolini had already complained that the only reply the socialists had made to his overtures was to call him a repentant Magdalene. When he resigned the *Avanti* came out with a complacent sneer which was not quickly forgotten.

The Socialist Party was in a worse fix than ever, for the pact had only increased its impotence. On August 10 the party executive approved the pact and on the 12th it passed a resolution against any form of participation in the government. Thus within two days the party made two decisions which cancelled each other out, and, which was more serious, without noticing the contradiction. Now that the pact was signed, what did it mean ? Was it a provisional truce between two armies in the field ? But from the military viewpoint there was only one army in the field, that of the fascist squads. The *arditi del popolo* movement had scarcely begun, and anyway by Article 5 of the pact the Socialist Party had expressly disavowed this organization. It was obvious that the agreement could only work on a basis which went beyond the ordinary doctrines of the two adversaries, namely, a certain consciousness of the country's interests endangered by the civil war, the recognition of a certain positive and intrinsic value in democratic liberty, which the working class had every inducement to protect.

The fascist rank and file protested everywhere, complaining in company with their backers, the big landowners and industrialists, ' legality is killing us '. In the actual conditions then prevailing the liberties won by the working classes could only be protected if the state remained neutral, interfering in certain districts to restore the essential components of the life of the community where fascism had destroyed them. The state was powerless without the country behind it ; it could only bring the fascists to reason if the workers themselves submitted to the general interest whose rule the unruly swarms of *squadristi* had to be compelled to obey.

But the Socialist Party was carrying on discussions with Moscow and with the Third International, to which, as decided in its last congress, it still belonged. In Moscow people only had a vague idea of what was going on in Italy, and anyway, after the failure of the Warsaw campaign and the removal of any immediate prospect of world revolution, Italy was no longer in Russian eyes anything but a rather unimportant pawn. The socialists made a point of keeping up the official connection with Moscow, which gave them some defence against the desperate rivalry of the communists. But this delivered the party into the hands of the communists. They bandied formulæ with each other, which, though much used for internal party controversy, merely confused the general political issue, where the fate of the working class and the Italian people was at stake. From time to time their eyes were opened by the fascist *manganello*, only to become blind again when it became necessary to proceed beyond the mere statement of facts to draw political and tactical conclusions. They wavered between boastfulness and slackness, between 'symbolical' firmness and resignation to the 'inevitable'. Occasionally there were signs that a new spirit would emerge from the blood spilled and the burnings, but each time their assurance and resolution failed them. They were much more afraid of appearing not to be revolutionaries than of allowing fascism to spread little by little all over Italy.

The communists had not signed the pact and their watchword was : 'Conciliation is not possible ; it is a fight to the death between us and fascism : fascism or communism.' In practice they fought the fascists neither more nor less than the rest, but their attitude was of the utmost help to fascism. To them everything was fascism : the state, the *bourgeoisie*, democracy, socialism. All these had to be fought, and it 'simplified' the struggle to lump them all together, and made it unnecessary to aim or control the blows struck. Actually the communists only fought seriously against the socialists and won their victories in attempts to outbid them. The Communist Party even opposed its members joining the *arditi del popolo*, which they denounced as a 'bourgeois manœuvre'. In a statement on August 7 the party executive declared :

> 'The *arditi del popolo* apparently propose to represent the proletarian reaction against the excesses of fascism, to restore "the law and order of social life". The aim of the communists is quite different : they are resolved to pursue the proletarian struggle to a revolutionary victory, and they believe in the unalterable antithesis between the dictatorship of *bourgeois* reaction and that of proletarian revolution.'

The armed bodies which were to fight everybody and carry out the revolution into the bargain must be organized by the Communist Party alone, without the socialists, in fact against them. This was simply a piece of narrow-minded and empty demagogy. Here and there a few shots were fired by communists, and a few, despite the party ban, joined the *arditi del popolo*, but the party as such practically kept out of the fight, and by its tactics did much to help on the victory of fascism.

There remained one course : to call in the state and employ its vast resources against fascism ; but this was barred by the Socialist Party's refusal to allow the parliamentary group either to support or to join the government. This party, which had rejected the constituent assembly, because it wanted ' soviets everywhere ', could make no political demands of the state which it proposed quite simply to destroy. They could not ask this state to rid them of their most dangerous enemies in order that they might carry out their own march on Rome. The pact was thus endangered by hundreds of incidents between workers and fascists who were determined not to yield the positions they had won, nor abandon the methods by which they had won them. There was no ' secular arm ' to enforce respect for the principles laid down by the pact. Nor did anything occur which might widen the breach in fascism, to make the difference between the two tendencies an irreconcilable one, or to compromise Mussolini and his friends and make it impossible for them to relinquish their new policy. Left to itself the fascist crisis could settle itself without much difficulty.

Mussolini's problem was how to regain control of the movement and make it a more manageable instrument to serve his own personal policy and ambition. In February, at the time of this Trieste speech, he had spoken against turning fascism into a political party, and at the end of May he had still been of this opinion.[1] The revolt of the squads and the important part they had played in opposing his orders convinced him, however, that the movement must be turned into a party so that it could be effectively disciplined. Although he abhorred programmes as ' dogmas and prejudices already out of date or easily left behind by

[1] P. 143.

the ceaseless stream of events ', he now rallied to the idea
of a programme, since a party implied one. On August 23,
six days after the Bologna declaration, a colleague on the
Popolo d'Italia published an article affirming that ' fascism
must make up its mind to become a party or perish '.
Mussolini took the opportunity of announcing his conversion :

> ' In another part of the paper a fascist writer raises a
> fundamental problem which may be summed up in the
> question, should fascism become a party ? After long
> reflexion and a careful study of the political situation I
> have come to the conclusion that it should. The causes
> and development of the fascist crisis force this choice on
> us : either a party or an army has got to be formed. In
> my opinion the solution lies in the formation of a party,
> so well organized and disciplined that it can be turned,
> if necessary, into an army capable of violent offensive or
> defensive action. The party must be given a mind, that
> is a programme. Theoretical and practical principles
> must be revised and extended, some of them abolished.
> The weeks which remain before the national gathering
> at Rome must be devoted to the elaboration of the
> platform of the Italian Fascist Party.'

This was very prudent talk. He was not suggesting the
abolition of the squads ; he only wanted to make sure that
squadrismo was not going to spoil the political role of the
party. The ministerial crisis of June and the peace pact
had shown him that fascism was in danger of forfeiting its
legal and political resources and having recourse to mere
civil war, a policy which would end by antagonizing the
greater part of the country and inviting suppression by the
state. Mussolini wanted to play a double game ; preventing
the intolerance and impatience of the *squadristi* from
forfeiting him the legal weapons that he thought fascism
still needed. At the beginning of September he was considering a Fascist Labour Party. This was the transition
from the abortive proposal of a ' Labour Party ' and the
new theory. ' The word " labour " is essential,' he insisted,
in the name of the new party. Two weeks later he proposed

quite simply ' Fascist Party '. The new party was not to be based on a coalition of syndicates, as he had contemplated in the beginning of July, but on an association of the *fasci* and their storm squads, by then amenable to party discipline. Instead of bringing about ' a united proletariat ', he would form his own syndicates. Mussolini was tacitly adopting the proposals of the Bologna heretics.

Although he had resigned in his letter of August 17 he had not given up the struggle, and although he was forced to give up his July 23 policy, there remained the struggle for leadership inside the fascist movement itself. Having now thrown his labour sympathies overboard he could act more freely in view of the approaching National Congress. He began by demanding, unsuccessfully, that it should be held in Milan, which was favourable ground, and not in Rome. At the same time he was perturbed by the attitude of Bonomi, who seemed determined to oppose fascist illegality. At Modena the Royal Guard had fired on fascist demonstrators, who had left several dead behind them. This caused a tremendous furore. Restrictions were set on the bearing of arms and the movements of lorries, which hampered blackshirt excursions. For the most part local authorities ignored the ministerial orders, or used them for hunting down the meagre beginnings of the *arditi del popolo*. Here and there, however, the fascist squads encountered difficulties. The *fasci* demanded that the parliamentary group should openly oppose Bonomi, but Mussolini was against violent anti-ministerial action, and insisted, on September 7, that they must first of all settle the fascist crisis and form the party. An attack at this stage would involve the risk of creating an anti-fascist coalition and government, and might even bring Nitti back into power. Bonomi was the lesser evil.

The *fasci*, whose growth had been due to every sort of help from public authorities, could not brook this new atmosphere of restriction. The heads of the Florence *fascio* published the following notice on September 30 :

' Very few citizens felt impelled to mourn for the tragic events at Modena, and no shops were shut, even for half an hour. In view of the open or secret hostility of the population, and particularly of the rich and pleasure-loving *bourgeoisie*, which applauded fascist action so long as it coincided with its own material interests, the fascists declare formally that from to-day they retire from the struggle. . . . We stand back, our weapons sheathed.'

Directly the people realized that the fascists no longer had the support of the state they gave them a wide berth and ignored their orders. The Venice *fascio* also ' withdrew from the struggle ' and left the *bourgeoisie* henceforward ' to provide its own defence '. Mussolini stood out against this wave of panic.

> ' This curious, paradoxical epidemic,' he wrote on October 8, ' affects the *fasci* who in August were agitating against the Rome pact. After the Florence *fascio* come those of Ferrara, Padua, Venice ; all of them " exterminating " *fasci*, which are now retiring " into private life." . . . The extreme seriousness of such a decision lies in the fact that they appear up to now to have protected the *bourgeoisie* which least deserved it.'

And since the motion passed proclaimed ' unswerving opposition ' to Bonomi, Mussolini retorted : ' What is the point ? And if to-morrow the choice lay between Bonomi and Nitti, can one tell which way the obstinacy of the fascist executive of Venice would tip the scale ? '

The party congress was approaching, and Mussolini outlined the new programme in the *Popolo d'Italia*. The liquidation of the 1919 programme was complete, and tentative socialism had given way to ' integral ' nationalism. The basis for everything was the ' national society ', for ' the law of life in the world is not the unification of different societies, but their fruitful, and if possible peaceful, rivalry '. The state must give up all its monopolies in the sphere of economics ; its specific task was to ' devote all its energies to the reinforcement, development and expansion of the Italian nation, which will thus be able to attain its great historical and social goals '. Appeal was made to individual energy and initiative, which constitute ' the most potent

factor in production ', and all ' state intervention, nationalization, municipalization ' was renounced. All ' demagogic '
fiscal measures must be abolished and freedom from taxation
granted to ' that part of revenue which is turned into technical or instrumental capital '. At home, ' restoration of the
authority of the national state ' ; an agnostic view of the
monarchy ; the creation, alongside parliament, of national
technical councils with legislative powers. Prohibition of
strikes in the public services. With regard to syndicates,
fascism would help proletarian minorities who were getting
themselves placed on a national footing. In religious matters,
' complete liberty to the catholic church in the exercise of its
spiritual office ; a concord with the Vatican '.

The paragraphs devoted to foreign policy began with the
affirmation, already repeated countless times, that ' fascism
does not believe in the vitality or the principles of the
so-called League of Nations ', and took up all the points
expounded in the Trieste speech of February.[1] As for the
army, the 1919 programme, in deference to the pacific and
democratic spirit of the ex-servicemen, had demanded the
' replacement of the standing army by a national militia
defensive in character and with short-term service '.[2] The
new programme called, on the contrary, for ' a military
establishment proportionate to the present and eventual
needs of a continuously developing nation like Italy '. The
absolute difference between these two proposals showed how
far fascist ideology had gone since March 1919. To those
who imputed a lack of originality to the new programme
Mussolini replied a few days later with a pompously expressed
summary :

> ' We are irrevocably separated from all the socialist
> sects, because we reject all forms of internationalism and
> all forms of state intervention in economic life. . . . We
> are separated from the various schools of democracy and
> liberalism by our conviction of the necessity for a very
> strong state, hence one reduced to its primal politico-
> moral functions, and by our demand for an expansionist,
> courageous, Italian foreign policy.'

[1] P. 132.   [2] P. 34.

Mussolini proposed at the same time a system of regulations laying down the functions and relations of the executive organs of the party (National Congress, Central Committee, Executive Commission, National Council, Political Secretariat), of its federations and sections. These regulations, published on the eve of the Rome Congress, placed the squads under the control of the political leaders of the *fasci*, rendering them 'subject to political disciplinary control by the heads of each section'. Any signs of independence were to be crushed. The 'political' element was to control the 'military'.

At the time of the Rome Congress (November 7–10, 1921) the fascists, who in 1920 had had only about 100 *fasci* with 30,000 supporters, now numbered 2200 *fasci* and 320,000 members, chiefly recruited from landowners and middle classes. An analysis of 151,644 members, made at the time by the party secretariat, throws some light on the social structure of the movement : 18,084 landowners, 13,878 tradesmen, 4269 manufacturers, 9981 members of the learned professions, 7209 state employees, 14,988 private employees, 1680 teachers, 19,783 students. These 90,000 composed the militant part of the *fasci :* the financial backers, the leaders, and active members of punitive expeditions. Besides them there were 36,847 agricultural labourers, mostly members of socialist ' leagues ' forced into the *fasci* by the offensive of the *squadristi*, and 23,418 industrial workers, taken largely from the civil service, the unemployed dock workers, and the districts under fascist military occupation. These occupations had brought the fascists a windfall of 138 co-operatives and 614 workers' syndicates, with 64,000 members, two-thirds of them from Emilia, Tuscany, and Venetia. The mass of the workers in the towns and even in the country were paralysed and in some cases completely subjugated, but they remained loyal to their socialist or catholic organizations. At the moment the squads provided the only real driving power of the fascist movement. Even the Rome Congress only succeeded because it became a sort of military parade, an *adunata*, as Mussolini realized very well.

The day before the opening Mussolini met the opposition leaders and struck a bargain with them. The opposition, conscious of being in a majority, agreed not to impeach him or the central committee on condition that there was no more talk of the peace pact. Mussolini accepted, for he wanted to avoid a vote at all costs, knowing that it would go against him, and he was so disconcerted at the prospect of being publicly disowned that he was ready to deny anything. Grandi explained the views of the opposition at the congress. We want to avoid a split, he declared, ' so long as there is no more talk of a peace pact, here or anywhere '. Mussolini, who had seen his popularity endangered, got up on the platform and announced that the ' treaty is definitely a thing of the past, and no more than a retrospective episode '. Grandi and Mussolini embraced each other, and the congress, till now divided into friends and enemies of the pact, reserving their applause for one or other of the two leaders, greeted them with a single ovation, singing and bawling : ' *Giovinezza*.'

The discussion on the first day had revealed the cleavage between the two tendencies. A Turin representative got on the platform to deplore the fact that ' fascism went arm-in-arm with the landowners and industrial bosses ' ; while a *squadrista* had declared : ' We must not sign a truce, for we are soldiers.' The reconciliation of the two leaders on the second day put an end to this bickering. Both made speeches in turn on the programme question. Mussolini repeated the points already published in the *Popolo d'Italia*,[1] emphasizing once more the need of opposing any state intervention in the economic sphere. ' In economic matters we are liberal in the most classical sense of the word ', and, after criticizing d'Annunzio's Quarnero constitution, he added : ' liberal though we are in economics, we are not so in politics '. He emphasized, too, the need for a swing to the right and for a more imperialist foreign policy, praising Crispi, who ' at a time when Italy seemed to be committed to a stay-at-home policy, had the courage to make her play a part in the Mediterranean and Africa, because he felt that greatness was not possible for a nation unless it was inspired by imperialism '. Without this spur nations are condemned to decadence and death.

[1] Pp. 161–2.

Grandi made a speech much richer in ideas and suggestions and mercilessly critical of Mussolini's recent posturings, though without mentioning his name.   Parliamentary fascism and national fascism were in conflict, he said. ' After the elections, fascism, which was a romantic movement, became a political one and was repressed by parliamentarism before acquiring any proper character of its own. That is why, up till now, it has been groping about and has not been able to find its way.'   Its organization needed completely renewing, beginning with its philosophy.   In the Fiume tradition and in the Quarnero constitution were to be found all the principles of this double renewal, whose meaning ' might be summed up in the words, *liberty, nation, syndicalism* '.   Instead of following in the wake of the conservatives, the Vatican and reformist socialism, fascism should be the moving spirit of a new national democracy, a syndical democracy, which would allow the masses to support the national state.   ' The state must consist of a great and powerful association of syndicates, for we see democracy not as a means, but as an end.'   This was a retort to Mussolini, who had said in his speech : ' Democracy may be a means, but never an end.'   Fascism, concluded Grandi, is slowly maturing inside it the germs of the future state.   ' Our congress is only the preface to a great book that the new generation is to write.'

For most of those present the debates were a kind of stage performance to which they listened without understanding very well, and the two speeches were greeted with lengthy and enthusiastic applause.   This made it easy for the leaders to close the discussion at once and get a motion passed leaving to the National Council the task of shaping the party programme, co-ordinating Mussolini's and Grandi's plans.[1]

Considering how much opposed in theory were these plans this task might well have appeared hard.   But the solution arrived at saved time and maintained party unity. The fascist rank and file had no interest in ideological niceties ; their main idea was to go on beating up socialists,

---

[1] This motion, put by Michele Bianchi, and passed on the 9th, also settled the transformation of the *fasci* into a political party, the *National Fascist Party*.

and it was enough that Mussolini and Grandi had agreed to drop the peace pact. The difficulties with regard to the programme were complicated by all sorts of equivocations. Mussolini, himself a ' conservative ', had for several weeks been considering collaboration with the socialists, whom his fellow conservatives wanted to see crushed for good and all by the fascist *manganello*. Grandi, who talked about a new *Risorgimento*, and wanted to win the confidence of the masses and impose the Quarnero republic on a national scale, had the backing of the fascists of the Po valley, inspired and led by the landowners, who were particularly selfish and hostile to the workers. Mussolini made no secret of his mistrust of the fascist syndicates, particularly as the foundations for a ' syndicalist state ', but Grandi, who wanted to be both revolutionary and syndicalist, was the leader of the fascism of the ' punitive expeditions ', which were uprooting syndicalism entirely over a third of Italy. Mussolini, who wished to collaborate with the General Confederation of Labour, opposed d'Annunzio, who looked forward to a ' national reconciliation ', in which the Confederation would play an important part ; while Grandi, who proclaimed himself d'Annunzio's disciple, wanted to destroy the Confederation root and branch. Mussolini, who hoped for a personal dictatorship, had been talking of pacification and collaboration right up to the eve of the congress ; Grandi, with his talk of democracy and syndicalism, wished the blackshirt offensive to go on until the enemy were wiped out. On neither side was there any connection between theory and facts, between principles and the forces which were to put them into practice.

This tangle of equivocations eventually helped the fusion of opposing tendencies. Mussolini's reactionary ideas inevitably combined with Grandi's reactionary forces, and from that moment unity was regained, particularly as Mussolini was prepared for any sacrifice to get back the *squadristi ;* he had gone back on the peace pact, he had been the first to sign a complimentary telegram to d'Annunzio from the congress, and he had become an out-and-out nationalist. Although he had, a few months ago, defended the treaty of Rapallo, he now interrupted the speech of a delegate who complained that Italy had only very weak armed forces on the Jugo-Slav frontier by shouting : ' We are there. We will send a punitive expedition to Lioublana.' ' Loud applause ' records the official account of the congress.

Another episode, which had an important influence on the internal development of fascism, speeded up the union of the two schools of thought. The Tuscan and Emilian squads had arrived in Rome equipped for a punitive expedition, and they began attacking anybody in the streets who wore a red tie or did not uncover as they passed, as if they were in their ' own ' Florence or Bologna. At the station they killed a railwayman, and there was a general strike in protest. The government was alarmed. Fascist activity in other towns was all very well, but in Rome there were embassies, the Vatican, pilgrimages. . . . There were further incidents, and the fascists began to feel themselves surrounded by an atmosphere of hatred and contempt. They revenged themselves by leaving behind them in the Augusteo, the hall where the congress had been held, piles of litter and dirt. In the Chamber Mussolini spoke of ' misunderstandings between the people of Rome and the fascists ', Grandi of forgetfulness and ' ingratitude '. But both had learned their lesson. Mussolini had discovered that the only fascism that counted was that of the squads, whose confidence he had to win back if he wanted a real force behind him. Grandi realized that the Po valley was not the whole of Italy, and that, even where it seemed to have triumphed, fascism could not last without support from the state. Shortly after he wrote in this connection :

' A violent and dictatorial seizure of the powers of the state seemed to us at times to be an immediate necessity ; all the more obvious because it seemed possible and easy . . . *the days in Rome destroyed this illusion.* There in November we all felt clearly that any attempt at a rising would fail, because understanding of the new state has not yet matured in the heart of the people.' ' Punitive expeditions ' were not enough ; political action was wanted : ' Slow, steady, everyday work.'

Which of the opposition leaders could undertake this work ? They were all inexperienced and young, suddenly faced with a reality which had so far escaped them. The only possibility was Mussolini, who for several months had been pointing out the danger of the split between the country and fascism, the existence of which had come as an unexpected revelation to the extremists of the opposition. It began to be admitted that his opportunism had been called for by the situation, that he alone could direct the political action of fascism, and that without him it would fail. So, shortly after his appearance in the congress as a minority leader, there emerged, as the only possible leader of fascism, the unrivalled ' Duce '. The revolt against him, which had forced him to abandon the untenable position he had taken up, died down and fascism passed into his hands once more, but not before various incidents had taken place on the last day of the congress. The opposition delegates proposed Rome, instead of Milan, as headquarters of the party, in order to reduce Mussolini's personal influence. On this point the two sides voted against each other, and the resolution was carried by a large majority. The opposition greeted the result with significant applause, very galling to Mussolini. The list of the Executive Committee of the *fasci* was read out : Mussolini was first, then Grandi. Mussolini rose and announced that he would not accept. The Assembly cheered him, to force his hand, but he replied : ' It is no good insisting. You do not know me. I will not accept.' But his friends, on the contrary, knew him very well, for though he made no formal declaration of acceptance, he attended the first meeting of the new committee. He realized perfectly that the situation was developing in his favour, and he only kept up the farce because he needed a little time to get over the rebuff he had suffered at Rome. If possible, he would have liked to get his own back with the fascists by letting them manage for themselves and staying in Milan with the *Popolo d'Italia* until they begged him to direct the movement once more. The political situation allowed him no time for this. The ' democratic ' groups in parliament, ranging from Nitti to Giolitti, had begun negotiating for union into a single group, and had completed their arrangements by the end of November. Between 150 and 160 deputies joined the new alliance. The fascists, quit of the peace pact, which had not worried them much, resumed their acts of violence, which included the assassination of the socialist deputy Di Vagno in Apulia, and of the socialist Boldori, president of the Cremona provincial council of deputies, who was beaten to death in the road. For funeral speech he had the fascist comment : ' It was not our fault his skull was so thin.' A new attack was made on the *Lavoratore* in Trieste, and a compositor was murdered. This caused a general strike in protest, proclaimed by the Printers' Federation.

The government issued fresh regulations on the ' disarmament of citizens ' ordering searches to be made and arms seized. These measures were ineffective, for the government only went half-way and left to local authorities the final responsibility for breaking up the armed leagues. According to the regulations : ' headquarters are to be occupied, arms confiscated, the bearing of arms forbidden to all members of armed bands, who are eventually to be reported to the legal authorities in extreme cases, such as are mentioned in articles 253, 254 of the Penal Code (on those who " organize armed bands and belong to them ") '. But how many of these prefects and sub-prefects, when left to decide for themselves, were likely to go so far ? The regulations left loop-holes for endless evasion and connivance. A few searches were made, chiefly in People's Houses and headquarters of socialist syndicates, to seize any arms that might possibly still be there, and leave the field clear for the fascist attack. Members of several *arditi del popolo* were arrested and sentenced by the magistrates without pity. Strict observance of the law would have meant the occupation by the authorities of each fascist base from which punitive expeditions set out, and the arrest of *squadristi*. They contented themselves with a few searches. But the arms which they should have found were often supplied by the military, and when a search was arranged the leaders of *fasci* were warned, and had plenty of time to take them to a safe place, sometimes even the cellars of police headquarters or of the prefecture. Nothing was ever found, therefore, and next day the squads would go off again, armed, in their lorries, passing unmolested under the windows of the police-station, where a report was being drawn up, explaining that a thorough search had failed to reveal anything that would justify the prefect taking any steps.

The government realized that the measures they had taken were useless and contemplated abolishing the squads by decree. As soon as the fascist leaders had wind of this they got their blow in first, and on December 15, 1921 they issued the following order :

> ' To all sections of the party ! To all *squadre di combattimento !* There is a rumour in the press of an imminent attack by the government on fascism. . . . Party sections and *squadre di combattimento* make up an indivisible whole. After December 15, 1921, all members of sections will join squads. . . . The dissolution of the *squadre di combattimento* thus becomes an impossibility, unless the government first outlaws the entire National Fascist Party.'

Such was their challenge : the government wanted to dissolve the squads, but the whole party belonged to them ; let them dissolve the party if they dare. The government obviously would not dare. Its leader, Bonomi, had been elected in Mantua in May, on a national coalition list which included the fascists. He issued more and more regulations, which everybody ignored. The fascists had staked boldly and the state gave way. At the same time the internal crisis of fascism was brought nearer to a solution by the common danger which united ' sections ' and ' squads '. Instead of breaking up, thereby giving Mussolini and his friends a chance to join the state, towards the end of the year fascism had united against the state.

IX

THE CAPORETTO OF SOCIALISM

A T the end of 1921 Mussolini was faced with the serious possibility of the left-wing groups forming a coalition government bent on putting a stop to fascist violence. There were 535 deputies in the Chamber, of whom 145 were socialists, communists, and republicans, 110 *Popolari*, and 150 'democrats'. In order to bring about a ministerial crisis on November 26, the socialists had tabled a resolution deploring the inertia of the government over the armed bands. If the fascists joined the attack, Bonomi would be defeated, as Giolitti had been six months ago.

But Mussolini was not ready for a parliamentary crisis, and spared the government in his speech. Those in power, he said, might attempt to crush the two extreme factions, communist and fascist, simultaneously :

' Let me say at once that as far as the fascists are concerned it would be very difficult and dangerous ; for to-morrow, fascists and communists, alike persecuted by the police, might arrive at an agreement, sinking their differences till the time comes to share the spoils. I realize that though there are no political affinities between us, there are plenty of intellectual affinities. Like them, we believe in the necessity for a centralized and unitary state, imposing an iron discipline on all, but with the difference that they reach this conclusion through the conception of class, we through the conception of the nation.'

The Bonomi government might still have used one faction to destroy the other, but, content to live from hand to mouth, it did not. At the present time there were only three solutions : a military dictatorship, which, said Mussolini :

' I have never believed in, even when it is suggested by unemployed generals, who always think they have an infallible remedy for the world's troubles,' besides, ' dictatorship is a high card, which can only be played once, and at a frightful risk ' ;   alternatively an appeal to the country through new general elections ;   or, finally, a coalition government.   But who was to form it ?   Not Nitti, for the fascists were strongly opposed to him.   ' Signor Giolitti ? This statesman has always enjoyed great popularity.   Besides, history is a succession of logical and sentimental points of view, and one does not fix one's loves and hates for ever. Yesterday's friends become to-morrow's enemies, and vice versa ;   such is life.'   With regard to the general situation, if it was necessary to choose between civil war and a policy of pacification, the fascists felt themselves strong enough to accept pacification.

' It is time the Italian people stopped fighting at home and looked beyond their own frontiers, watching the new developments which are destined once more to change the map of Europe.   For the choice lies between treaty revision and a new war.   Italy must enter the lists solidly united and undistracted by internal disorder, so as to show the world—since from now on our life is neither national, nor even European, but world-wide—that Italy is about to enter the fourth and most brilliant period of her history.'

Reading this speech again to-day, one is struck by its incoherence.   It would have been easy to refute it and show up its countless contradictions.   Nobody did so, because in order to drive Mussolini and fascism into a corner it would have been necessary to take a firm line and shoulder definite responsibilities, not only over fascism but over the whole field of Italian politics.   Mussolini could afford to be incoherent, because none of the others, from socialists to liberals, were ready to pay the price of a coherent policy. He knew the weakness of his opponents and profited by it. Their torpor gave him freedom to manœuvre.   What he was out to prevent was the hardening of vaguely democratic feeling in the Chamber into a definite coalition from which the fascists would be excluded. Faced with the threat of anti-fascist action by the state, he countered with the threat of an alliance with the communists. Rather than a centre government, which would eliminate both extremes, he favoured a coalition government led by Giolitti, ' yesterday's enemy and to-morrow's friend '. He ' accepted ' pacification, but as the necessary prelude to an imperialistic foreign policy. In short, he did his best to stave off a ministerial crisis whose outcome the fascists could not yet control, and he succeeded. The Bonomi government survived a few weeks longer.

The crisis came two months later. The new session was fixed to begin on February 2. The day before, the right-wing members, the fascists and the socialists decided to vote against the ministry, and, which proved decisive, the democratic group called on its members in the cabinet to resign. Only the *Popolari* favoured the *status quo*. The government was simultaneously blamed for not making itself felt at the Cannes conference, for the ineffectiveness of its measures for internal peace and disarmament, for its weakness with the fascists, for its subservience to the socialists, for being influenced inside the cabinet by the *Popolari*, and for its growing tendency towards anti-clericalism. It was also criticized for not having done its utmost to rescue the *Banca Italiana di Sconto*, which had had to close down and demand a moratorium. Amongst those responsible for the failure of this great bank were several of the financial backers of fascism and nationalism, who wanted to save their cash at the expense of the state, and whose efforts found support in some of the ' democratic ' papers, such as the *Paese*.

The French ambassador in Rome, M. Barrère, once more had a hand in the game. At Cannes Bonomi had shown his approval of Lloyd George's advances for a ' return to normal ' in the European situation and for a more intelligent policy towards Germany and Russia. To reassure France, England was disposed to give her the direct guarantee to which later she was never willing to pledge herself. Briand lent a ready ear to these advances, but Millerand and Poincaré staged a little *coup d'état* in Paris, to get him out of the way.

M. Barrère took the same line in Rome. The Genoa conference was about to take place, but Bonomi was fated to miss it, as Nitti had missed Spa.[1]

Once the crisis had begun Giolitti and Nitti exerted themselves to settle it, but as they both wanted to be the *deus ex machina* of the new government their efforts cancelled each other out. For his part, Don Sturzo, the secretary of the *Popolari*, renewed his ban against Giolitti. The Bonomi cabinet resigned and in the course of negotiations for a solution, Giolitti, De Nicola, Orlando were eliminated in turn. In face of this difficulty the king refused to accept the cabinet's resignation, but asked Bonomi to go before the Chamber to obtain a vote which would show clearly what form the new government should take. On February 16 Bonomi accepted a motion of confidence, the first part of which emphasized ' the necessity of giving back to the country the conditions without which all classes cannot live peaceably side by side, with a respect for freedom of labour and organization, and in obedience to the law '. This was drawn up by the reformist, Celli, with the idea of embarrassing the fascists and forcing them into opposition, which would allow the formation of a majority from which they would be excluded, and give the definite lead which had been sought in vain for months.

Speaking for the socialists, Modigliani said that he would vote in favour of the first part of the motion, but would refuse to give a vote of confidence in the government. Mussolini understood Celli's aims perfectly, and took the offensive. He drew attention to the contradiction between the ' maximalist ' decisions of the last socialist congress, and the present acceptance of ' all classes living peaceably side by side ' and of ' obedience to the law '. On behalf of the entire right wing he too, accepted the first part of the motion, which was passed by 388 votes to 11. Thus he once more managed to prevent the voting in the Chamber from pointing the way to the formation of any new government. After this the fascists could, without any risk, support the socialists in refusing confidence in the Bonomi cabinet. The crisis continued, the longest known in Italy since 1860.

[1] Pp. 62–63.

Giolitti tried in vain to get the ban put on him by the
Popolari removed, and sent his favourite envoy, the prefect
Lusignoli, to the Vatican. The Genoa conference was about
to begin, and somehow or other a government had to be
formed. The *Popolari*, who had cold-shouldered Giolitti,
agreed to join a ministry formed by his lieutenant, Facta.
This took a form very different from that envisaged by the
Celli resolution, and included right-wing elements, such as
De Capitani and Riccio, of whom the latter was to be the
fascist intermediary in the new cabinet. Thus the crisis,
which had been engineered so as to bring in a government
' further to the left ', had the opposite effect. Mussolini's
coup had succeeded ; he had staved off a democratic coalition,
socialist support of the government, in short a stronger
ministry, which as he clearly realized could have made an
end of the fascists. The long crisis, the equivocation of the
socialists, the *Popolari's* ostentatious show of power and their
rallying to support the Facta solution, all served further to
discredit the parliamentary system. The country looked on
amazed at the antics of the various parties and their leaders
and could make nothing of them. The nationalists took the
opportunity to demonstrate in Rome, Bologna and Florence,
in front of military headquarters, shouting : ' We want a
dictatorship ! Down with parliament.'

The sort of truce—only by comparison—which lasted as
long as the Genoa conference, barely served to hide the fact
that the parliamentary crisis was having an increasingly
serious effect on the country. Chiefly under the influence
of the National Syndicate of Railwaymen there arose in the
working-class movement a ' Labour Alliance ' (*Alleanza del
Lavoro*), covering all syndical bodies, headed by the General
Confederation of Labour. The formation of this ' united
front ' put fresh courage in the workers and might have had
a decisive effect. But though indispensable it was not sufficient. It was exclusively syndical, and as such all it could
do was to proclaim on a national scale one of those general
strikes of protest which broke out after every fascist outrage.
But as it could organize neither street warfare, nor the legal
conquest of power, it proved as ineffective as the workers'
political parties. Moreover party differences were aggra-

vated rather than settled by the Labour Alliance ; behind the facade they still fought bitterly. Maximalists and right-wing socialists were on the point of an open break. And what serious contribution could the communists make to the united front, believing as they did that ' If the *bourgeoisie* brings it off and white reaction strangles social democracy, it will create the most favourable conditions for its own defeat and for the victory of the revolution ' . . . ?

The *Popolari* soon became conscious of strong pressure being brought to bear on their right, from the direction of the Vatican. At the beginning of February the College of Cardinals, which met after the death of Benedict XV, elected Cardinal Ratti as Pius XI. The new Pope belonged to one of the typical conservative Lombard families who had always taken a narrow-minded view over social questions, and was an instinctive reactionary in everything. The Jesuits, always attracted by a novelty, whether dangerous or profitable, did their best to make an accord between the fascists and the Vatican. Early in 1922, in their church of Jesus in Rome, the favourite meeting-place of the ' black aristocracy ', they preached the beauties of the new move-ment in which they foresaw remarkable liberticide possi-bilities. One of them was so far carried away by his enthusiasm as to get up in the pulpit and cry : ' Long live fascism '. In order to get rid of the socialists, Mussolini needed the help of the *Popolari*, who were indispensable to a right-wing government, and he hoped to win it through the Vatican. On the occasion of the death of Benedict XV he discovered religion, hailed once more the universal mission of catholicism and the revival of religious feeling, a potent means of escape for the poor and wretched. At the same time he had recourse to the strategy he had used with the socialists : playing off the right against the left wing of the party and hoping for a split. In actual fact the right wing had almost no following inside the party, but could count on increasing support from the Vatican.

Lower down in the catholic syndical organizations the movement in favour of collaboration with the socialists, and particularly with the General Confederation of Labour, was very strong. Peasants and workers who followed the

Popolari had suffered from the attacks made by fascists on the headquarters of their organizations and on their labour contracts. At Cremona they forced the *Popolari* to sign a local agreement with the socialists ' for the defence of syndical freedom and the protection of their municipalities '. But this defence could not go very far, since neither could be guaranteed unless the state took active steps to make the law respected. The political secretariat of the *Popolari*, together with Don Sturzo, were unwilling to commit themselves very deeply with the socialists ; besides which the confusion inside the party, where the maximalists still clung to their 1919–1920 ideas, made any collaboration in a government out of the question. To make matters worse, the maximalist executive of the party, sheltering behind a question of procedure, censured the Cremona agreements, which thus become inoperative. People who a few months ago had rallied to the ' democratic concentration ' and the political solution it implied now began to hesitate, and to see no hope outside an alliance with the fascists for a great national government. With this in view Nitti was showing signs of favour towards fascism, as in the declaration of policy he made in Melfi on March 12.

Mussolini had no more trouble in settling the crisis inside the party, which had been most threatening on the eve of the Rome congress and now only manifested itself in stray incidents. Grandi and the supporters of ' national revolution ' understood the necessity of temporizing, and recognized that Mussolini was the only pilot who could keep them clear of the rocks. Even over the young extremists he wielded an undisputed authority. He took care to be always in touch with them ; he was at once curt and kindly, off-hand and affectionate, holding out to each man the hopes that were most likely to bind him to his service, talking confidentially, committing himself to nothing, but inspiring others with the wildest dreams. At the beginning of 1922, a few months after the congress, Italo Balbo, one of the opposition leaders, wrote in his *Diary :*

' Once a month, often once a fortnight, I go and see Mussolini at Milan. Unforgettable meetings. The Duce simplifies the most complicated problems, a great quality in a leader. He is, too, always very affectionate. He never lets me go without embracing me. His confidence is my viaticum. Without this certainty I could not continue the struggle. He tells me I am one of the elect. Such praise makes me proud. Ambitious, too, to surprise him by doing more than he expects. I am certain he was right when, despite the hesitation of many, myself included, he turned fascism into a party.'

The reconciliation with the extremists had far-reaching results. At the National Council of Florence (December 20–21, 1921) the programme question was relegated to second place. Attention was focused on the organization of the fighting squads, which, while being placed under the control of the political committees of the *fasci*, were to be turned into a more regular army, capable of more ambitious feats than the assassination of socialist leaders and the burning of Chambers of Labour. Mussolini explained to the ' military ' fascists that it was time to stop thinking in terms of local or regional action and aim at the conquest of power. Until they were really prepared they must play for time. In his own mind he was far from certain that he wanted to march on Rome, his own inclination being to get there by other and less risky methods. But he had to calm the impatience of those who until lately had been his opponents, besides holding in reserve the prospect of a military conquest in case all else failed. Early in 1922 work was begun on the reorganization of the squads on a unified, national scale. Italo Balbo and the Marquis Perrone Compagni, the leader of the Tuscan fascists, went to Oneglia to meet General Gandolfo, who had recently joined. It was at his house that they met to ' plan the transformation of the squads into a Fascist Militia '.

Mussolini had insisted in August that a programme was necessary. Now that he had shaped his instrument, the party, he must take care not to handicap himself with a programme that would make it unwieldy. His convictions were unchanged ; he merely wanted to win over the refractory *squadristi*. He wanted just enough doctrine to keep the

party together without making it inflexible.   But he did
not want to tie himself down to anything, or leave the world
of adventure, where he felt at his best, for the tricky and
difficult one of fixed principles.   He wanted to continue his
daily borrowing of ideas to meet all possible combinations
of forces opposing or supporting him.   Ideas were only of
value in so far as they helped him on his way.   And in this
connection he took plenty of precautions ;   before the
discussion was over he had thoroughly confused the issue by
a profession of exaggerated relativism.

' The fascist phenomenon,' he wrote after the Rome
Congress, ' is the highest and most interesting manifesta-
tion of relativist philosophy.   And since, as Wahiger
asserts, relativism is derived from Nietzsche and his *Wille
zur Macht,* Italian fascism has been and remains the most
formidable creation of an individual and national will to
power.'

This will to power embraced the entire fascist world, from
Mussolini, for whom life was just a ' wild adventure ' and to
whom success was the only sanction, to the landowners and
manufacturers who, after shaking in their shoes for two
years, felt themselves once more the absolute masters of their
land and their factories, and thus saw ' the relationship of
man's tyranny over man once more restored ' ; and from the
petit bourgeois, who only yesterday had felt himself crushed
between capitalism and the proletariat, and who now
considered himself the deciding factor between these two
forces, to the demobilized officer, who saw in the fascist
militia the possibility of another command and the daily
ration of power that he could not do without.

From one point of view the vagueness of the programme,
instead of hindering the growth of fascism, helped it to
attract recruits and adapt itself to local conditions.

' The pretexts adopted by fascists to justify their offensive are not important, since they vary from place to
place.   At Bologna and Reggio Emilia one is told that
the cowardly socialists must be driven out since they
could not or would not begin the revolution.   In Carrara

and the Valdarno, on the other hand, they proclaim that the time has come to make away with the anarchists, who are threatening fresh upheavals and hindering gradual and progressive conquests. In Turin and Florence they rant against Russian communism, in Rome and Milan against Nittian reformism, and so on.' (L. Fabbri, *La Contro-rivoluzione preventiva*.)

At the same time they fostered the illusions of allies whom later they were to repudiate and trample on, all of whom hoped to make use of the fascist movement for their own ends : 'Giolitti to force a reconciliation on the *Popolari*, Salandra and his supporters to break the ban the socialists had put on him, the constitutional parties to save themselves from being swept out of existence by universal suffrage.' (G. Ferrero, *Da Fiume a Roma*.) The extreme adaptability of fascism led them to think that one day they would be able to mould it and use it to serve their own purposes.

This same adaptability allowed the frequent and widespread local crises in the *fasci*, which had paralysed the movement in 1919–21, to pass off quickly, without deeply affecting the situation created by the Rome Congress. At the beginning of 1922 the *fasci* were in the throes of a crisis, but the advance of the movement was not affected. One executive ousted another, there was constant quarrelling, but recruiting scarcely slackened and revived again immediately. Crises are only serious when a question of principle is involved, which was not the case with the fascists, either leaders or rank and file. Hardly anybody was prepared to sacrifice the privileges assured by membership of the party or the militia. It would have meant giving up uniform, arms, expeditions, subsidies, loot, flattery, and all the other advantages reserved to fascists. As was the case later with the German S.A., the opposition fascists could not live outside the atmosphere to which they owed everything ; a break with the party meant the end. Every *fascio* affected disbanded itself and re-formed, joining the movement stronger than before.

It is important to remember, too, the unifying effect of violence and crime perpetrated in company. Umberto

Banchelli, an opposition fascist, explains that the existence of rival *fasci* at Florence did not hinder the good work. 'Relentless blows were still struck at the socialists and communists. There was even a joint expedition to Pisa. The provincial council was turned out and the red guards put to flight. We fought like mad, I remember, and the two *fasci* acquitted themselves with equal credit.' Men who have killed together, burned houses, terrorized whole country-sides could not stop or separate. To commit crimes at top speed became a law, for one crime could only be washed out by another. The bond uniting the aggressors was not their own blood, which was seldom spilled, but the blood of their victims. Feeling that nothing could quench the hatred in which they were held, they went to all lengths, for they knew that once they hesitated, once their enemy was given a breathing-space, they were lost.

Mussolini, sustained by so many interests, hopes and supporters, had no difficulty in dealing with the last echo of the party crisis, between February and April, 1922. A letter addressed to the secretary of the party by Piero Marsich, head of the Venice *fascio* and an opposition fascist of 'fascism of the first hour' principles, was published at the beginning of February in the journal of the Fiume legionaries. In this letter Marsich revived the theme of the divergence between parliamentary and national interests, and blamed Mussolini for advocating in an interview a coalition government led by Giolitti. 'Under the pretext of avoiding a Nitti-socialist collaboration, is the Italy of Carso and Fiume to deliver herself into the hands of the man who opposed the war and betrayed us at Rapallo?' He also proclaimed that d'Annunzio was the 'only great Italian' and inveighed against 'the iniquitous hegemony of a man' who was forcing his politician's tricks on to the party. This was published in the *Popolo d'Italia* on March 7. Mussolini, who was then in Germany, broke off his journey at once and returned to Milan to deal with this 'wretched attempt at secession'. The National Council of the party met at the beginning of April and unanimously disavowed Marsich, who was deserted even by his friends.

The same occasion served to frustrate opposition from

partisans of d'Annunzio. He had been infuriated by Mussolini's condoning the Treaty of Rapallo, by the way in which
he had been left high and dry in December 1920, and by the
fasci joining the electoral lists in May 1921, and he had
ordered his legionaries to quit the *fasci*. The congress of
legionaries, which met in September, declared itself firmly
opposed to fascism, which it accused of serving landowning and plutocratic interests. D'Annunzio's definition of
fascism, ' agrarian slavery ', was on everybody's lips. At
the fascist congress in Rome, d'Annunzio and the Constitution of the Quarnero provided the theme of the opposition.
But even in Fiume, after d'Annunzio had left, the initiative
had passed to the local *fasci*. At the beginning of March
1922, a fascist deputy, Giunta, and his squads seized a
destroyer, sailed to Fiume and opened fire on the government
buildings, where Zanella, ' the autonomist ', was installed,
and drove him out. A provisional government was formed
under the fascist deputy, Giurati. Thus, in Fiume itself,
fascists and legionaries became less and less distinguishable
one from the other, and this tendency spread elsewhere in
Italy. Some of the legionaries remained with the *fasci*,
contrary to d'Annunzio's orders, preferring to swim with the
fastest current, and having no Vittoriale to retire to. The
distinction between fascists and legionaries was not clear,
and actually only affected those who were in personal contact with the ' commandant '. The legionaries had been
attracted to Fiume by their taste for adventure, and fascism
offered them the chance of a life of war, often their only
chance of any sort of life. The more powerful the fascist
organization became the harder it was for the ex-legionary
to break away on an independent course, particularly as
many of his leaders were to be found, captive or suborned, in
the front ranks of the fascists.

It was d'Annunzio's attitude towards the General Confederation of Labour which chiefly served to unite the
Fascist Party against him. He dreamed of playing one day
the role of poet-prophet-dictator in a national revolution
inspired by his Quarnero charter, and supported by all the
forces of progress, especially the world of labour. Labour
was to recover its dignity, now menaced by fascism, and

thus pacified at home Italy was to return to her world mission. Mussolini had already lifted many of d'Annunzio's ideas and he took this as well, turning it as always to his own advantage. Peace at home, yes, but in order that he might attain power and one day direct Italy's foreign policy. Mussolini, too, spoke of a 'fourth Italy' and of Italy's mission in the world, but any idea of a crusade for the 'national and social' liberation of the oppressed was discarded. D'Annunzio's apocalyptic visions were reduced to a ferocious nationalism, an extension of the 'will to power' beyond the frontiers.

Both right and left fascists were disturbed by d'Annunzio's activities and his suspicious contacts. At the beginning of April 1922 he was visited at his home in Gardone by Baldesi, one of the secretaries of the General Confederation of Labour. In the *Mondo*, one of d'Annunzio's legionary friends[1] expounded all the possible points of agreement between d'Annunzio and the socialist movement :

'D'Annunzio,' he wrote on April 5, 'is concerned with present reality, national reality and European reality. The social question arouses his respect and interest. . . . It suffices, without going too far back, to remember that he chose a syndicalist, Alceste de Ambris, as chief of his Fiume cabinet, that he settled a general strike in Fiume in the workers' favour, and that from Gardone he has always condemned the legionaries who have become " yellow ", " white guards ", or " agrarian slave-drivers ". . . . Many of the legionaries are men of the people and in contrast to the fascists have very advanced ideas. . . . In the *Violet book* of Fiume there is an appeal for the freedom of peoples addressed to the Clarté group[2] . . . and the d'Annunzio government at Fiume had decided to renew not only commercial but also political relations with Soviet Russia.'

The press mentioned d'Annunzio's possible appointment as President of the Federation of Maritime Workers, along-

---

[1] Signor Nino Daniele, who later accompanied Antonio Gramsci, editor of the Turin communist daily, the *Ordine Nuovo*, to arrange an interview with d'Annunzio at Gardone.

[2] The French pacifist group founded by Henri Barbusse.

side Captain Giuletti. Baldesi's visit was only tentative, with both sides feeling their way. On May 26 d'Aragona himself, the secretary-general of the General Confederation of Labour, paid a visit to the ' commandant '. Next day d'Annunzio received Tchitcherin, the leader of the Soviet delegation to the Genoa conference, and had a long talk with him. D'Annunzio presented the Confederation with a portrait of Dante, and was thanked in a letter written in the ' d'Annunzian ' style. Dante, said the letter, is the symbol of the exile ; ' lit by the sacred lamp ', his face shows ' the restrained anguish of the child driven from town to town, longing for a great nation to be renewed in the greater empire of united nations, and abhorring the municipal squabbles ' which are raging in Italy to-day, ' more fiercely and less gloriously ' ; the Confederation, too, was to have ' its sacred lamp, fed by the constant tears of the humble and by the blood shed by the workers '.

This very unsuccessful effort in the style of the ' commandant ' was written by Turati, normally a plain and sober writer. The fascists treated this pastiche with appropriate sarcasm, and made the *sacra lampa* the subject of endless jokes. Actually they were extremely annoyed and disturbed at this *rapprochement* between d'Annunzio and the Confederation, which still threatened to hold up their work of destruction. Mussolini continued to treat d'Annunzio with formal respect, acknowledged his good intentions, but stated that : ' Henceforward the situation is beyond the control of human powers, even if they are as exceptional as those of d'Annunzio ', and on May 30 he passed a resolution in the Milan *fascio* denouncing the Soviet regime ' responsible for the treaty of Brest Litovsk ' and the socialist ' wreckers of victory ', remarking that ' all the forces of plutocracy and anti-national demagogy have tacitly chosen Gabriele d'Annunzio as the executioner of fascism ', and inviting fascists ' to remember nothing of d'Annunzio but his ardent support of Italy's intervention in the European conflict, his warlike heroism and his loyalty to victory, and to ignore his personal attitude, which will not succeed in damaging the National Fascist Party, henceforward victor over all its foes, and the sole interpreter and inspirer of the reawakened national conscience '. Separation was thus achieved without the Fascist Party being directly affected.

While the Confederation was lighting the *sacra lampa*, the *fasci* were pursuing and intensifying the struggle on its own ground of syndical organization. Here the economic crisis helped them. The number of unemployed, only 102,156 at the end of 1920, quickly rose to 388,744 in July 1921, 512,260 in December, and 606,819 in January 1922. The industrialists and landowners now had the whip hand and did not hesitate to act. The Confederation was paralysed in many country districts by the fascist occupation, and fell back on the defensive. On October 9, 1921, one year after the factory occupations which were to have inaugurated workers' control and begun ' a new epoch ', the administrative council of the Confederation proposed a suspension of the agitations caused by employers' efforts to reduce salaries and the setting up of a commission of inquiry, composed of state representatives, employers and workmen, to investigate conditions in various industries, causes of the rise in the cost of living and the possibility of an adjustment in wages. The government accepted the proposal, the Confederation of Industry opposed it. Postponement of the revision of wage rates until spring 1922 was, however, won in Lombardy by means of negotiation, and in Liguria as the result of a general strike. All the same it was obvious that the tables had been turned. The ' control of industry ' which was to have given the working class a new place in production, and had been hailed by some as a beginning of expropriation and socialization, turned out to be nothing but a means of defence against an excessive reduction of wages, already enforced in some places by the joint pressure of the crisis and fascist intimidation. The few steps taken towards the transformation of ' wage-earners ' into ' producers ' were lost ; once more they were simply wage-earners, their wage their only connection with the producer's world.

Free syndical association was no longer the church triumphant, whose every move was crowned with success ; it was only the church militant, whose service was hard and defences uncertain. Here and there the fascists were percolating into the working classes, having at their disposal radical recruiting methods : violence and terror. Important fascist syndical organizations only grew up in districts already conquered by armed squads and as a result of such conquest. Fascist syndicalism ' flourishes like a weed amid the charred ruins of houses '. Concentration of squads in a district was invariably followed by the destruction of the Chamber of Labour and other syndical offices, by the assassination or expulsion of local syndical leaders. This *razzia* was the necessary preliminary to the setting up of a fascist ' corporation ' in which all members of the organization just destroyed were forced to enrol. Having destroyed the former organization, the fascists were left with the workers on their hands, and to avoid letting slip all they had gained they were forced, as the heirs of the red organizers, to tackle the problems they had solved. ' Rather delicate, this organization,' wrote Italo Balbo in his *Diary ;* ' Labour is over plentiful, and only syndical discipline can ensure work and bread for all.' This ' discipline ' bore a close resemblance to the ' monopoly ' against which the fascists had been clamouring a few months before. Often, having no one at their disposal capable of running the syndical ' league ', the fascists would force the previous secretary to carry on, giving him an occasional thrashing, to keep him in his place and inspire him with a wholesome fear of his new masters.

Mussolini had always been suspicious of fascist syndicalism, as of all definitions and interpretations that might endanger his freedom of action ; besides, he had watched the opposition flaunt the flag of ' national syndicalism '. Nevertheless he permitted this independent syndicalism of the fascists, so long as it did not affect the balance of forces inside the fascist movement to his own disadvantage. He fully realized that this syndical activity widened the gulf between himself and the socialists and would give him a chance to hasten the internal crisis of the socialist movement and capture the leaders of the General Confederation of Labour. ' We never thought,' said Mussolini in later days, ' when a few dozen of us met in the Piazza San Sepolcro on March 23, 1919, that we should form syndical organizations. . . . *Fascism has become syndical owing to the physiological needs of its development.'*

In January 1922 the Fascist Party held a conference at Bologna which set up the General Confederation of National Syndicates. The question then arose, what was to be the relation of the new organization to the party? Was it to be a direct subsidiary, or independent so as to be able to increase its own membership? This was put to the National Council of the party at the beginning of April, and it was Mussolini again who provided the very typical solution that ' the organizations should be made either strictly fascist *or* autonomous according to conditions of time and place '. The public services' syndicates, for example, must be strictly fascist, since they would eventually have to be used as a starting-point for an action against the state. In spite of the conception of a syndical democracy and a syndical state, embraced—more and more half-heartedly— by Grandi and his friends, fascist syndical organization was accepted only as a weapon in the political struggle for power.

This was made clear at the first national congress of Syndical Corporations held in Milan in June. Mussolini summed up the significance of this phenomenon in his speech : ' Gentlemen, to win, one must harass and destroy the enemy in every one of his hiding-places and trenches.' The new organization announced a membership of 458,000, including 277,000 peasants and agricultural labourers (60 per cent) and 72,000 industrial workers (15·7 per cent) ; the rest were spread out among the public services, transport, local government officials, intellectual and technical workers. ' The bulk of the Corporations ', said Mussolini at the time, ' is made up of agricultural labourers ', and chiefly from districts where fascist agrarian violence had exterminated the ' red ' organizations.

Fascism thus had a new end in view, to win recruits for its ' own ' syndical organization, and its offensive became all the more methodical and determined. The debates in the Chamber at the end of November 1921 and during the crisis of February 1922 came to nothing. The socialist group returned to the attack in March, but the resolution they put forward only obtained a majority of 82 to 79, almost two-thirds of the Chamber abstaining. Under the Facta ministry the local authorities, now entirely reassured, placed themselves more and more at the service of the *fasci*. Italo Balbo noted this with satisfaction in his *Diary* : ' We are masters of the situation,' he writes, with reference to Ferrara. ' We have not only broken down the resistance of our enemies, but we also control the departments of state. The Prefect has to submit to the orders I give him in the name of the fascists.'

Justice had become a one-sided affair. In the early months of 1922, in Rome, Venice, Vercelli, Cerignola (Apulia), Reggio Emilia, Bologna, Florence, Alessandria, all fascists accused of murder and ' private violence ' were acquitted and borne away in triumph by their friends. Those who had gone too far were sent for a trip abroad, to Fiume, or simply to another town. In Signor Chiurco's *History* one can trace the wanderings during several months of one of the *squadrista* leaders, Giovanni Passerone, an ex-lieutenant, who had distinguished himself in several engagements at the head of the Montferrato squads. He had, for example, attacked the Chamber of Labour at Casale (March 6, 1921) ; he had taken part with his squad in puni-tive expeditions with the fascists of Lomellina (Marches) ; he had burnt the Balzola (Casale) Chamber of Labour ; he had gone to Valenza (Alessandria) to complete the destruction begun by the local fascists (June 9). After May his progress became more colourful. On May 19 he went to Casale Popolo, and ' as a revenge against the local Chamber of Labour band, which had refused to play at a fascist celebration ', he entered the hall where the band was playing, turned out the women and children and beat up the musicians, forcing them to surrender their instruments, ' which were carried in triumph to the Casale *fascio* '.[1] About thirty people were wounded on this expedition.

Next day he was arrested for robbery with violence, but the fascists mobilized, ' and the authorities were forced to free him a few hours later '. On June 12 he went to Asti with eleven *squadristi* from Casale. ' Avoiding the Royal Guards. the soldiers and the police, the *squadristi* did their work

---

[1] The passages quoted are taken from Chiurco's *History*.

brilliantly. Report for the day : 57 minutes spent in Asti, 10 buildings wrecked, Chambers of Labour, clubs, co-operatives, private houses ; twenty broken heads. Carters' whips were here used for the first time as weapons of war.' In July Passerone became even more active. On July 18 he marched with his battalion to Novaro, where he took part in the attack on the Chamber of Labour and on socialist and communist clubs. From there he pushed on to Arona and Meina on lake Maggiore, returning afterwards to Trecate, where the fascists installed one of their number as mayor, and destroyed the Chamber of Labour ' by hitching lorries to the pillars supporting the arcades, and blowing up the rest '. From Trecate, with 150 fascists from Casale, he drove by lorry to Magenta on the road to Milan. To keep their hands in they pillaged and wrecked, on the evening of July 23, the co-operative, the recreation club, the offices of the railwaymen's club and the People's House. As a result of their doings in Novara, Trecate, Magenta, a warrant was issued for the arrest of the ' consul ' Giovanni Passerone and his friend Natale Cerutti. ' They were forced to leave Casale to avoid arrest. But they continued to take part in various expeditions to Turin, Ivrea, Biella, and Santhià, keeping in touch all the time with the Montferrato blackshirts. Cerutti went to Sampierdarena (Genoa) to organize fascist action there, and at the time of the August general strike he summoned the Casale squads to Liguria and directed their operations.'

Life was very different for the socialist organizers exiled from their own districts. They generally began by hiding in the provincial capital, since it was easier to hide in a town, and persecution was more difficult. But later on the town, too, was ' occupied ' by the fascists, and they had to go further. Gradually the number of possible hiding-places diminished. Life was still possible in Rome, Milan, Turin, Genoa. Life ? Most of these exiles had no means of existence. The first-comers sometimes found work to start with in the workers' co-operative societies ; some were helped by their families, or by friends from their own district, who subscribed amongst themselves to send them a little money. Little collections were made everywhere, and the workers, whose sense of solidarity was tremendous, gave with inexhaustible generosity. But the increasing numbers who never stopped arriving rendered the sums collected more and more inadequate, and these men torn from their jobs and families led a precarious, and worse, a pointless existence. For the fascist a change of town meant a new arena for his exploits, whereas the socialist felt himself uprooted, and was lost to the movement, even if his energy was unimpaired. For the fascists diffusion made for wider and more effective action, for the socialists, constraint and feebleness.

The fascists could, with impunity, even persecute and expel public officials who would not place themselves at their disposal or who resisted their will. Captain Jurgens, who with a dozen men had defied 500 fascists outside the station at Sarzana,[1] was hunted like a ' bolshevist ' from town to town. He was recognized in Spezia, chased through the streets, and forced to leave the town in haste to escape from his attackers. On February 17, 1922, there was a fascist demonstration in Prato (Tuscany) ; the state forces blocked the road and prevented the column from passing. ' Next day,' Chiurco tells us, ' the *fascio* ordered all factories and concerns to remain closed until the anti-fascist police commissioner was dismissed.' A deputation approached the prefect, who granted everything that was asked : dismissal of the commissioner, permission to organize a big meeting, punishment of the ' guilty ' Royal Guards. ' When the lock-out had attained its object, the *fascio* ordered its termination.' In April, Balbo organized the occupation of Ferrara to obtain the concession of public works. A crowd of 45,000 unemployed from the province camped in the town for two days. Balbo would not demobilize until the prefect had promised, not only public works, but also the liberation of his friend Baroncini, a squad leader of Bologna, arrested a few weeks previously after countless acts of violence. The prefect gave in.

Towards the end of May, the prefect of Bologna, Signor Mori, issued a decree forbidding the movement of labour from place to place in a certain number of provincial communes, so as to put an end to the innumerable clashes between

[1] Pp. 144-155.

local workers and the blacklegs recruited and escorted by the fascists. On the 27th, the fascist directory in Bologna resigned in protest, resigning its powers to a committee of action. There followed fascist demonstrations in front of the prefecture, demanding the dismissal of the prefect, and the wrecking of the *Ente Autonomo dei Consumi*, the headquarters of the municipal provision stores, and the offices of the provincial Federation of Agricultural Labourers. The general secretariat of the Fascist Party published on the 29th the following order :

' GENERAL MOBILIZATION OF ALL BOLOGNESE FASCISTS

' The struggle in the province of Bologna is becoming intensified. The local political authorities, in league with the anti-national parties, are trying to destroy the political and economic organization of fascism. From now on the powers and functions of the Directories of all the *fasci* of the province of Bologna are handed over to the committees of action. All the Bolognese *fasci* are mobilized.

' The undersigned, in his capacity of secretary-general of the National Fascist Party, is transferring to Bologna until the end of the struggle.

' *Signed :* MICHELE BIANCHI.'

Why did the prefect's decrees give rise to such alarm ? Because, if the fascists were debarred from moving about freely from place to place and making use of unemployed workers from other localities, and even other provinces, to crush the resistance of local workers, the free syndical organizations could continue to function. The fascists had to be able to manœuvre the army of unemployed as they did the fighting squads, so as to crush ' red ' organizations and starve the workers who still upheld them into giving way. As soon as a body of ' fascist ' unemployed shepherded by a squad arrived in a district, the local landowners could ignore the syndical employment bureau and tear up the labour contract without fear of a strike, since the unemployed, brought to the district by armed fascists, were there to replace the local workers. Fascists and landowners were determined not to give up this terrible weapon, and that is why Bologna was occupied for five days by tens of thousands of fascists from every province of Emilia, who refused to leave the town until Mori was dismissed. The government did not yield immediately, and Mussolini ordered demobilization, fearing an incident which might force the government to interfere and also the possibility of public opinion turning hostile. But soon afterwards Mori was removed to Bari in Apulia, where the fascists prepared another hostile demonstration, announcing that they did not want 'this gift '.

The great gatherings in Ferrara and Bologna, the first to involve tens of thousands of fascists, were important in other ways. They sustained the fighting spirit of the fascists, which had little outlet locally : ' The fascists need to be inspired,' explains Signor Balbo, ' their fighting spirit must be kept at a high pitch. This is the responsibility of their leader. There will be trouble if they are left to themselves.' In addition, such manœuvres were invaluable training for operations on a larger scale.

' As far as immediate objectives were concerned,' wrote Balbo, who had directed the entire expedition, ' the Bologna affair was not of great importance. But it has demonstrated the mobility of the squads. They have left their homes and fought for political objectives quite outside the scope of their purely rural mentality. They have obeyed unknown leaders, have formed a flying column, have stood on the defensive for several days without complaint, have slept on straw and lived off tinned food. This means that the Bologna episode, which I regard as a sort of grand manœuvre of the fascists of Emilia, can be repeated on a larger scale in a revolt against the established powers. A dress rehearsal for revolution. If the manœuvre calls for the rapid transport of battalions from the north to the centre,[1] we can be certain that the squads will march, disciplined and enthusiastic, under any conditions. We must begin our work again, recruit more units. During the five days of the Bologna action 60,000 fascists were mobilized.'

[1] Rome.

In the Italian penal code there were clauses forbidding armed assemblies and punishing the formation of armed companies.[1] The Facta government made no more effort to apply them than had the Bonomi government which it succeeded. Decrees of dissolution were very rare, and were imposed only when the scum of the population, lavishly distributed among the *fasci*, and particularly in the fighting squads, got out of hand and threatened to compromise fascism and its allies too greatly. The following, for example, were the grounds for a decree of dissolution issued by the prefect of Venice against the squad of the ' Knights of Death ' in June 1922 :

'. . . The Association of the Knights of Death in the town and province of Venice largely consists of elements which, in view of their penal and political antecedents, must be adjudged dangerous to public order ; . . . the said Association, while affecting patriotic and humanitarian aims, actually directs its activities to personal ends and for unlawful profit, for it carries out unjustified and illegal reprisals ; imposes on traders, business men and private citizens levies which are fixed by the leaders of the Association themselves ; settles disputes of a private character by illegitimate means and through intimidation of the public by the arrogant bearing of its members ; seizes houses against the will and the interest of those who have the right to dispose of them ; aids arrested persons to escape ; forces citizens to submit to the violation of their rights of assembly and circulation ; imposes lock-outs and the closing of shops, the removal of badges and emblems and the flying or lowering of flags. . . .'

Similar crimes and worse could be imputed to all the *fasci ;* but they were allowed to carry on their illegal and even criminal activities quite openly, without being disturbed and without any legal sanction being invoked against them.

Nevertheless, in spite of this unending and widespread violence, and partly because of it, Italian public opinion was turning away from fascism. Mussolini referred to this

[1] P. 169.

fact again at the National Council in April 1922, and took advantage of it to impose his policy :

> ' Our position is not startlingly good. The aura of sympathy which surrounded us in 1921 has vanished. We are opposed by *Popolari*, republicans, communists, socialists, and democrats. We have got to keep up an armed organization, while preventing the *squadristi* elements from becoming so strong that they can impose their will on the political elements in control of fascism. We must not even exclude the possibility of the fascists co-operating with the powers of the state. We must assert that the fascists will not hesitate to lend their men to the government to-morrow, if the higher aims of the state demand it.'

In his speech Mussolini did not reject the possibility of a *coup d'état* and a march on Rome, but he emphasized his preference for a governmental coalition. The problem for him, as for every real tactician, was that of time, and conditions, as he pointed out, were not too favourable. To go on fighting indefinitely against the reds, while remaining outside the government, might become dangerous. What he feared was that a sudden change in the situation might force him to choose between collaboration and insurrection, at a moment when he was not free to make the choice. His constant fear was of being ' too early ' or ' too late '. He kept a close watch on daily events, always on the look out for a fresh enemy to fight or a possible ally to be gained.

By the middle of 1922 Mussolini was no longer enjoying the complete freedom of movement he always liked to possess. Fascist development since 1919 had got rather out of hand. Mussolini, who had simultaneously led and followed the movement, found himself well to the right, although reactionary forces and interests openly prevailed throughout the movement. The ' bolshevist ' danger had been crushed long since, and the masses were on the defensive, their leaders scattered, incompetent or powerless. Fascism took root precisely when it had no further excuse for existence, at any rate as a reaction against working-class and socialist ' excesses ', and had turned into reaction pure and simple.

This was most obvious in the Po valley, where socialism had been at its strongest a few months earlier, and where it had changed even the physical appearance of the country-side and its inhabitants, transforming the workers in a few decades from diseased medieval serfs into members of 'leagues' and co-operatives. So far from saving socialism, this historic feat was the main cause of the implacable war of revenge waged on it by the landowners. In this district fascism counted its greatest military, political, and syndical strength. 'As early as 1921,' writes Balbo, 'the great quadrilateral between Ferrara, Mantua, Bologna and Modena formed the arena of our collective action on a large scale. . . . Emilia provides Italian fascism's greatest reserve of man-power.'

The character of fascist action in this district determined the orientation of fascism generally. Agrarian attacks on labour contracts went hand in hand with fascist attacks on socialist organizations. This explains the syndical disputes which went on during the first half of 1922, during the months when fascist policy was becoming openly reactionary. In March the fascist 'corporations' in the provinces of Piacenza and Milan, and in April those of Parma concluded a new labour contract with the Agrarian Association.

The substance of these contracts was the same every-where. They sometimes retained, on paper, the former wages, or did not cut them down very drastically, but they did away with all the guarantees with which the socialists had hedged in the contracts to ensure their strict application. Wage-earners and farmers were once more individually at the mercy of their employers and landlords. For example, in the Milan provincial contract the rates were liable to be revised every three months, which, in the absence of any organization prepared to defend the workers' interests, left them to treat individually with their employers, who could easily impose their own conditions. Any collective character of the labour contract was suppressed by Article 26, which allowed 'the parties to add to the contract special or individual clauses which were to be written by hand on the copy signed by the organizations', stipulating that 'these clauses were not to

be subject to the jurisdiction of the responsible organizations, nor to that of the Commissions of Arbitration set up
by the general agricultural pact'. The collective labour
contract itself was rendered practically worthless by the
clause relating to the free employment of labour, which
eliminated all the old syndical employment offices, and
which, in the Po valley where unemployment was chronic,
gave the landowner power of life and death over the workers.

In the province of Brescia the Agrarian Association had
renewed the old labour contract with the red organizations,
but directly the fascist offensive reached the province and
began breaking up the workers' syndicates and forcing
socialist municipal councils to resign, the more energetic
members wanted to get out of the contract they had just
signed. With this object in view they left their Association
and formed a fascist Landlords' Syndicate, chiefly recruited
from the provinces already occupied by fascism. The new
syndicate signed an agreement with the Provincial Federation of the Fascist Party. The latter agreed to force the
destruction of the old labour contract, on condition that the
landowners dealt only with the fascist organization, refused
to recognize the employment offices of the red syndicates
and applied the new contract only to workers who belonged
to or were willing to join the fascist syndicate.

The red organizations declared a general strike against the
violation of the contract already in force. But, according to
the *Popolo d'Italia* of June 23, once the agreement between
fascists and landowners had been signed ' the struggle has
begun, and the enemy are alarmed to see streaming into the
southern end of the province hundreds of workers generously
provided by Lomellina, Venetia, and the provinces of
Cremona and Mantua, while the valiant blackshirts from
these provinces and from Brescia break down the bolshevik's
attempts at resistance '. For, in the Italy of 1922, to defend
a contract signed a few weeks earlier and to defend the
dignity of labour, was considered ' bolshevism '. ' The
masses were infuriated ' against the strike-breakers, but how
were they to fight simultaneously against squads armed to
the teeth, against an invasion of unemployed who, like
locusts, destroyed anything left alive of the old organiza-

tions, and against the police, who were there to protect the 'freedom of labour'? After a few days' struggle the 'leagues' gave way and hoisted the fascist flag on such of their houses as remained standing.

The same thing was happening in the province of Pavia, in the rice country. At the season of the *monda* (weeding the rice-fields) there was for a few weeks a shortage of labour, and *mondine* (for the work was done by women) had to be imported from other provinces. These provinces were now under fascist control, and consequently the fascists and landowners of Lomellina were able to organize the *monda* in such a way as to crush the local red organizations, whose members were not engaged but were replaced by *mondine* escorted by fascist squads. Here and there resistance was attempted, but the local squads, assisted by others from outside, occupied the district, destroyed what was left of leagues and co-operatives and firmly installed the dictatorship of the landlord. Sometimes the fascists did not even have to break strikes, but were able to take preventive action. For example, at the end of June, while the syndical organizations of the province of Vicenza were discussing the renewal of the labour contract with the Agrarian Association, the Vicenza *fascio* announced that 'without concerning themselves with the question at issue', they would 'use every means to resist a strike'. Thus the workers saw themselves deprived in advance of their only weapon, and since the landlords were inflexible their fate was certain.

Another typical situation was that of Cremona, where the *coloni* (small farmers) were organized in moderately left-wing catholic syndicates. It was in this province that an agreement was drawn up between *Popolari* and socialists, in April 1922, for the defence of syndical and municipal liberties.[1] In June 1921, after a bitter struggle in which the workers actually seized *cascine* (farms), the landlords were forced to agree to the drawing up by a committee of arbitration of an agreement involving 'the introduction of a profit-sharing contract and the responsible control of agricultural enterprise' by the workers concerned. In August the committee announced its decisions in a report

[1] P. 177

entitled *lodo Bianchi*, after its chairman, a professor who held an ' itinerant chair of agriculture ', a first-class technical expert. It recommended the creation of ' an agricultural administrative body based on the participation of the workers in the results of enterprise, collective participation with accounts to be settled yearly and at the end of the lease ' (R. Bachi. *L'Italia Economica nel* 1921). Immediately on publication ' this scheme of organization was recognized as technically efficient, and was praised by experts '. The principles were fundamentally the same as those of the *Popolari :* a share in profits for the workers, and the conversion of wage-earners into small-holders,[1] a policy which the fascists had revived in their 1919 programme and which aimed at the ' abolition of the wage-earner '. There was nothing ' bolshevik ' about it, since such principles were diametrically opposite to the ' proletarianization ' and ' socialization ' aimed at by the socialists. But the landowners of the province of Cremona went to law to evade the findings of the committee of arbitration, and when their action failed they simply refused, in January 1922, to abide by them. At this point 80 per cent of them combined in a fascist syndicate, as a prelude to the open attack that they were planning against the *lodo Bianchi*. ' The landowners,' Chiurco says, ' banded round the deputy Farinacci and fascism, rejected arbitration.' The fascists of the province went into a state of permanent mobilization ; the government gave way, and in May the prefect authorized a new committee to draw up another contract. The findings of the first commission and the decisions of the magistrates having been allowed to lapse, the new contract was imposed by law, and the landowners let themselves be bound by their signatures the moment they had a satisfactory verdict. The *lodo Bianchi* was thus safely buried.

The joint advance of fascism and ' agrarian slavery ' went

---

[1] At the end of June the fascist Federation of the province of Modena passed a resolution against a bill dealing with agricultural contracts sponsored by the *Popolare* deputy, Bertini. This bill aimed at establishing a term of three years for *mezzadria* contracts, introducing the notion of ' just cause ' for the cancellation of contracts, and creating special arbitration machinery for the settlement of collective labour disputes. It was not the fascist ' syndicates ' in this case so much as the political organization of the *fasci* which opposed all legal intervention for the reform of agricultural contracts.

beyond the purely syndical sphere. In the same province of Cremona the landowners had, in May 1921, got their own representative, Giannino Ferrari, elected on the national coalition list, and he had joined the agrarian group in the Chamber. But, by the beginning of 1922, the Provincial Federation of Employers' Syndicates, formed under the ægis of fascism, was dissatisfied with him, because, 'although a direct representative of the landowners, he always, in this very serious situation, adopted a passive attitude', and in the same resolution the Federation reminded ' the agrarian associations throughout Italy that the name of Cremona ought to be the signal for a great national movement to prevent liberal governments, by their foolish and untimely actions, from artificially reviving subversive organizations which are at the point of death '. The landowners wanted no state interference between themselves and the workers' organizations, and no ' legal ' obstacles put in the way of the attack that they were determined to carry through to the end.

So it was that the different elements to be found in fascism in 1919–20, although they did not totally disappear, became gradually absorbed in a more consistent movement, which by 1921, and particularly by the first half of 1922, could be defined as essentially ' a *bourgeois* assault on reformist socialism in municipalities, collective labour contracts, employment offices and co-operatives, and particularly against agrarian reformism—an assault led by the landed proprietors of the Po valley, Tuscany and Apulia '.

For this reason Mussolini, though he had not committed himself to any one policy to the exclusion of another, and though he admitted that fascism had lost many sympathizers,[1] was pinning his hopes more and more on a coalition government in which the socialists would have no share. The socialists were entirely paralysed by internal difficulties. At the time of the Bonomi crisis in February 1922 the party executive had in a lucid interval authorized the parliamentary group to act as the situation demanded, but it immediately took fright at its own daring and revoked this order in March. On one side—the right wing of the

[1] P. 194.

party and the General Confederation of Labour, under pressure from representatives of the districts occupied by the fascists—a less short-sighted and fatalistic policy was demanded, and on the other—the left wing—a group of third-internationalists was formed, who largely adopted the point of view of the communists. Under fire from these two quarters the executive stuck more and more uncompromisingly to such formulæ as justified it in maintaining its eternal passivity. The difference between the party executive and the parliamentary group came to a head suddenly. On June 1 the socialist deputies passed a resolution proposed by Zirardini, deputy for Ferrara, in favour of supporting ' a ministry that should guarantee the restoration of peace and freedom '. The executive, meeting on the same day, disavowed the resolution and summoned the National Council[1] to crush this sedition. The Council met in Rome on June 10–14, in the presence of the leaders of the General Confederation of Labour. After a completely vague discussion and the failure of four or five resolutions they finally approved by 13 votes to 6 (with 5 abstentions) a motion proposed by Serrati, the editor of the *Avanti*, condemning ' collaboration, whether direct or indirect ', that is to say, not only collaboration and support, but even abstention from voting, whatever the government in power ; deploring the attitude of the parliamentary group and reminding the Confederation of the respect it owed to its treaty of alliance with the party. This pact, signed on September 27, 1918, left the responsibility for political action to the party executive, which, although it had not been at all anxious at the time of the factory occupations in September 1920 to take advantage of this provision and ' make revolution ', now remembered it in time to prevent the socialist deputies and the General Confederation of Labour from having any freedom of action in the parliamentary crisis.

Serrati, it must be admitted, had hesitated. The night before the meeting he revealed his doubts to a friend, but to rid himself of them he decided in favour of an absolutely uncompromising attitude. To agree with the argument of

[1] Formed of delegates from the provincial Federations, not to be confused with the party executive.

the parliamentary group meant admitting that he had been badly mistaken right up to the present, and exposing himself to the taunts of the communists who were preparing to fall upon the ' traitors '. The communists asked for nothing better than that the socialists should definitely commit themselves, hoping thus to discredit them in the eyes of the masses, while benefiting from their rise to power. But the decision of the National Council destroyed any possibility of successful parliamentary action in support of public liberties. The parliamentary group rebelled, and appointed a new executive. This completed the split between socialists and maximalists, while at the same time the importance of an accession of socialist votes to a new government was reduced to a minimum. The ' collaborationists ' could only reckon 60 votes out of the 145 socialist and communist deputies. The new parliamentary weapon was destroyed as soon as it was drawn by this now unavoidable schism. Besides, as time went on, and the fascist squads continued their occupation of the country, socialist collaboration began to lose its value. A year earlier mere abstention from voting on the part of the socialists would have reversed the situation, driven the fascists into political isolation and prevented them from surviving the crisis of the second half of 1921. In February 1922 abstention was no longer enough, and socialist support would have been necessary to any government arising out of the Bonomi crisis if it wanted to instil a respect for law and order into the fascists. By the middle of 1922 neither abstention nor support would have been enough, only collaboration. This, too, was rapidly losing its value, as Mussolini noticed when commenting on the socialist National Council in June : ' In the meantime plenty of water is flowing under the bridges of the Tiber, and it is probable that the collaboration offered by the collaborationists will soon have so diminished in value that they will not be able to find a dog to collaborate with them.'

On June 16 the Fascist Party executive and parliamentary group both declared themselves opposed to any socialist participation in government, which would be ' an obstacle to the economic reconstruction of the country ' ; decided that ' other parties lending themselves in any way to such an experiment made themselves responsible for treason against the country's interests ' ; and reserved for themselves ' the right to take action accordingly '. In other words, they threatened to extend their hostilities to any parties that accepted socialist collaboration, which nearly everyone had sought in 1919–20, and which had been solicited by Mussolini himself a year earlier.

Other parties and groups besides Mussolini began to show a lack of enthusiasm for socialist collaboration, which in view of the general situation seemed more and more doubtful. The *Popolari*, whose secretary, Don Sturzo, had always been fundamentally opposed to an agreement with the socialists, had extracted a promise from Signor Facta that the three bills in which they were particularly interested, concerning the state examination, the agricultural contracts (Bertini's bill), and the *latifundia* should be considered by the Chamber before the recess, and they were anxious to avoid any ministerial crisis. The democratic parliamentary group, which was formed in the autumn of 1921, caused the fall of the Bonomi ministry, and should have been one of the mainstays of a left coalition, was broken up again in May. The implacable rivalry between Nitti and Giolitti, and the fascist sympathies of various followers of this group acted as a disruptive force. The two resumed their freedom of manœuvre, each one hoping to bring about, to the exclusion of the other, a great national coalition, in which the fascists would take part, just as earlier each had hoped to gain the upper hand by bringing the socialists into the government. Giolitti now felt that he could no longer rely on the socialists. In a conversation with them he made it clear that he would not be content with a sleeping partner, but would insist on their sharing all the responsibilities of government. Considering the internal state of their party, the socialists were less than ever capable of making any such agreement. Thus the possibility of collaboration seemed very far removed. But the events of the middle of July 1922 brought it again to the fore.

The fascists of the Po valley had undertaken the conquest of the towns and districts which still resisted them.

'Fascism,' explained the communist Bordiga in a report to Moscow, a month later, after the march on Rome, 'has collected all ex-servicemen who could not fit into post-war society and has taken advantage of their military experience. . . . It has attained a dominant position in Italian politics by what may be called territorial methods, which may be followed on a map. Starting from Bologna fascism has advanced in two main directions, on one side towards the north-western industrial district, Milan, Turin, Genoa ; on the other towards Tuscany and central Italy, so as to encircle and threaten the capital.'

On July 15 the *Popolo d'Italia* came out with an enormous headline across the front page : ' Imminent collapse of last strongholds of P.U.S. Congratulations to the fascists of Cremona, Rimini, Andria, Viterbo, Sestri Ponente. Fascist mobilization at Novara.' What was happening ? Mussolini himself explained in the editorial :

' Italian fascism is at present engaged in fighting several decisive battles to effect local clean-ups. According to the latest news fascists have managed to force their way into Rimini and gained control of it. This is the turning-point. With Rimini we hold the key position which gives us a hold on Emilia and the Romagna, and a passage to the neighbouring Marches. Active fascist advance guards at Pesaro, Fermo, Pergola, and Jesi are seeing to it that the Marches will not long resist our fateful advance. At Andria our militia is victorious, and the reversal of the situation in this town is of extreme importance to our campaign in Apulia. The Bari *fascio* must make up its mind to get a grip of the situation there. In Latium the last few days have seen the Viterbo affair and the fascist concentration that followed it. The time has come to show all friends of Italy that the fascist forces in Latium are very numerous ; each little township in this vast district has its *fascio*, and the whole movement is drawing strength from the fresh vitality with which the Rome *fascio* seems to be endowed. Further north we find the forces of fascism engaged in Liguria. There is nothing to worry about there. Sestri Ponente (where the socialist council has resigned) will never be won back by the reds ; neither will the vile socialist-masonic-*popolare* coalition succeed in winning back Cremona. At Novara, too, we are triumphant. One has only to read our adversaries' newspapers to see that the greatest confusion reigns in the enemy camp. One calls for help from the government, another threatens a general strike, another encourages individual crime, some recommend patience. . . . No orders, no plan. . . . They continue to call us bandits, scum, barbarians, slave-drivers, brigands, corrupt. A lot we care. You are printing useless insults, gentlemen. Our retort, political and syndical, is to break your bones : surgery, ruthlessly applied.'

This sort of talk, making due allowance for the element of blackmail it contained, gives a savage but veracious picture of the situation. However, the *Popolari* were somewhat perturbed by events in Cremona, and parliament with them. On July 12 the prefectorial commissioner and the police chief were discharged, because they had sided too shamelessly with the fascists. The executive of the *fascio* immediately replied by delegating its powers, as usual, to a secret committee of action, which organized a big meeting of protest the same evening. Here it was decided to shut every office, shop, and bank until the government withdrew the measures it had taken. There was a big demonstration before the army headquarters ; fascist squads began to arrive from the surrounding country, and the town was occupied. During the following afternoon, the Chamber of Labour, the offices of the socialist paper, a communist press, several co-operative societies, and the flat of a *Popolare* deputy were ransacked and burnt. Later, they forced the police cordon that guarded the prefecture and broke into it.

When the news reached the Chamber the government was savagely attacked. Mussolini feared that his friends might suffer, and ordered the immediate evacuation of Cremona. But nothing could stop a further cabinet crisis. The *Popolari* announced their willingness to ' shoulder their responsibility ' and form a more energetic government. This time Giolitti's friends did not respond, for Giolitti preferred to leave Facta, his lieutenant, whom he believed to be loyal, to keep his place until the autumn, when directly after the recess he meant to return to power. But the crisis occurred and Mussolini stepped in to prevent all his plans from being wrecked. The right wing had decided to vote for the Facta ministry, and the fascists were preparing to follow their example, when Mussolini hastily prevented them. The old danger, which he had believed to be over, was revived, and in spite of all he knew about the chaos inside the party, he feared that socialist collaboration might come to pass after all. What particularly annoyed him was the attitude of certain ' democratic ' groups, Nitti's followers for example, who held that a left ministry need not necessarily be a ministry committed to take legal reprisals against the fascists. This might attract the *Popolari* to the coalition and any others who were unwilling to declare openly their fundamental opposition to fascism. Mussolini was not taken in by this : the new cabinet would be further to the left than the Facta one, and would be all the more dangerous in that it would revive the pacification programme which he, Mussolini, had repudiated. Besides, even if the new government did not wish to be anti-fascist, it might be forced to take action against the squads, now more lawless than ever, and in any case could no longer assure them state aid ; without this, as Mussolini saw clearly, their final victory was impossible.

To get out of the difficulty he broke abruptly with the right wing. His reasons were not political ; in fact his opinions and wishes were more right-wing than ever. On the very day of the Cremona affair he wrote in the *Popolo d'Italia :*

' Four months after the Genoa conference European society displays a very pronounced right-wing—anti-socialist and anti-democratic—orientation. Having kept a close watch on this process of reaction, we have been able fundamentally to revise the historical and theoretical outlook of fascism, and fascism has gradually been stripped of its earlier trappings which might have made it appear a left-wing movement or something like it. To return to its origins,[1] as some would like, that is to go

[1] But see the article of July 27, 1921, where Mussolini himself called for a return to first principles (p. 147).

back to the 1919 programme which has already borne poisonous fruit, would be childishness, or senility. Fascism is and must be the organized expression of this tendency of contemporary feeling, this classical revival of life against all subversive theories and peoples. While Europe and the whole world are moving to the right, there are in Italy a few clowns in the Montecitorio theatre, who dream like half-wits of left-wing solutions. It is time for Italy too to move to the right. Let us have done with left-wing policy.'

Why then did Mussolini desert the right, to vote with the left against the Facta government? The answer is that he was repeating his manœuvre at the time of the Giolitti crisis in June 1921, and the Bonomi crisis in February 1922. If the fascists voted for the Facta government, it would still be in a minority in the Chamber, and, if it fell, would drag the fascists with it. Besides, Facta could be turned out by a left coalition which included *Popolari*, democrats, and socialists, which would be dangerous because it would indicate very clearly how the new government could be formed. Mussolini succeeded in making the fascists vote with their opponents. This alone was no longer sufficient to ward off the danger he had managed to avoid in February 1922 after the Celli motion. This time the *Popolari* were determined, against Don Sturzo's advice, to collaborate with the socialists ; and the syndicalists, whose organizations were being attacked by fascist squads, had made their parliamentary group come to the same decision. The *Popolari* deputies went so far as to demand a more united cabinet, and the exclusion of the right wing *puntarella* which was included in the Facta ministry.

On July 19 their leader, the catholic syndicalist Longinotti, moved on their behalf in the Chamber that ' The Chamber, noting that the efforts of the government have not resulted in the internal pacification that is necessary for economic and financial recovery, proceed to the order of the day '. Turati interposed to say that the socialists were voting against a government, ' which in five months has not punished a single offence against the penal code ', and that they supported the motion of the *Popolari*. But the maximalist deputies declared that they would ' not share any of the responsibility for solving the crisis '. This completed the split in the parliamentary socialist group ; and at this crucial point Mussolini declared that the fascists were also going to vote against the government, saying that the proposal for socialist collaboration cut both ways.

' It remains to be seen whether this marvellous collaboration is a mere windbag or a definite contribution to the government of to-morrow. Judging by figures it seems to be a pretty barren affair. There are only 50 socialist deputies ready to vote for a new ministry, even one with an anti-fascist programme. Such a ministry would be opposed not only by the fascists but also by a third socialist party which is bound to emerge at the Rome congress,[1] if the collaborationists go there already pledged to its support. Frankly it is to our advantage that socialism should split further into three or thirty mutually hostile sects. It is to our advantage to encourage these divisions which help us to exterminate the party.'

Mussolini did not object to the presence of the socialists in the new government, but accepted and tried to make his friends accept the possibility, regarding it simply as an opportunity for annihilating the socialist movement. What he wanted once more to prevent was a socialist-democratic-*popolare* coalition from which the fascists would be excluded. He finished his speech by offering the Chamber the alternatives of fascist participation in national life through ' legal conquest and saturation ', or armed revolt against ' anti-fascist reaction '.

The immense confusion of passions and motives which formed the essence of the Italian situation and which, even to-day, is hard to straighten out, underwent an extraordinary simplification in the mind of Mussolini, while it simply befogged his opponents. The latter, too timid to pursue boldly either their ambitions or their ideals, groped about encumbered by outworn beliefs and plans. Mussolini

---

[1] The Socialist Party executive had summoned an extraordinary national congress to be held in Rome on August 6 to 8.

outstripped them because, besides keeping a sharp look-out for anything likely to affect the disposition of political forces in the country, he could see further ahead. He wanted to attain power quickly and by any possible means, so as to direct Italy's foreign policy.[1] This alone could satisfy his ambition and round off the adventure which began with his break with the socialists in October 1914. A few days before the cabinet crisis broke out he delivered a violent attack, in the *Popolo d'Italia* of July 8, on Schanzer, the foreign minister in the Facta cabinet, who had just returned from London where he had been negotiating with the British government over the compensations promised to Italy by the April 1915 agreement. Once more Mussolini expounded his own foreign policy, which was to be followed by his own government after the march on Rome.

' What does Signor Schanzer's visit to London really amount to ? Setting aside the bombastic humbug about " European reconstruction ", have Italy and England really any interests in common ? Is there any identity of European interests with regard to Germany and Russia ? In appearance, yes ; in reality, no. This habitual anglo-phile policy is doing us harm throughout the entire Near East. It is alienating the sympathies of Islam. It is logical for London to try and maintain the *status quo*. London has arrived. She lives on her income. What she cannot stomach she rejects. The English are a *bourgeois* nation, we are a proletarian one. . . . We distrust Signor Schanzer's policy, we distrust his reconstructionist mentality. He is still infected with Wilsonism. He is too much of a European to remember that it is the duty of an Italian foreign minister to be Italian.'

Mussolini was eager to get power, because he wanted to make Italy play her part, that is to say to play Italy's part himself, in the concert of Europe. The old figure-heads beyond the frontier, the overfed and drowsy nations would meet the same fate as the old politicians and parties inside Italy, who were befogged by their scruples and humanitarian dreams and paralysed by their inability to put them into

[1] P. 133.

practice. This was a further reason for his not wanting the socialists in the government, except as prisoners. Internal pacification for him meant simply an effective background for a bold foreign policy, expansionist and aggressive. If the Socialist Party continued as a force they could prevent its being carried out ; therefore they must be relentlessly exterminated.

The socialist movement was doing its best to facilitate this task. On July 17 the new executive of the parliamentary group, which included Turati, Treves, Matteotti, Modigliani, D'Aragona, and Baldesi, passed a resolution appealing to the workers to support the action of the group, which aimed at ' the freedom of syndical organizations, the solution of the economic crisis with the least possible injury to the proletariat, and the pacification of Europe '. They were opposed by the maximalist ' parliamentary committee ', which was ' opposed to any programme which involved collaboration and joining a ministry ', and the party executive, which called for a declaration of allegiance from all deputies, allowing them four days to reply to this ultimatum. The communists were delighted, for, they said : ' The fall of the Socialist Party is raising the Communist Party to the leadership of the Italian working class and its revolutionary struggle.' As a matter of fact they were beginning to feel rather anxious. After the fascist occupation of Novara, with its direct threat to the Milan, Genoa, Turin triangle, the communists of Turin felt themselves cut off and surrounded. With the idea of saving what they could from the wreck of the situation, they made overtures to the left wing of the *Popolari* and even to the liberal group centres round the *Stampa*, edited by the senator Frassati, a great friend of Giolitti. After the first contacts had been made a delegation, consisting of a representative from the communist section and one from the Chamber of Labour, went to Rome to report on the situation as it appeared in Turin and to ask the Communist Party to take definite action, or at any rate to authorize the formation of a common front with the socialists and other anti-fascist groups. The delegates were coldly received in Rome by the party secretariat and sent home, having gained nothing but abuse.

The Communist International had appealed some time ago for a ' united front ' on the following grounds :

' We thought we should be able to wrest the support of the masses from the socialists by sheer propaganda and by opposing their organization with ours. It must be admitted, though, that the socialist movement dies hard and that our methods have proved ineffectual. They must be changed. The socialists are still our worst enemies, but we must pester them with proposals for a " united front " and in that way set the masses against them and against their leaders.'

The Communist Party executive in Italy refused to apply these tactics. While their objective was the destruction of socialist equipment and organization, the Italian communists chose to exterminate the enemy by frontal attack. Moscow preferred encircling movements. In this dispute the fate of the Italian working class and of the Italian people meant nothing. Russia looked on the workers, the Socialist Party and even the Communist Party as mere instruments for the working out of a plan whose trustee she was by historic right, after the victory of October 1917. A good deal of theorizing was done in Moscow, but the distinction between communist principles and fascist lack of them, and the antagonism of the social forces they stood for, were all one to the Italian working class. The plans that were made for them, whether to raise them to power or to depress them for ever, were drawn up without reference to them, and depended on other plans, beyond their control or even their comprehension. From the human and personal point of view it was just as impossible for Zinoviev to act contrary to his immediate interests and taste for power, as for Mussolini to escape the devouring fire of his ambition.

The cabinet crisis had begun with the fall of the Facta ministry, outvoted by 288 to 103 votes, and had become increasingly serious. Mussolini had taken steps to ensure his being in a winning or at least a strong position. He had sounded Nitti some time ago about the formation of a great united national cabinet, asking for himself a minister's portfolio and under-secretaryships for two of his friends,

' for party reasons, and to avoid giving the impression that he had carried out a purely personal operation '. The intermediary between Mussolini and Nitti was General Capello, an important dignitary of the Palazzo Giustiniani freemasons, voted president of honour by the Fascist Congress of Rome. He was later condemned to thirty years' imprisonment by the special tribunal for his alleged complicity in the attempted murder of the Duce by Colonel Zaniboni in November 1925. Without mentioning Mussolini's proposals, Nitti sounded the *Popolari* and the socialists, but did not succeed in making them accept his scheme. Mussolini's other hope was Orlando, to whom he had suggested a coalition ministry, to include the fascists and the representatives of the General Confederation of Labour.

One after the other Orlando, Bonomi, De Nava, Orlando again, and De Nicola tried unsuccessfully to form a government. The *Popolari* maintained their twofold ban on Giolitti and the right. The socialists went so far as to promise support, but refused participation. And right in the middle of the crisis, on the 25th, the press came out with a letter from Giolitti, who declared himself opposed to the pact between *Popolari* and socialists, the reason being that he wanted to avoid important changes until November, when he proposed to take office again himself. In this letter he criticized the ' unjustified impatience ' of those who had provoked the crisis, and attacked them roundly. ' What good can a Don Sturzo-Treves-Turati coalition do the country ? ' he asked, giving vent to all the bitterness he retained from his set-back of May 1921.

In face of all these difficulties and complications which threatened to prolong the crisis indefinitely, the socialist group decided, on the morning of the 28th, to take a step forward, and announced that they ' would not shrink from any action that could compel respect from those who owed it to the clearly expressed desire of the National Assembly for freedom and the right of organization ' ; in other words, they would not shrink even from participation in the government. But the *Popolari*, although they did not want the right wing included in the new government, were alarmed by the increasing seriousness of the situation and the prolonging of the crisis, and now accepted the *puntarella*. Once again the socialists had come too late. A week earlier, and their decision might have led to a ministry of the left, but they had stopped at giving only their support ; now that they were ready for participation, the *Popolari* deserted them and turned to the right. Next day (July 29) Turati, summoned to the Quirinal by the king, was all in favour of forming a ' centre ' government, excluding the right wing and the socialists, although the latter promised their support.

Turati received the impression that the king ' either does not know what he wants or is not saying anything ', and he made a point of describing the completely abnormal state of the country. The king only broke silence to hint that ' a constitutional king cannot do very much. . . .' The communist press was exultant and made clear what its attitude would be if the socialists joined the government : ' Turati has gone to see the king,' it announced ; ' the socialist movement is breaking up. This means one dead weight less to drag along in future.'

Events in the country encouraged and then annihilated the intentions and hopes aroused in parliamentary circles by the open crisis that followed the fascist occupation of Cremona. Fascist expeditions and outrages in Novara, Magenta, Macerata, Ancona, were followed by general strikes in Piedmont, Lombardy, and the Marches. The local organizations called on the Labour Alliance to announce a general strike of protest throughout Italy. The Alliance hesitated, allowed the local strikes to fizzle out, and promised to launch an attack at the first opportunity. Events in Ravenna provided this opportunity. Italo Balbo, who had already organized an expedition to this town in September 1921,[1] set out again, this time with the intention of ' exterminating ' the enemy. During the 26th and 27th a general strike was begun by one side, and mobilization by the other. Balbo arrived with his squads, forced the gate of the town and began his work of destruction. A few extracts from his *Diary* show the methods used and the objects gained.

[1] Pp. 121–122.

July 28, Ravenna.

' Last night the squads began the destruction of the vast premises of the Provincial Federation of Socialist Co-operative Societies. . . . As usual the fascist action was quite unexpected. The old palace, once the dwelling-place of Byron, was completely destroyed.[1] The fascists only do this kind of thing when they are driven by absolute political necessity. There are no half-measures in civil warfare. The supreme aim is to ensure the safety of our country. We carried out this exploit in the same spirit in which we used to destroy enemy depots during the war. During the night the burning of this huge building lit up the whole town with a lurid glare. We, too, must strike terror into the hearts of our enemies.'

July 30, Ravenna.

' I went to the chief of police, leaving Dino Grandi in command of the thousands of fascists who had collected in the suburb of San Roch. I announced that I would set fire to and destroy the houses of all the socialists in Ravenna, if within half an hour he did not place at my disposal the necessary means for getting the fascists away. It was a dramatic moment. I demanded an entire fleet of lorries. His officials completely lost their heads ; but half an hour later they showed me where I could find lorries, ready filled with petrol. Some of them actually belonged to the Chief's office. My ostensible reason was to get the unruly fascists out of the town, but in reality I was organizing a " column of fire " (as the enemy have described it) to increase our power of reprisal in the province. I took my place with Baroncini, Caretti of Ferrara and young Rambelli of Ravenna in a car at the head of the long column of lorries, and we set out. This journey began yesterday morning, the 29th, at 11 o'clock, and finished this morning the 30th. Nearly twenty-four hours of driving, during which no one rested for a moment or touched food. We went through Rimini, Sant'

---

[1] The Federation, which had bought this historic palace, was presided over by Nullo Baldini and united ninety-two co-operatives, possessed 6000 hectares of land and rented almost as much again.

Arcangelo, Savignano, Cesena, Bertinoro, all the centres and towns between the provinces of Forti and Ravenna, and destroyed all red buildings, and offices of socialist and communist organizations. It has been a terrible night. Our passage was marked by high columns of fire and smoke.'

As a result of these events, the general councils of the two Chambers of Labour at Rome (socialist and anarchist) met on the evening of July 28 and invited the central committee of the Labour Alliance to proceed ' immediately to a national general strike, while warning the central committee that if it hesitates, if it shirks its unavoidable duty, if it does not decide shortly on a general movement, the organs of proletarian defence in Rome will denounce its authority '. A general strike was proclaimed on the evening of July 31—to begin at midnight of that date—by the ' secret committee of action ' of the Labour Alliance, which issued the following appeal :

> ' By proclaiming a general strike the Committee means to defend the political and syndical liberties menaced by the reactionary factions. . . . It is the duty of all lovers of freedom to break, by the strength of their joint resistance, the reactionary attack, thus defending the conquests of democracy and saving the nation from the abyss into which it would be cast by the madness of dictatorship. . . . The government of the country must take a solemn warning from the general strike, so that an end may be made of all violation of civic liberties, which should find their protection and their guarantees in the application of the law. During the general strike the workers must refrain absolutely from committing acts of violence, which would impair the solemnity of the demonstration and would quite certainly be exploited by our enemies ; except only in the case of legitimate defence of persons or institutions, if by mischance enemy violence should be directed against them. Only those orders emanating from responsible organizations are to be carried out. Workers, arise, in defence of civilized man's most sacred possession, freedom ! '

The Rome correspondent of the *Popolo d'Italia* wrote the same day that :

> ' the extremist elements of the party have attempted to make a skilful diversion by imposing practically by force on their more lukewarm comrades the proclamation of a general strike, *which must be considered therefore as a tactical manœuvre against the reformists,* to stir up the masses at a moment when an attempt is being made to divert them from the class struggle '.

The executive of the Fascist Party, on the other hand, said : ' the general strike which is to begin at midnight is cowardly and contemptible, because its object is not to liberate the working classes from fascism but to establish the so-called Left Ministry '. Which of these two versions coming from fascist centres was correct ?

In actual fact the general strike was not called for either of these reasons, but was the direct and inevitable result of the situation created by the Ravenna incident. After the fascist occupation of Novara (July 16), which followed the fascist exploits in Cremona, Rimini, Andria, Viterbo, Sestri Ponente, a general strike was proclaimed all over Piedmont, then Lombardy, and would have reached Liguria as well, had not the ' autonomous ' socialist leaders of Genoa prevented it, thus breaking the pledges they had exchanged with the workers' organizations in Milan and Turin. The general strike infected the Marches, where a small fascist army from neighbouring Umbria had occupied Macerata, Fabriano, and Ancona, the ' red ' town of June 1914 and June 1920.[1] Everywhere the workers' organizations demanded that these protests should be immediately combined in a general strike which would show their desire to have done with fascist terrorism. The Confederation leaders hesitated and did nothing, for the ministerial crisis was in progress and they were afraid of compromising the issue. But pressure from the more militant elements was so strong that the central committee of the Alliance of Labour, while ordering strikes in progress to be broken off, promised to prepare a concerted movement which should be launched

[1] Pp. 1–2 and 68.

at the first opportunity. This was provided a few days later by the serious events in Ravenna. If it is true that the strike was proclaimed on July 31 under pressure from the anarchistic elements in the National Syndicate of Railwaymen—who had founded the Labour Alliance—and that some of them went so far as to threaten with a revolver Azimonti, representing the General Confederation of Labour on the secret committee, this was only possible because all the workers were looking forward to a decision in favour of a general strike. The reformist elements could hardly oppose it since they had themselves just been flirting with the idea of using a general strike as a bargaining weapon in the negotiations for solving the (ministerial) crisis. When the calling of the strike had become inevitable, the majority of the secret committee took care to launch it as a perfectly lawful demonstration, for the defence of legality : ' a " legalitarian " strike ', Turati calls it. The appeal was addressed to ' lovers of freedom ', in the name of ' the defence of political and syndical liberties ' and ' the conquests of democracy ', and called only for the re-establishment of the rule of law. But in spite of its cautious language and intentions, the strike swept away nearly all that remained of the ' political and syndical liberties ' it was supposed to be saving.

Here the drama of the collapse of the Italian working-class and socialist movement reaches its climax. The threat or at any rate the proclamation of this strike ought, according to some, to have brought a left government into power, or, according to others, to have revenged the working class in the class struggle. Actually it disappointed both expectations and brought failure to both projects.

The strike was certainly ' legalitarian ' since its only aim was the re-establishment of civil liberties and the rule of law. But the character of a movement is not confined to its own objects ; the reactions it provokes also form part of it, and end up by transforming it, willy-nilly, at the crucial moment. The reformist leaders had hoped in September 1920 to use the occupation of the factories as a means for compelling the Socialist Party and the workers to form a government. Their methods had had the opposite effect and had alienated the masses, while leaving the *bourgeoisie* resigned and even partly in favour of such an event. Not only was the July strike ten days too late, but it followed on a campaign in which maximalists, communists and anarchists had described it as the ' necessary and sufficient ' means for turning the tables and liquidating fascism, without any help from the state or compromise with non-proletarian forces. The authors of the appeal for the general strike had taken careful precautions in drawing it up to show the connection between the movement they were starting and state action, which they called upon to defend their outraged liberties. But if the working classes and the state were to work for a common end there had to be some sort of connection between them, in fact there had to be collaboration. By calling the strike on July 31, however, the working classes materially severed their connection with the state. Even supposing (quite unjustifiably) that the state had decided to cope with the fascist gangs, it would have been entirely paralysed by the strike in the public services and the railways, while the fascists, with several months' advantage in distributing their forces, could cover a wide area in their columns of lorries. ' A solemn warning to the government of the country ', said the secret committee's manifesto. But neither to those who took part in it nor to those who suffered it did the strike appear merely as a ' warning '. There was practically no government in existence, in consequence of the cabinet crisis which had now lasted a fortnight; besides, the ' warning ' could not be conveyed to the ' government ', for the strike had destroyed all points of contact between the workers and the state. Conceived as a ' demonstration ', it failed in its effect. In Rome the *Popolari*, worried by the length and gravity of the crisis, had decided to agree to the inclusion of right-wing elements in the new government. In the country the catholic syndicates, the same which had won over the *Popolari* to the idea of collaborating with the right-wing socialists, refused to take part in the general strike ; and thus at the critical moment allies were lost whose help in assuring the ' defence of liberty ' was indispensable. The king, who still had Giolitti in mind, broke off all negotiations, and on August 1—the strike having begun at midnight—summoned Facta and once again asked him to form a cabinet. At five o'clock it was re-formed exactly as before, and was to be the last of the parliamentary regime.

In the country the struggle was begun in the most unfavourable conditions. In Piedmont, Lombardy and elsewhere the workers had finished a few days previously a protest strike lasting several weeks. They were rather exhausted and many hesitated or did not come out. In northern Italy, in Genoa and Turin, the order to strike came forty-eight hours early, either through misunderstanding or treachery, and this added to the confusion and depression. The secret committee was so secret that the workers' organizations did not know where to apply for orders. Also the general strike was purely defensive ; the manifesto quoted above allowed fighting ' only in the legitimate defence of persons and institutions ' and on this ground the inferiority of the workers' forces, unprepared and unsupported, was obvious. On the whole, leaving aside any strategic consideration, the course of the movement, which really did have the support of the majority of the workers, showed how much more they were worth than all their leaders put together. As things were at the end of July 1922, the almost universal success of the general strike was an act of faith that, wonderful and moving as it was, was quite fruitless. These men who refused to resign themselves to slavery—railwaymen who were driven back to work at the point of the revolver, while their homes were burnt behind their backs, workers who ever since the war had been striking in support of principle and unity and were doing it once more because they were told it would check the fascist offensive— all these people who were allowed to wear themselves out in misapplied efforts deserved other leaders and a different fate.

The fascists had been expecting a general strike for some time and were preparing their counter-attack, profiting by the delay accorded them after the events of Novara by the hesitation and petty scheming of the socialist and syndical leaders. In fact, on July 31, immediately after these events, the secretariat of the National Fascist Party sent out to its branches a circular which announced : ' According to latest information the attempt at a national general strike is abandoned for the time being. Nevertheless, to save ourselves from being taken by surprise if another attempt is made with the help of the "red" railwaymen, the fascists should at once make sure of having the necessary means for rapid transport : cars, lorries, motor-bicycles. . . .' On July 31 the same secretariat, being well informed, sent out another circular letter, which read as follows :

NATIONAL FASCIST PARTY—ROME
Press Office.
Private circular letter   ROME,
   (to be read and destroyed).   *July* 31, 1922.
      TO THE PROVINCIAL FASCIST FEDERATIONS
   (Please pass on immediately to subsidiary *fasci.*)

It appears that the Labour Alliance means to proclaim to-day, as from midnight, a national general strike, including the state services. If this critical news is confirmed by the facts a manifesto by the Executive of the Fascist Party on this subject will be published in to-morrow's newspapers. The Federations and the *fasci* must fall in with the instructions given in the manifesto. Their more detailed orders are :

(1) To carry out the immediate mobilization of all the fascist forces.

(2) If within forty-eight hours of the proclamation of the strike the government have not succeeded in ending it, the fascists will make it their own duty to do so.

(3) If the strike continues after the forty-eight hours, the fascists will proceed to the provincial capitals and occupy them.

(4) The fascists of the Carrara and Lomellina zones and those of the province of Alessandria must keep some of their forces at the disposal of the fascists of Genoa. Those of the provinces of Bologna and Ferrara must keep some of their forces at the disposal of the *fasci* of Romagna and of the Ancona zone.

(5) To keep watch over the main road junctions.

(6) The fascists must only obey orders issuing from

responsible persons and organizations : the Party Executive, and Provincial Directorates, who will rely on the
Inspectors-General and the Consuls.

(7) Actions except under the command of responsible
people are absolutely forbidden.

(8) If reprisals are called for, they must be sudden and
ruthless.

Thus, before this pointless and illogical strike broke out,
the fascist leaders had drawn up their plan for changing
the socialists' ' demonstrative action ' against fascism into
a pitched battle of fascists against socialism. Their military
objectives were settled : they did not yet want to occupy
Rome, but hoped to take advantage of the strike to gain two
essential positions on the frontiers of the regions they already
occupied, namely the Genoa and Liguria zone on one side,
Ancona on the other. In the course of their campaign they
succeeded in reaching two unexpected and important
objectives, Milan, the capital of Lombardy, and Leghorn,
the last centre of working-class resistance in Tuscany.

The fascist executive issued an ultimatum addressed to the
strikers and the state : ' We give the state forty-eight hours
to assert its authority over all its dependents, and over those
who are endangering the existence of the nation. When
this time has elapsed fascism will claim full liberty of action
and will take the place of the state, which will once more
have proved its impotence.' In this way the strike, which
was to have made the state enforce respect for the law, only
succeeded in uniting the legal and the illegal forces of
reaction—the state and the *fasci*. The outlaws were no
longer the fascists who for months had killed, burnt, and
pillaged with impunity, but the railwaymen and the
workers in general who were trying to remind the state of
its duty. During July the fascists had left a trail of smoking
ruins, tortured bodies, and broken minds from Rimini to
Novara and Ravenna, and now they were presented with
a splendid opportunity of becoming the guardians of law
and order.

For the second time they joined the national bloc in the
Chamber, not, as in May 1921, as a result of the elections,

but because of the strike, the particular method of suicide chosen by the workers' organizations.

With the strike the situation took a definitely reactionary turn, and the cabinet crisis which had followed the Cremona acts of violence ended in fascist terrorism on a nation-wide scale receiving what was practically an official blessing. The conservative and 'liberal' press had shown no enthusiasm for the attempted peace pact and had blamed the fascists for contributing towards socialist participation by their excesses ; the *bourgeoisie*, with Giolitti, had expected nothing but harm to come of the crisis begun by the vote of July 19 in the Chamber ;[1] but now both showed revived anxiety for ' the authority of the state ' against the workers on strike, and congratulated the fascists who were continuing and extending, in the name of the state, the work of destruction to which they had devoted themselves with renewed fury in the past few weeks.

The Labour Alliance decided to end the strike at midday on August 3, prolonging it for twelve hours so as not to give the impression of having given way to the fascist ultimatum, which expired at midnight on August 2. But the fascists were not going to be baulked of their expected gains. Michele Bianchi, the secretary of the party, telegraphed the following circular to all the provincial federations : ' Although the attempted strike has, on the whole, failed and the Labour Alliance been forced to declare it officially ended, it must not pass unpunished. The " collaborationist " socialists are the most to blame, and the fascists, returning to their homes and demobilizing—where the situation allows—must not forget it.'[2] The fascist offensive, then, had a double political objective : to spread out and occupy other districts and to strike especially hard at the ' collaborationist ' socialists. The parliamentary offensive which Mussolini had planned against them from the beginning of the crisis was completed under arms throughout the country. The government connived at it, and wherever its authority was in the hands of the military, it was used almost every-

[1] P. 211.
[2] Referring to the strike while addressing the Central Committee of the Fascist Party on August 13, Bianchi repeated that ' it was conceived by " collaborationist " socialism '.

where to help the *fasci*. Their activity greatly increased after August 3, i.e. after the end of the strike. Mussolini was jubilant, and wrote in his newspaper on August 5 : ' If the three secretaries of the Labour Alliance had been fanatical fascists they could not have done more for the cause of fascism.' To prove it he published the list of fascist victories. This list (see Appendix) includes the names of forty-three towns in which the headquarters of socialist and communist clubs and co-operatives, Chambers of Labour and newspaper offices had been burnt down and socialist municipal councils forced to resign ; in addition, so lavish was the victory, there were a number of others which there was no room to print.

The fascist push went on for several days, and demobilization was not ordered by the secretariat of the party until August 8, five days after the end of the general strike. Even then, while demobilizing, the fascists were to ' act in accordance with the local situation '. The meaning of this phrase was explained in a circular letter of the 7th :

> ' If nothing has happened by the end of the day we shall give the order to demobilize this evening. In districts where the situation may not be favourable to us a garrison must be left. It appears, now that things are quiet, that the authorities intend to begin seizing arms. Issue strict orders on this subject so that arms and munitions can be taken at once to a safe place.'

The fascists had meant to take advantage of the general strike to attain various important strategic objects, in particular—as may be seen from the circular letter sent out from the party secretariat on July 31[1]—the Genoa district and the city of Ancona.

In Genoa the working-class movement was in the hands of the ' autonomous ' socialists, who were outside the official party, held right-wing views and had favoured Italy's intervention in the war. Their leaders had played a fairly important and somewhat ambiguous part in the central committee of the Alliance of Labour. They were supported by a powerful network of co-operative societies which

[1] P. 219-220.

monopolized all the work of the port and placed a formidable vested interest in the way of the fascist advance. But there was a gap in this imposing facade which the fascists intended to force. The work of the port—lading, unlading, caulking, and repairs of all sorts—was done by several thousands of workers who were members of the co-operative societies, each one of which performed a special function in accordance with strict rules reminiscent of those of the old corporations. These societies were 'closed' and their members given priority of employment. Each morning a list was prepared of the demands for various forms of labour caused by the arrival and departure of ships, and if there were any jobs to spare 'outside' workers were engaged. During the war and immediately afterwards there was work for everybody, and the system served to protect high wages, from which non-members also profited. But when the economic crisis broke out and the activity of the port was reduced, the system was threatened from two quarters. Owners and merchants wanted to bring down prices, while the growing number of unemployed, allowed fewer and fewer shifts of work, turned against the barriers of the co-operative societies and trade unions which were shutting them out of the promised land of the port. A few days' work a week was enough to give a livelihood, and wages were so high that members sometimes gave up their shifts to outsiders in return for a percentage of their earnings. During the time of prosperity, real or artificial, there had been enough profits for everybody, contractors, co-operative workers and *lumpenproletariat*. The margin of profit was now narrower and the fight for the spoil had begun. In this fight the contractor had a natural ally in the unemployed. Attacked on these two sides, the system could not hold out, and collapsed in a few days. The attack was led by the fascists. The shipping magnates placed a million and a half lire at their disposal to organize a punitive expedition against Genoa on a large scale. A fierce onslaught was made against the closed co-operative societies, in order to make them open to everybody. Work in the port was not unlimited, and for this reason alone some system of regulation was necessary. Actually once the victory had been won the societies were to be closed once more, and closed more firmly than before ; but socialist officials were to be replaced by fascist ones, or were to change their labels. In the meantime two great results were obtained : a death-blow was struck at the political and economic mainstays of the ultra-reformist socialism of Genoa, and wages in the port were considerably reduced.

The method by which this victory was gained is not without interest. The orders of July 31[1] had been carried out, and on the summons of the Genoa *fascio*, the squads of Carrara, commanded by Renato Ricci, reached the town in a short time ' after destroying the Chamber of Labour in Spezia on the way '.[2] Other squads came from Alessandria, led by the fascist deputy Torre. The Fascist Party attached exceptional importance to the conquest of Genoa, and the committee of action formed in the town included, besides Ricci and Torre, Massimo Rocca, a member of the party executive, Edmondo Rossoni, the secretary of the Confederation of Fascist Syndicates, and the deputy De Stefani, afterwards finance minister in Mussolini's first cabinet : in short, a small general staff for the direction of the campaign. During the strike there was fighting almost everywhere, and the workers held out until August 4. The state forces came to the help of the fascists ; armoured cars and machine-guns were brought into action and the last barricades destroyed. The railway staff were forced to give in, and on the morning of the 5th most of them returned to work. But the fascist leaders were determined to gain all the objects for which the ' march on Genoa ' had been planned. The co-operative societies and socialist unions in the port had to be destroyed. All the economic activities of the port were under the control of a public body, the *Autonomous Consortium of the Port*,[3] representing all the different interests and presided over by the senator Ronco. The Consortium controlled and distributed labour and without it the fascists could not have gained their hold over the ' system '. On August 5 the strike ended, but ' in the morning the committee

---

[1] P. 219, section 4.
[2] The passages quoted are taken from Chiurco's *History*.
[3] *Consorzio Autonomo del Porto di Genova.*

of action, now established in the Bristol Hotel, decided to
destroy a number of socialist organizations and to attack
the port '. Senator Ronco was invited to the Bristol where
a member of the committee cut short discussion by reading
him the following ultimatum :

1. The Executive Committee of the Consortium of the
Port of Genoa henceforward annuls all contracts with the
existing co-operatives, revokes any authorization to work
and re-establishes the freedom of labour in the Port itself.

2. The existing co-operatives henceforward will be
denied all concessions.

3. The same Executive Committee declares that it
recognizes implicitly the principle of different co-operatives
for each branch of work.

4. Within three months from to-day the revision of the
lists of the Consortium must be completed, and in them
inscribed all the members of the co-operatives formed
during that period.

5. The Executive Committee may dispose of the
guaranty funds of the co-operatives in the Consortium to
compensate at least in part for the damage done to trade.

The Committee of Action gave senator Ronco half an
hour to accept these conditions. Signor Ronco, an old
liberal, replied that he had received his appointment from
the king, and left the Bristol Hotel. But shortly afterwards
the fascist squads went to the Palazzo San Giorgio, the
headquarters of the Consortium, and forced him to sign the
following order :

' The Executive Committee of the Autonomous Consortium of the Port has decided to revoke the authorization
given to the co-operatives to work in the Port, and to
return to the free choice of the workers inscribed in the
list of the Consortium until such time as the co-operatives,
which are to be newly constituted with no limitation of
membership for each class of labour, can be authorized
according to regulations ; also to revise the lists of the
Consortium with power to inscribe new members.'

At the same time the committee of action published an indictment of senator Ronco, although he had yielded under the threat of fascist revolvers.

'Citizens! The Palazzo San Giorgio, formerly the seat of austere and wise justices of the sea, must return again to the dignity and impartiality of the law.

'The petty tyrant of the Palazzo San Giorgio, bogus protector of the poor, and clever speculator, must rule no more.

'President Blockhead, trembling and incapable, must learn to keep his place or go quietly into retirement.

'In our Port, according to the spirit and the letter of the law, the principle of liberty must be kept sacred, and no monopoly of organization must subordinate the dignity of human labour to one party.

'Men of Genoa! When we have several co-operatives, instead of a single one with exclusive rights, strikes will no longer be necessary or so frequent, and will no longer discredit and ruin our Port.

'Long live the free and multiple co-operatives.

'Long live freedom.'

'President Blockhead' gave way to all the demands of the fascists, who left the Palazzo singing *Giovinezza*. Their victory was complete. But before the 5000 fascists concentrated in Genoa returned home they carried out a few more minor operations. Two co-operatives, the office of the reformist daily *Il Lavoro*, a socialist printing-works and other workers' clubs were sacked and burned. A great number of syndical leaders were forced to leave the town within twenty-four hours. The fascists also occupied the Chamber of Labour and handed it over to the military authorities. For during the fascist occupation of Genoa the government had delegated full powers to the military authorities in the town.

The second objective had been Ancona, which the fascists of Umbria had occupied for the first time in the middle of July. This time the fascist concentration was more general : squads arrived from Bologna, Perugia, Foligno, Romagna, Ferrara, from the whole of Umbria ; more than 3000 men.

The offices of workers' organizations were set on fire, after the state forces had driven out the defenders. The battle raged furiously in the suburbs, and especially at San Lazzaro, where the strikers attacked and besieged the barracks of the *carabinieri*, and even tried to occupy the fort of Monte Acuto. In spite of the workers' heroism the struggle was too uneven and Ancona too, passed under the control of the *fasci*.

The speed acquired in action and the favourable military and political conditions made it possible for fascism to attack two more important positions, Milan and Parma. In Milan the fascist mobilization was carried out under the orders of Captain Cesare Forni, leader of the squads of Lomellina. On August 3 the Palazzo Marino, the town hall, was occupied, and d'Annunzio made a long speech from the balcony about the ' pacification of minds ' and the greatness of Italy, without making the slightest allusion to fascism. This was all part of his ' saviour ' performance ; but his presence among the leaders of the fascist bands amounted to support, since it sanctioned the violence perpetrated against the socialist council. His words were blown away by the wind, the gesture alone counted and served to swell the fascist success. Michele Bianchi, the secretary of the party, sent a congratulatory telegram from Rome : ' The National Fascist Party echoes your cries of " long live fascism ".' D'Annunzio had certainly not shouted ' long live fascism ' ; he was furious at the lie and at being thus annexed, and telegraphed in reply : ' My own cry is the only one that should be exchanged between Italians to-day, " Long live Italy ! " I know no other.' But the *Popolo d'Italia*, which had published Bianchi's telegram to d'Annunzio, took good care not to publish the poet's reply. For this piece of misrepresentation d'Annunzio had only himself to blame. The following day, August 4, the fascist squads decided to destroy once again, for the third time since April 1919, the offices of the socialist paper, *Avanti*. After considering bombarding it from an aeroplane :

' the fascists decided to attack it from three sides, with columns made up of strong groups of *squadristi* from Milan,

Pavia and Cremona, under the command of Farinacci, and with a column of forty lorries. While shots were fired into the air to distract the attention of the state forces, the squads climbed the gates, got into the premises and attacked the staff with bombs and rifles. The defenders switched an electric current through barbed-wire, which had been prepared in advance, and electro-cuted Emilio Tonoli ; while Cesare Melloni was blown up by a bomb. But finally the fire took hold, destroying the paper-stores and ruining the building.'

Eight fascists were wounded.

' In the Via Canonica another fascist was wounded by the rebels, a battle started and the communist club was sacked. The state forces were brought into action, but the resistance offered by this rebel district was extra-ordinary. Armoured cars had to be resorted to, bombs were thrown, and two were killed and several seriously wounded.'

During the fascist occupation the police made 600 arrests, exclusively among the workers and the ' rebels '. Mussolini was in Rome, where on August 2 he was holding a con-ference on ' the imperial task of fascism ', and he did not conceal his delight. As some newspapers had reported that he disapproved of the violence and crimes of the fascists in Milan, he sent the fascists a message of support : ' The acts of reprisal you have carried out have my entire approval. The Rome newspapers which have referred to an alleged disobedience of my orders should realize that if I had been in Milan I should have seen to it that reprisals were on a much bigger scale.'

Although they won in Milan the fascists failed to gain Parma, which remained a thorn in the side of Po valley fascism until the eve of the march on Rome. It was Italo Balbo once again who decided to take the opportunity of finally destroying this island of anti-fascist resistance. The working-class movement in Parma was peculiarly situated. Before the war the city had been the Mecca of revolutionary syndicalism. Its Chambers of Labour had been led by

Michele Bianchi, Rossoni, Amilcare De Ambris, Filippo Corridoni ; the last had joined up and been killed in the war, the first three had later gone over to fascism. The syndicalists, torn between opposing tendencies, had been abandoned by the workers, the majority of whom supported the federal Chamber of Labour controlled by the socialists. The growth of socialist influence was quite recent and the local workers maintained a certain spirit of independence, if not of mistrust, of political parties. Further it was the only town where, despite the socialist and communist veto, there was a proper and well-trained organization of *arditi del popolo.*

On the second day of the general strike, which the local socialist leaders had already decided to end, fascist squads began to arrive from the province and from Cremona.

'A hundred fascists from Cremona,' says Chiurco, 'with Farinacci, were received on the third day of the strike, at the Garibaldi gate, with rifle-shots and hand-grenades. The state forces intervened, armoured-cars were brought into action ; the battle lasted several hours. Thousands of fascists poured in from all directions and occupied the railway stations ; fighting broke out every-where ; bombs were thrown ; rebel squads penetrated right into the centre of the town and attacked the headquarters of the *fascio.*'

The same evening Balbo arrived with more squads, which destroyed two railwaymen's clubs and the presses of the paper, *Il Piccolo*. But the leaders of the *arditi del popolo* were determined to hold out to the end.

'At dawn,' according to the account of Guido Picelli,[1] who had not forgotten what the war had taught him, ' the workers went into the streets with picks, shovels, and other tools to help the *arditi* to take up the roads and pavements, tear up tram-lines, dig trenches, build barricades with carts, benches, beams, sheet-iron, and anything else they could find. Men and women were there, young and old,

[1] Guido Picelli was killed at the beginning of January 1937 fighting heroically in defence of Madrid for the freedom of the Spanish people and the peoples of the world.

of all parties or no party, bound by a single bitter resolve, to resist the enemy. In a few hours the popular districts of the town began to look like an armed encampment. The section occupied by the defenders was divided into four parts ; each squad was composed of eight to ten men and armed with 1891 rifles, carbines, service revolvers, S.I.P.E. bombs. There were only enough rifles or muskets for half of the men. The entrances to squares, streets and alleys were barricaded ; in some places entrenchments were reinforced by barbed-wire entanglements. Church-towers were turned into observation-posts. The whole fortified zone was put under the command of the *arditi del popolo*. The tradespeople were in sympathy with the rebels and supplied them with equipment and food.'

It is impossible here to give a detailed account of the fight. The fascist leaders insisted that the prefect should get the army to break up the ' rebels' ' fortifications. Troops occupied the Trinità district, where the men at the barricades welcomed them with shouts of : ' Long live our soldier brothers ', while in the Oltreterrente district the *Arditi* refused to disarm. The fascists were furious at the result of their action and determined to resume hostilities, issuing the following statement :

> ' The authorities have been fooled by the bolshevik strikers. The cessation of the strike has been made to look like an alliance between the troops and the demon-strators, who are betraying their country. If the chosen guardians of Patriotism, the most sacred ideal we possess to-day, are incapable of defending it, then it is for us to rise up in defence of the dignity of the nation and of the insulted army. To arms, fascists ! We return to the fight in the name of immortal Italy.'

The army had been insulted, according to the fascists, because the workers who were defending their liberties had welcomed and fraternized with the soldiers instead of shooting at them. The fascists' new attack, directed this time against the Oltreterrente districts of old Parma, wilted before the desperate and well-organized resistance of the *arditi* and of the entire population. Mussolini, who was still in Rome and whom Balbo consulted by telephone, advised demobilization.   The fascist leaders managed to save appearances by getting their powers delegated to the military authorities, who took over the job of occupying and clearing the working-class districts.

The reason that the workers and people of Parma were able to resist the fascist assault, although it concentrated several thousand *squadristi*, was that the defence of the working-class districts was organized on military lines, remembered from the great war. It was under a supreme command, which included ex-servicemen ; it was non-party ; it was supported whole-heartedly and with wild enthusiasm ; the orders of the *arditi del popolo* were obeyed ; it was backed by a stern determination to fight, if the fascists succeeded in breaking the front lines, from street to street, and house to house 'until every position is destroyed or burnt '. Another consideration, of decisive importance, is that in Parma the army took no part in the attack on the ' rebel ' defenders, who were wise enough to take up the sensible attitude towards them that so infuriated the fascist leaders.

Although the workers' resistance foiled the fascist attempt on Parma (as it did also in the old quarter of Bari), taken as a whole, the objectives aimed at by the fascist leaders in anticipation of the general strike were gained and in many instances exceeded. In the often-mentioned Milan, Genoa, Turin triangle, Milan and Genoa had succumbed. The general strike left the socialist movement and the working classes in a stupor. Could they be revived and saved ? The reformist socialists printed in the August 12 number of their paper, *Giustizia*, the tale of defeat :

' We must have the courage to admit that the general strike proclaimed by the Alliance of Labour has been our Caporetto. We emerge from this test well beaten. We have played our last card and lost Milan and Genoa, which seemed the strongest points in our defence. In the Lombard capital the party newspaper has once more gone up in flames, the administration of the town has been snatched from its lawful representatives, and our best fighters are threatened with banishment. In Genoa, which was strongly held by the seamen and the workers in the port, the headquarters of our organizations have been occupied by fascists, and nothing but ashes are left of the socialist newspaper there. It is the same elsewhere. Every important centre bears the marks of the fascist hurricane. We must face facts : the fascists are masters of the field. Nothing is to prevent them dealing more heavy blows in the certainty of winning fresh victories.'

After emphasizing the lack of proletarian armament and the absence of any organization or co-ordination during the strike, the article went on :

' Our present unhappy and disastrous situation is the result of solutions that were thought of long ago being tried out too late. Too late, the " collaborationist " solution, which to be successful should have been adopted after the elections of May 1921 ; too late, the general strike of protest, which was attempted after the enemy had already broken down some of our strongholds and had had time to build up a formidable army.'

After Caporetto the Italian army had managed to reorganize and hold out on the Piave. But could the workers and socialists find their Piave line to hold up the enemy and block the way to the capital ?

X

THE MARCH ON ROME

AFTER the ' legalitarian ' strike parties and politicians
expected a few months respite, to adapt themselves
to the new conditions and decide on their tactics
for the reassembly of parliament in the autumn, when
everything would at last be settled. Giolitti had only
intervened in June and saved Facta because he reckoned
on getting into power after the recess and holding fresh
general elections in the spring ; although he meant first to
strike a heavy blow at the socialists and *Popolari* by abolishing
proportional representation. This would make it possible
to form a coalition government in which the socialists, or
at least some of the leaders of the General Confederation
of Labour, would be only too glad to take part. His general
idea was to carry on with the plan already begun in May
1921, and this time there was a chance of success, thanks to
the achievements of the fascists, the new split in the Socialist
Party—now well under way—and the possibility of a return
to majority elections.

Accordingly when the second Facta ministry met the
Chamber on August 9 it easily secured a majority. Although
it contained neither socialists nor fascists it was a thoroughly
patchwork affair, comprising friends of Giolitti and Nitti,
Popolari, ' national ' socialists, genuine democrats like
Amendola, and right-wing extremists like Riccio. It was as
chaotic as the state of affairs it was supposed to be dealing
with, and, existing as it did only through the weakness and
mutual tolerance of its members, it had no strength at all.

The fascists took part in the discussion on the government's
programme, but this time Mussolini put up an obscure
deputy to state his point of view. In the set speech that had
been prepared for him Signor Dario Lupi put forward the

alternatives : ' Either the state absorbs fascism or fascism
absorbs the state.' Did he mean by this that fascism was
ready to join the state, to obey the law and share the responsibility of power ? That had been Mussolini's attitude in
April,[1] but now the same phrases did not bear the same
meaning. This is what Signor Lupi had to explain. Fascism
did not want equality of rights within the framework of a
state that guaranteed similar equality to all parties and all
its citizens. Fascism rejected the idea of a state that was
' restricted by such absurd limitations of neutrality ' ; the
party would join the state if it became a party-state. The
state must follow a fascist policy : ' To settle the present
crisis,' declared Signor Lupi, ' the nation's enemies must
be routed. If the present ministry is incapable of doing so,
fascism will press on with enthusiasm and faith to accomplish
the national task that has been entrusted to it by God and
by Destiny.' Mussolini's own style is easily recognizable
in this peroration. Two years ago he had spat upon ' every
form of Christianity ' ; now he invoked God through his
spokesman, while he announced his intention of carrying
on his drive against the socialists and the workers. This
invocation of God—coupled with Destiny, since some god
has to be found for those who do not believe in God—was
intended to disarm the Vatican, and was soon to bear fruit.

Two days later the National Council of the Fascist Party
reassembled in Milan to consider the situation. Michele
Bianchi, the secretary-general of the party, stated that recent
events had shown that fascism possessed ' greater strength
than had been imagined '. ' Our victory, for which we
cannot adequately thank our enemies,' said Grandi
ironically, ' has been shattering, complete beyond all
expectation.' Everybody agreed with Bianchi and Mussolini
that fascism must be merged into the state, either by legal
means through new elections, or if necessary by direct
action. The seizure of power had become an urgent necessity, and Mussolini's impatience matched the demands of
the movement. The fact was that the destruction of the
socialist organizations had thrown on to the hands of the
fascists tens of thousands of workers, and they had no idea

[1] P. 194.

what to do with them. As fascism triumphed it came up against the practical problems with which the free syndicates had been concerned. Thanks to the terror it could brush aside or postpone some of these, but there were others which it had to face.

The political offensive had pushed fascism towards syndicalism, and this in its turn was forcing it to conquer the state. How to make use of the resources of the state was the principal problem before the National Council. Farinacci emphasized the danger to the fascist syndicates of unemployment during the coming winter. Grandi, in an interview in the *Giornale d'Italia*, expressed the problem in a more definite form :

> ' A passive but numerically important force is growing up alongside fascism. I refer to the well-organized body of our syndicates which to-day contains over 700,000 members. The coming winter may hold surprises for all, ourselves included, whose effects no one can foretell. We are faced to-day by an insurrection of the middle classes, and by a political revolution. It must also be remembered that this insurrection is likely to be complicated by a social crisis. What would happen were these two phenomena to meet before we managed to take up our share of the responsibilities of the state ? '

This mixture of anxiety and blackmail was genuinely effective. Fascism displayed itself to the *bourgeoisie* as the only force ' capable of absorbing the anti-state forces without endangering liberal institutions ', and without having to pay the price of socialist collaboration. ' *Our* collaboration,' Grandi assured them ' has all the advantages and none of the dangers of socialist collaboration. Fascism must become the mainspring of government immediately ; and to bring this about general elections must be held in November.'

The alternatives, legality or insurrection, put forward by Mussolini and fascism, only affected methods, for the object was the same in either case : the attainment of power. Mussolini had succeeded in persuading Grandi and his friends, especially the deputies among them, that it would be better to take the path of ' legality ', and that by following it they had every chance of success. Nearly all parties, from *Popolari* to nationalists, were either in favour of or resigned to the fascists joining the government, though they meant to restrict them to a reasonable share of it. But now that the squads were closing in on Rome Mussolini was not going to be content to play the part of a mere lieutenant. The post he wanted, and regarded as his own, was the ministry of foreign affairs. He wanted his name to be reverenced beyond the frontiers. Europe groaned under the weight of the peace treaty, the League of Nations was ' utopian '. England was the most formidable guardian of this system, and it was against her, against the ' conservative ' powers, that Italy must align herself. Mussolini became obsessed with this idea, to the point of monomania. He proclaimed himself more and more revisionist and anti-British. In June 1922 he got the fascist parliamentary group to pass a resolution condemning the ratification of the Syrian, Libanon and Palestine mandates. He tried to stir up Egypt against England. In the middle of July he proudly quoted in the *Popolo d'Italia* a resolution of the Arab Nationalist Committee which congratulated the Italian fascist and nationalist press on its attitude towards Near Eastern problems. ' It is clear ', he wrote in this connection, ' that we hold excellent cards to play in the Eastern Mediterranean ', particularly ' Arab nationalism in full swing '. Certain Italian diplomats remained obstinately pro-British, ' goodness knows why ', but ' all that will soon come to an end '.

In August the National Council of the Fascist Party passed another resolution, proposing ' to prevent by all possible means the ratification and carrying out of the Italo-Jugoslav conventions of Santa Margharita and Rome '. On August 28 Mussolini once more denounced the foreign minister Schanzer,[1] for ' sacrificing the independence of Italian foreign policy to the League of Nations '. On September 6, referring to Asia Minor, he demanded that Italian foreign policy should ' take up a realistic attitude and abandon completely all hollow theorizing, breaking away once and for all from its subjection to England '.

[1] He was minister for foreign affairs in both the Facta cabinets.

Later, on October 1, four weeks before the march on Rome, he explained his hostility to England and the League of Nations.

'During the four years that have followed the armistice England has practised the most complete deception possible on Europe and the world. It is from London that the post-war doctrine of reconstruction has emerged. . . . We have never for one moment been taken in by that solemn league of tricksters which sits at Geneva oblivious of the ridicule that surrounds it. Nor have we ever believed in English pacifism or English reconstructionism, or any of the nebulous league theories which are wafted over from the Anglo-Saxon world.[1] We must be ready for an essentially anti-English policy. It is not in Italy's interest to support the British Empire ; it is in her interest to contribute to its downfall.'[2]

There was a close theoretical and practical connection between this view of foreign politics and Mussolini's fight for power, both in cause and effect. Hatred of ' Wilsonism ', of European reconstruction, of the ' league spirit ' abroad, went hand in hand with hatred of socialism and democracy at home ; the one was a function of the other, its counterpart on a different scale : an easily grasped parallel.

'The century of democracy is over,' wrote Mussolini on August 19. 'The ideals of democracy are exploded, beginning with that of " progress ". Ours is an " aristocratic " century which followed the old democratic one. The state of all will end by becoming the state of a few. The new generations are not going to let the corpse of democracy block their way into the future.'

He stressed this again on September 17 :

'It is not our programme which divides us from democracy, since all programmes are alike, but our

[1] In Tsarist Russia the ' nationalist populist ' Prougavin foretold a fatal conflict between *bourgeois* and parliamentary England and the Holy Russian Empire, autocracy incarnate, supported by the will of hordes of *mujiks*. ' The historian,' remarks Tchernoff in his memoirs, *From Nijni–Novgorod to Paris*, ' cannot help remarking how in periods of reaction dictatorships, of whatever kind, are fundamentally hostile to the English parliamentary regime.'
[2] See below, on p. 257, the end of Mussolini's speech in Milan on October 4.

conception of the future trend of history ; and it is from this that our mentality and methods are derived. For we are more and more convinced that the world is moving towards the right, the ideas and the institutions of the right, and above all in the direction of anti-socialism. . . . We are more and more convinced that for our salvation we have got to establish a new order, no matter how reactionary our methods. . . . The democratic conception of life is essentially political, the fascist essentially warlike.[1]

'. . . The masses are so much cattle ; the prey of spasmodic, fluctuating, and irresponsible forces ; inert matter, without volition, and without future. We must overthrow, therefore, the altars raised by Demos to their Holiness the Masses. This does not mean that we must neglect their well being. On the contrary we must bear in mind the statement of Nietzsche, who desired that the masses should enjoy the highest material well-being so that their complaints and troubles should not disturb the higher manifestations of the spirit.'

It is from the people, according to the principle of democracy, that power is derived. But according to the fascist conception they are simply the masses, a sort of primary material which must be immobilized, though not obliterated. And as soon as the people lose all independent existence, all self-determination, they nourish and serve the ' will to power '. Fascism is like the barbarian horde marshalled against the city ; but marshalled in a new way,

---

[1] So far as it is possible to speak of a mussolinian doctrine it may be summed up in a single phrase—the glorification of war. In the article on fascist doctrine that Mussolini himself wrote for the Italian Encyclopædia he gives the following definition : ' Above all, as far as concerns the future and development of humanity in a general way, fascism does not believe in either the possibility or the usefulness of eternal peace. It repudiates pacifism, which runs away from the struggle and shrinks from sacrifice. War alone screws all human faculties to their highest pitch and sets the seal of nobility on the peoples who have the courage to face it. . . . Consequently a doctrine founded on the assumption of peace is no more consistent with fascism than are international institutions with the spirit of fascism.' And in his speech in the Chamber of May 26, 1934, which may be regarded as the starting-point for fascist action in Africa and in the Mediterranean, Mussolini proclaimed that : ' War is to man what maternity is to woman. I do not believe in eternal peace ; in fact I think it wastes and denies the essential virtues of man, which can only be fully displayed in bloodshed and strife.'

with iron discipline, trains running to time, the mobilization of the body and mind of every member. A horde which will become a modern army, before which in its turn the free city will seem a confused mob. Modern war is mass war, involving the entire resources of a country. Dictatorship becomes a necessity, for the masses must be compelled to march, either by force or by isolating and exciting instincts and reflexes which social habits, democracy and city life have weakened and bridled. Hence it is that the struggle to guide a nation into knowing and obeying no other law than that of war demands the destruction of social institutions, those stages by which civilization consolidates its slow and difficult advance. To deprive the people of their communes, their syndicates, their co-operatives was like pushing them backwards down a slope from which everything that might arrest their fall had been removed. To ensure its own freedom of movement, fascism had to suppress all liberty, and substitute for bodies which might use it as a means to a freer social life others devoted to absolute stagnation. Mussolini thoroughly understood that to impose a ' warlike mentality ' on Italy he had to destroy democracy and in particular its only serious support, the working-class and socialist movement. Socialists and *Popolari*, the two great popular parties, which really reflected the hopes of the masses, were genuinely pacifist. Nowhere on his European journey did Wilson receive more spontaneous and disinterested homage than in Italy. To make such a people ' warlike ', democracy and socialism had to be exterminated ; and fascism had to have not only power, but a monopoly of power.

In the course of its violently rapid growth the character of fascism became more and more military, a foreshadowing of the pattern of organization and life that its chiefs were to impose on the Italian nation. In order to turn the nation into a barracks fascism had to begin by being a barracks. To those who looked for a breakdown owing to the immense number of new recruits Mussolini replied on August 26 : ' The river of fascism continues to increase its waters, which have already burst through several dams and soon will be in full flood. Our enemies pretend to be pleased at this impressive and rapid growth of our numbers which they hope to see ebbing with the same speed.' But the Fascist Party is not like all the other parties. There is no argument, no formation of ' tendencies ', no fear of schism. ' Fascism is quite different. Its members are first and foremost soldiers. The party ticket is a mobilization paper. The politico-military structure is now firmly established. Military discipline involves political discipline. People are there to fight and not to argue. With this type of organization the dangers of proselytism are greatly reduced.' A year earlier Mussolini had faced an internal crisis in fascism by backing the ' political ' elements against the ' military ' ; now he congratulated himself that fascist organization was military in structure, performance and mentality, as was fitting for an army of occupation. It was also favoured not only by the neglect, blindness and self-deception of its adversaries, but by the concrete support of a combination of interests ; primarily the landed interests, and, more or less directly connected, the most reactionary groups of Italian society : big bankers—especially the shadier sort, heavy industry—armament manufacturers in particular, some sections of the army, and the Vatican.

Between August and the beginning of October the energies of the fascist movement were completely absorbed in turning to account the immediate results of its victory over the general strike. In Genoa Senator Ronco, president of the Consortium of the Port, ended by resigning, and the government approved the work of the fascist Committee of Action. On August 15 the municipal council of Cremona was dissolved. A month earlier the first Facta cabinet had been turned out of office for not saving the town from fascist violence ; now the second Facta cabinet sanctioned this violence with the decree of dissolution. Two weeks later Milan suffered the same fate ; there also the state merely ' legalized ' the occupation of the Palazzo Marino.[1] At the end of the month came the turn of Treviso, which the fascists had attacked in July, 1921.[2] At the beginning of September the fascists took two strategic positions which were to help them in their march on Rome : Terni, in

[1] P. 227.   [2] P. 149.

Umbria, and Civitavecchia, some few dozen miles from the capital. The great steel works of Terni had been closed since July, as there were no government contracts, and the 'red' syndicates had obtained a promise that the works should be reopened on September 1. But the directors of the Terni works had joined forces with the fascists, and on the first, despite the promise, the hooters were silent. The fascists trooped in from all the towns of Umbria and the Marches, and occupied and terrorized the town. The fascist Committee of Action placarded the town with the following notice : ' Liars as usual, the socialists promised you the reopening of the works to-day. They have not been opened. Incapable of admitting their cowardice, the socialists did not promise what has actually happened— their flight.' The fascists ' punished ' the socialist deputy, Nobili, who had remained in the town, by beating him with a *manganello* (bludgeon). The two Chambers of Labour, confederal and syndicalist, were burnt down. Socialist and communist clubs in the neighbourhood were similarly destroyed. As soon as this affair was ended the directors decided to reopen the works, but henceforward they would only deal with fascist ' syndicates '.[1]

In Civitavecchia, where the socialists had won control of the municipality at the 1920 elections, the local fascist movement was insignificant. In 1921 the Rome fascists had several times tried to gain access to the town, but without success. On August 4, 1922, again, after the general strike, the fascists of the Maremma, ' by previous arrangement with the fascists of the town, entered Civitavecchia. But the

---

[1] A month later a somewhat similar episode occurred at Leghorn. The Orlando shipbuilders had at the time an order from the government for eight destroyers, but on various pretexts they were demanding an appreciably higher price than the one agreed upon. Upon the refusal of the government to submit to these fresh demands, which amounted to several millions, and after an attempt at compromise which failed through the obstinacy of the shipbuilders, the latter closed down their works. The fascists intervened and the Marquis Dino Perrone Compagni issued an ultimatum inviting the ' Orlando company and the government to reopen the works by October 12 ; if not the fascists would occupy them.' The government gave in and the same day ordered the re-opening of the works. Messrs. Orlando, who had inspired the fascist ultimatum, obeyed joyfully : in giving these orders the government accepted all their demands. And the fascists, who had thus gained much wealth for their friends, the shipbuilders, appeared absolute saviours to the workers of Leghorn. Fascist syndicalism scored heavily in this town.

action, though well planned and commanded, was a failure '.
Chiurco gives no other details and blames the under-
prefect of the town for his ' hostility ' to the fascists, which
only amounts to saying that he did not help the *squadristi* by
every means in his power, as was usually the case. About
four hundred of them had arrived and occupied the station,
after firing a grand fusillade, before leaving the train, to
frighten and disperse the railway workers. The troops,
who should have opposed the entry of the fascists into the
town, did nothing, and the colonel commanding the local
military college put himself at the head of the fascists and
with them forced the cordons of police. The alarm was
given and the workers in the port and in the working-class
districts rushed to the centre of the town to meet the fascists.
The *carabinieri* tried to disarm them, but had to give way
before the firm attitude of the crowd. Thus the fight began,
and the invaders, for once unsupported by troops and
demoralized at being attacked, gave way, and began to
escape down side-streets. Their leaders' appeals, insults
and blows were in vain. Finally the troops appeared and
the squads left the city under their protection, leaving behind
them one dead and six wounded. This had to be avenged ;
and at the beginning of September the fascists arrived in
greater strength from Maremma, Rome, Pisa, the Roman
Campagna, Orvieto and all over Umbria. Though the
workers resisted the fascists entered the town on September 4,
the socialist council resigned, and the port authority
accepted the terms laid down by the victors.

The fascists continued to crush the few centres of working-
class resistance and to impose their will generally. On
September 7, for instance, when eight fascists were arrested
at Massa : ' The fascists of the area,' Chiurco relates,
' assembled in the town. The affair was organized by
Renato Ricci and Edmondo Rossoni, members of the party
executive. Over six thousand blackshirts paraded in full
war equipment through the town. The ultimatum to the
authorities demanding the release of the fascists expired the
same evening. The fascist mobilization covered all Lunigiana, and on the morning of the 8th there was a further
demonstration : an endless column, headed by fascist

cavalry, marched through the town. Meanwhile the magistrates had hastened to examine fresh witnesses, with the result that at 3 p.m. the arrested fascists were set free.'

Again in September the fascists attacked Molinella, a large rural centre where the working-class population, under the leadership of the mayor, Giuseppe Massarenti, was entirely socialist. Here the authorities had taken strong measures to prevent fascists from outside approaching the neighbourhood. The local *fascio* and the landowners were furious and demanded that this ' scandal ' should be stopped. Mussolini supported them by declaiming in the *Popolo d'Italia* against this ' silly comedy '. ' The situation,' explains Chiurco, ' remained the same for several days. The leaders of the *fascio* protested against the excessive police precautions, which amounted to martial law and unfairly restricted the liberty of honest citizens. Landowners declared a lock-out against socialist labour, and were joined by manufacturers and tradesmen. The fascists occupied the country-side.'

A month later they occupied the town hall. These were but a few events among thousands which were occurring every day, especially on Sundays, all over the country. In the meantime what changes and vicissitudes had affected the different parties ?

The working-class movement was beginning to disintegrate. Before the end of August the National Syndicate of Railwaymen and the Italian Syndical Union (anarchosyndicalist) broke away from the Labour Alliance. The extremists who had forced the Committee of Action into proclaiming the strike were the first to quit the sinking ship. The Printers' Federation, very right-wing, declared a few days later that it ' reserves the right to decide for itself on each occasion as to its participation in political strikes ', that is to say it no longer recognized the alliance between the General Confederation of Labour—to which it belonged— and the Socialist Party. On October 6 the Confederation itself renounced the pact and declared its independence. This pact had subordinated the actions of the syndicates to the foolishness and inefficiency of the political party, and had helped to bring about the workers' failure. But at this moment such a decision could only signify a hasty retreat before the foe, whose demands were accepted under the illusion that damage could thus be limited and complete ruin avoided.

During August and September the Socialist Party was still a prey to internal dissension. On August 28 the right-wing section, the ' concentrationists ' (a last homage to the ghost of party unity) issued an appeal, declaring themselves frankly in favour of legality and collaboration with the government. This division, which had been in virtual existence for several months, led to a fresh cleavage at the socialist National Congress, which took place in Rome early in October. Since the end of 1920 the Socialist Party had lost a great part of its strength, now reduced to 73,000, of whom 61,000 were represented at the congress. Its maximalist leaders proposed the expulsion of the ' concentrationists ', on various grounds, accusing them first and foremost of ' manœuvres which aim at helping to solve the ministerial crisis by the promise of eventual support to government policy '. The voting went in favour of the maximalists by a small majority—32,106 against 29,119 ; the two tendencies being thus more or less equal, as at Leghorn. The split was dramatic because it seemed so unusually pointless. Separation from the reformists was not going to make the new majority of the party less feeble or incapable. The speech made by its leader, Serrati, showed an appalling misapprehension of the real state of affairs :

> ' You say,' he thundered at the reformists, ' that we can help to settle the *bourgeois* crisis and pick up some trifling advantages, as we did in 1912. You seek alliance with democracy and say that socialism too is democratic. But socialism is proletarian democracy, real democracy, while the other is *bourgeois*, the falsification of true democracy. . . . Let all who wish to work for the revolution come with us and all who wish to thwart it go with the *bourgeoisie*.'

Serrati was simply persisting in his pre-war hostility towards the reformists, and all the events of 1919–22 had passed over his head without effect. The problem raised by the right-wing socialists—it is to their credit that they did raise it and to their shame that they had not done so earlier and more boldly—was not how to 'pick up trifling advantages', but how to rescue, together with 'bourgeois' democracy, in short with democracy altogether, the bare conditions for the existence and development of the working-class and socialist movement. By the beginning of October 1922, and even earlier, the question was no longer whether the 'revolution' was being thwarted, but whether the victory of fascism and its attainment of power could be prevented. The rather dull minds of the Italian maximalists had not grasped this fact within four weeks of the march on Rome.

For the reformists, who had now regained their liberty of action, the situation was no less dramatic. What use could they make of the freedom they had gained ? Breaking with the communists in January 1921 and with the maximalists in October 1922 had meant breaking with so great a porportion of the masses that even if their new policy was still practicable it could only count on a very limited support in parliament and in the country. The article in the reformist paper, quoted at the end of the previous chapter,[1] after pointing out that the policy of collaboration and that of the general strike had been adopted too late, had reached the following conclusion : ' The cause of this delay lies in the fundamental confusion of method which is still the bane of the Socialist Party. The Rome congress ought to tear up the Bologna programme of 1919 and go back to the Genoa programme of 1892 '.[2] Actually it is doubtful if this return to first principles would have been of any assistance in face of the existing situation, for by then there was just as much risk of its being inadequate and too late.

But even after August 1922 the triumph of fascism was not absolutely inevitable. In spite of everything fascism was still only an army of occupation. Its numbers were increasing in swarms, but it was not a solid force, and it was very far from sweeping away the nation. A victory for the forces of anti-fascism alone was no longer possible ; nothing short of a complete mobilization of the nation would have

[1] Pp. 231–232.   [2] P. 54.

served.   The reformists were too routine-bound, too paralysed by their fear of alienating the masses and endangering syndical unity to be able to initiate any such movement.   They were vaguely aware that such a way out of the difficulty might be found, but they were almost ashamed to consider it.   They tried out new catchwords which sounded false even to their own ears and attempted to give them a literary turn by vague references to the *sacra lampa*.[1]   For to them the idea of the nation was just another means to an end, which had turned up at the last moment and which they had snatched at in the hope of evading the enemy who were at their heels.   But between ' nation ' and ' working class ' there was an unbridgeable void ;   years of propaganda and the slogan of ' red versus tricolour ' made it impossible for the workers to see what their place could be in this ' nation ', or why they should associate themselves with this new attitude.   Besides, the fascists were not going to give up their monopoly of patriotism.   The result was that the right wing suspected a trap and the left thought it was treason.   The only way of ending the deadlock would have been for the united working class to face the problem of forming a government aiming not only at smashing fascism, but also at building a new Italy.   At no less a price could fascism be abolished.   Only by fulfilling to the utmost the duty they owed to themselves and to the community, whose conscience and driving power they should have been, could the workers defend their own rights.   Duty, responsibility and initiative were the price of liberty.   Only in such conditions could fascism have been beaten back in the second half of 1922.

From August to September the fascist movement gained momentum by means of a series of political and syndical congresses, mobilizations and *adunate*.   Provincial or regional congresses of *fasci* took place in Pescara (for the Abruzzi), Rimini (for Romagna), Pola (for Istria), Porto Maurizio, Tolentino (for the province of Macerata), Avellino, Ferrara, Modena, Iglesias (for Sardinia), Foggia, Messina, Como, Parma, Vicenza, Siena, Pesaro (for the Marches).   Congresses of fascist syndicates were held in Padua, Arezzo,

[1] P. 184.

Turin, Genoa (for the sailors' organizations), Leghorn, Ravenna, Andria (for the whole of Apulia).

In addition the party organized great regional *adunate*, where tens of thousands of blackshirts assembled—September 20 in Udine, Novara, Piacenza, on the 24th in Cremona, the 29th at Ancona.

All these demonstrations served as useful training for the militia and increased the pressure on the government. In the meantime the fascists had other and more definite aims in the territorial as well as the political sphere. There were two regions still exempt from fascist control : the south, except Apulia, and the part that the Italians call Alto Adige and the Austrian South Tyrol. The question of fascist penetration into the south was raised at the National Council in Milan (August 14), when it was decided to hold a special meeting to form a ' complete political, economic and military plan of action ' for this part of the country. In an interview with the *Mattino* of Naples Mussolini praised the workers of the south as being ' less infected with the germ of subversiveness ', and the south itself as ' the nation's storehouse of man power, an inexhaustible reserve of soldiers'. He also stated that the next National Congress of the National Fascist Party would be held in Naples on October 24. A conference of delegates from the south, arranged by the National Council, took place in Rome on September 6 and 7. In this part of Italy fascism had to contend with political forces of some strength and importance, contributing a great number of deputies to various ' democratic ' groups under leaders ranging from Nitti to Amendola.

Backed by strong local influence these forces were firmly entrenched, and in certain regions, such as Sardinia, they developed autonomous tendencies, harnessing the ex-servicemen's movement and certain sections of the petty *bourgeois* to new parties (' Sardinian Party of Action ') far removed from fascism.

In the ' redeemed ' country of the Adige valley the majority of the population were German born. The South Tyrol had returned four deputies, all German, in the March 1931 elections. Where the Italian element prevailed, as in Trent, the whole administration was in the hands of the

Popolari. It was impossible for the fascists to reach Rome while this area of opposition existed on the frontier. As early as September 1 Michele Bianchi had sent a memorandum to Facta, the prime minister, demanding from the government an active policy for the Italianization of the district. Early in October the fascist forces of Venetia and other provinces of Northern Italy, led by the deputies, De Stefani, Giunta, Farinacci, occupied Trent and Bolzano and forced the government commissioners, Credaro and Salata, to resign and clear out. All the fascist demands were at once agreed to in Rome. The fascist leaders ordered demobilization and handed over the headquarters of the Trent deputies, which they had occupied, to the military authorities. ' At their request this transfer of authority from fascist squads to regular troops was accompanied with all the ceremony of changing guard and saluting colours.'

In the purely political sphere Mussolini had other objectives. Whatever policy circumstances might compel him to follow, he needed the neutrality, if not the support, of the monarchy and the army. The relations of fascism with the monarchy would depend largely on its relations with the army, since the latter continued deeply loyal to the house of Savoy. Mussolini was sufficiently contemptuous of the king to do no more than blackmail him. The *Giornale d'Italia* had published a letter by a group of officers who showed their sympathy with fascism, but at the same time were anxious about its republican tendency, and declared that they were prepared to fight for the Crown, even against the fascists. Mussolini replied in the *Popolo d'Italia* on August 23 :

' Nobody drags the Crown into our quarrels to-day, though there are plenty of reasons for doing so. We have given up stressing the famous republican " tendency ", and furthermore, Fascism has in many towns—Lucca, Reggio Emilia, Trieste—paid formal homage to the king. We have banished from our minds the threefold amnesty to deserters. After which we have the honour to assert that Fascism follows the wide law, " *do ut des* ". The Crown is not at stake, so long as it keeps out of the game. Is that clear ? '

About a month later in his speech at Udine Mussolini went still further, continuing his policy of blackmail, and even raising his price :

' I think that the regime in Italy can be profoundly altered, without touching the monarchy. On its side the monarchy can gain nothing by opposing what may in future be known as the fascist revolution. It can gain nothing, for by so doing it would become a target which we with our lives at stake could not spare. Those who sympathize with us should not stay in the background ; the king must have the courage to be a monarchist. Why are we republicans ? In one sense because we see a king who does not play his part. The monarchy could well represent the continuity of the nation, a great task and one of the utmost historical importance.'

The effect of the *squadristi* and the fascist syndicates had been to win the landowners in a body over to fascism, to such a degree that it would be more accurate to say that the fascists had rallied in a body to the side of the landowners. They had still to gain the upper middle classes, of whom only a few, though very important, sections had taken any direct part in the fight. To do this Mussolini extended the action he had already begun for the ' demobilization ' of the state, and he launched the party on a systematic campaign for ' restoring the national finances '. One may well understand how attractive to Italian capitalists were the pictures drawn by Mussolini in his Udine speech on September 20 :

' We want to strip the state of all its economic functions. Enough of the state which acts as railway owner, postman, insurance company. Enough of the state which functions at the taxpayers' expense and exhausts the finances of Italy. With the police, the education of the rising generation, the army to ensure the integrity of the fatherland, with foreign policy, no one can say that the state thus restricted is diminished in stature. No ; it is still very great, retaining all its spiritual realm and renouncing the material one.'

Such vague and incoherent language enabled Mussolini to offer everybody the fulfilment of his dearest hopes. The capitalist saw all the public services restored to private enterprise, the shopkeeper saw himself released from taxation and all state supervision and trivial regulations ; and the petty *bourgeois* idealist was delighted to turn over the ' material realm ' to them, imagining himself something—minister or hall-porter—in the ' spiritual realm '. Meanwhile the party did not stop at these grand principles, but prepared a long report, drafted by Signori Corgini and Massimo Rocca, for a series of meetings on the financial restoration which continued to be held in the principal towns of Italy from early September up to the eve of the march on Rome. In this report and at the meetings were demanded : the reform of the civil service ; the transfer of state industries to private firms ; the abolition of useless state bodies ; the abolition of subsidies and privileges granted to officials, co-operatives, and municipal shops in receipt of ' preferential treatment to that shown to private traders ' ; simplification of the tax system ; reduction of duties on inheritance, on business transactions, and in some cases on luxuries, for such duties led to the ' destruction of the family and of private property ' ; the balancing of the budget, not by raising taxes, but by extending the number of taxpayers and increasing taxes on consumption goods rather than by directly taxing riches.

In the course of 1922 Italy's financial and economic situation was showing signs of improvement, as a result of measures adopted by the various governments, especially after 1921. The adverse trade balance was diminishing, savings bank deposits were increasing, the note circulation was gradually getting back to normal. Here are the relevant figures up to December 31 of each year :

	Adverse trade balance	Deposits at general and post office savings banks	Note circulation
		(in thousands of lire)	
1919	12,694	10,643	18,551
1920	10,557	13,213	22,000
1921	15,048	15,576	21,475
1922	8,647	17,250	20,279

Taking into consideration the state budget alone it is clear that between 1919 and 1922 Italy had made an effort of recovery in which fascism had taken no part at all. The state had included war debts in its ordinary budget, instead of budgeting for them specially, and provided for them from its own normal resources. The deficits of 1919–22 were due, not to the normal functioning of the state, but to the payment of the heavy costs of war which entirely absorbed all budgetary surpluses and affected all this period particularly strongly.

The following figures, based on the elaborate evidence given by Professor F. A. Repaci in his great work on the Italian budgets of 1913 to 1932,[1] show the actual progress of Italian finance during the years immediately following the war :

Budgetary period[2]	Receipts	Annual increase of receipts	Expenses	Total deficit	War costs paid off	Percentage of war costs of total expenses
		(in thousands of lire)				
1918–19	7,512	—	30,857	23,345	25,683	83·23
1919–20	10,210	2,698	21,704	11,494	12,424	57·24
1920–21	13,184	2,974	34,139	20,955	22,339	65·43
1921–22	15,444	2,260	32,612	17,168	18,264	56
1922–23	15,912	468	19,172	3,260	4,867	25

There are several conclusions to be drawn from these figures. Between July 1, 1918, and June 30, 1922—four months before the march on Rome—the state received a total of 64,350,000,000 lire ; during the same period it spent 78,710,000,000 lire on war expenses, that is to say more than the total deficit, which was 72,962,000,000 lire. In the 1922–23 period, of which the first four months were previous to the march on Rome, the deficit was 13,908,000 lire less than that in the previous period, but at the same time the amount devoted to paying off war costs was reduced by 13,397,000,000. This shows that the successive Italian governments since the armistice had already effected a considerable improvement in the financial situation

[1] *La Finanza Italiana nel Ventennio* 1913–1932, Turin, ed. Einaudi, 1934. See also Marcello Soleri, *Note sul bilencio*, in the *Rivista di Politica Economica*. March 31, 1927.

[2] The budget year begins on July 1.

without having recourse to foreign loans, and had in four years paid off some 79,000,000,000 of war costs.

The campaign that Mussolini and his party launched in September had rather different aims ; more precisely their intention was to gain the confidence and the support of Italian financial circles, by proving how completely fascism had abandoned its ' demagogic ' programme of 1919–20, and that it had decided to attack the workers on financial, as it already had on syndical and political ground. The *Corriere della Sera*, the great ' liberal ' paper of Milan, gloated over the Corgini-Rocca programme, which it regarded as a triumphant return to the pure tradition of the Manchester school. . . . . Thus on September 6 this paper was ' delighted that a party, whatever it may call itself, is returning to the old liberal tradition, drinking the pure life-springs of a modern state, and it hopes that this party will not falter, but will strive earnestly to achieve the liberal programme pure and unadulterated '. The editor, Senator Albertini, had applauded the fascist occupation of the Palazzo Marino, and a month earlier, on the presentation to the Senate of the new Facta ministry, had spoken against socialist collaboration, ' in view of the danger it involves in the present financial position of the state '. Whenever the *Corriere della Sera* mentioned a punitive expedition it gave the fascist version, as if the lorry loads of blackshirts were out on innocent jaunts which were spoiled by the inevitable ' communist ambush '.[1] The kidnapping of deputies by fascists, which became common as time went on—Miglioli in Cremona, Fradeletto in Venice, Benedetti in Pescia— was recorded in its columns without a word of regret. After the congress held in Bologna on October 8–10 it was obvious how far this party had moved to the right, although it still called itself liberal. The moving spirits of this congress

---

[1] The cowardice and collusion of the press before fascist terrorism shows clearly the anti-working-class and anti-socialist feeling of Italian ' liberalism '. The economist, Luigi Einaudi, one of the principal contributors to the *Corriere della Sera*, in one of his articles compared the ' proletarians ', whose birth rate, according to him, was falling, with the ' *bourgeois* women, who breed healthy children, skilful wielders of the bludgeon ' (allusion is to the fascist *manganello*). Later on Senator Albertini suffered the same fate as Senator Bergamini (see p. 153n). The fascist government deprived him of his property and the control of his paper. Professor Einaudi's review, *la Riforma Sociale*, was also suppressed.

were the fanatically conservative Sarocchi and Belotti, Senator Albertini and various nationalists. A proposal to call the party ' liberal-democratic ' was crushed by 45,426 to 21,091. The congress was definitely hostile to collaboration with the socialists, and the *Giornale d'Italia* commented as follows on the results : ' The Liberal Congress of Bologna has declared for the pure party tradition and decided to steer firmly to the right. . . . By rejecting the adjective " democratic " it clearly wished to indicate that the association of liberalism with democracy is to cease.' Grandi, though he reproved the congress for not having made quite clear how liberalism stood in relation to fascism, remarked : ' Once more it was really Mussolini who presided over the Liberal Congress. The right wing had its way over the question of the name to be given to the party ; the word " democracy " is the *bête noire* of fascism, and it was thought that its rejection would please the fascists.'

In these circumstances it is hardly surprising that the attempt, revived in August, to build up a great democratic party should have been doomed to failure. The earlier ' democratic coalition ' of autumn 1921 had broken up early in June 1922.[1] The new attempt was faced with all the difficulties that had wrecked the old one, in an aggravated form. Rivalry between Nitti and Giolitti was as before, while most of the politicians of the centre had succumbed either to fear of fascism or to the desire to come to terms with it. The members of the ' democratic ' groups had planned a great campaign of meetings to introduce to the country the new political party, which was going to play the part of mediator between the extremes of right and left. Signori Cocco-Ortu, Bonomi, De Nicola, Orlando, and even Giolitti and Nitti were to speak. But the scheme of amalgamation broke down, even in the form of a federation of the various parties. Cocco-Ortu was to have made the first speech of the series at Naples, at a conference of the southern deputies, but he cried off on the grounds that ' very few democratic deputies have agreed to support the plan '. Later on, in September, Giolitti delivered the *coup de grâce* by expressing

[1] P. 202.

in print his dislike of the proposed coalition. The leaders of the centre parties were either on holiday or else preferred to hold their tongues and not compromise the future. Senator Albertini made caustic reference to this in his speech :[1]

> ' Our rulers are not conspicuous for their courage. See : they hardly ever speak ; they commit themselves as seldom as possible. Last Wednesday[2] we were expecting an important debate. Well ; neither Giolitti, Nitti, Salandra, Orlando nor Bonomi turned up. I watched this sad spectacle from the top of our gallery, while fascists and socialists fought it out amid the indifference of nearly everybody else.'

After August, Mussolini and his friends rained alternate threats and reassurances on public opinion and the government. At the beginning of the month, during the fascist mobilization, the *Avanti* explained the fascist ' plan ' for the march on Rome :

> ' The fascist plan of campaign,' wrote the socialist paper, ' skilfully drawn up by the generals and officers who command the squads, is being carefully and methodically worked out. . . . At the moment there is a hitch. But only for a few days, or even hours. The fascist army is getting ready for its last task, the conquest of the capital ; and not just for the fun of burning down the People's Houses and the headquarters of a few socialist organizations. Now that they have finished their campaigns in Emilia and northern Italy, the fascist forces, who are possibly better armed than the regular army, supplied with rifles by the military authorities, and led by regular officers, are concentrating in Ancona, in the south of Umbria and near Civitavecchia. It is common talk everywhere among the fascist leaders that it will be Rome's turn next.'

The *Popolo d'Italia* declared that the scheme was ' fantastic ' and attributed the article to socialist ' funk '. The fascist press bureau began its series of disclaimers which continued

---

[1] P. 252.   [2] August 9.

right up to the march on Rome : 'The rumour that has been circulated that the fascists are aiming at Rome in order to bring about a *coup d'état* is entirely baseless.' A few days later, on August 11, in an interview with *Il Mattino* of Naples, Mussolini said :

'The march on Rome has begun. It is not a question of the actual march of the three hundred thousand black-shirts that form our redoubtable army. Such a march is strategically possible by three routes : by the Adriatic coast, the Mediterranean, and the Tiber valley, all of which are in our power. But it is not yet politically inevitable. Remember the alternatives I suggested in my speech in the Chamber.[1] They are still open, and the next few months will provide the answer. It is quite certain that fascism means to become the state, but it is not so certain that the attainment of this objective involves a *coup d'état*. Still, that possibility must be regarded as a possibility. Apart from this I repeat, the march on Rome has begun, if not from a strictly insurrectional aspect, at least from an historical one ; since at this very moment a new political class is in process of being formed, to which will be confided quite soon the difficult task of governing—I say governing—the nation.'

Rumours of a march on Rome quickly spread and multiplied. Everybody was discussing it ; only government circles remained sceptical. Baron Beyens, the Belgian ambassador at the Vatican, relates in his memoirs :[2]

'In September I travelled with an Italian manufacturer, Baron Blanc, an enthusiastic supporter of fascism, to whom I offered a seat in my reserved compartment . . . he informed me that quite shortly, in a few weeks' time, Mussolini was going to bring off a *coup d'état*. The blackshirt bands would be mobilized and provided with rifles and machine-guns. After assembling for the Naples Congress they would march on Rome.'

Towards the end of the same month, September, Mussolini made a speech at Cremona, the meaning of which was

---

[1] Pp. 207, 234.   [2] *Quatre Ans à Rome*, Paris, 1934.

clear to anybody, though its menacing frankness failed to shake the inertia of the government :

'What we have done so far is nothing to what remains for us to do. A strong and healthy Italy is getting ready to make a clean sweep of the scum of Italian society. Let our enemies have no illusions. We mean to make our organization even more effectively disciplined, military and forearmed, so that should a decisive stroke become necessary, all of us down to the last man—let traitors and deserters beware !—all of us will do our duty. In short we mean Italy to become fascist. That is simple. That is obvious. We mean Italy to become fascist because we are fed up with seeing her governed at home by men who continually waver between carelessness and cowardice, and above all because we are fed up with seeing her looked upon abroad as a negligible quantity. . . . Our banners were raised at Vittorio Veneto. It was on the banks of the Piave that we began this march, which cannot end till we have reached our final goal, Rome. Nothing can stand in our way, no man can prevent us.'

Mussolini knew that the critical moment was at hand and redoubled his care and his activity. Political parties were in such a state of disruption, the air was so full of animosity and reaction that he could allow himself to make proposals of the most violent kind without causing any unusual stir. On the evening of October 4 he spoke at Milan before the *squadristi* of the Sciesa group, and explained his intentions :

'Those who help us will be well treated. Those who harm us will be harmed. Our enemies will have nothing to complain of if they are treated as enemies, harshly. . . . To-day there are two governments, that is to say, one too many : the liberal government and the fascist government. The state of yesterday and the state of to-morrow. . . . The fascist state is infinitely better than the liberal state, and it is therefore worthy to take over the mandate from the liberal state. . . . The citizens are asking, " What state will end by imposing its laws on the

Italians ? " We have no hesitation in replying, " The fascist state ". How are we to give the nation this government ? In this way : if they have not become completely soft-witted in Rome they must summon the Chamber early in November, pass the new electoral law, and call on the people to give their votes during December.'

Any further parliamentary crisis would be futile. If the government did not follow the method indicated by Mussolini, fascism would have to adopt the other method :

' Observe that our tactics are perfectly open. In any case, when one is attacking an entire state, one can hardly stop at the sort of petty conspiracy which remains secret up to the last moment. We have to give orders to hundreds of thousands of men, and it would be expecting too much to hope to keep them dark. So long as it is necessary, our cards are on the table.'

Mussolini then expounded home and foreign policy :

' We shall not give liberty, even if the demand for it is couched in the faded forms of immortal principles ! This election frippery is not the only thing that separates us from democracy. Do people want to vote ? Well, let them vote. Let us all vote till we are sick of it, till we go crazy ! Nobody wants to abolish universal suffrage. But we are going to introduce a policy of severity and reaction. We divide the Italians into three categories, the indifferent, who await events at home, the sympathisers, who will be allowed to come and go, the enemy, who will not.'

As to foreign policy, he again summarized his usual programme, unaltered :[1]

' By hurling the Italians as a single force towards world tasks, by turning the Mediterranean into an Italian lake, by allying ourselves with those who dwell on the Mediterranean and driving out those who are its parasites, by accomplishing this difficult, long, cyclopean work, we

[1] Pp. 236–238.

shall truly inaugurate a magnificent period in Italian history.'

A few days later, on October 6 and 7, the cabinet met to consider the situation. It was rumoured that they meant to call up two classes to the colours, that they were going to take energetic measures to suppress the trouble. Facta and Taddei, minister of the interior, held long discussions with General Diaz, who was summoned to Rome by telegram, with General Badoglio and with Soleri, the minister for war. General Badoglio was certain that the fascists could never reach Rome : ' After five minutes under fire fascism will collapse,' he said. Mussolini was rather perturbed and wrote in the *Popolo d'Italia* :

> ' We do not think that General Badoglio's sinister intentions will materialize. The national army will not march against the blackshirt army, for the simple reason that the fascists will never march against the national army, for which they cherish the highest respect and infinite admiration. . . . In spite of everything we are confident that General Badoglio will not attempt the useless task of butchering Italian fascism.'

The fascist leaders also feared an immediate political crisis, which was constantly suggested in the papers, and Bianchi and Grandi visited Facta, who reassured them. The *Corriere della Sera* explained that the fascists did not want Facta's resignation, ' since they could not hope for a more obliging ministry than the one over which he presided '. The Facta ministry survived ; the Chamber was to be assembled at the beginning of November, when the crisis would solve itself. In this way the fascists gained three weeks, which enabled them to defeat all the schemes of their opponents.

The Facta ministry were becoming more hopeful. Against the march on Rome Facta and his friends had one supreme weapon : three days before the opening of parliament, on November 4, Gabriele d'Annunzio was to make a great speech in Rome, in which, from the summit of the Capitol, he was to make an appeal for the pacification of the country.

He would be surrounded by thousands of disabled soldiers, who had assembled in Rome to celebrate the great event. Orlando went to see the poet at Gardone, and on his return to Rome on October 13 he said : ' D'Annunzio's love for our Italy reaches at once such a height of exaltation and perfection that to hear him speak is to imagine oneself at the very source of our national life.' So the fascists ran the risk of encountering d'Annunzio actually in Rome, and with him ' the heroes and martyrs of the war '. D'Annunzio would in fact be making a sort of preventive march on Rome, likely to make Mussolini's impossible.

In the first half of 1922 many people had looked on d'Annunzio as a possible rival to Mussolini and the eventual ' executioner '[1] of fascism. Even his presence in Milan among the occupants of the Palazzo Marino[2] had not discouraged those who rested their last hopes on him. A deputation of ex-soldiers, ' legionaries ' of Fiume, with Alceste de Ambris, Luigi Campolonghi, and former comrades in arms of the ' Commandant ', went to Gardone after the general strike, on August 6, and appealed to him to intervene and save the country from fascist dictatorship. D'Annunzio replied that he meant to summon to Rome a great *adunata* of ex-soldiers of all parties, to restore order, while retaining parliamentary government ; three months of dictatorship being followed by normal free elections. According to his idea the dictator would, of course, be himself. He exhorted his visitors to get to work and bring together in Rome as many ex-soldiers as they could, and for slogan he gave them ' *sine strage vici, strepitu sine ullo* '. The deputation met together again in Milan immediately afterwards ; Colonel Amleto Pavone, now a general and a fascist, suggested dividing Italy into ten areas and sending emissaries to recruit anybody who was prepared to ' march ' and ultimately to fight in order to win a victory for the ' Commandant's ' plan. The latter did his best to strengthen his connections with some of the working-class organizations. Shortly after the meeting of the Central Committee of the National Syndicate of Railwaymen (August 19), at which they had decided to quit the Labour Alliance and had sent

[1] P. 184.   [2] P. 227.

a telegram to d'Annunzio hoping for his return to health, one of the leaders of the syndicate said :

'A few days before his accident some of the railwaymen's delegates had a long conversation with d'Annunzio. We are certain to have the support of the majority of the railwaymen, and with d'Annunzio we shall soon have a formidable organized bloc of workers. At the moment we have only the sailors and the railwaymen, but other strong and important federations are ready to follow our example.'

A Rome paper announced that ' for some time there have been signs of d'Annunzian tendencies among the post office workers, and it is not impossible that before long the P.T.T. may make a decision similar to that of the railwaymen '. The Federation of Legionaries of Fiume busied itself about preparing a ' Syndical constituent assembly ', which was to build up working-class unity afresh round d'Annunzio and his programme.

All this time d'Annunzio was also trying to gain the support of various politicians, among them Nitti, who at the time of Fiume had been his *bête noire*. But he preferred Nitti to Giolitti, because he could not forgive ' that butcher' for turning him out of Fiume. Besides, to the poet Nitti seemed an ' expert ' in economic and financial matters, and, moreover, an expert with culture and imagination. D'Annunzio's envoy went to Agnano, where Nitti was taking the waters, and laid before him the soldier-poet's scheme for a great ' reconciliation of all ex-soldiers '. Nitti agreed to meet d'Annunzio, but on certain conditions. He refused to go to Gardone, because d'Annunzio had too heinously insulted him in the past ; he knew that d'Annunzio would never so humiliate himself as to come to him. So it was arranged to meet at a neutral spot, half-way between Gardone and Rome. Nitti also pointed out that no pacification would be possible if Mussolini were not present. Further he demanded guarantees for his personal safety, since to reach the rendezvous in Tuscany he had to go through country swarming with riotous fascist squads to whom he would be fair game. All arrangements on these lines were

completed ; Mussolini agreed to meet d'Annunzio and
Nitti, and the latter was to travel with two cars, accompanied
by the fascist deputy, Aldo Finzi, his friend, Schiff Giorgini,
and one Brambilla, the owner of the villa in which the three
chiefs were to meet. All was ready when a telephone message
came through : ' D'Annunzio is dying.' The Commandant
had fallen out of a window of his museum-convent-bachelor
retreat of a villa after a quarrel between two of his lady
friends, his ' sisters ' as he liked to call them. This put
him out of action for some weeks and left him in a very weak
state, though he did not abandon his plans. On September 12, the anniversary of the march on Ronchi, he issued
an appeal, in which he regretted that he had not his legionaries round him, hoped that in their minds ' liberty and
light would be one ', and to the slogan they already knew,
sine strage vici, added a word of hope, ' *insperata floret* '.

The *Popolo d'Italia* published this message on its fourth
page without comment. Mussolini's craving for power was
stronger than ever. The idea of a march on Rome was in
the air. It would be the natural outcome of the fascist
' offensives ', which were becoming wider and wider in
scope, moving on to the annexation of new territories from
those which were already subdued.[1] The whole Po valley,
all central Italy, Tuscany, Umbria and the Roman
Campagna were occupied by the blackshirts. By October
only a few towns still remained ' free ' : Turin, Parma,
besides the south, more or less neutral. The impetus
attained by the expeditions and fascist *adunate* was bound to
reach Rome ; it was logically inherent in the whole movement just as much as in the determination of Mussolini
and the other fascist leaders. During the strike in August
Facta had yielded up Milan, Genoa, and Leghorn to the
fascists in return for a promise that they would not occupy
Rome. Accordingly the advance of fascism and the feebleness of the government combined to make Rome the last,
the key position, on whose fate depended that of the regime,
and which the fascists had got to seize or lose all their
previous gains.

There were other pressing reasons why power must be

[1] See Mussolini's article of July 15, quoted on pp. 203-204.

captured immediately. Already, at the Central Committee of *Fasci*, held in mid-August in Milan, several delegates had expressed anxiety at the increasing numbers of working men whom fascism had somehow to take in and shelter after destroying their organizations.[1]   To cope with this pressure, control the masses and satisfy their most elementary wants was only possible if fascism had the full resources of the state at its disposal.   Various events emphasized the danger that fascism might have to face inside its own improvised and overgrown syndical system.   In the province of Siena the fascists had occupied, in Poggibonsi, San Gemignana, Casole, and Serre di Rapolano, various agricultural properties (*tenute*), evoking protests from the provincial federation of the Agrarian Association, whose paper, *Il Solco*, wrote at the beginning of September :

> ' The fascists of Siena want the landed proprietors to employ a constantly increasing number of labourers, there being now so many unemployed.   They have threatened to invade and actually have invaded farms, because proprietors have refused to take on more hands. We freely admit that these proprietors are not saints, but this is no justification for invasions, real or threatened. Otherwise the socialists too would be justified, since they used the same arguments to support their own violence.'

Mussolini, irritated, sent a telegram calling on the fascist federation of Siena to account for its actions.   In Ferrara, too, for the same reason, the situation was strained.   The landowners had profited by the complete victory of *squadrismo* to lengthen working hours and reduce wages.   The sugar manufacturers, of whom there were many in this province where beet was widely grown, reduced wages by from six to eight lire a day.   All this caused discontent and even disunion among the fascists of Ferrara.   The party executive ordered an inquiry and the branch was dissolved, while dissension between ' official ' and ' autonomous ' fascists broke out.

The fascist militia was becoming a serious problem. These tens of thousands of men could not be left to terrorize

[1] Pp. 234-235.

and rob the population. Having once slaughtered, burned, and occupied as widely as they could, some other form of activity had to be found for them under the ægis of the state. They were extremely expensive to maintain ; and although landowners, manufacturers and bankers subscribed lavishly, the money had to be solicited and could not go on for ever. The financial problem became acute as the numbers of the militia rose. A regular source of income, such as the state only could provide, had to be found. The militia was to become an organic part of the new state, the fascist state. In an article of October 24 the *Popolo d'Italia* foreshadowed its character and functions :

' To the question, what shall we do with the *squadre di combattimento* when we are in power ? will they be dissolved ? a voice, instinctive rather than rational, answers from the bottom of our heart and says : no, *squadrismo* cannot, must not die. For us it would be suicidal ; if force is needed to seize power, it is needed all the more to hold it. The *fascist* militia will be transformed. The squads will cease to be organs of a party and become organs of the state. Transformed by pre-military instruction, they will be the living ideal of the nation in arms. Once *squadrismo* has been militarized the danger of rivalry between it and the other national armed forces will end, as its task will be separate. The volunteer army incorporated in the organization of the new state will be the surest guarantee of the future.'

The nationalists were still a potential source of danger and rivalry.[1] They, too, had their squads, they had their blue shirts as the fascists their black shirts. On September 9, at Genoa, one of these squads seized the *Vulcania*, a ship belonging to the *Navigazione Generale*, because a nationalist member of the crew had been discharged. The nationalist flag was hoisted to the mainmast. Elsewhere there were various brushes between nationalists and fascists, one particularly serious at Taranto, at the ceremony of presentation of colours to the local nationalist section. The fascists attacked the nationalists in the street, fought with fists,

[1] P. 155.

bludgeons, and pistols, and even threw ' hand-grenades, which spread terror through the town '. The treasurer of the nationalist group was killed and many were wounded. The fascists were angry because several deserters from the local *fascio* had joined the ranks of the nationalists. The executives of both parties, fascist and nationalist, intervened and deplored these incidents, ' which could only help the common enemy '. In a speech in Milan on the morning of October 15 the nationalist deputy Federzoni heaped compliments on Mussolini and fascism, but that afternoon in the same town there was an *adunata* of ' blueshirts ' from Bologna, Vicenza and Genoa. This did not fail to disturb Mussolini, who had no intention of letting the nationalists rob him of the fruits of his labour at the first opportunity.

The possibility of the formation of a Giolitti ministry was the gravest danger that still remained. On October 7 the cabinet had decided not to resign ; nevertheless a crisis might break out at any moment. For Mussolini the problem was rapidly resolving itself into the concrete question of the direct seizure of power. At the last meeting of the Central Committee of the National Fascist Party (August 13), Italo Balbo and Michele Bianchi had proposed the following resolution, which was passed unanimously : ' The Central Committee, after examining the military situation of fascism, entrusts to a supreme command of three the task of carrying out any military action that circumstances or the needs of the fascist programme may demand.' The party executive appointed as triumvirs Italo Balbo, De Vecchi and General De Bono. The last two met on September 15 to draw up the new regulations of the fascist militia, which were first published in the *Popolo d'Italia* on October 4. On October 6 Balbo went to see Mussolini, who questioned him on the ' possibilities of success for a revolutionary action against Rome, asking not for general assurances, but for precise information and accurate details '. Balbo's impression was that Mussolini was inclined to attempt an insurrection. The march on Rome was decided in principle on October 16 at a meeting of the general staff, which took place in Milan in the presence of Mussolini and of the party secretary, Bianchi, and at which the generals Fara and Ceccherini were also present.[1] The following account of the meeting is taken from Italo Balbo's *Diary*, for October 16 :

' Mussolini goes straight to the heart of the question. In the course of a particularly clear general summary he declared that events are moving fast and that fascism may at any moment be led to start an insurrection. He thinks the movement should culminate with a march on Rome to force the government to resign, and induce the Crown to form a fascist cabinet. He adds that we cannot wait for a parliamentary solution, which would be against the spirit and the interests of fascism. The manœuvres of the last few days are serving to distract the attention of public opinion and even of the government. The direct seizure of power is the only solution worthy of our movement, which has acted outside and above the laws of a decrepit regime. We will not lower ourselves to compromise, we will make our strength felt. Mussolini asks all present, demanding absolute frankness, if they believe that the military forces of fascism are ready, morally and materially, for their revolutionary task.

' De Bono and De Vecchi, who, like me, have visited in person during the past few weeks all the centres of their zones,[2] inspected the legions, and been in direct contact with the men, consider that the fascist forces are not yet ready and that we ought to wait some time.

' I say that I am worried by the turn taken by political affairs in the last few days. I consider any delay dangerous. The old political parties are beginning to play a cautious game. In spite of itself fascism risks being caught up in the plot that is being hatched against it and in the snare of the elections.

' I think that if we do not attempt a *coup d'état* at once, by the spring it will be too late. In the mild atmosphere

[1] On October 22, 1924, General De Bono resigned from the general staff of the fascist militia. Mussolini thanked him on this occasion for his services ' since October 16, 1922, the day he had summoned him with other generals to Milan, 46 Via San Marco, to arrange for the march on Rome.' Via San Marco was the headquarters of the *Popolo d'Italia*.

[2] At the Oneglia meeting (p. 178) of January 1922, Italy had been divided into military zones ; a division that was modified in October (pp. 282–283).

of Rome liberals and revolutionaries will come to an agreement ; it will not be difficult for the new cabinet to take more energetic police measures and to engage the army against us. To-day we have the advantage of surprise. So far nobody seriously believes in our revolutionary intentions. In short a six months' delay would multiply our difficulties by ten. Much better make our final attempt to-day, even if we are not completely ready, than wait till to-morrow and give our enemies time to complete their own preparations.

'. . . Michele Bianchi supports my views and adds important political arguments. Mussolini says he agrees with us and De Bono and De Vecchi are won over without pressing their views further.

' The Duce concludes this rapid survey by saying that it is impossible to decide if the insurrection should take place at once, but that it must be attempted at the first opportunity. He suggests fixing the date of the rising after the review of fascist forces which takes place in Naples on October 24.

'. . . The leadership and organization of the action is then discussed. Mussolini explains that the party is to invest its powers in a Quadrumvirate consisting of the three commanding officers—De Bono, De Vecchi and Balbo—and the party secretary, Michele Bianchi. Once the military action is begun all the political hierarchies,[1] local or national, are to disappear. The military command, imbued with full powers, will take their place.'

Thus in the middle of October Mussolini thought that insurrection was inevitable, but, as in all the circumstances of his life, he wanted to reduce the risks of the enterprise to a minimum. He would have liked everything to happen as if the march on Rome had taken place, without actually having to carry it through. At the beginning of the month he had prepared the call to action which the Quadrumvirate was to announce to the fascists and the country when the

---

[1] Italian *gerarchie*, official fascist expression describing the higher members of the party, the leaders.

moment came, and he reserved the right to modify it at the last minute to suit the circumstances. Rome could not be annexed like any ordinary town or province occupied by fascist squads. From such a step there could be no retreat. Tremendous political skill was needed to allay the suspicions and aggressiveness of rivals, to gain fresh allies, and to ensure the neutrality of the various armed forces of the state. During the last three weeks before the march on Rome Mussolini made frenzied efforts in every direction to ensure such political advantages. He neglected nothing, from d'Annunzio to Giolitti, Salandra to Nitti, the monarchy to the republicans, the freemasons to the Vatican.

The first step, which he took charge of himself, was to eliminate d'Annunzio. To do this he had to make him a few concessions and let him think that he could go on playing the part of the saviour of Italy, ' without bloodshed and without upheaval '. D'Annunzio was closely associated with the Federation of Maritime Workers, led by Captain Giulietti, who had secured the return of Malatesta to Italy and had helped greatly in the provisioning of Fiume.[1] This federation had placed itself under the protection of the ' Commandant ' and made him large gifts of cash, which were badly needed for the ' franciscan ' retreat at Gardone. After the fascist ' conquest ' of Genoa the federation was threatened ; the local shipbuilders and the local fascist leaders demanded its liquidation. At the beginning of September a congress was held at Genoa by the ' National Maritime Corporation ', a fascist organization which meant to displace that led by Giulietti. Bianchi and Rossoni, secretary of the fascist syndicates, were present, and Mussolini sent a personal message. The congress decided that war must be declared on Giulietti's federation, and also called on the government to give up all its levies on excess war profits and its demands on the shipbuilders, so as to ' help in the resumption of maritime activity ', for the sake, of course, of the unemployed. Thus commenced a desperate struggle which could only end in the victory of the new fascist monopoly. Giulietti, however, was cunning and though he hung on to d'Annunzio he began

[1] P. 50.

making advances to Mussolini. The ' Commandant ' was at this period on very bad terms with the fascists. On October 13 he had announced the mobilization of his legionaries in Fiume. On the 18th the Fascist Party press bureau published a communiqué forbidding fascists to go to Fiume. On the 19th Captain Coselschi, d'Annunzio's secretary, made the following announcement in the Rome *Tribuna :*

' As you are aware, the Commandant has decided to convert the federation of his legionaries into a genuine and powerful organ of national propaganda, destined for the pacification of the country and the spiritual uplifting of the Italian people, divorced from all party tendencies. . . . The headquarters of the federation will be moved from Milan to Florence. The organization of the legionaries will not represent a party, but will be a group of disciples united to defend the faith of Gabriele d'Annunzio.'

As for the agreement between Mussolini and d'Annunzio, Coselschi continued :

' I cannot give any details, as we are pledged to secrecy. I can, however, confirm that this agreement, which has to do with syndical forces, really exists and concerns an event of great importance for national pacification, with consequences affecting political as well as syndical affairs.'

Mussolini, d'Annunzio and Giulietti had in fact just signed a pact dealing with the Federation of Maritime Workers. The text of the pact, signed at Milan on October 16, was not published till October 22 in the *Popolo d'Italia.* These are its essential points :

' In Milan, between the Italian Federation of Maritime Workers, under the protection of Gabriele d'Annunzio, and the executive of the National Fascist Party, represented by Benito Mussolini, after declarations of mutual esteem, the following pact has been ratified to protect the integrity of the Italian mercantile marine and to ensure national peace :

' 1. The Federation, which is considering demanding from the shipowners fair treatment for their crews, will gladly submit any request of this type for the examination of the fascist representative before agitating in parliament or making direct application to the shipowners ; with a view to proving the legitimacy of such a request and giving an opportunity to take common action in the matter.

' 2. The fascist representative will examine these requests with the representatives of the Federation, so as to arrive at an agreement as soon as possible, and in any case within three days at the latest.

' 3. As soon as agreement has been reached on these requests the representatives of the Federation will communicate them to the shipowners and open negotiations with them.

' 4. If these negotiations are broken off, fascism, which is personified in Mussolini, will fight with all its forces, joined to those of the Federation, to obtain justice by direct action.

' 5. Within a maximum of thirty days after signing this pact the Fascist Party solemnly promises to dissolve the Maritime Corporation and to order its members to return immediately to the ranks of the Federation, which shall continue in the same functions and under the same control as at present.'

This pact, which was signed by d'Annunzio, Mussolini, and Giulietti, stupefied the fascists of the maritime towns, who had been fighting Giulietti's federation ever since August, and meant to replace it by the fascist ' Maritime Corporation '. The fascists did not understand how the decisions of the Genoa congress[1] could be reversed at the wish of three people who had taken no part in it. The ' liberal ' and conservative press gave a place of honour to their protests. The *Corriere della Sera* expressed the fear that, thanks to Mussolini and d'Annunzio, Giulietti would be confirmed in his all-powerful position, and would take the opportunity ' to continue his demagogic and anti-national

[1] P. 267.

policy '. Three days later at the Naples congress a fascist representative from Genoa said that in signing the pact the executive had perpetrated ' a colossal blunder which has cut the ground from under our feet in the syndical as well as in the political sphere '. The reaction was such that on October 24 the *Popolo d'Italia* declared that : ' It was a question of an agreement in principle, drawn up with the intention of making peace ', and that further agreements should be made during the thirty days ' to make the treaty a really effective peacemaker '. ' We postpone,' added the paper, ' our comments and impressions for thirty days.'

Nothing in the text of the agreement warranted such an interpretation. Article 5 was explicit ; the promise made by the executive of the Fascist Party to dissolve the fascist ' corporations ' was subject to no condition. But Mussolini was forced to trim his sails. The fascists, the uncomprehending mob, must be allowed their howl of complaint, being unable, like Mussolini, to conceive of subordinating everything to the plan for which he was feverishly working. He had no doubt that the operation he had just carried out was both opportune and useful, and his confidence was justified. The advantages of the treaty were numerous and important. On the eve of decisive events it bridged over the difference between fascism and d'Annunzio, and made Mussolini look like a peacemaker and a supporter of d'Annunzio's political designs. By temporarily saving the Federation of Maritime Workers from the fascist attack, he led d'Annunzio to believe that the victory of fascism would not mean the abolition of national syndicalism, and of the ' labour ' idea which Mussolini himself had had in mind in 1919 and early in 1921, and which d'Annunzio still hankered after. It flattered d'Annunzio to be able to show what his protection was worth, while on the other hand he felt rather in the debt of Mussolini, whose personal intervention had been decisive. On October 20 he ordered the demobilization of his legionaries, whom he had summoned to Fiume a week earlier.[1] It is true that it was announced in the press on October 21 that he would speak in Rome on

---

[1] P. 268.

November 4, as arranged by the ex-servicemen in conjunction with Facta, Orlando and Amendola. But as early as October 25 his secretary, Coselschi, gave out in Florence that the Poet was ' very tired after the hard work of the last few days ', that his doctors had ordered him rest and that ' in the circumstances it is impossible to guarantee that he would be able to go to Rome on November 4, as he would have liked '.

By signing this treaty Mussolini fostered the hopes of members of the General Confederation of Labour and other workers' organizations which they had begun to fix on d'Annunzio. The Federation of Maritime Workers, which played such an important part from the technical point of view, since it controlled practically all sea transport, would no longer obstruct fascist action. Captain Giulietti, it was announced in the *Avanti*, had even placed the ships of the federation at Mussolini's disposal for the transport and supplying of the fascist army in the event of a campaign in Dalmatia. In case the advantages he expected turned out disappointing or too many difficulties arose in the application of the agreement, Mussolini had taken his usual precautions. It did not come into full force for thirty days, and before they were past the march on Rome or the accession of the fascists to power by some other means would have taken place. By then he would have no particular need of d'Annunzio or Giulietti and he could maintain, transform, or destroy the pact as circumstances demanded.

Giolitti was more difficult to dispose of. He was an unimaginative man, and not a great initiator of policy. He was quite willing to hold new elections, but not just yet ; he would prefer the spring, after a few months of office. Mussolini was negotiating with him through Lusignoli, the prefect of Milan, who had already acted as intermediary between them at the time of the action against Fiume.[1] Giolitti wanted the fascists to join his cabinet and he insisted that they should be represented there by Mussolini. But the demands of the fascists, who felt or believed themselves to be masters of the country, were more ambitious than a few months ago, and this made negotiations difficult.

[1] P. 84.

' It is said that the fascists,' said the *Corriere della Sera* of October 19, ' have asked for representation in the new cabinet proportionate to their real strength in the country and not merely to the number of seats they won at the last elections ; that they have asked for three important portfolios and the right to appoint a new foreign minister. Giolitti, on the other hand, would like Mussolini to join the government and would offer him a place as minister without portfolio. As to the electoral reform, agreement should not be difficult since Giolitti and Mussolini both want a revision of the existing law to favour absolute majorities, applying the proportional method to minorities.'

On the same day the *Popolo d'Italia* denied the existence of a political understanding between Mussolini and Giolitti, and even denied that discussions had taken place, while Michele Bianchi explained at Montecitorio that the negotiations had fallen through because the fascists had not been offered adequate representation. Actually relations between Mussolini and Giolitti were not broken off, but Giolitti announced that he was prepared to form a government at all costs, even without the fascists, if they insisted on their exorbitant conditions. On October 23, when opening the session of the provincial council of Coni, he explained his attitude towards them :

' A new party has entered Italian political life, attended by much commotion, violent in some parts of the country, less so in others. There it should take the place to which the number of its supporters entitles it ; but by legal means, which alone can give a party, within the constitution, real and lasting authority, and which alone can enable it to realize the fundamental part of its programme, which is to restore the authority of the State for the safety, greatness and prosperity of the country.'

Up till the last minute Mussolini allowed Giolitti to believe that they were in agreement on essentials and that they only differed over the sharing of places in the cabinet. Giolitti, for his part, thought he could get the best of the bargain by passing the word round among his friends that he would eventually do without the fascists altogether.

On October 23, at Turin, Giolitti met Corradini, his one-time Under-secretary of State, the prefect Lusignoli, the ministers Bertone (*Popolare*) and Teofilo Rossi, Zanetti, editor of the *Sera* of Milan, and Giovanni Borelli, who, at the last liberal congress in Bologna, had spoken in favour of alliance with the fascists. These discussions and negotiations had in view the formation of a new government, but any decision was postponed until after the speech Mussolini was to make in Naples. The same day Lupi, who had acted as Mussolini's mouthpiece in the Chamber in August,[1] announced that the fascists agreed to the elections being held in March ; this would have been a concession to Giolitti and a possible basis of compromise with him.

Salandra fell straight into the trap set for him. He cherished the secret hope of gaining fascist support and becoming prime minister once more. When the *fasci* of Capitanata held a congress in Troia, his native town, they sent a delegation to pay him their respects. Much flattered, Salandra replied ' that he considered himself an honorary fascist, and would sign on as a militant one if he were not seventy years old.' Pointless to talk of a dictatorship in Italy : ' There is no danger of it,' he insisted, ' the right man, the dictator, is missing.' Italy was to have another Salandra ministry, in which there would be, of course, plenty of room for the fascists.

As for Nitti, Mussolini knew that he was suspicious, and that a tempting bait must be prepared. The accident which put d'Annunzio out of action in August had also interrupted the negotiations between Nitti and Mussolini.[2] But Mussolini resumed them on his own towards the end of September. He sent Schiff-Giorgini to Acquafredda, who told Nitti :

' I have come from Mussolini. Italy is being ruined. Facta is an idiot. Mussolini has been approached by Giolitti, he has an understanding with Salandra, but he is convinced that only you can succeed. An extra-parliamentary crisis must be provoked. You must make a

---

[1] P. 233.　　　[2] Pp. 260–261.

speech which will prepare the way for the summoning of parliament, the resignation of Facta, and the formation of a coalition government.'

Nitti replied that he could not deal with Schiff-Giorgini, who had no proper authority. He wanted serious guarantees to avoid compromising himself to no purpose. Mussolini must send someone of importance on such a mission. Mussolini yielded and charged the ambassador Romano Avezzana to continue the discussions. The latter went in person to Acquafredda, confirmed Mussolini's first message, and insisted that Nitti should as soon as possible make the declaration asked for by Mussolini. Nitti then asked a number of definite questions : (1) What were Mussolini's immediate demands ? Would he be content with one ministry and two under-secretaryships ? (2) Why had Mussolini also approached Giolitti and Salandra ? (3) What would he do with the *fasci* ? (4) Was he prepared to go so far as to take military action to suppress them ? Mussolini replied : (1) It is now impossible for us to be content with one ministry and two under-secretaryships. The *fasci* have expanded. They have liquidated the general strike. Circumstances have altered, and we want two ministries and three under-secretaryships of State, though we do not want the political or military ministries. (2) I am surprised that Nitti should take exception to my negotiations. I carried on negotiations with Giolitti because his friend the prefect, Lusignoli, allows me a free hand in Milan and I have to go carefully with him. Salandra does not count. (3 and 4) The *fasci* will be dissolved at once.

Baron Romano Avezzana once more went backwards and forwards between Milan and Acquafredda and a course of action was finally decided upon. Nitti was to make a speech enlarging on the seriousness of the situation and emphasizing the need for new elections. The *Popolo d'Italia* would publish it without comment. Mussolini, who preferred to know nothing of any march on Rome, would speak at the Naples congress and damn everybody except Nitti. The crisis would take place and a fine new ministry with Nitti and Mussolini would be formed for the salvation of Italy.

Nitti carried out his part of the plan and made a speech on October 20 in the little theatre in Lauria, in Basilicata, devoted chiefly to financial questions. The *Popolo d'Italia* enumerated the principal points as follows :

1. Italy needs the restoration of the economic unity of continental Europe.
2. In the present unsettled European conditions, Italy must keep her army ready for action, concentrating on the officer class, and strengthening aviation.
3. To obtain the necessary means for the defence of the country, credit must be restored, strict economy practised, and confidence given back to capital. Now that the enquiry into war contracts which has seriously disturbed so many industries has been completed, the question of excess profits must be settled, the stock market revived, and any scheme for the registering of stocks by actual holders abandoned at once.
4. The state budget must be balanced.
5. The state must give up all services not essential for its proper functioning, re-establish the security of the public services and declare any strike in these services a criminal offence.
6. All reforms likely to impede production or discourage the investment of capital must be abandoned.

This speech was followed by a banquet at which Nitti said exactly what Mussolini had asked him to say.

' The present government is incapable of coping with a single one of the fundamental problems that face the country or with any of the live forces outside the government. After what has happened in the last few days one is compelled to ask oneself if the present difficulties ought not to be dealt with by methods outside the ordinary administration, and if it is not time the country were quickly consulted. There is a distinct cleavage between the situation in parliament and the situation in the country. . . . Democracy exists, socialism exists, but fascism too exists as an ethico-social phenomenon and has developed to such an extent that no statesman can neglect it. . . . We should utilize all live forces, and welcome

the idealistic part of fascism, which has been the cause
of its progress, and we must at the same time make use
of the healthiest and most industrious sections of the
working classes, guiding both into the legal framework of
our institutions. We must have a strong government,
and the only way to get it is to go to the country as soon
as possible.'

Nitti thus echoed most of the Fascist Party's demands for
the financial restoration of the state, the very ones which
had won for it the sympathy and help of Italian financial
circles. His views on the military question were very
different from those he had professed in 1919–20, while
finally he supported the fascist argument on the necessity
for immediate elections, a further point of disagreement
with Giolitti, who wanted to go to the country in six months'
time. The *Popolo d'Italia* published Nitti's remarks without
comment, as arranged, but with an unsympathetic headline,
' Flippant speech by Nitti '. Italo Balbo in his *Diary* says :
' Nitti's aim is a little straighter in his last speech ; but the
old pirate has nothing to hope for from fascism except a
firing squad.' His comments might have been different
had he realized that the Lauria speech had been prepared
in collaboration with Mussolini and at his request.

Up till now Italian freemasonry had been rather in favour
of fascism ; the lower middle-class sections through patriotic
and nationalistic feelings, or because they were attracted by
the republican tendency Mussolini had made so much of ;
the industrialists and capitalists through instinctive conservatism and reaction against the socialist advance, and the
Order as a whole because its hopes were raised by the
violently anti-clerical terms of the fascist programme of
1919 and the fascists' growing hostility towards the *Popolari*.

In Milan there was a group of freemason industrialists
closely connected with Mussolini, amongst them Cesare
Goldmann, who had been a candidate in 1919 on Mussolini's list, and Ceresola, who later brought De Bono a large
subsidy from freemasonry for the march on Rome. General
Capello[1] was at once a fascist and 33 ∴ of the Grand Orient.

[1] P. 211.

A large number of fascists belonged to the Grand Lodge of Piazza del Gesù :[1] Cesare Rossi, Italo Balbo, the Marquis Perrone Compagni, the deputies Edouardo Torre, Acerbo, Terzaghi, Lanfranconi, Oviglio, Capanni. Between 1919 and 1922 a fair number of *fasci* were formed through masonic influence, and Domizio Torrigiani, Grand Master of the Palazzo Giustiniani freemasonry, boasted, although he afterwards regretted it—too late—that he had several times put the Milan *fascio* on its feet again. Dissension inside the Florence *fascio* had its repercussions among the masons, leading to the creation of rival lodges and mutual excommunications. However in some fascist circles the feeling against freemasonry hardened as fascism gradually became more and more anti-democratic. At the end of September, 1922, the deputy De Stefani moved at a meeting of the secretaries of the *fasci* of Vicenza a resolution affirming that ' membership of the National Fascist Party is incompatible with active participation in freemasonry '. A few days later he asked Mussolini his views on this subject and was told : ' As to freemasonry—which I have always disliked—the question you raise seems to me inopportune. It can be revived when things are calmer. We must not bite off more than we can chew.' He thus checked De Stefani's zeal, which might have lost him valuable support. On October 19 the Grand Master, Domizio Torrigiani, sent a circular letter to all the lodges of his order in which he emphasized the importance of the masonic contribution to fascism in its earlier stages :

' When the terrible post-war crisis began we decided that our order must give all its energies to the defence of the state, and we are glad to say to-day that groups of our Brothers, who enjoy high authority, have contributed to the birth and development of the fascist movement. The number of our Brothers in the *fasci* is still increasing. In the conflict of tendencies that accompanied the evolution of the fascist phenomenon, they have done their best to encourage the elements most consistent with the spirit of freemasonry. As with all our other Brothers in the

[1] P. 48.

different parties, we have never attempted to control their liberty of action, which is limited only by our fundamental precepts. The fascist leaders, I feel sure, realize and appreciate the loyalty of fascist freemasons.'

Freemasonry had helped in the work of national settlement and recognized the salutary part that fascism had played in it.

'And when we saw,' continued the letter, 'that youth was turning enthusiastically towards the fascist movement, we were among the first to notice and point out that this great political phenomenon must correspond, however indirectly, to a great national need. We believe it would be superficial to judge it solely from the theoretical declarations of its leaders. We must observe its content and its real meaning. In politics it shows a desire for violent change. Economically, fascism already controls several hundred thousand organized workers. Considered in relation to masonic principles these facts controvert the fascist theory of opposition to all democratic doctrine. A large mass of workers, organized for economic conquests, cannot succeed in disowning liberty, fraternity, equality. The ordinary idealistic middle *bourgeoisie* who are the backbone of the *fasci* are incapable of wanting to build up oligarchies and diminish liberty. One may criticize the parliamentary democracies and worn out parties, but one cannot deny the reality of the mass movements of the day nor the fact that they are irresistibly democratic.'

This optimistic analysis, which bears witness to the deliberate blindness of the Grand Master and his friends, did not altogether succeed in allaying a certain uneasiness, which was nevertheless quickly overborne :

'If freedom were suppressed, if essential private liberties were interfered with, if a dictatorship or an oligarchy were established, every freemason would know where his duty lay ; he knows that it would be a sacred cause for which, as our glorious tradition shows, men can live and die. But we do not believe these threats. A new force is entering the life of the nation. Freemasonry hopes that it will be for the good of Italy, which it looks on as its religion.'

And so it was that it contributed three and a half millions towards the march on Rome.[1]

Mussolini did not want the question of the freemasons raised just then, because, though he did not want to alienate them, he was equally unwilling to appear to favour them in case he should alienate the Vatican and check the *Popolari's* drift to the right.   As early as September 19 a group of eight *Popolari* senators had sent a letter to Don Sturzo emphasizing the impossibility of any collaboration with the socialists : ' It is worth while reaffirming once again one's conviction that there are unions so lacking in all the most sacred and vital principles of social life that they cannot be tolerated and still less invited.'   A month later, on October 21, the National Council of the Italian *Popolare* Party issued an appeal to the country, which, although it contained vigorous and even courageous declarations in favour of liberty and democracy, nevertheless reflected on the whole the general turn to the right taken by all political forces in the country after the end of August.   It was in favour of new elections, but in ' the atmosphere of liberty through which alone the sovereignty of the people can be made clear ', and on the basis of proportional representation, which Mussolini, Giolitti and Nitti wanted to abolish.   The elections must turn on ' the policy of financial recovery and the willingness of the new forces that have grown up in the nation to rally to the constitution and give up their hankering for rebellion and armed organization'.   This ' centrist ' appeal of the *Popolari* passed almost unnoticed, for the authority of the party was diminished by the numerous communications from the Vatican.   The Italian press published almost at the same time a letter sent out by Cardinal Gasparri, a secretary of state, to the ecclesiastical authorities, which in the circumstances seemed to disavow the *Popolari* :

' Your Most Illustrious and Most Reverend Lordships are aware that recently the Holy See has been accused

[1] Eugenio Chiesa, a freemason and one time deputy, revealed in 1926 that a group of high officials of the order had spent three and a half millions in contributing to the cost of the march on Rome.

and attacked in the press for its alleged connection with the *Popolari*, as if the latter were an emanation of the Holy See or represented the Catholics in the country or in parliament. Against these insinuations the Holy See has always energetically protested, constantly declaring that, faithful to its principles of keeping outside political rivalries, it has remained and means to remain in the future totally separate from the *Popolari*, as from all other political parties ; and that it intends to censure or blame them, like any other party, if they act in opposition to the principles of religion and Christian morality.'

The right wing of the *Popolari* won an important victory over the list for the municipal elections in Milan after the ' legal ' dissolution of the socialist council. At an early meeting the idea of putting up a separate list had prevailed, but on October 23, after a referendum, over which the Archbishop of Milan brought all his influence to bear, the proposal simply to support the list of the national bloc was carried by a large majority.

At that time the Republican Party was greatly reduced in strength, though it had important centres in the Romagna and in Genoa, the city of Mazzini. In the Romagna hatred of the socialists had thrown some of the republicans into the arms of the fascists, who had made a point of showing republican tendencies. In August, after the general strike, the republicans withdrew the ' moral support ' they had given to the Alliance of Labour.

During the second half of 1922 the many ' loyalist ' declarations made by Mussolini and other fascist leaders had diminished their enthusiasm and their hopes of founding some sort of republic with the aid of fascism. But Mussolini was busy fostering a separatist movement inside the small Republican Party. Towards the end of August ' republican *fasci* ' began to appear, the first of which, in Genoa, announced ' its perfect agreement with the methods used by the National Fascist Party to combat the political and economic aims of every sort of anti-nationalist party '. On October 16 there was founded in Rome the ' National Mazzini Union ', on the initiative of an adventurer of the worst type, Carlo Bazzi, a freemason and one of the chiefs of the (fascist) 'National Syndicate of Co-operatives', the funds of which were used to subsidize the march on Rome.

It was to the Quirinal, where in the last instance the fate of fascism would be settled, that Mussolini devoted his most serious attention. From the time of his controversy with the *Giornale d'Italia* up to his Udine speech he had not ceased to address his 'advice' and threats to the Crown, in public, so that Rome might know what to expect. He unhesitatingly applied to the Crown the same policy of internal disintegration that he had used against the socialists, the *Popolari*, the liberals, and the republicans. The king was too faithful to Giolitti, whom he hoped soon to see in power, dragging behind his triumphal chariot the pinioned forces of fascism and socialism, the latter now entirely harmless. In the middle of October, when he was in Brussels during the engagement of the crown prince Umberto to princess Marie-José, he told king Albert how optimistic he was about the Italian situation. Giolitti had the ministry in his pocket and would form a government immediately after the reopening of parliament on November 7. Mussolini, however, had strong support even inside the royal household.

The king's cousin, the Duke of Aosta, married to a member of the Orleans family, was ambitious and ready to favour the plans of Mussolini, who dangled the hope of a regency before him. The duke as early as 1920 had suggested to the king that he should set up a regime like that of Horthy in Hungary, that is a ruthless anti-working class and anti-socialist dictatorship. In 1919–1920 he had applauded the Fiume enterprise. Now he thought he was near his goal, for d'Annunzio, the freemasons of Piazza del Gesù, and some of the fascists, including Mussolini, had all considered him as a possible candidate for the throne, in case King Victor Emmanuel refused to accept the new situation. In any event Mussolini allowed the most alarming rumours to circulate. The duke was only an instrument to him, a pawn in his game, though an extremely valuable one.

Another influence was being exerted at court in favour of fascism ; that of the queen mother, Margaret of Savoy, widow of Umberto I, and the inspirer of the despotic policy which had led to his assassination by Bresci. When the three commanding officers of the fascist military forces, De Bono, De Vecchi and Balbo, went to Bordighera to complete the preparations for the march on Rome, Queen Margaret asked them to dine at her palace. De Bono and De Vecchi accepted, realizing that she knew the reason for their presence in the town. When they took their leave she ' gave them her best wishes for the success of the fascist schemes, which aspire to the safety and aggrandisement of the nation ' : so wrote Balbo in his *Diary*.

The fascist high command drew up its plan : General De Bono decided to concentrate the fascist troops at Santa Marinella, near Civitavecchia, Monterotondo and Tivoli. They were not counting on the southern forces. The headquarters of the Quadrumvirate were to be in Perugia ; in Foligno, also in Umbria, they could concentrate, as a reserve force, the troops that arrived late. On October 20 there was a meeting in Florence of the three officers with Michele Bianchi and the deputy Giurati. They made the final arrangements for the Naples *adunata* and appointed ' inspectors general ' for the twelve zones into which Italy had been divided.[1] The 1st and 2nd zones (Liguria, Piedmont, the province of Pavia, Lombardy) were allotted to Captain Cesare Forni ; the 3rd (Alto Adige, part of Venetia), to Italo Bresciari ; the 4th (part of Venetia, the whole of Julian Venetia) to the deputy, Major Giovanni Giurati ; the 5th (Emilia and the Romagna) to Major Attilio Teruzzi ; the 6th (Rome, Perugia) to Lieutenant Ulisse Igliori ; the 7th (Tuscany) to the Marquis Dino Perrone Compagni ; the 8th (Marches and Abruzzi) to Captain Giuseppe Bottai ; the 9th (Campania and Basilicata) to Captain Aurelio Padovani ; the 10th (Apulia and Calabria) to the deputy Captain Giuseppe Caradonna ; the 11th (Sicily) to Captain Achille Starace ; the nomination to the 12th (Sardinia) was postponed. The fascist columns

[1] P. 265.

of Santa Marinella were to be commanded by the Marquis Compagni jointly with General Ceccherini ; those of Monterotondo by Ulisse Igliori and General Fara, and those of Tivoli by Bottai. General Zamboni was later to be put in command of the reserves in Foligno.

The review of the fascist forces took place in Naples on October 24, and Mussolini made an opening speech in the morning at the San Carlo theatre. After recalling the victory of 1918, marred ' by the absurd and false democratic conception of war, which managed to prevent our victorious battalions from marching into the " ring " in Vienna and through the streets of Buda-Pest ', Mussolini announced that the moment had come ' when the arrow flies from the bow, for the string is stretched to breaking point '. He went on to explain how fascism and its demands stood in relation to the Italian political situation :

' You remember ', said he, ' that my friend Lupi and I propounded a question, which concerns Italy as well as fascism : Legality or illegality ? Parliamentary or revolutionary conquests ? How is fascism to become the state ? For we mean to become the state. Well, on October 4, in my speech at Milan,[1] I had already solved the problem. . . . I ought not to have had to make any choice. The feeble government now sitting in Rome (where the weak, honest and ineffective Facta is attended by the three black spirits of the anti-fascist reaction : Taddei, Amendola, and Alessio) see the problem in terms of the police and public order ! . . . To the question—fascists, what do you want ?—we have already replied very definitely that we want the dissolution of the Chamber, electoral reform, elections at short notice. We have asked the state to abandon its grotesque attitude of neutrality towards the national and anti-national forces within it. We have asked for drastic financial measures, the postponement of the evacuation of the third Dalmatian zone, five portfolios, as well as the Emigration Commissariat. We have categorically demanded the Ministry of Foreign Affairs,

[1] Pp. 256–257.

the Ministry of War, the Admiralty, the Ministries of Labour and of Public Works. I am sure none of you will think these demands excessive ; and I may add that by the terms of this " legalitarian " solution I was to have no personal share in the government, and I will tell you why. To keep control of fascism I must have great freedom of movement in journalism and in discussion. What was the reply ? Nothing. Worse still, ridiculous offers were made to us. Ministries without portfolios, undersecretaryships were talked of, all of which is contemptible. We have no intention of getting into the government by the back door, of selling our wonderful birthright for a ministerial mess of pottage. This problem, as a problem of history, has been misunderstood ; now it has to be faced as a problem of force.'

Mussolini ended his speech by singing the praises of the monarchy and the army, and with a hymn to Naples, ' future queen of our Mediterranean '.

On the afternoon of the 24th Mussolini was present at the march past of 40,000 fascists concentrated in Naples, and later at a meeting in the Piazza del Plebiscito, where he took leave of the blackshirts in these terms : ' I say to you with all the gravity that befits this moment, henceforward it is a question of days, perhaps of hours, whether we are given the government or whether we seize it by hurling ourselves on Rome.' The *Corriere della Sera* in its editorial the next day remarked that ' the march on Rome, daily disavowed in articles and interviews, makes a definite reappearance in these parting words spoken by Mussolini ; instead of " marching on Rome ", the words used were actually " hurling ourselves " on Rome, as if on some prey '. Blind and deaf by choice, the great ' liberal ' paper added, ' We are willing to believe that the Naples speech is a sign of impatience rather than the announcement of a decision.' This view was not shared by the blackshirts who were shouting ' To Rome, to Rome ' in the Piazza del Plebiscito.

After this frenzied occasion and in this over-heated atmosphere a last meeting was held at 10 p.m. in Mussolini's

private room in the Hotel Vesuvio to make the final decisions.
Teruzzi, Starace and Bastianini were there as well as
Mussolini and the Quadrumvirate, De Bono, De Vecchi,
Balbo and Bianchi. Mussolini proposed that the political
leaders of the party should hand over their powers to the
Quadrumvirate at midnight on October 26 : ' The aim of
the movement must be the seizure of power, with a cabinet
including at least six fascist ministers in the most important
posts.'[1] Immediate mobilization was fixed for October 27.

' Then, on the 28th, action against the nearest objectives, prefectures, police stations, post offices, telegraph
exchanges, wireless stations, anti-fascist newspapers and
clubs, Chambers of Labour. Once the towns are conquered, swift concentration of the squads on Santa
Marinella, Monterotondo, Tivoli in columns ready to
march on Rome. Where the entire population is fascist
and conquest of the towns is assured, as in the Po valley
and Tuscany, a limited number of fascists will be left to
guard the positions ; all the rest must be sent to the
concentration points. But where the conquest of a town
is impossible or doubtful no attempt even is to be made
on the public buildings, and every single fascist must be
sent to the meeting place. The plan must follow the lines
laid down in Milan and Bordighera and under the command of the officers chosen in Florence. On the morning
of the 28th the three columns will leave simultaneously
for the capital. On the same morning, Saturday, the
Quadrumvirate's manifesto will be issued from Perugia.
. . . As for arms, the Quadrumvirs have fixed on two or
three depots on which an attempt may be made. In any
case the fascists will be able to disarm the small detach-
ments of *carabinieri* in the country districts. Separate plans
for the offensive in Milan, Turin and Parma have been
drawn up.'[2]

[1] Details of this meeting are given by Italo Balbo, who kept the minutes.
[2] The day before, another meeting had been held in Naples at the headquarters of the *fascio*, which had been attended by the commanding officers,
zone inspectors and officers commanding the columns. The same plan was
under discussion : ' The action will be carried out in two parts, first, mobilization of forces during the night of Thursday, 26, to Friday, 27, so that by
Saturday at midday all movements are complete and the fascists are in a
commanding position. Secondly, all possible pressure must be brought to

On the evening of October 24 the squads began to disperse. The fascists who had come to Naples from all over Italy were taken home in special trains. Mussolini left the town early in the afternoon next day, and other fascist leaders left as well, carrying the order of mobilization to their own districts. The march on Rome, then, was going to take place. . . . Did Mussolini really want it?

The official historians of fascism are sure that he did; others deny this, quoting the evidence of various colleagues of Mussolini's, who describe him as vacillating and anxious to compromise, even saying that he had to be ' kicked into Rome '; others describe him as a double-dealer, treating with everyone and letting everyone down, leaving his decision to the last minute, to see how the land lay and to suit his own selfish interests. Each of these ' close-ups ' portrays a genuine attitude of the Duce at a given moment, but does not answer our question. Between the spring of 1921 and the general strike of August, 1922, Mussolini was considering an accession to power by taking part in a coalition government : a government of the three ' mass parties ' in July, 1921 ; a national coalition (with a right-wing slant) in 1922, with eventually a socialist *puntarella*. After the August strike he still considered, for a few weeks longer, the formation of a coalition ministry, not led by himself : he thought of Giolitti, Salandra, and Nitti in turn. Perhaps he only wanted to trick them, to conceal his preparations for the ' march '. That would have been possible had Mussolini been entirely free to choose his own path, and able to ignore the time factor. He had already begun to feel, after the great fascist offensives, that he must reach power as

bear on local authorities so as to influence official action and seize all organs of State control, while avoiding as far as possible any disturbance in the normal functioning of the public services and the daily rhythm of public and private life. The fascist legions will remain in occupation of the towns, while those who are to form the columns for the march on Rome will proceed to the appointed places.' (Chiurco, *History*, V, p. 20). The general strategy of the march anticipated an ' ultimatum to the Facta government, calling on it to surrender the authority of the State ', followed by an entry into Rome and the occupation of the ministries. In the event of defeat, the fascist militia were to ' fall back towards central Italy, covered by the reserves concentrated in Umbria ', and this would give them the chance to ' set up the fascist government in a central Italian town ' and then resume the action against Rome, ' with a swift concentration of blackshirts from the Po valley, until victory was assured '.

quickly as possible, and now the urgency was even greater. But he was not at all certain that violence could lead to a fascist success. He knew very well that the state, feeble though it was, could crush any outbreak with the greatest of ease. The idea of celebrating his victory by a spectacular entry into Rome at the head of the fascist legions sometimes appealed to him, but he was instinctively on his guard against any romanticism and preferred to turn to less brilliant and less risky solutions. If the march involved too many risks other methods must be found at all costs : hence the negotiations with the old politicians. In putting forward the alternatives of legal conquest or violence he was sincere, because he was following the situation and his own interests to their logical conclusion, and because this was the real choice that was being forced on himself and the fascist movement. On the one hand he knew how much the situation had changed in his favour, and how much fascist violence, the negative attitude of the state, and the mistakes of his enemies had contributed to his own strength. He wanted to exert this strength to the utmost and convert it into political power.

On the other hand he realized that matters had gone so far that a decision could not long be postponed. Even at the beginning of October he was afraid he would be forced to choose between a Giolitti government and insurrection, and he did all he could to avoid the dilemma. Towards the middle of the month, of all the reasons which were driving him to make up his mind two in particular forced his hand : Giolitti's determination to form a government with or without the fascists, and the demonstration in Rome that the Facta government were staging on November 4 for d'Annunzio and the ex-servicemen around the ' altar of their country '. It was at this moment that the National Fascist Party called for the immediate convocation of the Chamber and new elections. According to Italo Balbo this was only a manœuvre. ' We are playing hide and seek ', he wrote in his *Diary*. ' The election scare is more than enough to take in the old parliamentarians, who are tumbling over each other to gain our alliance. With this bait we shall do what we like with them. We may have been born yesterday but we are cleverer than they.' Probably this was the explanation given him by Mussolini; but his manœuvre was subtler than it appeared to his enthusiastic colleagues. Mussolini could well afford to talk about elections, as he was sure to win big successes in them. On October 16 and 23 the administrative elections in the provinces of Rovigo and Reggio Emilia resulted in big majorities for the fascist lists. The socialists, victorious in November, 1920, had to give up the struggle. In Milan *Popolari* and democrats joined the national coalition list together with the fascists in order to win the town council from the socialists.[1]

The negotiations with Giolitti had fallen through, but Mussolini still thought of the ' march on Rome ', or rather the mobilisation of the military forces of fascism, as a means of enforcing the solution that Giolitti did not want. As he had explained at the meeting in the Hotel Vesuvio, the movement must insist on ' the formation of a ministry which includes at least six fascists in the most important posts '. Even after October 16 Mussolini did not surrender himself entirely to the myth of the ' march '. For him it was still a means like any other, more dangerous than the others, and one which in his heart he hoped he would not have to use.[2]

The officers of the militia and the leaders of the squads, on the other hand, could conceive of no other solution. At the Naples meeting it was they who had demanded ' immediate mobilization to gain our ends '. Mussolini tried to keep his hands free and went on negotiating without giving the other fascist leaders any detailed information, and sometimes without saying a word, as in the case of his dealings with Nitti. It must have been about this time that, according to Massimo Rocca, he exclaimed in irritation against the impatient partisans of direct action : ' For the second time I have made myself a personal force in fascism, and if fascism does not obey me I will crush it.' The deputy

---

[1] P. 280.

[2] According to the instructions drawn up in Naples for the march : ' If armed resistance by the government is encountered, avoid clashes with the troops as far as possible, and show them sympathy and respect. Do not accept any help that regiments may offer to the squads. This possibility will be examined by the Quadrumvirate only if fighting actually takes place.'

Gino Olivetti, secretary of the General Confederation of Industry, who was concerned in the political parleys with Mussolini on the eve of the march on Rome, said later to a socialist deputy : ' Mussolini manœuvres with diabolical cleverness. He negotiated with everybody up till the last minute and, when he had made sure of being well placed in any ministry, he launched, or allowed, the march on Rome.' Mussolini's wish was not only to deceive and distract his enemies but to be able to fall back on alternative solutions. He looked on the march as a means of forcing his negotiations to a conclusion.

Finally by delegating full powers to the Quadrumvirate he rid himself of all direct responsibility for the adventure and left himself free to act in a wider field. At heart he had more faith in his own diplomatic skill than in all the military resources of the ' high command '. Gaetano Salvemini is right in drawing attention in his penetrating study ' The Advent of Mussolini '[1] to the fact that after leaving Naples on the 25th, he went through Rome without stopping and straight on to Milan instead of joining the Quadrumvirate in Perugia. If he had been confident in the success of the movement ' he would surely have gone to Perugia to claim all the glory of the fight and the victory at the very heart of the insurrection '. He preferred, however, to stay in Milan, five hundred miles from Rome, but only two hours from the Swiss frontier, thus keeping open, not only a line of retreat but even the possibility of flight in case things took a turn for the worse.

After the events of the 24th the fascist congress in Naples, which opened the next day, lost all significance. It was held all the same. ' The congress,' remarks Italo Balbo, ' is almost empty. But there are a few determined people who have prepared their speeches and want to make them. The congress farce must go on, at least till to-morrow night. It is the only way that we can take in the government and public opinion.' Actually the congress could only take in those who wanted to be taken in, for there were frequent allusions to the impending adventure. Michele Bianchi made a brief speech in which he said : ' It is we who count

[1] In the review *Res Publica*, October 1932, p. 598.

for most in politics and in the Italian nation to-day. We may pride ourselves on the present situation. Until a few days ago we hesitated, but you feel, as I do, that during the last twenty-four hours all hesitations have vanished and given way to a firm and clear determination which must and will conquer. How are we going to obtain v ictory? A full congress is no place for such a discussion, nor is the secret committee with its more than seventy members. We need only look at each other to understand, and I think that we do already fully understand.' And as the discussions still went on Bianchi interrupted, shouting : ' Fascists, it is raining in Naples ; why are you still here ? ' The next day, however, the discussions still went on. Resolutions were passed on various questions, but without settling them, for quite soon they had to be faced again when the party was in power. For instance, on the electoral question Grandi remarked : ' The political officials no longer count ; they have delegated their powers to the general staff. To-day there is no need of discussion, but only of obedience.' Dudan's report on foreign policy provoked a short discussion, during which a member of the congress, after demanding a solution of the problem of the Italians in Tunisia and rejoicing that ' international chaos is favourable to our cause, since we can hope for a revision of treaties and an improvement in our position ', advised prudence, on the grounds that ' a party which finds itself on the eve of occupying the *Consulta* does well to promise nothing '.

In Rome government circles had followed events in Naples with mixed feelings. Those who had feared that the fascist squads would march straight on the capital were reassured. Those who had hoped for incidents which might lead to vigorous repressive measures were disappointed. But Mussolini's speeches, his threats and his allusions drove the Facta cabinet into an intolerable position. They had to make some decision, and it was no longer possible to wait until November 7 and the reassembly of the Chamber. The right wing were on the look-out and decided to precipitate the crisis and make any Giolitti coalition impossible. At the request of the fascist deputies, De Vecchi and Grandi, Salandra invited Facta to resign. He hesitated, so the

minister, Riccio, the friend and confidant of the right wing
and the fascists, threatened to resign alone. This made
possible a compromise, on the afternoon of the 26th, after
a meeting lasting from six till seven, by which ministers did
not resign but placed their portfolios ' at the disposal of
the premier, so that he could examine the situation with
greater freedom'. At one in the morning on the 27th
Bianchi described the situation to Mussolini by telephone
and received the reply, ' No change in decisions taken.'

The cabinet met again on the 27th and after a three hour
discussion, ending at 7.30, it resigned. At the same time,
since it was known that the fascist mobilization had begun,
various measures, planned in advance, were decided upon,
and after midnight the military authorities were put in
charge. The resignation of the cabinet made things worse
and still further weakened the government, which was giving
up its authority at the very moment when it should most
vigorously have asserted it. The right-wing parties wanted
to prevent the march on Rome by forming a coalition under
Salandra and getting it accepted by exploiting the fascist
menace : the tactics that had succeeded in 1914. All the
conservative and liberal papers, from the *Corriere della Sera*
to the *Giornale d'Italia*, demanded a ' strong government '
in which the fascists should have a share. The *Idea Nazionale*,
a nationalist paper, openly called for an extra-parliamentary
solution of the crisis. ' Facta,' wrote this paper, ' has shown
that he understood the needs of the moment by handing
in the resignation of the cabinet without waiting for the
result of a vote in parliament. But the resignation of the
cabinet is not enough. . . . The solution of the present
crisis cannot come through parliament. It was not caused
by any shifting of parliamentary forces, but by a revulsion
of conscience in the country and the maturing of fresh
energies that have been waiting to break out at any moment.'
Meanwhile negotiations and manœuvring continued. Orlando and the prefect, Lusignoli, went to Cavour to see
Giolitti, whose eightieth birthday was being celebrated.

After his agreement with Mussolini, d'Annunzio had
become rather dubious about going to Rome on November 4;[1]

[1] P. 271.

now he became more and more hesitant. The leaders of the Association of Disabled Soldiers, Ruggero Romano and Carlo Delcroix, went to Gardone to persuade the ' Commandant ' not to depart from his plan. This step failed, for on the 27th it was announced that the ceremony of November 4 would not take place, ' to prevent the noble impulse of the wounded and the name and person of d'Annunzio from being made to serve the ends of shady political intrigues.' Facta got in touch with the king and with Mussolini, and asked both of them to come to Rome. The king, who was enjoying a country holiday in San Rossore, was in the capital by eight in the evening. Mussolini refused. That evening Facta called on the king and handed him the resignation of the cabinet. The king, apparently, was not at all pleased at the turn taken by events, but Facta reassured him and tried to show that the situation was not too serious, and that the measures taken left time for a solution to be found. For he too had his solution. In his Naples speech Mussolini had praised his ' straightforwardness ' and censured the ' anti-fascism ' of the ministers Taddei, Amendola, and Alessio.[1] Might not a third Facta ministry be possible, in which they would be replaced by three fascist ministers ?[2] But the statements made to the press by Bianchi on the evening of the 27th and on the 28th removed any hope of such a solution : ' This is an extra-parliamentary crisis,' he said, ' the Chamber is left out of it. It has made no sign. The succession therefore must pass to those who, outside parliament, have precipitated the crisis ; that is the fascists. . . . In the light of common sense there ought to be a Mussolini cabinet. . . . A Salandra, Giolitti, Orlando or Giolitti-Orlando cabinet does not make sense ; and in

[1] P. 283.

[2] Count Sforza, in his *Builders of Modern Europe*, has divulged the confidences imparted to him after October 1922 by Giolitti and the senator Taddei : ' When I expressed my astonishment to Giolitti that he had not thought it his duty to come to Rome and take power in autumn 1922, the reply I received was that he was probably wrong, but that the objections of every kind raised by Facta to prevent him stirring from his country house at Cavour were endless and inexhaustible. Facta even telegraphed, once his departure from Cavour to go to Rome had been determined on, to say that the floods had made the journey dangerous. Giolitti's explanation was that Facta had allowed himself to be taken in by private overtures from the fascists, who had dangled before him the hope of remaining premier in a new cabinet containing Mussolini and other fascists.'

any case remember that any combination that includes the
fascists must reserve the Ministry of the Interior for them.'[1]
Bianchi ended his statement by giving ' a new and definite
denial to the rumours of a march on Rome, a general
rising and *coup d'état*'. ' The conquest of Rome is in process
and we have no need of any mobilisation or *coup d'état*.'[2]

At the same time news arrived in Rome which could no
longer be ignored of the fascist mobilisation which was
taking place, and of the occupation of barracks and public
buildings in various Tuscan towns.   The *Popolo d'Italia*
came out the next morning with the headlines : ' Italian
history at the cross-roads—Mobilization of fascists in Tuscany
—All the barracks in Siena are occupied by fascists—The
soldiers fraternise with the blackshirts.'   Facta was thus
forced to summon a cabinet meeting during the night,[3]
and it was decided to proclaim martial law as from noon
on Saturday, the 28th.

Italy's fate was settled during the morning of the 28th.
The resignation of the government had suddenly put the
king into the position of arbiter of the situation. Round the
Quirinal and the Viminal the tragi-comedy was being played
out, hour by hour. At 9 o'clock Facta brought for the
king's signature the decree proclaiming martial law, of
which the country had already been informed by a government announcement.[4] But before this interview took place

[1] On the other hand the Interior was the only important ministry that
Mussolini had not demanded in his Naples speech.

[2] A few hours later, Bianchi, who had gone to Perugia, headquarters of
the Quadrumvirate, went to the prefecture and rang up the Ministry of the
Interior. ' It so chances,' relates Balbo in his *Diary*, ' that Facta himself rushed
to the telephone, thinking it was the prefect. Michelino Bianchi then informed
him of the forced changing of the guard at the prefecture of Perugia and the
occupation of the town by the fascists.'

[3] Though the cabinet had resigned this was still possible, as the king had not
summoned anyone else.

[4] Here is the text : ' Seditious demonstrations are taking place in certain
Italian provinces, organized with a view to obstructing the normal functioning
of the powers of the State, and capable of bringing the most serious trouble on
the country. The government has tried every form of conciliation in the hope
of restoring harmony among conflicting views and of assuring a tranquil
solution to the crisis. Faced with attempts at insurrection it is the duty of the
resigning government to maintain public order by any means and at any price.
It will discharge this duty in full, for the safeguarding of citizens and of free
constitutional institutions. Citizens should keep calm and trust in the measures
of security which have been adopted. Long live Italy ! Long live the King ! '
This proclamation was only published in Rome, while the telegram declaring
martial law had arrived everywhere early in the morning, and was in some
places received by the fascists themselves who had seized the telegraph offices.

steps had already been taken to try to prevent the execution of the ministerial decree. Pressure had been brought to bear on the king from the early hours of the morning. At 7.30, says Chiurco, ' Doctor Ernesto Civelli,[1] who came by himself and before anyone else, explained the situation to the king, telling him of the concentration of 70,000 fascists, who were surrounding Rome. He assured him that the fascists were with the king, certain that the king would be with them.' On the other hand, at 6 o'clock in the morning, the nationalist deputy Federzoni and Roberto Forges-Davanzati, editor of the *Idea Nazionale*, went to Facta and asked him if he still was in touch with the leaders of the fascist movement. When he said that he was not they offered to put him in touch again, and from the very office of the president of the council they telephoned to De Vecchi at Perugia, headquarters of the Quadrumvirate, and to Mussolini at Milan, inviting both to Rome. De Vecchi accepted, Mussolini refused once more. Facta returned to the Viminal and told the cabinet that the king was hesitating. The cabinet instructed him to return to the king and insist on his authorising the declaration of martial law already proclaimed. It was probably between Facta's first visit and the second, which took place at about 10 o'clock, that others started to intervene : Federzoni, who announced the mobilization of the Nationalist Party, and Admiral Thaon de Revel, who asked the king to avoid any conflict between the fascists and the army. News also reached him that his cousin, the Duke of Aosta, was at Bevagna, not far from Perugia, in touch with the Quadrumvirate and ready to allow himself to be placed on the throne if the king abdicated or was deposed by the fascists. Consequently Facta was faced with a second and absolute refusal[2] and the cabinet had no alternative but to withdraw the decree.

---

[1] Civelli, with the engineer Postiglione, had been told off to attend to ' all the services required by the mobilized fascist militia '.

[2] Again according to the very trustworthy evidence of Count Sforza, the senator Taddei, Minister for the Interior in the retiring cabinet, was convinced on the evidence of a number of small signs which at the time had seemed insignificant, that Facta, disregarding the formal mandate twice entrusted to him by the cabinet, had advised the king not to sign the decree of martial law. The reason he put forward was the lack of authority of the cabinet, which was resigning, an action to which he was holding them.

At 11.30 a.m. the Stefani agency was authorized to publish the fact that ' the measure concerning the proclamation of martial law was withdrawn '.

The king's decision, disavowing his own government, removed its last scrap of authority and completely altered the situation. In fact it proved decisive.

' By cancelling the declaration of martial law,' writes the historian, Salvemini, ' the king had not only paralysed the outgoing cabinet ; he had renounced his right to appoint the new premier. Up till 12.15 on October 28, the time when the Stefani message was transmitted to the newspapers, it was open to Salandra and the king to negotiate with the fascists to bring them into the cabinet in a subordinate capacity. But after that moment Mussolini became the master.'

Throughout the afternoon of the 28th the king continued to take counsel. De Vecchi arrived in Rome at 1 o'clock and saw the king, who also received the president of the chamber, De Nicola, and the deputies Cocco-Ortu, Orlando, De Nava and Salandra. Giolitti and Mussolini were summoned but did not appear. At 5 o'clock the king received Facta once more and, for the second time, De Vecchi, who ' explained to the king the highly patriotic aims of the movement.' While speaking thus, the papers related, the ' quadrumvir' was greatly moved ; so was the king, who embraced him and declared that it was he alone who had refused to sign the decree, and that he would give to Italy, ' while scrupulously observing the limits of the constitution, the government which would answer best to the needs of the nation '. To form this government the king summoned Salandra at about 6 o'clock. He at once got into touch with the fascist leaders, De Vecchi, Ciano and Grandi, and explained his intentions. The *Giornale d'Italia* brought out a sixth edition[1] between 9 and 10 p.m., with the news of the formation of the Salandra-Mussolini cabinet, in which four portfolios were reserved for the fascists.

It is probable that this was a mere manœuvre designed to prepare public opinion and involve the fascists. But

[1] Which was dated the 29th.

behind it lay the fact that the fascist leaders accepted it in principle, on condition that Mussolini agreed, which they had no doubt of his doing. According to an article by Giovanni Marinelli, the administrative secretary of the National Fascist Party and treasurer of the march on Rome, the majority of the fascist chiefs wanted to accept Salandra's proposal. He described later how the negotiations were broken off :

'At 11 p.m. on the 28th, after the final conversations at the Quirinal in which Salandra, De Vecchi and others had taken part, there was a further meeting at the Rome office of the *Resto del Carlino* at which De Vecchi, Marinelli, Grandi, Postiglione and Polverelli were present. After a level-headed discussion of past events, of the negotiations they had just been engaged in, and of their intentions for the future, they decided with surprising forbearance in favour of a Salandra-Mussolini coalition. The present writer and Postiglione were entrusted with the unpleasant task of describing this difficult business over the telephone to the Duce. We did so with the feeling that the result would be something very different. We entered the almost deserted Viminal at one in the morning. We went up to the office of the Minister of the Interior. Taddei was nowhere to be found, and we saw only the under-secretary, Fumarola, and the permanent under-secretary. Our coming surprised and alarmed them, but they allowed us to get through to Milan, which was the object of our visit. Postiglione, as soon as he was connected with the Duce, read out the details of the suggested coalition. Mussolini listened without interrupting, and when it was finished, after asking if there was anything further to say, replied : " It was not worth while mobilizing the fascist army, causing a revolution, killing people, for the sake of a Salandra-Mussolini solution and four portfolios. I will not accept." And we heard the click as he hung up the receiver. Deeply moved we reported the Duce's refusal to De Vecchi, who was waiting for us at the *Moderno* hotel.'[1]

[1] According to one account Mussolini was in two minds over his friends' offer, when the deputy, Aldo Finzi, who was with him in Milan, snatched the

When Mussolini was rung up by Postiglione (1–1.30 in the morning of the 29th) he had already written the leading article for the *Popolo d'Italia* of the 29th :

'This is the position : a large part of Northern Italy is in the hands of the fascists. The whole of central Italy, Tuscany, Umbria, the Marches, Upper Latium is occupied by the blackshirts. Where they have not taken the police stations and prefectures by storm the fascists have occupied the stations and post-offices, the nerve centres of the nation. . . . We have already won an extensive victory. We are not going to spoil it by last-minute coalitions. It was not worth while mobilizing for the sake of making a deal with Salandra. The government must be purely fascist. . . . Any other solution must be turned down. The people of Rome must understand that the time has come to make an end of pretentious formalities, which on less serious occasions have been frequently disregarded. They must understand that there is still time for an orthodox and constitutional way out of the crisis to be found, though to-morrow it may be too late. It is up to them to decide. Fascism wants power and will get it !'

By the evening of the 28th Mussolini had begun to realize that the first part of the fascist plan had succeeded almost without a hitch, and that the cancelling of the decree of martial law had delivered Rome and power into his hands. In Rome the notion of a Salandra-Mussolini coalition was still current, for several fascist chiefs such as De Vecchi and Ciano, the king, the army leaders and the nationalists were in favour of it. Mussolini would probably have accepted it a few days before, and would have fallen back on it if the

telephone and answered for him : 'A Salandra cabinet is no good, we must have a Mussolini cabinet.' On the same evening (the 28th), however, the *Giornale d'Italia* published the news that 'Mussolini has wired to Facta and told him that he had attempted to get into touch with Salandra, but had not succeeded ; that he had asked Facta to give Salandra a message on the subject of the crisis, to the effect that he had no intention of joining a Salandra cabinet and his friends would have nothing to do with any such arrangement either. Mussolini added that he had a cabinet all ready ; but he would not leave for Rome until he saw a chance of carrying out his plan.' On the morning of the 29th, at seven o'clock, De Vecchi and Acerbo made another attempt to draw Mussolini into the new coalition.

fascist mobilization had failed, but now he did not see why he should not exploit to the full the victory he had just won.

On the eve of the adventure he had written to d'Annunzio to suggest the formation of a triple dictatorship, himself, d'Annunzio, the Duke of Aosta. D'Annunzio had refused. But that evening Mussolini was in a position to send another message to Gardone :

> ' My dear Commandant, the latest news assures our triumph. To-morrow Italy will have a government. We mean to be intelligent and cautious and not to abuse our victory. I am sure that you will hail it as the greatest dedication of the resurgent youth of Italy. *A voi, per voi.*'

D'Annunzio was told by those who brought him this message that the king had refused to sign the decree of martial law and ' it appeared that he was certain to ask Mussolini to form the new government.' Mussolini's assurance was based not only on the general trend of events but on the solid support that he was being given. While Rome was chasing the illusion of a Salandra ministry, hard work for Mussolini's cause was being done in Milan. There were lively discussions between Mussolini, the prefect Lusignoli and the leaders of the General Confederation of Industry, the deputies A. Stefano Benni and Gino Olivetti. The heads of the Banking Association, who had financed the march on Rome to the tune of twenty millions, the heads of the Confederation of Industry and of the Confederation of Agriculture telegraphed to Rome to tell Salandra that a Mussolini government was the only possible way out. Senator Ettore Conti, a great electricity magnate, and Senator Albertini, editor of the *Corriere della Sera*, which the fascists banned next day, telegraphed to Facta, asking him to request the king to entrust Mussolini with the formation of a ministry. On the same day the Pope made an appeal for peace, which amounted to an appeal for disarmament and the condonation of fascist sedition. Chiurco informs us that the Vatican took its precautions in good time : ' At this point the Holy See sent word through an important emissary that it would be obliged if Mussolini would state what were the political intentions of fascism towards the Church.' The fascist reply ' gave the most loyal assurances '. Mussolini was therefore the favoured candidate of the plutocracy, of the ' liberals ', who preferred him to the old politicians such as Salandra, and of the Vatican. In a few hours' time he was to have the backing of the monarchy as well.

Salandra had postponed his reply to the king till the following morning (Sunday the 29th), when, at 10 o'clock, he went to the Quirinal, declined the task of forming the new cabinet and said that Mussolini was the only man capable of doing so. The king then asked De Vecchi to telephone to Mussolini and ask him to come to Rome. Mussolini's answer was that he would not leave Milan until he received a telegram from the king definitely charging him to form a cabinet. General Cittadini, the king's A.D.C., sent the following telegram at once : ' H.M. the King requests you to come at once to Rome, and desires you to form a cabinet.' Mussolini decided to leave for Rome by a special train at about 3 p.m., but changed his mind and did not leave Milan until the evening on the 8 o'clock train.

During the crisis caused by the resignation of Facta's cabinet, between the afternoon of the 27th and the morning of the 29th, the fascist officials had carried out the first part of the plan whose final details had been settled in Naples on the 24th. Power was to be handed over to the Quadrumvirate on the night of October 26, and the squads were to mobilize secretly during the night of the 27th. Local objectives were to be attained during the morning of the 28th and the three columns destined for Rome were to begin their march. The fascist delegates who left Naples between the 24th and the 26th took with them orders for universal mobilization and instructions for local actions. According to the original plan, practically all the fascist forces were to go to the meeting places from which the columns were to set out for the ' march on Rome '. Mobilization and local action were only the first stage of the march, to which everything was subordinated. But between the morning of the 25th and the 26th or 27th this plan was greatly modified. Only a few 'legions' from Tuscany, some 'centuries' from the Po valley,[1] the squads of the Abruzzi and of the province of Rome were appointed to 'march' on the capital. The local actions now became the most important part of the plan. This was due to a change in the political plan ; for Mussolini and his closest advisers reckoned that mobilization and local action would exert sufficient pressure to enforce the solution demanded by the fascists. The fascist political leaders were now largely concerned to keep the blackshirt columns as far from Rome as they could without spoiling the stage effect of the 'march'. This was to be kept as a threat, though without hindering the normal development of the crisis that resulted from Salandra's refusal to form a ministry.

On the night of the 27th the prefects delegated their powers to the military authorities, who made no attempt to prevent the fascists seizing buildings or to evict them when in occupation. Practically all senior officials, civil or military, displayed a benevolent neutrality, amounting occasionally to open complicity, in face of the fascist mobilization. The few cases of resistance were due to the individual initiative of a few officials and soldiers during the period of martial law on the morning of the 28th. When the Stefani agency announced its cancellation the authorities felt themselves more than ever encouraged in their attitude, and there was a rush to welcome the new government directly it was learnt that the king had summoned Mussolini to form it.

The Quadrumvirate had decided to direct the conquest of the capital from Perugia, and installed themselves openly at the Brufani Hotel, opposite the prefecture. A platoon of soldiers could have seized the 'high command' of the fascist revolution if some N.C.O. had taken the initiative. Actually the reverse happened, for three fascist delegates called on the prefect at about midnight on the 27th and summoned him to give up his powers to the fascist command. Although the prefecture was defended by the Royal

---

[1] According to the *Regulations for the formation of fascist squads* drawn up at the beginning of 1922, the *squadre* consisted of from twenty to fifty men, the 'centuries' included four *squadre*, the 'cohorts' four centuries, the legions from three to nine cohorts.

Guard, the government representative agreed within half an hour. Squads of blackshirts replaced the Royal Guard and also occupied the post office, the provincial administrative headquarters and the police station, all without a shot being fired. ' The worthy citizens, most of whom were ignorant of the night's events, learnt of them from a notice which the new fascist authorities posted up on the walls.'[1] By the morning of the 28th it almost seemed as if the prefect had played the traitor for nothing, as the military authorities had been ordered to take over the powers that had been yielded to the fascists. But in spite of a few disagreements the military and the fascists remained on excellent terms. At 11.45 a brigadier-general went to the Brufani Hotel to negotiate with General De Bono, and was received with military honours. ' At 12.30 the fascist supreme command intercepted another telegram from Rome which enlivened and cheered both legionaries and citizens : martial law was revoked. Radiant with joy the fascist deputy Pighetti rushed to the Divisional Headquarters to pass on the good news. From now on they were all confident of complete victory.'

The events of Perugia were repeated almost identically in a number of towns that the fascists had been able to occupy without resistance. At Alessandria in Piedmont, at three o'clock on the 28th, the general commanding the division summoned the fascist chiefs who had already occupied the prefecture, the police station, the station, the telephone exchange and a barracks, to inform them that he was ' awaiting precise orders from the government '. At Casale ' the prefecture was rapidly occupied, for the subprefect handed over his powers immediately '. At Bergamo in Lombardy, ' after some parley the military authorities recognized the fascist occupations '. At Brescia ' the principal centres were occupied and the fascists were in complete command of the situation '. At Como an army major, a fascist, ' saw to it that the troops did not oppose fascist occupation of the public buildings '. In Sondrio the fascists managed to occupy the garrison command, a barracks and a customs office without a shot being fired.

[1] This and future quotations for which no reference is given are from Chiurco.

At Pavia, when the fascists made an attempt on the pre-fecture, ' the Royal Guard had levelled their rifles against the fascists when the timely action of the fascist officers and the Chief of Police averted a tragedy '. In Venetia the chief aim of the fascists squads was to isolate Venice and occupy the great railway junctions of Mestra and Verona, which were the key to all local communications. At Venice ' on the evening of the 27th, the Consul[1] Magrini met Admiral Mortola, commanding the naval division and the fortifica-tions of Venice. The interview, which had its dramatic moments, revealed the great Italian heart of the Admiral, who, without forgetting the sacred call of duty, showed that he understood the great ordeal of deliverance to which the country was called '. He understood so well that, certain of his ' neutrality', the fascists were able to ' isolate Venice from all communication with the government ', garrisoning it with only one cohort of from four to five hundred men. . . . The remaining fascist forces could be concentrated in Mestra, where the station was occupied, and take part in other local operations. Belluno, Udine, Trevisa, Padua, Vicenza were all occupied. In Julian Venetia the good terms that had existed between military and fascist authorities were maintained under fresh con-ditions. The fascist deputy, Giunta, has recorded what happened in Trieste :

' On the evening of October 27 there was a banquet in honour of the governor Mosconi. Signor Mosconi was popular in the town and we ourselves were on very friendly terms with him because, admittedly, he well understood and favoured the valuable function of fascism in Julian Venetia. Thus there was nothing strange in the fascist leaders being seen that evening at the dinner table while I continued to direct the mobilization and drink in *Asti spumante* the health of the representative of the government I was preparing to overthrow. On the 28th I entered the prefecture with 3,000 blackshirts. . . . The prefect, Crispo Moncada, was awaiting us in his

[1] In the fascist military system a ' consul ' corresponded to a general and commanded a legion.

office. When I told him that I was taking possession of the prefecture in the name of the revolution which at that moment was knocking at the gates of Rome, the prefect, pale with emotion, replied that he accepted our conditions and begged us with tears in his eyes to think only of Italy. Knowing as I did his patriotic soul and noble loyalty, I asked him to remain at his post and carry on with his routine work. There was still an unknown factor : the army. What were its orders ? Extreme prudence was necessary, for the Jugo-Slavs had considerable forces on the frontier. Accompanied by my little general staff I went to army headquarters. On the way I met General Sanna, the commandant, in his car. Directly he saw me he got out and came to meet me. " Now I shall have you all shot," he said with a would-be serious air. " Do, excellency, but you will need more than one firing squad." '

The conversation continued on these lines until finally, ' his heart won and the general came with us to the prefecture, where we decided that the army should remain neutral, unless orders to the contrary came from Rome '. In the meantime the fascists occupied the general post office and telephone exchange and cut all communications with the peninsula. The whole of Istria passed under their control and in Gorizia ' relations between the civil and military authorities and the leaders of the revolt were entirely cordial '.

During the 28th the fascists took over, unresisted, in almost every town in the Po valley ; at Piacenza, where the prefect ' enthusiastically ordered that the fascists should occupy every administrative office ' ; Parma, and Ferrara, where ' in view of the correct attitude of the prefect who had shown tact and understanding, the prefecture and the police station were not occupied ' ; Modena, Reggio Emilia, Rovigo.

In Tuscany they took action as early as the 27th, which threatened to start the movement too soon. For instance, at Pisa the fascist executive had put up a notice announcing the march on Rome, and at Siena ' handfuls of fascists had walked peacefully into the barracks of the local garrison without meeting any resistance ; after taking possession of the arms and munitions they found there they marched through the middle of the town, singing, up to the head-quarters of the *fascio* '.   In Florence the general post office was occupied from midnight on the 27th onwards.   On the afternoon of the same day news had come of the mobilization in Tuscany, which, according to the *Stampa* correspondent ' people had been talking about for days '.   There had been a fascist demonstration in favour of General Diaz, the com-mander-in-chief of the army, who happened to be in the town and made no secret of his sympathy for the movement. During the morning of the 28th, the fascist military and political leaders, the consul Tamburini and the barrister Marziali called on General De Marchi.   ' The object of the interview,' according to the *Stampa* correspondent, ' was to examine the situation resulting from the declaration of martial law.   General De Marchi explained that it was his duty as a soldier to turn the fascists out of the public buildings that they had occupied.   Signori Marziale and Tamburini replied that there were claims of feeling stronger than any oath, especially one that conflicted with conscience, logic and justice.   " But," replied the general, " after forty years in the army I cannot disobey the king."   " The king is with us," they assured him, " and we are with the army." General De Marchi then advised them to telephone to the fascist leaders, while he telephoned to Rome for confirmation of the reassuring news that the consul Tamburini had given him.'   To calm the fears of the military authorities the fascists brought out a special edition of a newspaper announcing that the king had asked Mussolini to form a government. At the time this was pure invention, but it served to put a stop to any steps taken by the military authorities, who were already inclined to a benevolent neutrality by the contra-dictory news they were receiving about the enforcing of martial law.

The situation thus caused, resulting from two years of collusion everywhere between fascists and army officers, could not be changed in a few hours, especially as the govern-ment in Rome was resigning and in disagreement with the king over the measures to be taken. Nevertheless in the few places where the authorities even partly carried out their duties, the fascists were crushed or held up. At Turin they had to be content with holding an evening meeting on the 28th in front of the police station, and when, next day, they occupied the railway station the mere order of a police officer was sufficient to turn them out. In Milan they were thrown on the defensive, and built barricades round the headquarters of the *fascio*. The deputy Finzi and Stefano Benni, leader of the General Confederation of Industry, came to an arrangement with the prefect Lusignoli to avoid incidents. An attack on the offices of the *Avanti* was beaten off by the Royal Guard, and the fascists who had entered the Manara barracks were forced to leave at once by an energetic colonel of Alpini who refused to budge even when Mussolini intervened in person. They were not able to occupy the prefecture of Bologna until October 30, and in Cremona, on the evening of the 27th, an attack was repulsed ; and the fascists, leaving three dead and four wounded, had to fall back for the moment. In Genoa the fascist mobilization fell foul of the measures taken by the military authorities, but the latter, instead of arresting the fascist leaders for sedition, entered into negotiations with them. ' The fascist Triumvirs of Genoa were summoned before General Squillace, the divisional commander, who informed them of the declaration of martial law and said that the orders from Rome would be strictly carried out.' This did not prevent the fascists from occupying the prefecture on the 29th without meeting the slightest resistance.

In Rome during the night of the 27th troops were posted at all strategic points, with barbed wire entanglements, *chevaux de frise* and armoured cars. The two principal railway lines connecting Rome with the north were cut, and yards of rail torn up. The Royal Guard occupied the headquarters of the *fascio* after negotiations with the fascists, who left by agreement. ' The fascist officials,' said the correspondent of the *Corriere della Sera*, ' went away taking their documents with them and installed themselves in a restaurant in the Piazza Barberini ; consequently nothing came of the search made at their headquarters.' However, during the morning of the 28th the fascists kept very much in the background, and it was not until early in the afternoon, when it became known that the king had not signed the decree enforcing martial law, that fascists and nationalists appeared in the streets, though they contented themselves with a demonstration in honour of the king.

In the south of Italy the fascist mobilization was slow ; the fascist squads did not leave Naples after the Congress until October 29, and concentrated at Foggia. There they occupied the prefecture and a barracks. In Apulia they seized various public buildings without meeting any resistance.

The proclamation of martial law ought to have brought the authorities down on the mobilized fascists who were attacking public buildings, stations and barracks. The fascist plan of mobilization and occupation should have been countered by measures for the restoration of public order. This was done nowhere save in Rome, Turin, and partially in Milan. The military authorities sat waiting for instructions, as if they were not automatically obliged to take the necessary steps against rebellion.[1] Nearly everywhere, on the contrary, a compromise was arranged, as a result of which the fascists did not occupy military headquarters, nor, with a few exceptions, attack barracks. Everyone waited on events in Rome, as if such inaction made no difference. Up till noon on the 28th the government in Rome could still have saved the situation, for the army was intact and the fascists could not have stood up against a serious attack. The rapid development of the crisis and the king's appeal to Mussolini on the morning of the 29th, which was practically common knowledge by the afternoon, created an optimistic atmosphere which made any serious clash between the army and the fascists impossible.[2]

[1] Apparently there was only one exception. ' In Casale,' says Chiurco, ' the fascist leaders went, on the morning of the 27th, to the colonel commanding the 1st artillery regiment to inform him of the situation and suggest that he should at least remain neutral in the conflict. The colonel said nothing, but drew his revolver and fired at the handful of fascists, luckily without hurting anyone. He then hurried into the street to return to his barracks, where he shut himself up to prepare for defence.'

[2] Apart from Cremona the only serious resistance was put up by the *carabinieri* in three small places, who defended their barracks against the ascists. Three fascists were killed in San Giovanni in Croce (Cremona),

Owing to Mussolini's influence the fascist leaders in general scrupulously carried out instructions concerning relations with military authorities.[1] In their proclamations they took the utmost care not to offend the army's loyalty to the crown. These all ended with ' Long live Italy ! Long live the king ! ' and were couched in the most reassuring terms. For example the fascist governors of Umbria announced, when installing themselves in the provincial government building at Perugia : ' Our occupation affects nothing except the government and the spirit of the government . . . for Italy, for the King, for Fascism ! ' The appeal issued from Foggia to ' the Italians of Apulia, Calabria and Basilicata ', assured them that ' we do not want to overthrow the regime, nor in any way upset the established order. We only want to give the Nation a government worthy of its superb vigour '. The fascist executive committee of Reggio Emilia explained : ' The fascists are not acting against the existing constitution nor against the king, His Majesty Victor-Emmanuel III of Savoy. We only want him to be truly king of Italy and to govern by getting rid of his present half-witted collection of ministers.' The fascists of Verona addressed the army direct : ' Officers and men, our brothers. Our hearts beat as one. We have a common passion, Italy ! We have defended her in war and in peace and we want to save her to-day from those who, but for us, would have left the monarchy defenceless and sacrificed the King. Listen to the voice of your hearts, which is the true voice of the country. It bids you open your arms to us. Here are we, brothers. Long live Italy ! '

The proclamations of the fascist supreme command were in the same vein. The Quadrumvirate published one on the 27th in Perugia, which had been drawn up by Mussolini in the middle of October. In its original form, after announcing the delegation of authority to the secret Quadrumvirate of action ' with dictatorial powers ', it went on to say :

two killed and two wounded in San Ruffillo (Bologna), one killed and eight wounded in Fiorenzuola d'Arda (Piacenza). The total fascist losses in fights with the state forces between October 27 and 29 were thirteen dead (six in the attacks on the *carabinieri* barracks) and forty-seven wounded, of whom four died ; the rest for the most part only had slight wounds or mere bruises.

[1] P. 288, n. 3.

'The secret Quadrumvirate of action declares the present government fallen, the Chamber dissolved and the Senate adjourned. The army is confined to barracks and is to take no part in the struggle. Members of the state forces must realize that fascism is not marching against them, but against a political class of cowards and incompetents who have been unable for the past four years to give the nation a government. Workers in the fields, in the factories, in transport and in the civil service have nothing to fear from fascist tenure of power. Their just rights will be loyally protected. We shall be generous to our enemies who submit, towards the rest we shall be ruthless. Fascism draws the sword to cut the too numerous Gordian knots that clog and degrade Italian life. We call God and our 500,000 dead to witness : we have one impulse, one will, one passion : the well-being and the grandeur of our country.'[1]

At the last minute important alterations were made to this text. The passage about the government, the Chamber and the Senate was suppressed. The passage about the army was altered so as to make its neutrality all the more certain. The fascist Quadrumvirate no longer ordered it to be confined to barracks. It addressed it in the following terms : ' The army, the last reserve and safeguard of the nation, must not take part in the struggle. Fascism repeats its great admiration for the army of Vittorio Veneto.' In addition, the passage intended to reassure the workers was preceded by another, far more eloquent, to reassure the *bourgeoisie* : ' The producing classes of the *bourgeoisie* must realize that fascism desires to impose a single discipline on the nation and to help all the forces capable of augmenting its economic expansion and well-being.' On October 29, at the very gates of Rome, the officer commanding the forces assembled in Tivoli made an announcement that the sole aim of the march was ' to give the nation a strong and wise government '.

The Quadrumvirate at its headquarters in Perugia was in reality exercising none of those ' military, political and

[1] The MS., in Mussolini's handwriting, of this first version is reproduced in Chiurco, V, pp. 22–25.

administrative powers of the party executive ' which were supposed to have passed into its hands. The mobilization, as arranged in Naples, took place in the different parts of Italy, but without the Quadrumvirate being able to follow its fortunes and its growth. In northern Italy the fascist leaders kept in touch with Milan and occasionally with Mussolini himself. The fascist deputy Torre brought Mussolini's instructions from Milan to Alessandria and kept in touch with him during the days that followed. The Quadrumvirate only intervened once during the mobilization : Balbo was sent to Florence on the afternoon of the 27th, because the fascists in Pisa had begun too soon, and in Florence as well the squads had ' given the alarm to the military authorities '[1] by going into action too soon. The same evening Balbo was back in Perugia and from that moment the Quadrumvirate ceased to have any direct connection with the mobilization, and was therefore incapable of controlling the movements of the columns assembled for the march on Rome which it was supposed to be directing. It had already had some difficulty in meeting at all. On the very morning of the 27th Bianchi, who was in Rome, after looking everywhere for De Vecchi and failing to find him, left a letter at his hotel at 9 a.m., saying, ' I leave for Perugia in a few hours' time. From now on there can be no retreat. The latest events favour our plan.[2] We must see things through to the end. You must do your utmost to get to Perugia to-morrow morning. Enormous responsibility rests on the Quadrumvirate and it is essential that we should be in full agreement so as to avoid a fatal confusion of orders and counter-orders.' This letter shows that a few hours before the morning of the 28th when, according to the Naples programme, the three columns were to leave simultaneously for Rome, two of the Quadrumvirs had not even managed to get into touch with each other. It shows too that as yet their political views were quite divergent. De Vecchi was trying for a compromise with Salandra, and went on trying until the morning of the

---

[1] Pp. 303–304.
[2] Bianchi was alluding to the decision, made by ministers the day before, to place their portfolios at the premier's disposal.

29th ; while Bianchi, Balbo and De Bono wanted a Mussolini government.[1] It so happened that the four members
of the Quadrumvirate represented severally the forces which
had contributed most to the growth of fascism. The pre-
war ' interventionist ' syndicalists, the remains, now older
and wiser, of the *Fasci d'azione rivoluzionaria* were represented
by Michele Bianchi, party secretary and politically the
closest to Mussolini ; the old conservative and monarchist
classes by De Vecchi, himself a great landowner ; the new
elements, ex-servicemen, the natural products of the war,
by the *squadrista*, Italo Balbo ; the regular army, representing virtually the tolerance and complicity of the state, by
General Emilio De Bono. But as Mussolini was not there
to hold together the divergent tendencies, its unity was
impaired and the importance of its role diminished.

De Vecchi finally appeared in Perugia on the morning
of the 28th, only to leave almost at once.[2] Italo Balbo
describes how the Quadrumvirs used on the 28th the full
powers with which they had been invested :

'De Vecchi described the situation in the capital. It
is still uncertain and chaotic. Some say that martial law
has been declared, others contradict it. Such information
as he was able to get before leaving for Perugia confirms
it. . . . De Vecchi went straight back to Rome. From
this moment we in Perugia are in utter ignorance of the
government's intentions. The news which arrives from
time to time is mostly bad. The government is apparently
making intensive preparations against us. We are badly
in need of reliable information. At any moment we may
find ourselves quite out of touch. Our plan of action is
also dependent on the government's attitude and the
measures it takes. . . . There is a good deal of appre-
hension at headquarters. We know that even the day
before the fascist leaders had not made up their minds
to act. Some thought it too soon, others would have
preferred a parliamentary solution. The rumours that
continue to arrive in Perugia, becoming more definite

---

[1] At the last minute the Quadrumvirate had co-opted, as their chief of
staff, Grandi, who favoured compromise.

[2] P. 294.

towards the evening, seem certain of a cabinet in which Mussolini will not be premier and in which the fascists are to be oddly mixed up with people of every kind of political complexion.'

Very worried, Balbo went off to Rome. But first he signed, as De Bono and Bianchi had already done (De Vecchi at this moment was not in Perugia) a curious document to the effect that : ' The undersigned members of the supreme fascist Quadrumvirate, invested with full political and military powers, have decided, now the fascist forces are mobilized, that the only acceptable solution is a Mussolini cabinet.' Was this meant to be a kind of precautionary guarantee taken by three of the Quadrumvirate against a last minute surprise coalition ? Against whom was it directed : the fourth Quadrumvir, De Vecchi ;[1] Grandi and Ciano ; or Mussolini himself? In any case the document is of purely academic interest, for the Quadrumvirate never had the slightest opportunity of affecting the outcome of the crisis. All the negotiations took place between the king, the right-wing parties (Salandra and the nationalists), Mussolini who remained in Milan, and a group of fascist leaders, who remained in Rome (De Vecchi, Ciano, Grandi). And directly the king's A.D.C. telegraphed to Mussolini, on the morning of the 29th, the invitation to come to Rome to form the cabinet, Mussolini prepared his list, took it with him to Rome, and altered it at the last minute, without once consulting the Quadrumvirate, who were still officially in possession of ' full powers '.

Luckily the situation in Rome took the most favourable turn for the fascist designs when martial law was revoked.[2] General De Bono, who published his journal of the campaign in a fascist review[3] a short while ago, quotes for October 8, 1922 :

[1] During the few hours he spent in Perugia, before going back to Rome to follow the discussions, De Vecchi is said to have had a fairly violent quarrel with Bianchi on the subject of the monarchy.

[2] Balbo, who left for Rome on the evening of the 28th, was not at all clear as to what was going on : ' Is martial law in force, or is it not ? ' he asked in his Diary. ' It was announced and then revoked, but the military preparations which are being carried out at the Rome Divisional Command prove that in practice it is in force.' For even after the revocation the military authorities were still in charge.

[3] The *Ottobre* review for October 28, 1930.

' The Quadrumvirate is almost entirely cut off from the actions that are taking place in the provinces.

' We are fairly well in contact with the columns marching on Rome.[1]

' Zamboni[2] sends me word from Foligno that he has mustered about 3000 men, of whom rather more than 300 are armed. Rifles have got to be found for them.

' Bianchi is trying in vain to telephone to Milan and Rome.[3]

' All telegrams are sent up to us from the telegraph office, and at about 10 a rather discouraging one arrives : martial law is proclaimed and orders given to arrest all leaders of the movement, wherever and whoever they may be.

' 12.45, a cipher telegram arrives ordering that no account is to be taken of the telegram proclaiming martial law.

' Michelino (Bianchi) and I embrace each other.[4]

' 21.30 Much coming and going at the Hotel Brufani, crowds staring, cameramen appear. The whole drama is beginning to look like a play with a happy ending.'

Next day the Quadrumvirate did not trouble to carry out its plan of seizing the arms factory at Terni, and shifting its headquarters south to Narni, so as to be near Rome. Thus the ' supreme command ' of the Quadrumvirate came to an end without having commanded anything.

As for the march on Rome, we have seen that, contrary to the original plan, the forces to be used were reduced. The fascist columns were to be concentrated in three places, distributed as shown on the adjoining plan.

According to the Naples plan, ' On the morning of the

---

[1] We shall see that they were in contact, rather ineffectively, at the beginning only, early on the 28th, but later on hardly at all.

[2] The general commanding the ' reserves ' concentrated in Foligno.

[3] Bianchi had telephoned to Rome during the night. Thanks to Facta, Federzoni was still able to telephone to Perugia at 6 a.m. to summon De Vecchi to Rome (p. 294).

[4] At the news of the withdrawal of martial law all the fascist leaders were overjoyed. In Perugia the fascist deputy Pighetti ' beamed with joy ' (p. 301) and in Rome, according to Chiurco, ' Ciano, De Vecchi and Grandi wept with emotion on exchanging the news that the king had refused to give his consent '. Clearly they all felt that they were at last safe.

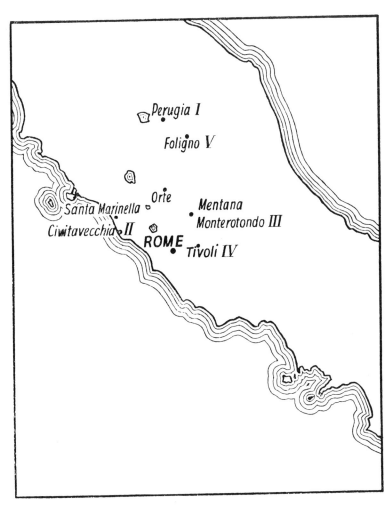

I.   Headquarters of Quadrumvirate.
II.   Perrone column, with general Ceccherini.
III.   Igliori column, with general Fara.
IV.   Bottai column.
V.   Reserves, with general Zamboni.

28th, simultaneous departure of the three columns for the capital '. By following the adventures of each of these three columns it may be seen that this part of the plan was not carried out at all.

The Marquis Dino Perrone Compagni, who commanded the second column, arrived at Civitavecchia just before midday on October 28, and found the fascist squads of the provinces of Pisa, Lucca, Leghorn and Tuscan Maremma already in Santa Marinella. No preparations for billeting them in this tiny place had been made, and it was pouring with rain. The Carrara squads had been delayed by difficulties met with chiefly during the occupation of Massa. They had to be waited for, and did not appear until the next day, the 29th. Moreover, no trains could go on to Rome, because, on orders from the capital, the regular troops had torn up yards of rail.

At the Monterotondo-Mentana rallying point (III) about 2000 men arrived during the night of the 27th from upper Latium, ' in every sort of conveyance, lorries, antediluvian motor cars, bicycles, carts of every description, and some on foot '. But the forces from the north were held up at Orte, on the Florence-Rome main line, where the line had been torn up by the troops. One train, bringing three thousand men from Siena, by going back and using another line, managed to get to Monterotondo towards noon. In addition five hundred men arrived from Orvieto during the course of the day, three hundred from Sabina, and the first Florentine legion with two thousand men. Lieutenant Igliori, ' seeing his little army beginning to grow, cast about for food and lodging '. On the evening of the 28th Italo Balbo arrived from Rome, where he had gone to find out what was going on, and was back on his way to Perugia. Igliori ' told him that he had not yet had any news from headquarters, and that the continual arrival of new forces was making his position impossible '. But they had to wait until the railway line was repaired, so that the contingents coming from Tuscany and Bologna could leave Orte and get to Monterotondo.

The concentration of 8000 men under Giuseppe Bottai at the Tivoli and Valmontone meeting place (IV) comprising the militia of the Abruzzi and the Sabines was completed in the morning of the 28th. But he was faced with the same problem. 'There was a shortage of food,' for the train ' with the provisions collected by the Intendant-General to feed the revolutionary army could not get through because of the break in the line.'

A reasonably accurate reply can thus be given to the question asked by Salvemini[1] on the number of fascists ready to pit themselves against the regular army on the morning of October 28. There were about 4000 at Civitavecchia and Santa Marinella under Perrone, some thirty-eight miles from Rome, and without rail transport ; 2000 at Monterotondo under Igliori (for the Siena legionaries did not arrive until noon), nineteen miles north of Rome ; and about 8000 men at Tivoli under Bottai, fifteen miles east of Rome. Altogether 14,000 men, armed with rifles, muskets, revolvers, daggers and some only with bludgeons, with almost no machine guns and not a single heavy gun,[2] against whom the government could have brought 12,000 men of the Rome garrison equipped with all the resources of modern offensive and defensive warfare. A few tanks and aeroplanes could easily have scattered these troops, who were without proper arms, without food, and, in spite of the heavy showers with which they were continuously drenched, without water ; quite apart from the fact that the columns were almost entirely out of touch with each other and with the headquarters in Perugia.

The Foligno reserves were a long way away, and according to De Bono only 300 of their 3000 were armed.[3] A raid on Spoleto enabled general Zamboni, who commanded them, to supply them with rifles, but the column did not get

[1] In the study, already quoted (p. 289).
[2] The Spanish journalist, Rafael Sanchez Mazas, correspondent of the Madrid A.B.C., described the equipment of these troops as follows : ' There was an infinite variety of equipment and uniforms. . . . They carried rifles, muskets, sticks, whips, clubs, shot-guns and carbines. . . . In their belts they wore daggers, pistols, sickles and other agricultural implements.' The evidence from widely differing sources is in agreement about this.
[3] In his Diary, on the 28th, Balbo speaks of 5000. The Quadrumvirate did not even agree on the number of effective forces near Perugia with whom they were able to keep in touch. Balbo at least realized that the reserve forces were inadequate, particularly as they ' might play a decisive part in the revolution '.

back to Foligno after this adventure until 7 o'clock on the morning of the 29th.

On Sunday the 29th the Perrone column was still in the same plight. The legion from Carrara had arrived, it is true, but this merely increased the difficulties attending the concentration. At 9 in the evening Perrone despatched a *squadrista* on a motor bicycle with the following message to the supreme command :

> ' Up till now 6143 blackshirts have arrived at Santa Marinella, of whom 2413 are in Santa Marinella and 3730 in Civitavecchia (station). Our forces are divided, because no more shelter can be found in Santa Marinella in this frightful weather.
>
> ' *Needs*—we are short of water, food and money.[1]
>
> ' *Liaison*—it is impossible to keep in touch with the supreme command. It took nine hours to get from Perugia to here going at top speed in a Fiat 510. I am asking for an immediate connection through Rome, which would ensure us quicker communications with head-quarters. At present no order, however urgent, can reach us in less than nine or ten hours.'

All day long on the 29th more troops kept arriving in Monterotondo, for the railway line, broken near Orte, had been repaired. There were 2000 men from Arezzo and Valdarno, 3000 from the second Florentine legion, 500 from Bologna, making a total of available forces of 13,000 men. During the afternoon there arrived General Fara,[2] who was to command part of the militia, and De Vecchi, on his way back to Perugia. De Vecchi promised to send orders, but

---

[1] Igliori, commanding the third column, complained, too : ' Not a brass farthing to hire cars and send out orders for the meeting.' (Chiurco, V, p. 175.) All the same, from the contribution of the Freemasons and the Bankers' Association alone, the sum set aside for the march on Rome amounted to some 24 millions. Other substantial subsidies had been provided by the Agrarian Confederation, by the National Syndicate of Co-operatives, by other associations and by private individuals. The fascist leaders in fact had several tens of millions, of which only a very small fraction was used for the march. The ' intendants ' of the march, Civelli and Postiglione, only played a secondary part ; the real treasurer was Giovanni Marinelli, administrative secretary of the National Fascist Party, who, by arrangement with Mussolini, was keeping the money in reserve in case of a reverse.

[2] Six generals took part in the march on Rome : De Bono, Fara, Ceccherini, Zamboni, Novelli and Tilby.

when by 8 p.m. nothing had arrived, Igliori decided to organize the departure for Rome the next morning. The rain and the lack of food were getting on the nerves of the legionaries and their leaders, and forcing them to close in on the capital. Igliori sent a letter to Bottai in Tivoli to explain that ' in view of the impossibility of remaining in Monterotondo ', he was leaving for Rome, and to ask him to do the same.

That evening at about 10.30 Bottai, who was in command of the Tivoli concentration, sent the following reply to Igliori's invitation :

' I must point out to you that your decision may seriously affect the outcome of the political conversations now in progress, which are leading up to a complete victory for us. Our deputies, Grandi and Ciano, were here to-day, and they emphazised this danger and the necessity of obeying orders. Mussolini will be in Rome this evening,[1] and he it is who must tell us the exact moment to enter. I am in touch with Rome all the time.'

After saying that he too intended to go as near Rome as the Ponte Mammolo, Bottai continued, ' I advise you to do the same ; in this way we can get nearer Rome, while awaiting the orders that will certainly be given us by Mussolini as head of the government.' Thus on the evening of the 29th, the Perrone column had no intention of marching, the Igliori column only wanted to leave because it was so horribly uncomfortable at Monterotondo, and the Bottai column was waiting for Mussolini to open the gates of Rome in his capacity of head of the government.

On Monday the 30th Mussolini went by train to Civitavecchia on his way to Rome. At the Santa Marinella junction he wanted to talk with the leaders of the fascist columns. Neither Perrone nor General Ceccherini, who had arrived during the night, were there. However, he met Renato Ricci, leader of the blackshirts from Carrara, and asked him for news of the men who were bivouacking in Santa Marin-

---

[1] Mussolini had, in fact, decided to leave Milan on the 28th early in the afternoon ; but he then postponed his departure (p. 462).

ella.   ' When he learnt,' relates a representative of the
Stampa, who was travelling with him, ' that these men,
about 3000 in number, had neither tents nor lodging, he
ordered that they should be moved to Civitavecchia so that
they could have food and shelter.'   The marquis Perrone
was busy holding a review of his militia in honour of general
Ceccherini, ' one of the very gallant generals, as he says in
his *Journal*, beloved by the army, whom Mussolini wanted
to accompany the fascist troops in uniform, so as to avoid,
as far as possible, any clash with the troops.'

A superfluous precaution, for Mussolini arrived in Rome
before the fascist columns, and they did not begin their
march until he gave them their orders, after becoming head
of the government.   The Perrone column received the order
on the evening of the 30th and arranged to depart the next
morning, after instructions had been given for billeting the
legionaries in schools in Rome.   On the morning of the
30th two trains took the Igliori columns from Monterotondo
to the bridge of the Via Salaria.   It was pouring with rain.
Igliori ought to have waited there for orders, but, as he
himself put it, ' there was not a single house in the neighbourhood to shelter our men, who were soaked to the skin
and had eaten nothing since the day before '.   He was
' extremely worried at having to keep a column in such bad
conditions at the gates of Rome ', and so he went off to
find shelter in the outskirts.   The column arrived near the
city towards midday and put up in the railwaymen's garden
city near Villa Savoia.   Chiurco, who was in command of
the Siena legion, has preserved the telegram he sent his
friends as soon as he could get out of the deluge which had
driven them all into the city : ' Fascist command, Siena.
Arrived victoriously among the first, machine guns to the
fore ;   all goes well.'   The other column commander,
General Fara, had gone ahead in his motor car to within
a hundred yards of the garden city.   ' The general was
nearing the bridge when a cavalry colonel presented himself
and informed him that the order had been given to remove
all troops defending the bridges.   On behalf of the army
corps commander the colonel placed himself entirely at
General Fara's disposal, and announced that His Excellency

Mussolini had been sent for by the king.'[1]   The Bottai column left Tivoli ' in a terrific deluge ' on the morning of October 31 ; it went by special train to Tor Sapienza and then marched to the quarters that had been specially prepared in the town.   The Foligno ' reserves ' also left on the morning of the 30th : ' ten trains in succession brought them to Rome for the great *adunata* ' which took place on the afternoon of the 31st.

Why did Mussolini, who had done his utmost to prevent the fascist columns from converging on Rome, now want them to enter the gates of the city on foot?   Because now that he had formed his government it was absolutely essential to produce something resembling a ' march on Rome '.   The advantage of coming to power in a haze of heroism and violence was that it gave him an excuse for an eventual repudiation of time-honoured procedure and combinations.   Dangerous and useless as a means for acquiring power, the ' march ' became a precious means of consolidating the power already won.   It gave satisfaction to thousands of *squadristi*[2] who had been rotting in the rain for three days, giving them the feeling, confirmed by their march through the streets of Rome, that they had won a grand victory, while at the same time it showed the old parties and politicians that Mussolini now had the joint forces of the state and of the Fascist Party at his disposal.   Powerless against the state, if it had made the slightest attempt to defend itself, fascism became supreme as a ' state party ', and by creating the ' party state ' that Mussolini and the other leaders had aimed at.

When he received the king's invitation at Milan, Mussolini, instead of leaving at once, preferred to keep Rome

[1] This is how the ' Bulletin N.4.', published by the local fascist leaders in Ferrara, described this event : ' The three fascist columns commanded by Generals Ceccherini, Fara and De Bono have reached the gates of the capital. A cavalry regiment which was to have opposed the advance of General Fara's column has enthusiastically put itself under the general's orders.'

[2] The total numbers of the columns converging on Rome amounted to about 37,000 men, of whom 6000 were from Civitavecchia and Santa Marinella, 13,300 from Monterotondo-Mentana, 8000 from Tivoli, 4000 from Valmontone, and 5000 from Foligno.   But the number of blackshirts who marched through the streets of Rome during the afternoon of October 31 was much greater ; the current of success swept along towards Rome new contingents from near and far, increasing hour by hour.

waiting for a few hours, so as to make himself more valuable, and the better to prepare his cabinet. He had a long telephone conversation with the deputy Acerbo, to whom he entrusted various missions in Rome and confided his plan of forming a broad bottomed administration, including even certain members of the General Confederation of Labour. He made a short speech to those who came to cheer him off in the evening at the Milan station : ' If I have the chance of taking power, I can tell you that henceforward the Italian State is going to exist to the fullest extent of its powers.' In the train he declared that he would come before the king, ' in a black shirt, as a fascist ', and that he would give no demobilization order until he had formed his cabinet. The list he had ready contained the names of the economist Einaudi and the deputy Baldesi, one of the leaders of the General Confederation of Labour, whom Acerbo had asked on Mussolini's behalf and who had accepted. But neither Einaudi nor Baldesi, nor any other leader of the Confederation, were to appear in the Mussolini ministry, for the leaders of the right, disappointed by the failure of their manœuvre, had vetoed it. Mussolini kept for himself from the first the premiership, the Ministry of the Interior and—his ambition at last achieved—the Foreign Office. The cabinet included representatives of all parties, except socialists and communists. The fascists had five ministries, the *Popolari* two, the various kinds of liberal democrats had three, the conservatives one and the nationalists one. The fascists had nine under-secretaryships, the *Popolari* four, the liberal democrats two, the conservatives one, and the nationalists two.

The share of the right-wing parties in the new administration was strictly limited, but there were compensating advantages : the socialist movement and the workers' organizations had been put out of action, parliament was curbed, the inquiry into war expenses was suspended, the fiscal measures dealing with excess profits and the registration of securities were quashed. Above all there was no longer any opposition to the foreign policy that the nationalists had always advocated. A few weeks after the march, Alfredo Rocco, under-secretary of state, called this to mind in a speech : ' We await with confidence the imperial Italy which is to come.'

The population everywhere stood by, surprised but passive, while these decisive events were taking place. There were a few incidents here and there, such as took place every Sunday in Italian towns and countryside. Barricades were set up in Parma ; in Rome shots were fired in the suburb of San Lorenzo, through which the black-shirts of the Bottai column passed on their way to the centre of the town. That was all. The fascist squads, on the other hand, took advantage of their mobilization in almost every district to occupy newspaper offices, set fire to Chambers of Labour, ransack private apartments and turn out such socialist councils as had survived previous offensives.

The so-called leaders of the working class lost no opportunity of showing their incapacity, right up to the last moment. The communists, although persuaded ' that no defence is possible against such overwhelmingly powerful forces ',[1] suggested that the Alliance of Labour should be immediately reconstructed and a general strike proclaimed. They were quite aware that nothing could come of this, but their own reaction to the tragic events which had sealed the fate of the Italian people was to suggest this feeble manœuvre, which would give them a chance to do nothing and cry ' treason ' at the General Confederation of Labour. The leaders of the Confederation very properly denounced this as a piece of communist provocativeness, but did so in a statement which contained this shameful passage : ' The General Confederation of Labour feels that it is its duty when political passions are running high and forces alien to the workers' syndicates are disputing the power of the state, to warn the workers against the speculations and incitements of political parties and groups which would drag the proletariat into a struggle in which it must take absolutely no part.'

Most of the anti-fascists did not realize how serious things were. People's nerves had been on edge for too long and the first impression was of relief and resignation. They mostly thought : ' On the whole, things are better

[1] *Rassegna communista*, 31 October, 1922, p. 1454.

so. *They* cannot last two months.' In Montecitorio a group of deputies were speculating about the future. Amendola was optimistic : ' There is nothing to be frightened of. Mussolini too will get caught in the constitutional toils, and finally we shall have a government.' A socialist deputy replied : ' That is an illusion ; the fun is only just beginning and you will be eliminated in your turn.'

Mussolini had as yet no very clear idea of what he was going to do, but behind him he felt the irresistible and intoxicating impulse of his success. He had reached power and he meant to keep it.

At the exhibition of modern Italian art in Paris in the summer of 1935, there was a large picture showing Mussolini on horseback at the head of the legions marching into Rome, Mussolini plunging into the heat of battle like Bonaparte at the bridge of Arcole. As an antidote to this outrage against art and truth, there was fortunately a few hundred yards away an exhibition of classical Italian art from Cimabue to Tiepolo. But where can the Italian people turn for forgetfulness or a new mode of life, when realization comes of the loss suffered by themselves and humanity when they allowed Mussolini to ride to power in a wagon-lit on October 31, 1922, a day before the March on Rome, ' which never took place '.

EPILOGUE

I

WHEN the post-war crisis began, Italian national unity had been established for barely fifty years, and the part played by the masses in winning it had been small. After 1870 the old oligarchies had only one aim in view : to suppress the fourth estate and deprive it of every means to direct action and power. On this point the conflicting forces of Vatican and monarchy were agreed. There were no democratic or revolutionary traditions, and the parliamentary system had remained an artificial improvisation grafted on to the life of the nation, whose growth had not been helped by the corrupt methods of Giolitti's reformism. The only really democratic force was the working-class and socialist movement, but this was handicapped by its narrow outlook and concentration on municipal affairs. Nevertheless the people—workers, artisans and peasants—with the traditions of their own independent institutions, were slowly making their weight felt in the state, when their progress was interrupted by the war. This was begun and carried on in Italy as a civil war, and coincided with a grave crisis in the ruling classes. The war was followed by depression and disorder : economic crisis in the country, which was exhausted and dislocated by the effort of victory ; moral crisis among the people who, 'while being and feeling victorious, were suffering the humiliation and crisis of the vanquished'.

Within these wider causes there were other factors which helped to alter the course and the outcome of Italy's post-war history : the failure of the socialist movement ; the reactionaries' and particularly the landowners' offensive in the form of military action and territorial conquest ; the economic crisis of 1921 ; the help and complicity of the state and its dependent bodies ; the discrediting of Parliament ; the part played by Mussolini.

.   .   .   .   .   .

Most important were the socialist feebleness and mistakes, which were the direct cause, not of fascism itself, which appeared in every country after the war, but of its success in Italy. This becomes evident if one follows from day to day, as we have done, the policy of all the proletarian parties—socialist, maximalist, communist—in the years 1919–1922. It is helpful, though, to look still further into some of their failures and mistakes.

In so doing we may lay ourselves open to a charge of injustice towards the Italian working-class and socialist movement. But this is not the history of that movement, nor the biography of some of its leaders (Matteotti, Turati, Treves, to mention only those who are dead), whose moral greatness was sometimes actually a cause of political inferiority. Nor is this the valley of Jehoshaphat, where faults and merits are meticulously scrutinized. . . . We are combatants who accept, as they come, the tasks imposed on us by the time in which we live. It is our object to record the causes of a catastrophe where results have been grave in the extreme and will take long to repair. But we can only bear the responsibility for the past by a firm determination to avoid, so far as it is within our power, a recurrence of the same mistakes and the same disasters. Only candid and ruthless self-examination can give us the right to draw publicly the conclusions from our experience, and can transform our suffering into a message for others.

The fundamental weakness of Italian socialism in every sphere was due to its lack of true revolutionary spirit. This spirit is drawn by two allegiances : the refusal to accept the injustice, disorder and meanness of existing society, and the will to arrive at a new economic regime, new institutions, arising out of new relationships between men. Condemnation of the present must be enlightened, strengthened and justified by affirmation of the future. Only in this sense is there any truth in Bakunin's saying, ' the passion for destruction is a creative passion '. But it has been truly

said of Italy that ' hatred of everything old deadened even
the desire for a new order ', and that is why this hatred was
so impotent.

For a class to be really revolutionary it must, says Marx,
' first be aware that it is not a particular class, but the
representative of the general needs of society '. Italian
socialism lacked this leaven, which alone could have raised
it to victory. With a middle class crippled, clinging to its
class point of view in the midst of the great upheaval which
had intensified its egoism and its greed, the socialist movement had a great part to play. If it had been strong enough
to remain faithful to it, it might have saved the Italian
people.

Instead it shirked its task. It lurked in the background
all through the post-war crisis. This desertion is the sole
explanation of the fascist success. Society, even more than
nature, abhors a vacuum, and the forces of barbarism are
ever ready to rush in and fill it.

The Italian socialists waited for the middle class to die
off naturally, without considering whether its death struggle,
as they assumed it to be, if unduly prolonged, might not
generate seeds of decay which would infect the whole nation,
the socialist movement included. They behaved like the
sole heir to an estate who prefers not to turn up till the last
minute, just before the will is read. While they waited they
confined their activities to ' separating their own responsibilities from those of the ruling classes '. This separation
was, up to a point, justified and even necessary. But responsibility for evil committed is always shared by those who
have failed to prevent it ; and we have no right to connive
at others' actions unless we are prepared to step in at the
right moment and succeed where they have failed. It is
all the easier to separate our own responsibilities from those
of the ruling classes if we are able and willing to shoulder
our own responsibilities on behalf of an entire nation. If
not, it is quite simple to avoid ' legal ' responsibilities by
pleading a kind of alibi, the last resort of all scoundrels.
(' Nothing like a alleybi ' was the advice given by Sam
Weller's father to Pickwick.) In so doing we incur a much
heavier responsibility to history, whose judgments go

much deeper than any legal code. Useless, then, to say ' We were not there.' The masses, who have lost all, will want to know why not.

The policy of the Italian communists and maximalists was to let things get as bad as possible. A policy which depends on aggravating a situation the better to control and direct it is justifiable so long as one is ready and willing to intervene at the right moment and restore order in the chaos that follows. Such tactics, which must be employed with the utmost precision, become too easily a game of chance, depending as they do on the blindest and least reversible of forces.[1]

The Italian maximalists and communists had no idea of tactics : theirs was a state of mind that combined demagogy with inactivity and was quite devoid of the prophetic passion which calls down evil in order that virtue may triumph more brilliantly, and of the creative spirit which is capable of bringing about a vigorous transition from lowest to highest.

Such failings always imply a lack of humanity : the syndicate, section, party or class remains hidebound by its own limitations, and instead of regarding them as such, ends by making a fetish of them and loses that power of transcending them, which is the supreme necessity and spirit of socialism. This was the sole cause of the hiatus between the labour organizations, political and syndical, and the mass of the people.

Many of the socialist leaders thought that the vague popular movement which followed the armistice was just a ' war psychosis '. This was doubtless true, but it was not the whole truth. Those who fought in the war came in contact with the ' system ' and were swept up and controlled by it for four years. The war had torn them abruptly from their parish pump outlook and given them a stormy

---

[1] The revolutionary defeatism of the bolsheviks in 1917 had an instantly paralysing effect on the October revolution. For not only did Kerensky find it impossible to carry through the offensive measures demanded by the Allies, but Lenin too was unable to pass from defeatism to revolutionary war ; hence Brest Litovsk. To-day it may be argued that this worked well, as the central powers were forced to quit the Baltic countries and the Ukraine, and Soviet Russia was saved in spite of all. But this resulted not from the military paralysis of the revolution at the beginning of 1918, but in spite of it, and from a combination of quite unexpected circumstances.

introduction to real politics. A whole generation was united in a common experience of an extraordinary nature. Afterwards the mass of ex-servicemen everywhere felt that they were on the threshold of a new life. They revolved vague, half-formulated ideas which led them to seek contact with each other and to feel conscious of the need to fight for their common salvation. As was to be expected after the shock and the bloodshed, their reactions were not always normal. But there was a real feeling that ' we must not be taken in again ', a feeling which ought to have been directed towards definite ends. Instead all that was noble and potentially humane in this emotional upheaval remained inarticulate, ignored, until finally it was exploited only to rescue from the past what had better been left there.

The socialist movement failed to realize how the war had thrown the great unorganized masses into the foreground. A movement on such a scale was beyond the old syndicate or party standard. The soldier back from the front found a society at once too unstable and too orderly for his liking. The revolution itself was too orderly—party card, syndicate subscription, membership of the co-operative, difficulties he could not get over, faced as he was by mistrust or tolerance, both equally insufferable. The Italian socialist leaders could no more understand the ex-servicemen of 1919–1920 than the German syndicates understood the unemployed of 1929–1932. Even Turati, so humane and so enlightened, felt that his chicks had turned into birds of prey. His socialism was a matter of conscience and education. In this he was right, but the time had come for the pedagogues, however noble, to give way to the prophets and missionaries. The sheltered flock in the party and the syndicates ought to have been neglected a little in favour of the lost sheep wandering in their thousands over waste land, so that they too could be saved.

Owing to the immense success of their co-operatives, Chambers of Labour, and town councils, the socialists of the Po valley believed they were simply going to absorb the old regime. Every day new institutions were growing up which to some extent foreshowed a society freed from the obsession of profit. But in legitimate pride in the results obtained they lost sight of their limitations, and socialism by remaining local and provincial became the victim of its own success. It went so far as to make a virtue of its faults. It was no longer only the old Italy, but socialism itself, the socialism of Reggio Emilia, which *farà da se*.[1] There was no point in considering the problem of the state, which supplied credits, grants and public works on demand. ' Here,' explained the socialist chiefs, ' we are already in power. If the whole of Italy becomes a Reggio Emilia the revolution will be made.' This ' socialism in a single province ' lost in breadth what it gained in depth ; and breadth for socialism is not a matter of mere dimensions, but forms part of its very essence. The rate of its spread decides its nature and its destiny. Through its ignorance or neglect of the peasants of Apulia and the herdsmen of Sardinia it lost contact with the nation and with the reality of socialism. It lost too the sound knowledge that none of its work would last while the ' oases of socialism ' were still isolated in a desert whose sands might at any moment submerge them. This kind of socialism not only fails to lead to revolution, but risks losing all its conquests, as it did in Italy. The real essence of local and gradual action is to keep in touch with the state on the one hand and to further the aims of socialism on the other. In the absence of this twofold outlet the political capacity, to use Proudhon's phrase, that the working class develops in its own institutions is lost to the community. The Italian socialists were utterly incapable of relating their ideals to the tasks imposed on them by circumstances.

Through this lack of perspective a prodigious quantity of devotion and human material, far superior to that behind many other political or religious movements, was wasted, and the chosen people, who had already arrived at the threshold of the new city, were disarmed and vanquished.

The socialists of the extreme left, on the other hand, invoked at every step their final aim of ' proletarian revolution '. On principle everything was sacrificed to this. For them there was no question as to whether their aim was consonant with the general interest ; it was an accepted

---

[1] ' Will act on its own,' a phrase which appeared during the *Risorgimento*, expressing independence of outside help.

dogma, an historical fact, that it was so. Henceforward human emancipation was the work of the proletariat, and of the industrial proletariat in particular, acting through its leaders and its political party. And in their turn the party leaders became the trustees of the general interest and identified themselves with its progress and its demands. To look back and see if the sanctity of the apostolic succession had survived so many stages was pointless. There resulted a sectarian frame of mind dominated by a theological hatred of all who refused to recognize the divine quality of their mandate. So at the decisive moments in the Italian crisis the communists were fiercely opposed to a ' united front ', which they had never seriously or loyally supported.

The ideas and behaviour of the communists over the alliance of the proletariat with other social classes were characterized by the same sort of trickery. These were used as mere pawns in a strategy which was carried on over their heads. The alliance was not conceived of as depending on a common principle to which the proletariat and its allies were bound in equal measure. On the contrary ' partial demands ' were discussed, for the sake of an agreement that was only provisional and involved no deep or lasting obligations. While all goes well such differences pass unnoticed, but when the pace slackens the other classes begin to take notice and to claim their independence. This is what happened in Italy.

The alliance was founded on a very impermanent community of interests, and not on a desire for emancipation, which alone could have made it worth while or durable, and it ended not in mere disruption but in actual conflict. For the middle classes fell easy victims to manœuvres aimed at turning them against the proletariat. Fascism gave them an ideology which flattered their worst instincts by allowing them to believe that they were playing an independent and decisive part. The ' arbitration ' of the middle class between capitalists and workers was set up against the ' hegemony ' of the proletariat. One conception displaced another and the human raw material of the ' revolution ' was sacrificed to it.

.   .   .   .   .   .

The working-class and socialist movement in Italy was therefore defeated largely because, as Filippo Turati said, it was reduced to 'teaching the proletariat to shirk at a time when the country was faced with the most urgent and burning problems'. A graphical representation of the two movements would show them to be in some degree complementary. The socialist curve rises until the spring of 1920, when it fluctuates (defeat of the Turin general strike), hesitates, then rises suddenly with the factory occupations in September. Then there is a continuous fall till the march on Rome. The fascist movement, powerless until the early months of 1920, scarcely revived by the employers' great offensive which led to the occupations, rose steeply during the last three months of 1920 and continued to rise rapidly in 1921. The decline of the working-class and socialist movement was due entirely to internal causes, and preceded and made possible the victorious outbreak of fascism. In an article written at the end of 1920 Mussolini said : ' In the past three months . . . the psychology of the Italian working class has changed profoundly,' and on July 2, 1921, sixteen months before the march on Rome, Mussolini recorded : 'To say that a bolshevist peril still exists in Italy is to accept a few disgraceful fears as the truth. Bolshevism is beaten.' Mr. Bolton King, who has written the best history of the *Risorgimento*, has rightly come to the following conclusion :

'Fascism had no part in the Bolschevist collapse ; it was as yet not strong enough to make itself felt effectively, and Mussolini indeed had smiled approvingly on the occupation of the factories. There is no substance in the myth that it saved Italy from Bolschevism. But the myth is a convenient one and it still lives in dark corners.'

In Italy this myth has become the object of an official cult very useful for the purposes of the internal and foreign policy of the fascist regime. It is nevertheless true, however, that it was not fascism which defeated the revolution in Italy, but the defeat of the revolution which determined the rise and victory of fascism.

Why did fascism only begin really to take hold when its historical necessity, or as much as it had claimed for itself, had disappeared ? Because the movement was not merely defensive, but a deliberate attempt to wipe out the forces and strongholds of the enemy. In this way alone could the privileged classes and especially the landowners attain their object, which was, not to restore equilibrium, but to profit by its destruction. The retreat of the enemy only whetted their appetite for reaction and revenge. When, for a few weeks towards the middle of 1921, Mussolini toyed with the idea of a general settlement on the basis of a compromise, the fascists in the country districts frustrated his plans and found support for their intransigence in all conservative centres. Aggressive fascism of the *squadrismo* type was born of the union of the capitalist offensive with the ambitions and appetites of various sections of the middle class, left by the ebbing of the tide of war which had carried them along nicely for four years. Thus, to borrow another expression from Turati, ' a revolution in words ', which had broken down after October 20, was followed by a ' bloody counter-revolution ', a ' posthumous and preventive counter-revolution '. . . .

Just as the capitalist and fascist attack was being launched another factor began to weaken the workers' resistance. The slump became serious after the beginning of 1921, and the industrialists did not hesitate to use it as a weapon, proceeding to make wholesale dismissals of their staffs. The workers' committees and syndicates began by opposing them with their veto, but they could not hope to hold out long with purely passive resistance. The industrialists threatened to close the factories, and the workers no longer had any enthusiasm about occupying them. They tried compromise ; with their strong sense of self-preservation and unity, the syndicates and internal factory committees imposed reductions in the hours of work of the whole staff, which they still had power to do, so as to avoid dismissals. This sacrifice by all for all considerably reduced wages all round. Those who were afraid of losing their jobs accepted this as a lesser evil, those who were or who believed themselves safe, eventually began to feel slightly uneasy and incapable of resistance. They became resigned to the elimination of one and then another category of workers : those who had a patch of ground in the sun, those who had no families dependent on them, the latest comers to the factory. This policy of despair gradually impaired the solidarity of the workers' front. Those who were sacrificed, with the tacit or formal consent of those who remained, departed embittered, sometimes desperate. Such a state of affairs could only be tolerated if it led to something better. But the workers, on the contrary, felt that they had reached an impasse, and that their sacrifice was useless, since anyhow the employers managed in the end to reduce their staff as much as they liked. The deadlock might have been ended by a firm policy uniting all the national resources to end the depression and assure at all events a minimum living wage to all workers. But who could have carried out such a policy ? Not the socialists, who had been explaining for two years that this was a crisis of the capitalist system, that it was actually the final crisis of this system, and that the *bourgeoisie* must be left to shift for itself. Still less the ruling classes, whose one aim and obsession was the political and industrial enslavement of the workers. Fascism was there to simplify their task.

Consequently the slump, which the socialists had reckoned as an asset, proved their undoing. For every slump starts a process of social disintegration, with results that cannot be foretold dependent as they are upon uncertain human reactions. An exasperated desire to ' put an end to things ' somehow may lead to despondency and panic unless it is directed towards some concrete aim, and allowed a glimpse of a new order. The slump crushes those who cannot thus look ahead and are therefore without hope. Its value as a revolutionary factor lies in the forces of order it sets in motion ; if these are not the forces of a new order, it only serves to consolidate the old.

.   .   .   .   .

The economic crisis in Italy coincided with a political one. Every branch of the state, police, executive, magistracy and army, gave its support to the fascists, in ways varying from tolerance to direct complicity. The ground was prepared for them, they were supplied with arms and transport, and they were promised immunity from punishment. Government decrees mouldered in files or were used exclusively against socialists. The government itself preferred not to be too deeply involved. For everybody was hoping to make use of fascism : Giolitti, to push the socialists into the government, the conservatives to keep them out, employers and landowners to liquidate working-class syndicalism, the monarchy and the Vatican to buttress the established order. They all relied on fascism as a temporay ally which could easily be disposed of later.[1] As matters stood, the state could only live a hand-to-mouth existence, going from compromise to compromise, from concession to concession. It had no source of strength. The mass of the people was estranged and hostile, and parliamentary crises followed one after the other continuously and without any signs of a solution appearing. Confusion, lassitude, and disgust, skilfully enhanced by controversy, and a kind of ' planned defeatism ' prepared public opinion for the justification of dictatorship. Liberty, in whose cause nobody, whether individual or party, was prepared to sacrifice either ambitions or personal wishes, was left defenceless. The threat to the state became a threat to democracy.

.   .   .   .   .   .

In addition to the failure of the socialists, capitalist and fascist aggression, the economic crisis, state complicity, and the breakdown of parliamentary institutions, there must be taken into account the personal influence of Mussolini.

During the war he severed all that connected him with his ancient beliefs. At heart, though, he had never been a real socialist. As a young man, consumed by pride and the desire to assert himself, and obsessed by the idea that society was oppressing him, he had broken away and taken refuge in Switzerland. As society would not give him the position

[1] We know how mistaken such calculations were. At the 1921 elections Giolitti got the fascists included in the lists of the ' national bloc '. When Count Sforza warned him of the danger of such a combination, he replied : ' These fascist candidatures are nothing but fireworks ; they will make a great deal of noise but nothing will come of it.' The king shared the illusion, saying to Briand as late as December 1924 concerning fascism : ' It is not serious, it will not last.'

he wanted, his will to power took the form of individual revolt. The experiences of his years of exile had a decisive effect on him. Sometimes he had been dependent for his daily bread on the help and goodwill of mere artisans or simple decent socialists, or on petty dishonesty. Sometimes he had had to take the roughest kind of work; he had fallen low, and known extreme poverty. Such a life might have turned him into a saint or a criminal, but he was too ambitious and too unscrupulous to take either way out. He learnt to set his teeth, to calculate, to reject the romantic outlook and to grab his opportunity. Socialism could give him a start and serve for shelter. In a few years he reached the highest position that the party could give him, the editorship of its paper, *Avanti*. By the outbreak of war socialism in its turn had become the obstacle that society had been to him in the years 1900 to 1908. Mussolini did not hesitate to break away a second time. After the armistice he realized that he had to begin all over again and start a third struggle for existence. From that time on his personal fortune is so closely linked with the history of fascism as to be often indistinguishable.

If Mussolini had simply joined forces with the reactionaries in 1919 the flood would have passed over him and he would have been left behind; he would not have found himself in March supported by the ex-members of the ' *Fasci* of Revolutionary Action' of 1914–1915, nor, a short time later, would he have managed to collect a number of young men and ex-servicemen. Even if he had formed the new *fasci* they would have perished with him. By the end of 1920 the situation had altered : the *squadristi* and the ' slave-drivers ', spreading from the valley of the Po, were advancing rapidly and overthrowing the socialist strongholds one after another. Mussolini hastened to make use of this movement, and revised his programme, declaring that ' the reality of to-morrow will be capitalist '. Towards the end of 1921 however, the movement was showing signs of getting out of hand and compromising his political plans. So he tried to frustrate it, denouncing its 'greedy egoism which refuses any national conciliation '; he contrasted the ' urban fascism ' of Milan with the ' agrarian fascism ' of Bologna, 'fascism of the first hour' with that which stood for the defence of 'private interests and of the darkest, most sordid and most despicable classes now existing in Italy'. Having announced in Florence : 'Our programme is based on facts', he now clamoured for a 'return to principles'. A few months later still, when the situation had developed further, he trampled on the vague tendencies of Grandi and his friends towards 'democracy' and 'syndicalism', and from their opposition movement he took nothing but the bare principle of armed organization, stripped of any political significance ; a simple weapon for the capture of power. Besides, although he disguised his plans in 1921 under a pretended 'return to principles' Mussolini declared one year later that 'to go back to the beginning, as some would have, that is to get back to the 1919 programme, is to give proof of childishness and senility'. His versatility and complete lack of scruple proved an invaluable asset to fascism. It was he who prevented the attack on the Bonomi cabinet in autumn 1921 ; he who persuaded the group to support the Celli resolution in February 1922 (p. 174) and in July succeeded in preventing the formation of an anti-fascist group which might have become a government. If this had taken place fascism would have lost the support, or at least the connivance, of the state, and risked defeat. Finally, if Mussolini had not acted as he did, the march on Rome would have taken place in earnest and fascism would have met its doom.

Mussolini is not a genius ; he merely has, as Mr. Bolton King so justly remarks, 'the minor arts of a statesman'. But these he possesses to a very high degree. Much of his strength has come from the weakness of his enemies. In 1919 he was simultaneously outbidding the demagogues and working for the cause of reaction. This could never have happened if socialism had not allowed it. Faced with a constructive, which does not mean a watered-down Socialist Party, based on the traditions, institutions and powerful resources of the Italian working-class movement and free from delusions about soviets, Mussolini's tricks and man-œuvres would have fallen flat. From the second half of 1921 up to the march on Rome Mussolini managed to exploit parliamentary action and *squadrismo* at the same time, thus, in Lenin's phrase, combining ' legal with illegal action '. But it was the socialist movement which gave him the necessary freedom of movement, by refraining from all action, legal or illegal, and thus delivering the country into the hands of its enemies. If it had been attacked through these inconsistencies fascism might have been crushed, but because they were neglected and allowed to flourish they became a direct cause of its strength and success.

The Italy of 1919–1922 lacked political leaders. Giolitti's mentality was pre-war, and when he returned to power in 1920 he was in his seventy-eighth year. The others, Nitti, Bonomi, Orlando, Salandra, all suffered from the same handicap : they were good scholars, but too academic to be able to deal properly with the post-war situation. The socialists had a few first-rate men, mostly on the right, but they were hampered by the conflict of doctrines inside the party and the working-class movement. The personal qualities of some of the communist leaders, such as Gramsci and Bordiga, could not outweigh the damage done by hopelessly wrong-headed tactics, and sometimes aggravated it. The maximalist socialists were a body without a head. Lamartine's description of a Girondin chief applied to most of their leaders : ' One of those complaisant idols of which people make anything they wish except a man.'

Italian socialism had need of a man, several men, in order to win, or, which came to the same thing, to avoid being wiped out. This was why Mussolini was able to reduce Italy to his own size and fill the entire horizon. With his advent the rule of ' principle ' came to an end, and his own personal adventure became that of Italy itself. For the better understanding of this crisis it is possible and indeed essential to trace back over centuries its remote and fundamental causes : the configuration of the land ; the economic and social structure ; the long enslavement of the people ; the recent liberation, barely tolerated by some, barely assimilated by others. But these causes were not bound, inevitably, to lead to the events of the years 1919–1922 as they actually took place, with all their changes, their possibilities and their final result. New forces were growing up in Italy, alongside the prevalent lethargy, and for a certain space of time these balanced each other. In such cases momentary influences, including luck, may be decisive. The slightest variation may upset the balance and change the whole situation. Then it is that the actions of one man become of first importance, and history becomes a drama in which everything is linked up and nothing pre-determined, in which the epilogue may be changed up to the last minute, so long as the actors—individuals or groups—do not themselves rush towards the catastrophe. Contrary to a common belief, circumstances do not always of themselves create the men who are needed. Past history now provides a proof.

II

Fascism is a dictatorship ; such is the starting-point of all definitions that have so far been attempted. Beyond that there is no agreement. Dictatorship of capitalism ' in the period of its decline ', dictatorship of large-scale capitalism ; dictatorship of finance-capitalism ; ' openly terrorist ' dictatorship ' of the most reactionary, chauvinist and imperialistic sections of finance-capitalism '; dictatorship of the ' two hundred families ' ; and so on, until sometimes one meets the definition of fascism narrowed down to the personal dictatorship of Mussolini or Hitler. Someone has said, ' Italian fascism is Mussolini '.

Each of these definitions contains some truth, but none can be accepted as it stands. Further, we shall take care not to produce a new one, which would of course be the right one, a pocket formula, which could be brought out at any moment to clear up our own and everybody else's doubts. Our way of defining fascism is to write its history. We have tried to do this for Italian fascism of the years 1919–1922. A theory of fascism can only be evolved through a study of all its forms, latent or open, modified or unrestrained. For there are many different fascisms, each one made up of numerous, sometimes contradictory tendencies, and capable of developing in such a way that its most characteristic features may be altered. To define fascism is to surprise it during this development, and, in a given country and at a given time, to seize upon its essential differences. It is not a subject with definite attributes which need merely be selected, but the product of a situation from which it cannot be considered separately. The mistakes of the workers' parties, for instance, are as much part of the definition of fascism as the use made of them by the proprietary classes.

The present study of fascism has not been carried beyond the march on Rome, but there is no reason why we should not glance further.[1]   Although conditions in Italy ought to be comprehensively reviewed and compared with those in other countries during the years that followed, the present less enterprising method may at least enable us to point out a few common characteristics from which some conclusions can be drawn.   For this purpose fascism must be considered in relation to the economic, social, political and psychological conditions from which it sprang ; to its own social background and the class struggle ; to its tactics, its organization ; to its consequences and the regime that it set up ; finally to its own programme and ideology.

.   .   .   .   .   .

Fascism is a post-war phenomenon and any attempt to define it by looking for an historical precedent, e.g. in Bonapartism, is fruitless and bound to lead to false conclusions.   Foremost among the conditions that made fascism possible was the economic crisis.   No crisis, no fascism ; and this refers not to any economic crisis, but specifically to the one that settled permanently over the world after the war.   The war left the world with industrial capacity beyond its immediate needs and a complete lack of co-ordination between the various branches of production, complicated by a reduced purchasing power in all countries. The result was over-production and famine, inflation and paralysis.   We are no longer faced by classical crises, which rise from a terrible slump to a still higher rate of production and consumption.   The ' periodic ' crises have been

[1] Some use has here been made of research work undertaken for a more general history of the post-war world, which, given sufficient time, means and strength, I hope to complete and publish later on.

succeeded by 'chronic stagnation with slight fluctuations', the 'alternation of relatively short boom and relatively long depression', foretold by Engels more than fifty years ago. Even in the United States, where crises are more oscillatory owing to the possibilities of the home market, the existence of an irreducible mass of several million unemployed points to a new kind of depression. Fascism is bred in these depressions and forms part of the reaction to them. In countries without the large home market of the U.S.A., the British Empire, the U.S.S.R., depressions are more or less incurable. Economic discomfort fuses readily with nationalist aspirations and talk of 'a place in the sun'. This results on the one hand in isolation and the aggravation of the more artificial and parasitical aspects of the economic system, on the other in the illusion that the 'encirclement' can be broken by seeking some violent solution beyond the frontiers. The capitalist system, having to a great extent lost its resiliency, oscillates no longer between depression and boom, but between autarchy and war.[1]

In every country the end of the war and the beginning of the depression saw fairly considerable alterations in social status. The creation of a mass of *nouveaux riches*, and distinct changes in the traditional forms of capitalism resulted in the emergence of a new *bourgeoisie*. Practically all producers had become so used to exceptional war-time profits that they had lost sight of the notion of the rigidity of cost price, while the stimulus of competition had been entirely removed. Such considerations were always resurrected when workers'

---

[1] In this sense, therefore, it is true that fascism is the fruit of capitalism in decline and the expression of a retrograde economic system. It is also true, though inadequate, to say : ' to conquer fascism we must conquer the depression ', and ' fascism must be fought in the world of economics '. Economic revival undoubtedly checks fascism, but by itself it cannot eliminate the danger altogether. In March 1937 the socialist minister Spaak, speaking of the Rexist movement, said : ' I used to think the eventual success of our steady campaign against the depression would be enough to stamp out this lawless, bold and dangerous propaganda. I frankly admit that I was wrong, and I realize to-day that a movement like Rex cannot be fought by a mere improvement of economic conditions. Although the work of improvement must go on, we have got to carry the struggle on to political and even sentimental ground.'
    In addition, national boundaries to-day render the struggle against the depression hopeless. And a decisive victory against fascism can only be gained on the political plane by the reconstruction of Europe, after the deadly magic circle of autarchies has been broken and the way found once more to collaboration and unity.

wages had to be discussed, but they had really ceased to operate, and almost everywhere capitalists were conscious that they could no longer manage without the direct help of the state.   Its seizure by any possible means became for them a matter of life-and-death importance.

On the other hand, the war had set the popular masses in movement, and after the war this movement was accelerated.   The organization of the workers' parties and the syndicates was breaking down under the pressure of the hundreds of thousands and millions of new members.   They had no great stability, and the high tide was quickly followed by a rapid ebb.   Moreover, in spite of the growth of the old organizations, there was a large body of waverers who remained outside, ready to rush in any direction.   This body has been referred to as the ' middle classes ' ; but it must be emphasized that they were not the middle classes of the classical period of capitalism, absorbed after each crisis into the machinery of increased production and into a new proletariat.   The post-war middle classes no longer had even the chance of joining the proletariat ; the depression barred both their rise into the *bourgeoisie* and their descent into the proletariat.   This petty and middle *bourgeoisie*, which found itself everywhere excluded, formed the backbone of fascism in Italy and everywhere else.   But the expression ' middle class ' must be given a wider meaning, to include the son of the family waiting for a job or for his inheritance to *déclassés* of all kinds, temporary or permanent, from the half-pay officer to the *lumpenproletarier*, from the strike-breaker to the jobless intellectual.   It includes workers who are more conscious of being ex-servicemen or unemployed than of their class, from which they break away in spirit to join the ranks of its enemies.

With the coming of peace the long pent-up demands of the masses were released, at a time when, as a result of the war, there was less than ever to satisfy them.   A tendency to hoard available resources rather than find better ways of sharing them brought the problem of power into the foreground.   Three factors combined to lead the way to fascism : the intensification of the class struggle, its increasingly political character, and the relative equality of the opposing forces. Given the first two, the third is of crucial importance. Such equality is paralysing to any form of government, whether it be a national coalition, a combination of left-wing parties, or a social democratic majority. So long as it continues and no better form of government is found, the state is at the mercy of blind upheavals caused by some instinct of self-preservation, by the defence of threatened privileges, and by the aspirations of classes that have been upset and thrown out of gear by the depression. By abandoning the attempt to gain a solution by legal methods, the working classes turn to the creation of a 'second power', within the state and opposed to it; the *bourgeoisie* then has recourse either to 'reactionary transformation of the state' or to fascist violence.

Amongst the general conditions of fascism that should be mentioned is the existence of a kind of 'climate', a special atmosphere of excitement and frenzy; this is so indispensable, both before and after victory, that the party leaders have to strain every nerve to keep it up. In this atmosphere all reactions are strained, all sense of proportion is distorted, and ordinary standards vanish. Psychological shock becomes as necessary as drugs to an addict. Delirium is exalted as normality. Fascism cannot be dismissed as mere war psychosis (any more than the Commune could be dismissed as a '*fièvre obsidionale*'); the history of fascism, however, is one of the most remarkable and disturbing chapters of social pathology.

.   .   .   .   .   .

Fascism finds its chief support in the post-war middle class, whose main characteristics we have just described. Must fascism, therefore, be defined as a middle-class movement taken up and exploited by reactionary capitalism? There is much truth in this definition, but it cannot be accepted without reservations. The social significance of a movement is not entirely decided by its social make-up. Although most of the supporters of fascism are recruited from the middle classes, its first historic role is that of the exterminator of working-class parties and syndicates. Afterwards, whatever its pretensions or its supporters, it takes a hand in the capitalist offensive. The suppression of the independent workers' organizations permanently alters the balance of social power. Fascists and capitalists can no longer behave as if these organizations had not been suppressed. Even when fascism pretends to play the part of arbitrator between capital and labour, it puts one of the parties in an inferior position—by destroying its independence—from which it can only free itself by throwing off fascism altogether.

It was chiefly the urban middle classes which were swept into fascism. In July 1919 Mussolini believed, not only that fascism was fated to remain ' a minority movement ', but that it could not ' spread outside the towns '. And although Italian fascism was chiefly established, after 1921, through the influx of countryfolk into its ranks,[1] its leaders were largely drawn from the middle classes in the towns, or were the sons of landowners—officers, students—town-dwellers with no desire to play the part of Cincinnatus, once they were back from the front. They were much more anxious to conquer the towns, the first step towards political power, than to be the leaders in their village. Further, fascism was never successful when confined to purely country districts, and the impulse to victory came less from the Po valley campaigns than from Rome and Milan. The big cities always played the leading part.

Fascism finds its chief support in those members of the middle class who either have or think they have no independent economic standing, and are thus easily ' liquidated ' or absorbed into the new political framework provided by fascism. It is not pure chance which makes the French peasant oppose fascism so obstinately : he will obviously continue to do so as long as his economic basis—the patch of ground he owns and tills—and his more or less real independence are threatened. In the Balkans all the authoritarian regimes—bred in the great cities—were set up in face of the violent resistance of the peasants, who mostly supported opposition parties (National-Zaranist party in Romania, the Croat peasant party in Jugo-Slavia, the

[1] Pp. 198–199.

' Agrarians ' in Bulgaria)[1] In all these countries the land
reform carried out after the war had created an important
class of peasant proprietors, who remained anti-fascist even
in subjection ; while in contrast the absence of such reforms,
or excessive slowness in carrying them out, have made
of fascism a danger or a success in Italy, Germany and
Spain.

Another theory that will not hold water represents fascism
as a revolutionary movement turned reactionary under the
influence of the ruling classes. Fascism is reactionary from
the start. Its first steps are helped and guided by reactionary influence, and its intervention completely upsets the
political and social equilibrium.[2] The coincidence of fascist
development and the political and economic offensive of
the possessing classes is a common phenomenon. Italian
fascism did not begin to be important until 1921, when
' agrarian slavery ' appeared in the Po valley, Tuscany and
Apulia, at the same time as the industrialists' attack on
workmen's wages and collective labour agreements. National
Socialism, in embryo in 1923, did not begin to get under
way until after 1928-29, when wages were being cut and
the policy of deflation had begun. After 1922 Mussolini's
policy coincided with that of the ' liberals ' of the *Corriere
della Sera*, the conservatives of the *Giornale d'Italia*, the great
landowners and the Vatican, namely, to keep the socialists
from any share in power ; just as Hitler, in 1930, insisted
on the breaking up of the great coalition and the exclusion
of the socialists from the Prussian government.

The middle classes had to some extent been caught up
by the wave of popular feeling in the years 1919-20, but
the inability of the socialist movement to find any solution
had cooled them off. Tactless insistence on the ' dictatorship
of the proletariat ', although this was nothing but a form of

[1] This also shows how difficult it is for the peasants to defend themselves
against attacks from the towns and capitals, unless they have dependable allies.
The alliance of the peasants with the urban proletariat is a necessity and a
safeguard for both.

[2] The importance of this intervention and of its effects depends on the
balance held between the two great opposite forces, a balance which may be
upset by the appearance of marginal or ' interstitial ' forces. It is therefore
impossible to judge the influence of the middle classes simply from a numerical
point of view.

words, had helped them to change their minds. Feeling that their pockets and their beliefs were threatened by the socialist movement, they turned towards fascism. All their latent hatred of the man in cap and blouse now came to the surface, finding expression on the one hand in savage attacks on the workers,[1] on the other in a vague desire for independence, and even a kind of idealism. This idealism and the new language it created made its own contribution to the victory of the possessing classes, winning over for them a section of the masses with which they had entirely lost touch.

The relations between middle-class fascism and the capitalist offensive were very close at the start, and have remained so for a long time. Does this mean that they are incapable of development and change ? Only a very detailed analysis of these relations in the different countries at different times could lead one to any conclusion on this question ; while it must be remembered that, whatever the relations may be, they are always affected and distorted by the absence of a third power, that of a freely organized labour group.

.   .   .   .   .

Fascism is not reaction pure and simple, but reaction employing mass effects, which alone are of any use in the post-war world.[2] Hence the use of demagogic slogans and even of socialist terminology : for a long time Mussolini called his paper a ' socialist daily ', and the *Führer's* party still styles itself National-Socialist. As a result the old political parties often find themselves left high and dry.

But the real originality of fascism lies not so much in its mass tactics or its demagogic programme, as in the all-important and independent part played by tactics at the expense of programme.[3] Giolitti used to say, ' Mussolini

---

[1] A Tuscan squad chief, U. Banchelli, in his *Memoirs of a Fascist*, explains that those who carried out these attacks acted, ' not as fascists, but as sons of lawyers, doctors, tradesmen . . . ', and, he adds : ' for long these gangs had only to meet people who looked like workers to attack them without pity.'

[2] Even the Vatican during this period was aiming at strengthening or creating mass Catholic parties nearly everywhere (the *Centrum* in Germany, the *Popolare* party in Italy, *Acción Popular* in Spain).

[3] The fascist myth of the ' leader ' leads to the same result and necessarily involves the claim to absolute power.

has taught me that it is not the programme but the tactics of a revolution against which we must defend ourselves.' The fascist method is tactical rather than doctrinal. Its supreme resort is the *fait accompli*, which is of no effect unless it finally leads to the seizure of power. Absolute power alone enables fascism to overcome its inherent inconsistencies and to maintain its advance, for the spoils can be used to satisfy the most varied appetites, the prestige of victory to attract supporters, and the power of the state to crush its enemies into submission for a long while. This is how the fascist writer Curzio Malaparte, in his *Technique of the Coup d'Etat*, describes the political crisis which preceded the march on Rome : ' These same liberals, democrats, conservatives, while they were summoning the fascists to join the National Bloc, were eager to install Mussolini in the Pantheon of the " saviours of the country " . . . but they were not so ready to resign themselves to the fact that Mussolini's aim was not to save Italy in accordance with the official tradition, but to seize the state, a much more sincere programme than the one he had proclaimed in 1919.'

.   .   .   .   .   .

Hence the importance to fascism of organization, especially armed organization. Every fascist movement has its armed organization, without which it is powerless. This does not mean that every fascist goes about armed, or that the movement has immediate access to arms dumps and arsenals. But its organization is military, with its cadre of officers, discipline, meetings, training, and the firm belief of every member, from top to bottom, that this organization is a necessary and effective instrument for the conquest of power. Fascism always begins by declaring itself ' anti-party ' and ends by turning itself into a political party ; in all the great countries, however, its military organization remains its chief characteristic. Mussolini was able to enrol the entire party in the squads in December 1921, and in 1936 de la Rocque could convert his squads into a party, with the same aim of saving the military organization by disguising it. This organization lies at the heart of fascism and determines its very nature.

Must fascism be resisted by military means? The question of force is undoubtedly involved. But the force behind a sound policy must come as a natural consequence of that policy. Military organization may be very extensively developed, but if it is out of touch with the country its position becomes desperate; this was the case with the fascist squads in the middle of 1921 and the socialist *Schutzbund* in Austria in February 1934. Both Mussolini and Hitler, on the other hand, won their chief victories on the political field (the Facta crisis in October 1922, and the von Schleicher crisis in January 1933).

It is essential for any anti-fascist movement to be always in close touch with the masses. It must also associate itself with the state.[1] In the event of a complete fusion of the ruling classes and the machinery of state with fascism, there may be no other alternative but direct revolutionary action or fascist dictatorship. Even so the consequence is not inevitably the slippery dilemma of 'bolshevism or fascism', which limits the possible courses of action at a time when they should be as varied as possible. Every example that can be quoted (Italy, Bulgaria, Germany, Austria) proves that a union of the state with fascism is the worst thing that can happen. The policy of the working classes fighting fascism must be to do their utmost to avoid being faced with such a situation.

The working class and the masses should try to cut fascism off from the state, and to neutralise and oppose the influence of those who would subordinate the state to fascism. Fascism can do nothing without the help of the state, and less than nothing as its enemy. But it is difficult for anti-fascism to win if it is simultaneously fighting the state and fascism in their entirety. The Italian communists who declared in 1921 that 'the issue lies between

[1] Matteotti, who was very far from being a coward, advised the Polesina workers not to be drawn by fascist provocation, saying: 'Even silence and cowardice are sometimes heroic.' Turati wrote to the workers in Apulia that they must 'have the courage to be cowards'. But apart from the fact that the fascists needed no 'provocation' to destroy what they had quite decided to destroy, the plan of local non-resistance was pointless, unless the struggle in Rovigo or Bari was given up so as to concentrate every effort on Rome, and afterwards intervene in these places with the more powerful resources of the state. But it was absurd simultaneously to discourage local resistance and leave the state in the hands of the accomplices of fascism.

proletarian dictatorship and fascist dictatorship ', and the German communists who in 1932 gave the order for a war on two fronts : ' Against Weimar and against Potsdam ', ended by fighting neither fascism nor the state.[1] The struggle against fascism is three-cornered—the anti-fascist front, which must be on as broad a base as possible, the fascist bloc, which has to be broken up, and the state, whose resources must be mobilized for the defence of democracy. Victory is only possible through a political strategy that takes these three elements into account and aligns them in such a way that force is on the side of democracy.

. . . . . .

To complete this analysis of the nature of fascism we must study the fruit it bears : its consequences, not only inside each country, but also on an international scale, which are closely inter-connected.

Wherever fascism is established the most important consequence, on which all the others depend, is the elimination of the people from all share in political activity. ' Constitutional reform ', the suppression of parliament, and the totalitarian character of the regime cannot be judged by themselves, but only in relation to their aims and their results. Fascism is not merely the substitution of one political regime for another ; it is the disappearance of political life itself, since this becomes a state function and monopoly. Political doctrines circulate, are abandoned or modified, but the people have nothing to do with their adoption or their fluctuations. Even when syndicates, or even a party, continue to exist, they are mere instruments, subordinate branches of the state. By becoming part of the machinery of state their nature does not undergo any change ; they merely become instruments in the second degree, the instruments of instruments. With the removal of all freedom and independence from their institutions the people are reduced to a malleable raw material whose properties of resistance and yield can be calculated and

---

[1] Working-class unity is one condition for victory over fascism. But this depends on another condition, namely, that unity must not impair power for political manœuvre. For the value of working-class unity eventually boils down to the value of the policy it lays down and carries out.

controlled. They still take part in parades and demonstrations, and may be kept in a constant state of alertness
and tension ; but this is simply part of the drill and never
approaches the level of political consciousness.

In this system there is no room for the fatal illusion, long
held by the communists, that fascism might do some good
by destroying ' democratic illusions '. The Italian communists actually announced in May 1921 that : ' It is true
that White reaction is celebrating a few ephemeral victories
over an enemy which is paying dear for its unpreparedness,
but it is destroying the democratic and liberal illusion and
breaking down the influence of social democracy among
the masses.' And in the resolution of the Presidium of the
Communist International, published in January 1934, the
following statement concerning Germany may be read :
' The establishment of an undisguised fascist dictatorship,
by dispelling the democratic illusions of the masses and
liberating them from the influence of social democracy, is
accelerating Germany's advance towards the proletarian
revolution.' This is not the place for a detailed criticism
of this conception, which the Communist International has
never abandoned in spite of all its changes of front, and we
need only record that fascism suppresses not only ' democratic illusions ', but the workers' and socialist movement
which is subject to them. Fascism is like a completely
successful operation : the patient dies and all his illusions
are removed.

By reducing the people to a mere instrument, fascism
destroys the nation. This aspect of the system tends to
pass unnoticed, disguised by the violent nationalist frenzy
that fascism cultivates. National conscience as conceived
in the nineteenth century by Mazzini, the prophet of the
nation state, is ousted by state expediency. For him
nations could not exist without free peoples, any more than
humanity could exist without free nations. The winning
of political liberty and the winning of national independence
spring from the same instinctive urge, and in the best
Jacobin and romantic tradition, ' patriot ' and ' democrat '
are identical. For Mazzini the awakening of national
consciousness was no more than an essential step towards

the formation of European consciousness : ' Young Italy ' could only fulfil itself in ' Young Europe '.

Such conceptions take us far from fascism, while at the same time explaining why the fascists mean to destroy the working-class and socialist movement. Since the end of the nine-teenth century socialism has almost everywhere taken the place of democracy in initiating the masses into national life. They have taken their place in the nation and state on social grounds. This has brought difficulties in its train and sometimes confusion and crisis, but it remains a great historical fact that the masses brought the whole weight of their needs and hopes with them into national life, and thenceforward it was impossible for this life to be organized on any but a higher level of conscience, liberty and individual well-being. For the fascists, on the other hand, the people are only the tool of their ' will to power '. This is inspired by a furious nationalism, which takes over the socialists' demands only to adapt them to serve their own purposes. The slogans of the class struggle in its narrowest sense become the passwords of armed strife between nations : ' young ' nations versus old, ' poor ' nations versus ' satiated ', ' proletarian ' nations versus ' plutocratic '. Hence in all forms of national socialism the nationalism inevitably absorbs the socialism, and in every fascist ' armed nation ' the army swallows up the nation.[1]

This leads equally to autarchy and war. The economic difficulties and contradictions of the fascist regimes speed up the process,[2] but they are not the sole causes. The fascist systems are not only ' driven ' into war, all their activities lead up to it, and it provides the opportunities and the atmosphere they need. Though choice there may be, they cannot do otherwise than choose war. Preparation for war at a given moment ceases to be a means, and becomes an end in itself, completely changing the economic, social and political structure of the country. Fascism is

[1] In fascist jargon, the very expression ' armed nation ' has become suspect and is being replaced by that of ' military nation ', ' warrior nation ', etc.

[2] In his speech in the Chamber of May 26, 1934, Mussolini said : ' Three-quarters of the Italian economic system, industrial, and agricultural, is supported by the state. . . . We touched bottom some time ago : it would be difficult for us to fall any lower.' This situation must be considered one of the immediate causes of the Italian attack on Ethiopia.

committed to this preparation and can only fight its way out. For fascism preparation for war does not mean leaving one of many doors open just in case war should unfortunately break out, but leaving only one open and shutting all the rest. War is not merely a possibility which the state must bear in mind, but a certainty and a necessity to which everything is subordinated. Speaking at the meeting of the Corporations on March 23, 1936, Mussolini explained his policy and his ideas for the future as follows :

> ' Italy can and must attain the maximum of economic independence for peace and war. The whole of the Italian economic system must be directed towards this supreme necessity, on which depends the future of the Italian people. I now come to the crux, to what I might call the plan of control for Italian economic policy in the coming fascist era. This plan is determined by one single consideration : that our nation will be called to war. When ? How ? Nobody can say, but the wheel of fate is turning fast.'[1]

The fascist economy is a closed and planned economy with war as its objective. Cost price, competition and even profit are of no importance in the general scheme. The political aim of preparation for war is more important than any economic consideration, and equally the resulting economic organisation can serve no other aim. In his speech of May 26, 1934 (quoted above), Mussolini said : ' If I wanted to introduce state capitalism or state socialism into Italy, I should now have all the necessary external and objective conditions for doing so.' Can it be said that fascist economy is state capitalism ? In spite of several points of resemblance, we believe not. Under fascism the state does not simply take the place of private capitalists as the organizer of the economic system, but forces them to follow its own policy. Fascism is interested in power, not profit. Naturally profit may one day have to be added to power, but between the two there is a wide gulf which

---

[1] Those who thought or pretended to think that the conquest of Abyssinia would appease fascist Italy and turn Mussolini into an apostle of European peace can now see how arbitrary were their conjectures.

the capitalist class, as such, would refuse to cross unless it were forced.[1]

But it is being forced to do so by a new political class, which is a product of the economic evolution of fascism, and which in its turn reacts on this movement by forcing it towards its most extreme consequences. The proletariat, as such, is entirely excluded from this new class. Preparation for war may relatively reduce unemployment and improve the lot of some classes of workers, but under a system of autarchy it is only achieved by sacrificing the standard of living of the working class as a whole. And since it involves a great concentration of industry, trade and credit, and necessitates large-scale agriculture and mass production of cereals[2] a great proportion of the urban and the whole of the rural middle class is more or less ruined. The increasing concentration of industry, the monopoly of foreign trade, the fixing of prices and the many forms of state intervention all tend to the elimination of the lesser industrialists and the small traders and farmers. On the other hand those members of the urban middle class who have no direct share in production[3] benefit considerably from the regime and pocket a nice share of the profits. They are to be found everywhere, occupying numerous places on the executives of the party, militia, syndicates, state institutions new and old. They form part of the immense fascist bureaucracy which is now the country's ruling class. Generally speaking this new class is the result of a compromise between the capitalists and the middle and lower middle class in the towns. It is interspersed with army chiefs, and members of the aristocracy, but the *homines novi* are in a majority, and theirs is the prevailing mentality : a mixture of furious nationalism and state worship, in keeping with both their

[1] The ideal of every Italian capitalist is that war should never come, because it is so risky, but that preparation for war should continue, if possible, for ever.

[2] In spite of poetic appeals for a ' return to the land ', the fascist regimes, in which some people imagined they saw a revival of agricultural life, only tend to encourage town life by their zeal for industrial methods. One of the conditions and results of preparation for war under fascism is that the relations between the country section and the town section are always being modified to the advantage of the latter.

[3] It was this class which contributed most towards forming the fascist organizations.

ideology and their interests.[1] This new ruling class battens on the state, indulging in shameless scrambles for gain, runs through fortunes with ease, exploits and fleeces others, but has no definite place in the economic life of the country. Even when he becomes a landed proprietor or a capitalist this new fascist ruler continues to draw the best part of his resources from the political monopoly of which he is assured, and from the perpetual expansion of the machinery of state, which he encourages with all his might.[2]

Autarchy and preparation for war make this expansion inevitable. The expansion of state machinery in its turn is bound to involve autarchy and war. Nothing inside the country can break this vicious circle. Fascism has successively wiped out the working-class movement, the people, the nation, every restraining influence. Such is the tragic balance sheet of the fascist attack of the years 1921–1922, whose effects stretch far beyond the boundaries of Italy. The flames which destroyed the Peoples' Houses were only the beginning of a greater blaze which threatens to set Europe alight. The blows that shattered the headquarters of workers' syndicates, co-operatives and socialist sections have struck at the foundations of the new Europe : the Europe loathed by fascism, since it means the end of war and fascists alike.

III

For fascism the political programme is a mere makeshift, concocted to meet the immediate needs of political strategy. On the eve of the march on Rome, as at the time of von Schleicher's resignation, the fascists, like the national socialists, based their candidature to power on the reality of their strength and not on their old or new programme. And it was their strength, directed against the working class

---

[1] The ' left-wing ' fascists, to be found chiefly amongst syndical officials, are the greatest extremists in foreign policy and are always asking for state intervention in internal policy and in the economic sphere. In this connection there is, for example, a considerable distinction in tone and even in attitude between the syndical paper, *Il Lavoro Fascista*, and *Il Sole*, the ' organ of commerce, industry, finance and agriculture '.

[2] In its present phase Italian fascism may be defined as a ' triarchy ', in which power is exercised by the big capitalists, the bureaucracy and Mussolini himself.

and the socialists, which the conservative classes meant to exploit when they helped them to power.

' Our programme is based on facts,' said Mussolini at the fascist congress in October 1919. This remark described not merely the party's intended tactics, but an entire conception of life, which reduces everything to its value in relation to the ' will to power ' standard. This is the major difference between fascism and socialism, over which no compromise is possible. The fate of humanity for a long time hangs on the outcome of this conflict, and the issue lies, not, as it may appear, between two rival philosophies, but between philosophy and the negation of all philosophy.

' Action has dug a grave for philosophy,' said Mussolini on his train journey to Rome, where the king was going to charge him with the formation of the new government. This ' realism ' that fascism perpetually claims for itself is the high-water mark of its so-called doctrine. Having once arrived in power, fascism, like any other parvenu discovering his noble quarterings, provides itself with antecedents. It goes back to the Guelph tradition, to the Counter-Reformation, to Romanticism : history is ransacked in a feverish search for ancestors. All that survives of these efforts, before as after victory, are the by-products of a crude pragmatism, and the glorification of force, of which a furious nationalism and worship of the state are the outstanding manifestations. Behind it all is the ' pagan ' conception of life as struggle and effort which are their own justification. Hence the exaltation of war : ' War alone,' writes Mussolini in the *Italian Encyclopædia*, ' brings all human energies to their highest tension, and sets a stamp of nobility on the peoples who have the courage to face it.'

Certainly fascism always preaches duty, self-denial and discipline, and condemns individual egoisms. But actually fascism is ' anti-individualist ' the better to suppress the universal instinct of humanity in the individual conscience, which it frees from its inhibitions so as to avoid the necessity of reckoning with its demands. It sacrifices, not the attributes of individuality, but the conscious being. Apparently everything is saved, since moral life is simply transferred to the state. ' For the fascist everything is in the state, and nothing human or spiritual exists or, *a fortiori*, has any value outside the state.'[1]

'For fascism the state is the absolute, before which individuals and groups are only relative.'[2] And since it is impossible to base a moral imperative on the 'relative', we may well ask the meaning of this 'absolute' which fascism finds in the state. Mussolini himself gives us an answer : 'The fascist state is a " will to power " and to domination.'[3]   Having started from the will to power, and subordinated the individuals to it, fascism is bound to find it again in the state. Moral life itself, and all its possible foundations, are locked out. The 'will to power and to domination' has nothing in common with morality, even if, following the Hitlerian formula, this serves the 'vital needs' of a people.

Allowing for its defects, socialism is the greatest attempt to subordinate to the needs of the human conscience everything which, in reality, is hostile and alien to it. Socialism aims at putting human before economic necessities, at 'humanizing' and 'moralizing' nature and preventing its brute forces from spreading unchecked. It studies natural 'laws' in order to make use of them and not to remain bound by them. It fights to save the human soul from outside restraints, and to impose its own internal law on the outside world. Its aim is to control the industrial machine with its huge productive powers as well as the state machine with its great power of coercion, particularly as both the powers and the machines are tending more and more to merge into one. Socialism is a finalist, fascism an instrumental doctrine, a sort of drill, a discipline, a stimulant, and as such it can neither found nor replace a system of ethics either for individuals or for the state.

The negation of philosophy, fascism is thus the negation of politics and religion. 'The democratic conception of life is essentially political, the fascist essentially warlike,' wrote Mussolini in September 1922. Fascism can only tolerate religion if it surrenders what was apparently its own private domain, that of the individual conscience. By

---

[1, 2, 3] These passages are from the article on 'fascist doctrine' written by Mussolini for the *Italian Encyclopædia*.

helping to break down the resistance of individuals and groups to their absorption by the fascist state, the Church has accepted and smiled on the omnipotence of this state which denies freedom to the independent conscience and to religion itself. Even, or rather particularly, when official honours are being heaped on it, religion only survives under fascism by allowing itself to be used as a tool. Like fascism it becomes merely a discipline, a useful means of consoling and restraining the common people, an indispensable resource that so many atheists, from Voltaire to Mussolini, have invoked. 'Religion for the poor' is thus added to 'imperialism for the proletariat' in the well-filled fascist armoury of '*raison d'état.*'[1]

.   .   .   .   .   .

Since fascism exalts action and denies philosophy, must faith in philosophy be signalized by the denial of action? The pundits who take this line betray philosophy twice over by betraying both philosophy and action. No conception of life is true or workable unless it is universally applicable, and in this case 'universally' applies to each individual man, and so to humanity as a whole. Man and humanity are identical terms. It is impossible to affirm what is human in individual man without realizing it in the whole of mankind. Hence the human must be supreme, and impress itself on every branch of life. There can be no giving way to *faits accomplis*, no surrender to success ; the responsibilities that are owed to all men cannot be avoided by an escape into the realm of good intentions. Good intentions by themselves do no good. It is not enough to be in the right ; one has got to succeed.

Methods and tactics are necessary therefore ; weapons must be chosen, forces combined, the decision made as to where they are to be applied ; certain positions must be abandoned in order to win others ; progress must be made through advances and retreats and cunning manœuvres whose meaning only becomes apparent with their comple-

[1] Thus on February 26, 1937, a week after the Addis Ababa massacres, the Cardinal Archbishop of Milan, Monsignor Schuster, compared Mussolini to the most glorious of the Roman emperors, and hailed ' the Italian legions who are occupying Abyssinia in order to ensure to its people the double advantage of imperial civilization and the catholic faith '.

tion. But tactics, like all the realities of life and history—classes, technique, institutions—have a tendency to develop on their own, forgetful of the end towards which they are directed. Everything tends to grow like a cancer regardless of its surroundings and of the very reasons which brought it into being. This is all the more serious, since a truth derives its value from the importance which is given to it and the position it occupies, for it is one thing if it is kept in the background and quite another if it becomes the centre to which all other factors are subordinated. On the other hand a certain degree of independence in tactics is inevitable and even essential for final success. The tactical ' theme ' must be hit upon and renewed in each new situation. The forces available to support it must be summed up and used accordingly, and victory comes only as the resultant of the calculation.

Victory has not only to be won, but won in a given time. Each situation has a ' potential ' which is variable but not infinite. Its curve is mobile, but man's action must take place within it, for one day it will fall under the influence of the very forces that have caused it to rise. The point of incidence may be varied a thousand times, but not for ever. Circumstances arise in which a general sense of exhaustion and saturation makes it impossible for action to be postponed any longer, or the opportunity is lost for a long while. Tactics which are inoperable within a given time are valueless ; the time factor, itself a variable function, must be taken into account and controlled. In post-war Italy, as elsewhere, there was a great fund of hopes and desires turned towards a new order, but the workers' parties acted as though this capital could be left unproductive or wasted at will. Ten years have been enough to dissipate what seemed inexhaustible, and no one can tell when the impulse and the opportunity will come again.

To win, and to win in time, contact must be made with the great masses, and the help of an organization is indispensable. This does not eliminate the role of individual appeal and protest, the need for both prophets and skirmishers. The chosen few strike the new coinage, but it must be put into circulation, and everything depends on how widely and how quickly this is done. Contact between the idea and the people can be achieved only with an organized system keeping always in close touch with them. This is a liability as well as an advantage, for the go-between, the party, tends to become an independent unit and builds up machinery, which in its turn becomes more or less independent. This hardens into party loyalty, with its defensive and conservative instincts. But it would be a grave error to treat this as a sign of inertia. Some defence mechanism is as necessary to collective bodies as to individuals. The herd instinct is the first victory over chaos ; it is a bulwark against the outside world and prevents destruction or dispersal by outside influences before the individuals have found time to get their bearings or realize what is happening. The mass character of post-war social and political action has profoundly altered the conditions for this action. The very fact that action must take place through and on behalf of the masses has made it to some extent inevitable that the struggle should be centralized and more confidence placed in the leaders. A general staff which has to make a public explanation of its tactics every five minutes and justify every step is doomed to defeat. On the other hand, the modern political campaign cannot be carried out without publicity, stage management and much significant symbolism. In it agitation ('the putting of a single idea into many minds') counts for more than propaganda ('the putting of many ideas into each single mind'). Regrettable though this may be, a movement which refuses to adapt itself to these new necessities cuts itself off from the masses and from its goal.

What chiefly stands in the way of this adaptation is an illusion, cherished largely by 'intellectuals', who are inclined to overestimate the value of the tools that they themselves have learnt to handle. For them it is important not only to be right, but to have been right in the past. They are content to prove their enemies' arguments weak or their programme contradictory. The man in the ranks knows that this is only the beginning of a fight which must be constantly renewed. The ideas, plans and promises of the enemy must doubtless be criticised, but it must be remembered that the human mind, as well as the mass mind, is a stream which needs replenishing. If you block the spring, however muddy it may be, another must be provided : one idea can only be replaced by a greater, one passion by a stronger. The masses forget easily ; their judgments are based not on the 'contradictions' of the past, but on the consolations of the present and the hopes for the future which are held out to them. But it is the greatest paradox of political life that any war of principles is also, and particularly at critical moments, a war of positions. For no battle is fought without a battle ground, without positions from which to start the attack, put up defences, dig oneself in and hold on in face of the enemy assault. These strategic reasons are obvious, but there are others which go deeper. It is wrong to suppose that an idea goes on living after the men and institutions in which it was embodied have disappeared. In certain conditions it may be resurrected, but there is no certainty that such conditions will return. The fascist experiment proves that an idea is jeopardised when its background is destroyed. 'Ideas cannot be killed ' is a sublime and dangerous commonplace, which ignores the fact that an idea needs material support if it is to last. An idea is a generation, or a succession of generations. If the generation disappears and the succession is cut, the idea is submerged and the inheritance lost. When the fascists kill, banish or imprison their enemies, burn their houses and destroy their institutions, they know what they are about and do not strike in vain ; especially when they borrow some of the principles of socialism ; ideas are menaced as much by falsification as by the destruction of their protagonists. The use of socialist terminology by the fascists is a caricature of socialism, its negation ; this hostly survival is more baneful than death itself.

.   .   .   .   .   .

To make headway and to win, socialism—with the conception of life it champions—must take stock of the inconsistencies it meets with in all its forms of action. These are not mere obstacles standing in its path, but lie at the very roots of the problems it hopes to solve.

Pre-war social democrats looked upon themselves as the trustees of 'truth' and the representatives of interests which some time or other were bound to prevail. When? That did not matter very much. Left and right agreed that a majority must be won for socialist ideas, and that once this happened all the rest would follow. The growing menace of a European war had led Jaurès to consider the problem of a race between socialism and war, which socialism must win in order to prevent war; but this idea never decisively influenced the movement as a whole. Pre-war socialism existed in a void and took no account of time.[1]

The experience of the war led a section of the socialist movement to see the problems of conflict and victory in quite a different light. Thanks to their revolutionary traditions Lenin and the bolsheviks were to the fore when the historic moment came. Taken by surprise, like all the other parties, by the March revolution, they plunged into it determined to make the most of it in the time at their disposal. They argued that a political and social movement cannot always wait until all the perfect conditions for victory are offered, but that circumstances may arise—the collapse of the autocratic regime in Russia, the wear and tear of the world war—that impose a responsibility which cannot be postponed, even if it has not been catered for in the handbook of the perfect marxist. Then the problem of action, the necessities of time and place have to be squarely faced. Victory must be won in Petrograd on November 7, or the game is lost. The problem of the majority is no longer the same : majorities must be gained in critical places at critical moments. At this moment all that matters is victory over the enemy, the creation of the 'torrent' of which Gorki speaks, and which must sweep away all resistance. In Max Eastman's phrase the Marxist ceases to be anything but a 'technician of revolution'. The myopic and abstract mentality of the social democrat's approach to tactical problems gives way to a new spirit, which, before every

[1] After the elections of September 1930, which saw the first great advance of national-socialism, the German social-democratic paper *Vorwärts* wrote : ' The question whether a socialist majority in the *Reichstag* will be attained in the next few years or in several decades is of secondary importance.'

goal to be attained, every step to be taken, considers what are the real forces to be used, how they are to be acquired, and how each step can lead to the next.

In this search for ' means ' there is a danger that bolshevism has not avoided. The ' means ' now fill the entire horizon. When the workers have come to power in the belligerent countries, thought the bolshevik leaders in 1917, or when socialism is ' constructed ' in the U.S.S.R., announced the rulers of the Soviet State in 1928, then the era of ' principles ' will begin ; until then they can be dispensed with. Meanwhile everything becomes a ' means ', people, parties, tactics, individuals. Revolutionary, like industrial or any other kind of technique, tends to develop independently and subordinate to itself the men and purposes that it ought to serve. In consequence technique becomes such an important part of political action that specialists are required, ' professional revolutionaries '. It is they who draw up plans of campaign for dragging the masses from objective to objective up to the final victory ; they who hold in their hands the thread which leads eventually to the promised land of ' principles '. This idea, the roots of which may be found in the Russian revolutionary tradition (Bakunin, *Narodnia Volia*), and which was fostered by the struggle against the Tsarist regime, flourished again after the failure of the plans which Lenin made during the war, and which inspired his activities in the years 1917–20. Lenin thought that in the conditions created by the war the working class was bound to take power anyhow and anywhere, in the first country in which the ' imperialist front ' could be broken. Russia offered the first chance because the Tsarist regime collapsed under the weight of its own helplessness. It did not much matter that Russia was a backward country in which the proletariat was a small minority ; what did matter was to profit from the country's social weakness so as to seize power and hold on until revolution had broken out in other countries, especially in Germany. Then the Russian working class would pass on the torch to the proletariat of the more industrialized countries. Meanwhile the position had to be held and all necessary compromises made with the Russian peasantry until the main body of the troops—the world proletariat, and above all the Germans—had caught up and gone ahead. When Lenin said at the time of Brest-Litovsk that 'land must be sacrificed to gain time', he was still thinking of the time needed for the victory of the world proletariat to free Russia from its contradictions and isolation. For Lenin Russia was only a pawn, the first available on the chessboard of world revolution.

World revolution never took place, and for several years Russia's isolation was enhanced by the policy of the ' *cordon sanitaire* ' followed by other states, particularly by those of the Entente. So the process was reversed, and the bolsheviks had to rely on their own resources. Although this reversal was forced on them by the necessity of keeping a hold on power, the lustre of its more dramatic aspect for long hid from them its real significance and consequences. The Soviet State, which was to have brought 'direct democracy' with it, the 'people's State' of which Lenin had talked in 1917, set up a dictatorship which became more and more severe and gradually swept in every kind of organization inside the community—soviets, syndicates, the Communist Party itself, and in other countries utilized any force, party, or principle that might serve its needs, as interpreted solely by the leaders. Use is made indifferently of anti-militarism or Chauvinism, the *Reichswehr* or the Red Front; the League of Nations is denounced as a ' fortress of imperialism ' or exalted as the ' bulwark of peace '. The defence of democratic liberties becomes alternately an unforgiveable sin of the ' hangers-on of capitalism ' and the supreme aim of the Popular Front. Léon Blum is criticized in 1934 for saying in the Chamber that the socialists would resist a German attack on France, and violently attacked in 1936 because as head of the government he received Dr. Schacht. Family feeling, which once stank of the *petit-bourgeois*, is honourably reinstated, not because socialism may be enriched thereby, but because the Soviet State wants France to have a big army and consequently as many recruits as possible.

This method of completely subordinating the material interests of the working-class and socialist movement and of other nations to the strategic needs of the Soviet State puts all the problems and actions involved in a wrong light, even when the slogans that go round and the solutions advocated are irreproachable. This subjection of all tactics and principles to the Russian scale has caused a great number of people, who joined the communist movement because they saw it as a perfect combination of theory and practice, to break with it rather than betray the motives which first impelled them to join it. Their experience of fascism has had a great deal to do with this ' return to principle '. Those who have fought against fascism have come to the conclusion that they cannot take up the fight starting from the standpoint of bolshevik communism or treat principles as mere matters of expediency which may be modified or abandoned at will.

The struggle against fascism is primarily a struggle for the liberty and rights of the human being. One can only carry it on if one really believes in these principles and is prepared to demand and fight for them under any regime. The communists have adopted the doctrine attributed (wrongly) to Louis Veuillot : ' When we are the weaker party we demand liberty in the name of your principles ; when we are the stronger we refuse it to you in the name of our own.' This attitude offers certain advantages which attract the average combatant who finds things very easy the moment truth becomes ' one way only ' and is found to be on ' this side of the Pyrenees '. Some intellectuals, who had never been able to stand much of the heady wine of principle, were delighted to find that their weakness was a virtue and grateful to bolshevism for having rid them of their inferiority complex. But such advantages are false and dangerous, and people must have the courage to give them up if they want to go on fighting against fascism. It is a hard fight involving real values and calling for more than a merely temporary conviction. The absence of such faith is bad for the fighting power of the combatants, for their moral sense cannot be so crushed as to deprive them of all consciousness of wrong-doing when the fascist victory takes away all their landmarks, ' facts ', and leaves them adrift. Besides, other members of the community who are asked to help may wonder if the unscrupulousness of which the proletarian party boasts as a virtue is not likely to be turned against them to-morrow, and if, in the absence of some common imperative, any agreement they make will not become one-sided.

Much of the individual and collective demoralization that has followed the victory of fascism in certain countries is due to the so-called communist ' realism ', which has infected the very heart of resistance with doubt and feebleness. No individual deed of heroism can make up for this blow at the very source of anti-fascism ; especially as fascism must, in order to win, succeed in destroying the faith and the material aids that have made working-class and popular conquests possible. It must break the framework and the ties that give the masses power to unite and resist, shattering them until each man is isolated and uprooted and can no longer stand out against the organization that is forced upon him. All fascist methods have the same aim ; they destroy workers' organizations, suppress democracy and political life itself, use and falsify socialist principles, by stirring up hatred and passion they evoke the maximum of blind mass reaction, they hold eternal principles up to scorn. Their intention is to destroy the hope, on which all great revolutions have been nourished, of a truth in which men may recognize their common safety and their highest destiny.[1]

Socialism, therefore, cannot be a form of ' red fascism '. Though the possibility of its manœuvring in the same way is not excluded, it cannot use the fascist creed as the fascists use the socialist creed. It cannot go far that way and avoid the risk of going too far. To copy fascist tactics, either deliberately or in panic, is to play the game which suits both the nature and interests of fascism and in which it excels. By suppressing conscience and free thought fascism creates just the atmosphere and the weapons it wants, and in these conditions it is bound to outclass its enemy. By following it on to its own ground socialism, without opening

[1] Hence the sympathy of the various forms of fascism for ' philosophies ' of power and instinct, their borrowings from pragmatism, relativism, vitalism, their generous consumption of ' dynamism ' and ' myth '. Fascism only extols the irrational so as to substitute reasons of state for the human reason.

up any new possibilities, betrays its own nature and its real and only claim to superiority. The adoption of the amoral means and ends of fascism implies the abandonment of the historic role of the proletariat, which is the ' fulfilment of philosophy '. Its mission is to bring back into the world that sense of universal and human needs which other classes refuse to admit. Socialist society and the action leading to it can only be conceived of *sub specie philosophiæ*, which means *sub specie generis humani*.[1] The worth of the working class lies in its philosophical and, consequently, its human content.

By sacrificing this it prepares its own collapse and defeat, and delivers itself into the hands of fascism. This is not a merely academic point. The world to-day is suffering from a profound confusion of material and spiritual values and from the lack of a common truth and a common task. Exaggerated nationalism is only one aspect—the most formidable—of this confusion : each country writhes in isolation like a sick man. Fascism glories in this situation, intensifies it, and recognizes no connection with the rest of the world except through war. Consequently it detests anything that brings nations together in any other way, be it international socialism, Christian ethics or the League of Nations. Thus it marches on, dragging us with it towards the abyss. There can be no illusions about this. The human race was barely able to endure the war of 1914–18, though it possessed great material and spiritual reserves, accumulated over a long period, which saved it from collapse. To-day we should begin a new war with less resources and greater powers of destruction, after a prolonged period of crisis which in several places has nearly cracked the thin crust of civilization on which we live. The chances are that the next war will be a purely fascist one, introducing and compelling the general adoption of fascist methods ; a war carried on with the finest technical equipment backed by the mentality of the cave man.

In face of this threat more is needed than to meet ' automatism ' with ' automatism ', coercion with coercion, cor-

---

[1] ' Philosophy cannot be fulfilled without the suppression of the proletariat, and the proletariat can only be suppressed when philosophy is fulfilled.' Marx. *Contribution to the Critique of the Philosophy of Law.*

ruption with corruption, white army with red army, or to befog everyone with a cloud of formulas, as if the only hope lay in confusion. In point of material and military strength we must be superior to the fascists, since that is the ground on which they are trying to force a decision. But unless some great moral force emerges to prevent war altogether, or if it comes, to keep its aims clearly defined, some force that endures unchanged through all events, however frightful or overwhelming, victory cannot be won, or, if won, signifies nothing. Such a force is only to be found in the popular masses, the common people, the workers. Theirs are the fundamental feelings : love of peace, desire for social justice, respect for humanity, the sense of brotherhood which are the mainsprings of humanity. Naturally these feelings do not predominate all the time ; they have often to be unearthed, and they can be suppressed or deflected. But not a single man of the people in any country really believes that war is ' the hygiene of the world ', or joins in the jeers of the fascist leaders at the massacres of Addis Ababa or the martyrdom of the children of Madrid. He has to be educated up to this stage, trained to forget his genuine impulses. But once the fever has worn off, or he is brought hard up against problems from which his attention has been distracted, his strong instinct to regard war as a curse reasserts itself. This is the focus of resistance to fascism.

It is not the side with the last cartridge or the last ton of steel that is going to win the next war. The most indispensable raw material will be human energy, inspired and sustained by lofty hopes and aims. Technical efficiency alone cannot win, especially if the war becomes, as it is bound to, one of slow attrition. It will be more than ever a war of the masses, an infantryman's war. And still more certainly than in the Great War it will be the last comers and the non-combatants who will tip the scales. Public opinion will play a decisive part and its judgments will be worth armies.[1] In a war lasting a few months the fascist formula, *automatism plus fanaticism*, may show to advantage, but in a prolonged struggle moral

---

[1] The fascists are well aware of this : for though they affect to despise the ' foolish weathercock of so-called public opinion ', no regime has spent and plotted so much to corrupt and influence it.

values will tell.   Humanity must find salvation in its deeper self, and the deepest and most enduring feelings are those pertaining to enlightened moral consciousness.   After the deluge, if any countries survive, the sun will shine on those who have managed to preserve those foundations of humanity that fascism is trying so hard to destroy for ever.

APPENDIX

List of fascist ' victories ' during the general strike (see p. 222) published in *Popolo d'Italia* of August 5. This list, which is given here in full, only includes information which reached the *Popolo d'Italia* previous to the night of August 4, 1922.[1]

Alessandria	Occupation of the town hall and People's Theatre.
Ancona	Chamber of Labour, anarchist club, railwaymen's club, ' Soviet ' club, Melloni club.
Antignano (Leghorn)	Socialist club.
Ardenza (Leghorn)	Communist club.
Campo Canneto (Parma)	Co-operative and socialist club.
Chiappa (Spezia)	Socialist and communist clubs.
Falconara (Ancona)	Socialist club.
Figline Valdarno	Resignation of socialist town council.
Florence	Railwaymen's bar, Chamber of Labour, socialist paper, *La Difesa*.
Fornovo (Parma)	Co-operative and socialist club.
Genoa	Railwaymen's club.
Gravina (Bari)	Chamber of Labour.
Intra (Novara)	Chamber of Labour and co-operative.
Leghorn	Chamber of Labour, Socialist Provincial Federation, communist club, socialist divisional headquarters, the ' Swan ' club, occupation of the town hall, forced resignation of socialist town council and socialist deputies for the province.
Milan	Socialist club, tramwaymen's club, railwaymen's club, two communist clubs, railwaymen's co-operative, occupation of Palazzo Marino, headquarters of socialist town council.
Naples	Headquarters of Harbour Federation.
Noceto (Parma)	Co-operative and socialist club.

[1] Unless otherwise stated, the offices of the organization mentioned were destroyed, almost always by fire.

Novara	Resignation of socialist town council.
Novi Ligure	Chamber of Labour, resignation of socialist town council.
Oderzo (Treviso)	Communist club.
Padua	Chamber of Labour.
Pavia	Chamber of Labour.
Peicastagno (Genoa)	Socialist and communist club.
Piacenza	Chamber of Labour.
Pisa	Socialist paper, *Era Nostra*.
Pistoia	Occupation of town hall.
Ponte a Signa (Florence)	Proletarian league of ex-servicemen.
Rebosco (Genoa)	Socialist and communist club.
Rimini	Marine Labour co-operative, railwaymen's co-operative.
Ronco (Parma)	Socialist co-operative and club.
Saliano (Parma)	Co-operative and socialist club.
Sampierdarena (Genoa)	Chamber of Labour, railwaymen's co-operative.
San Jacopo (Leghorn)	Socialist club.
San Secondo (Parma)	Socialist co-operative and club.
Savona (Genoa)	Socialist co-operative.
Schio	Chamber of Labour.
Spezia (Genoa)	Federal Chamber of Labour, Syndicalist (dissident) Chamber of Labour, Marine Federation, Metalworkers' Syndicate.
Torre (Padua)	Chamber of Labour.
Turin	Several communist clubs.
Trieste	Van belonging to the paper *Il Lavoratore*.
Vicenza	Chamber of Labour.
Vigevano	Chamber of Labour.
Voghera	Railwaymen's club.

The harvest was so abundant that the *Popolo d'Italia* was unable to quote the full honours list. The following is an attempt to fill the gap, always confining itself to August 4 as the limiting date.[1]

Ancona	Home of the communist deputy Corneli, and socialist printing works.
Binasco (Milan)	Chamber of Labour.
Leghorn (Tuscany)	Railwaymen's club.
Legnaia (Florence)	Mutual aid society.
Legnano (Milan)	Occupation of town hall.

[1] The information given is almost all taken from Chiurco's *History of the Fascist Revolution*.

Ovada (Alessandria)	Chamber of Labour, paper *l'Emancipazione*, resignation of socialist town council.
Padua	Railwaymen's club.
Parma	Railwaymen's clubs, printing works of *Il Piccolo* twice burnt and pillaged, occupation of town halls of Salsomaggiore, Borgo San Donnino, Sissa, San Lazzaro, Lusignano, Palma, and other socialist communes in the province.
Pavia	Resignation of twelve socialist town councils in the province.
Pisa	Chamber of Labour, occupation of railwaymen's club.
Quiliano (Genoa)	Occupation of town hall.
Riva Trigoso (Genoa)	Chamber of Labour.
Sala Braganza (Parma)	' General conflagration.'[1]
Savona	Railwaymen's club, occupation of town hall, Chamber of Labour, Consortium of Harbour Co-operatives.
Siena	Chamber of Labour (for the third time), anti-fascist newspaper stall, mutual-help club *Il Risorgimento*, anarchist clubs *Germinal* and *Pietro Gori*.
Tavernuzze (Florence)	Communist club.
Varese	Occupation of the town hall.
Vigevano	Communist club, printing works of *L'Independente*, fascist expeditions in the district to Siziano, Sairano, Piccolini di Vigevano, Mezzanino Po, Casorate, Carbonara, Mezzana Corte.
Voghera	Resignation of socialist town council.

These are only outstanding episodes among thousands of individual and collective outrages which it is impossible to relate in detail.

[2] Chiurco IV, p. 214.

INDEX

The Mayflower Press, Plymouth.   William Brendon & Son, Ltd.